# RUNAWAYS, COFFLES AND FANCY GIRLS: A HISTORY OF SLAVERY IN TENNESSEE

## BY BILL CAREY

Clearbrook Press

Printed in the United States of America


ISBN: 978-0-9725680-4-3

Library of Congress Control Number:  2018903570


Book and cover design by: One Woman Show Design


Clearbrook
Press

Nashville, Tennessee 37205
www.clearbrookpress.com

# TABLE OF CONTENTS

# PREFACE AND
## ACKNOWLEDGEMENTS

A few months ago I went to the Tennessee State Library and Archives intending to look over some of the early issues of the *Knoxville Gazette*. My plan was to write a column about some of the things I found in the *Gazette* during its first year of its publication (1791).

As I started looking over old microfilm, my eyes were drawn to the runaway slave ads and to the legal notices published by sheriffs who had caught runaways and locked them up. I got to thinking about the stories behind these published items. I thought about what it must have been like to have headed across the countryside with no food or supplies and little idea of what direction you were going. As I read the sheriffs' items, I thought about these slaves being sent back to their slaveholders, where they would be beaten for having run away in the first place. I reflected on the irony that, while Tennessee's early settlers were migrating west, these slaves were trying to go back where they came from, to their families in Virginia.

I was also taken aback by how much information there was in the runaway slave ads: Name of the slave, physical description of the slave, description of the slave's clothes, notes about personal habits of the slave, etc. It occurred to me that some of this data gave us more information about slaves than we had about their slaveholders.

I decided to make a list of every runaway slave ad published in the

*Knoxville Gazette.* After I did that, I decided to keep going and find runaway ads in early copies of the *Tennessee Gazette* and the *Nashville Whig.* Fifty ads became 100; 100 became 200; 200 became 500; and eventually I found and made copies of more than 900 runaway slave ads purchased by Tennessee slaveholders. As I logged the information in each of these runaway slave ads, I realized that the tidbits in them, put together, told us a lot about life at that time.

Runaway slave ads were usually printed alongside other slave-related items such as advertisements for slave sales and "slave wanted" ads. Inevitably, I started collecting and logging those as well. As I started reading various ads, I became enthralled about some of the discoveries I was making (some of which, I later realized, had been made by other researchers before me, but some of which had not).

Along the way I purchased and read several articles and books on the subject, the best of which was Frederick Bancroft's 1931 book *Slave Trading in the Old South.*

In the process I came to realize that I hadn't known very much about slavery. I have written several books, hundreds of articles and thousands of pages of content for the non-profit organization Tennessee History for Kids (which I co-founded), but I didn't know much about slavery. I didn't realize how deeply entrenched slavery was at every level of society; how vital it was to Tennessee's economy; how just about every judge, every newspaper editor, every factory owner and every banker was, for lack of a better phrase, "in on it." I was also stunned about by how out in the open the system was. I had suspected that slaves were involved in the construction of the Tennessee State Capitol, for instance. But it never occurred to me that you could find ads in which slaveholders were asked to hire out their slaves to work on it.

I eventually concluded that some of us who teach Tennessee history don't talk enough about slavery. We talk about westward migration; about Tennessee becoming a state; about the Battle of King's Mountain, the War of 1812, and all the other fascinating chapters of Tennessee history. We talk about Andrew Jackson, David Crockett, John Sevier and Nancy Ward. But many of us don't talk about slavery until we start going over the causes of the Civil War.

Meanwhile, in recent years we have begun teaching about

Tennessee's small abolitionist movement and about the short-lived newspaper known as the *Emancipator*. Our avoidance of the realities of slavery, combined with the addition of the *Emancipator* as mandatory Tennessee trivia, has created a situation where we are misleading our students into thinking that Tennessee was "different" than the rest of the South—that slavery "wasn't as bad" and wasn't as entrenched in this state as it was in other parts of the South. That bothered me and (to be honest) kept me up at night as I worked on this book.

I still haven't written that column. But, after several months research and writing this book (in my spare time), I've at least learned something about slavery. My hope is that people who read this book will be able to say the same thing.

During the course of researching this book, several people asked me what I hope to accomplish by writing it. I hope this book results in a greater understanding of slavery in Tennessee. I hope teachers start incorporating more lessons about slavery into their classes, and I'd like to see students doing research about slaves in their home counties. I'd like to see historic markers about slavery in places such as the corner of 4th and Charlotte in downtown Nashville; the Niota Train Depot in McMinn County; and the Williamson County Courthouse. I'd like tour guides to start telling the complete truth about slavery in Tennessee. I'd like us to realize, when we talk about life in Tennessee before the Civil War, that slavery was everywhere.

The last thing I want is to do is add to the animosity that already exists in our society. Instead, I hope we can all get a better understanding of our collective story and agree that this part of it must be told.

I need to thank the following people who helped me while I researched this book.

Let's start with the staff of the Tennessee State Library and Archives. Not only were they helpful, but they also came to work on a couple of days when it was snowy and icy and I was the only member of the general public using the place.

The board members of Tennessee History for Kids, without whom I could not do what I do. For several years, these people have been

volunteering their time to help me try to help public school students.
I greatly appreciate it, Jay, Ed, Karen, Ron, Steve, Christina, Meredith, Tracy, Mark, David, Dennis and Will.

Eddie Weeks, librarian for the Tennessee General Assembly.

The staff of the Metro Nashville Archives, especially Ken Fieth, Kelley Sirko and Drew Mahan.

David Ewing, Ridley Wills II and Tina Jones.

Nicki Wood and Debbie Tilbury, who helped me edit the manuscript.

Angie Jones, the incredibly talented designer.

Most importantly, my wife Alicia and my sons Will and Ben.

LOCAL.—Nothing of importance since our last issue. A negro, committed to jail as a runaway, cut his throat on Monday evening, and a pair of horses attached to a wood wagon made a break on Tuesday.— No damage done in the latter case, except arousing the captain and first lieutenant of the loafers from their afternoon siesta.

*Athens Post*, **April 11, 1851**

# INTRODUCTION

Everyone has their reason for moving to Tennessee. In Emanuel's case, he came because the government of Nashville bought him.

Born sometime between 1796 and 1806—that's all we know from official records—Emanuel was raised on the Petersburg, Virginia, plantation of a man named Edward Stokes. Sometime in Emanuel's life he was sold to William Finch of Chesterfield County, Virginia. Finch may have been another plantation owner. He may have been a professional slave trader. If Finch was a slave trader, then Emanuel would have been locked up in a slave pen while he waited to be sold again.

In December 1830, the government of Nashville paid a man named William Ramsey $12,000 to go to Virginia on a slave-buying trip. Ramsey bought 24 slaves who ranged in age from 14 to 45. Their names were, in the order they appear in government records, Ben, Emanuel, Jim, Frank, Lewis, Moses, Salem, Anthony, Charles, Lucinda, Lilburn Henderson, Allen, Jim, Moses, Allen, Isaac, Vincent, Peter, Bob, Granville, John, Isaac, John and Jim.

Emanuel cost $450.

How those 24 slaves made the 600-mile journey from Richmond is something we will probably never know. The slaves may have sat in wagons for the long, bumpy ride through fields and across rivers and mountains. They may have been shackled and chained together and forced to march two-by-two in what was then known as a coffle—a common sight in those days on the road through Blountville, Knoxville, Kingston and Sparta. If so, they may have all slept, chained together, on the side of the road (now known as Highway 70).

Either way, the 24 slaves who made the journey would have been escorted by armed guards, like prisoners today.

Once in Nashville, Emanuel settled into life as a slave, which meant taking orders from the mayor of Nashville and from Albert Stein, the German engineer in charge of the city's new water system. According to records, he and the rest of Nashville's slaves worked mainly for the water department.

By 19th century slave standards, it may not have been such a bad life. However, Emanuel must not have been happy. Perhaps he missed home. Perhaps he wanted to be free. Around July 20, 1834, he ran away. A few weeks later, the following advertisement appeared in Nashville's newspapers:

## $30 REWARD.

RUNAWAY from the Corporation of Nashville, Ten. on the 20th ult. a negro man named EMANUEL. He is about 35 years old, is five feet three inches high, dark yellow complexion, rather a sulky countenance, a small scar on his left eyebrow. He was raised by Edward Stokes, of Petersburg, Va. and purchased of Wm. Finch, Chesterfield county, Va. Ten dollars will be given for him if taken within the county of Davidson; $15 if taken out of the county of Davidson and in the limits of the State, and $30 if taken out of the State and confined in jail so that we get him again. All reasonable expenses will be paid in either case if brought home.

Aug. 5  2w                    JNO. M. BASS, Mayor.

PART ONE

# GRAND DIVISIONS

# INFORMATION,

## To whom it may concern.

ON the 20th of October next, the annual escort through the wildernets, for families, will leave the block houses, at South West Point, for Bledsoe's Lick, (distance 110 miles.. At the same time and place, the contractor for cutting a waggon road thro' the said wildernets, means to be in readiness to commence the opening of it, and to proceed with sufficient celerity for the families to take through their waggons and baggage to the Cumberland settlements in safety.

Jan. 6, 1795.

---

The SUBSCRIBERS for

Toplady's Translation of Zanchius on PREDESTINATION, are informed that the work is now published and ready to be delivered to the subscribers, who are requested to send for their books.

☞ The prizes are to be paid on demand.
Knoxville, March 17, 1794.

---

ESCAPED from the subscriber on the 27th of March, a negro fellow called JEMMY who had been taken up as a run away, at Connor's creek block house, on the 14th of the same month.

He had with him a horse, and was making for Cumberland to his master, Joseph Davis, who he says left him with one John Hays, on Holston. Said negro is about 5 feet 7 inches high, about 35 years old; has a scar in his forehead; had on when taken up, a green coat and jaket, leather breeches, yarn stockings, & moccasons.

The negro confesses he stole the horse he says he took him in the woods, but cannot tell where abouts. This horse is a bay colour, about 14 hands high, all four feet white, a star in his forehead, marked with saddle spots, is poor and appears very old. The owner is requested to prove the horse, pay charges, and take him away.

ALEXANDER CARMICHAEL.

Knoxville, March 17, 1795.      6. ¾ t.

*Knoxville Gazette*, May 8, 1795

CHAPTER ONE

# SLAVES ACROSS THE MOUNTAINS

When people think about East Tennessee, they often think about bluegrass music, the Great Smoky Mountains, Dolly Parton and waterfalls.

When people think about the *history* of East Tennessee, they often think about frontiersmen, John Sevier, the Overmountain Men and Cherokee Indians.

East Tennessee's history generally doesn't bring to mind the institution of slavery. But slaves were there. Slaves were there when it was known as the Washington District of the Southwest Territory and when the state of Tennessee was organized. Slaves were there in East Tennessee before some of the counties were formed. They were there before communities such as Maryville and Sevierville were even conceived. Slaves were there, being bought and sold, being given away in lotteries and even running away from their owners.

Sixteen years before Tennessee became a state, there were slaves on the Donelson Party flotilla, which left Fort Patrick Henry (present-day Kingsport) and floated downstream on the Holston and Tennessee Rivers, bound for present-day Nashville. The first person to die on that journey was a slave. "Camped on the north shore, where Captain Hutchings'

**An excerpt from John Donelson's journal of the migration from
East to Middle Tennessee in the winter of 1779-1780**

negro man died, being much frosted in his feet and legs, of which he died," John Donelson wrote in his journal.

Slaves—dozens of them, in fact—were killed and kidnapped during the frontier battles with the Chickamaugan Indians. Many of the people who first cleared East Tennessee's forests and planted the land with cotton and corn for the first time were slaves.

Tennessee's first newspaper was the *Knoxville Gazette*—a publication which, oddly enough, was first printed at the Hawkins County Courthouse. In the very first issue of the *Gazette* (dated November 5, 1791) at the Tennessee State Library and Archives, there is an ad that reads: "Wanted to Purchase: A NEGRO FELLOW, about the age of 20 or 24—one who can be recommended for honesty and sobriety. Apply to the printers."

A few issues later, the *Gazette* ran an ad for a merchant named James Miller. Having just arrived from Philadelphia and

RANAWAY from the subscriber, living in Sullivan county, a mulatto man, named JACK, twenty three years of age, five feet ten inches high; took with him a brown great coat, striped jacket, pair of black velvet breeches, pair of overhalls, pair of wooden hose, ditto thread, pair mockasins, and a smoothe bord gun. —Whoever will take up and secure said fellow, so that I get him again, shall have if taken in Sullivan, three pounds, if out of the county, five pounds, and if stolen, I will give ten pounds for the taking the said fellow, and having the thief brought to conviction.

JO N SHELBY, Sen'r.
Sullivan county, 28th, May 1793.

*Knoxville Gazette*, June 29, 1793

Richmond, Miller had a lot to sell—clothing of various kinds, tools, Bibles and spelling books, teas and coffee. Also, a "few young, likely Virginia born Negroes."

The October 6, 1792, *Gazette* had an ad for a runaway slave (possibly the first such ad ever published in present-day Tennessee). Thomas, who was about 20, had run away from the lead mines in present-day Wythe County, Virginia. "It is probable he may make for the Cherokee nation," the ad stated.

Two weeks later, William Smith of present-day Hancock County published an item in the *Gazette* saying he had "three Negro Men, One Woman and two Children" to sell.

In December, the *Gazette* reported the capture of a runaway slave named Matt—caught by Washington County Sheriff George Gillespie. "The owner is desired to come and prove his property, pay

RAN AWAY from the subscriber, about the 10th of September last, a negro fellow named ISAAC, about 18 or 19 years of age, five feet six inches high, and yellow complexion. I expect he will attempt to make for Maryland, and pass himself as a free man. The clothes he had on when he went off were nearly worn out. Any person who will apprehend said negro, and secure him, so that I get him again, shall receive FIVE DOLLARS reward, and all reasonable expences paid, by
JOHN SINGLETON.

Little River, Knox county,
November 19, 1793.           25. 3t.

*Knoxville Gazette*, **October 19, 1793**

charges and take him away"—a sentence that would be repeated in many, many similar items published by sheriffs across Tennessee during the next seven decades.

Starting in 1793, it is hard to find an issue of the *Gazette* without a runaway slave ad. In several April 1793 issues, one can find an ad offering an $8 reward for tracking down Jim, a "country born negro" who "laughs very loud, and is fond of children," according to slave owner Joseph Erwin of present-day Claiborne County. In June, Sullivan County slave owner John Shelby ran an ad in search of "a mulattoe[1] man, named Jack, twenty-three years of age, five feet ten inches high." At about the same time there was an ad for a runaway called William Bundle, who was said to be heading for the Clinch River. A couple of months later, John Singleton of Knox County offered $5 for the return of a slave named Isaac. "I expect he will attempt to make for Maryland, and pass himself as a free man."

---

[1] The term "mulattoe," more often spelled "mulatto," refers to a person of mixed African and European blood.

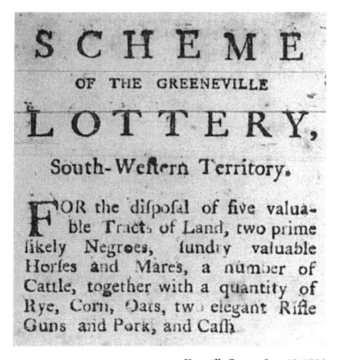

*Knoxville Gazette,* June 19, 1794

RAN AWAY from South West Point, on the 10th instant, two negro men, and a negro woman — One of the men called *Dave*, is about 36 years old, 6 feet high, very black, a very likely, active fellow. The other fellow called Bob, about 38 years of age, yellow complexion, inclined to be corpulent; each of them armed with rifles. Dave had an excellent new rifle. Bob's rifle was not so good, and was breacked with pewter. The woman is named *Pegg*, pock marked, very ugly, and about 40 years of age. Whoever takes up said negroes, or either of them, and delivers them to their master, or secures them so that he can get them, shall be generously rewarded for their trouble.
                      JAMES RICHARDSON.
April 15, 1795.                 8.        3.

*Knoxville Gazette*, April 24, 1795

In the spring of 1794, the *Gazette* worked with a group of men from Greeneville to organize and promote a lottery. Like many lotteries on the American frontier, winners received prizes rather than cash. The prizes given away in the lottery included (among other things) 500 acres of land on the Nolichucky River, 136 acres of land on the Big Pigeon River, several horses and several cows.

Also given away in the Greeneville lottery of 1794: "two negroes, Joe and Luce." Lottery tickets cost $3 and could be purchased from George Roulstone, editor of the *Gazette*.

The Southwest Territory was divided into two districts: the Washington District (present-day East Tennessee) and the Mero District (present-day Middle Tennessee). Between the Washington and Mero Districts sat the wilderness of the Cumberland Plateau,

# TO BE SOLD

TWO lots, on one of which is a house in the town of Knoxville, for Cash or a Negro, will be taken.---Enquire of the Printers.
Jen. 12, 1795.                    2 3 ·

*Knoxville Gazette*, January 23, 1795

which was still Cherokee territory at the time. In the mid 1790s, it was considered unsafe to cross the Cumberland Plateau except with armed military escorts which occasionally departed from Fort Southwest Point on the east side and Fort Blount on the west side. This was, after all, an era in which relations were extremely poor between the settlers and Native American tribes such as the Cherokee and Creek.

Nevertheless, some slaves took their chances and chose to run away, regardless of how dangerous it may have been. In early 1795, a slave named Jemmy ran away and was said by his slaveholder to be "making for Cumberland." In April 1795, the *Gazette* contained an item announcing that three slaves named Dave, Bob and Pegg had run away from Fort Southwest Point. "Dave had an excellent new rifle," the ad stated. "Bob's rifle was not too good, and was breached with pewter. The woman is named Pegg, pock marked, very ugly, and about 40 years of age." That summer, people living in and near Knoxville were on the lookout for three other runaway slaves— Phillip, George and Allard—all from Virginia, and all thought to be heading toward Tennessee.

Also of note, an unknown person ran an ad in the January 23, 1795, *Knoxville Gazette* offering to sell two lots in Knoxville for a payment of "Cash or a Negro."

In the spring and summer of 1796, residents of the Southwest Territory were excited to become citizens of the new state of

Tennessee. A look through the *Gazette* makes you realize just how much was happening. Early in 1796 came the announcement that lots would be laid out and sold in a new town called Maryville. Shortly thereafter came the news that another town, called Sevierville, would be created between Knoxville and the mountains to the east.

In the same issue in which the town of Sevierville was announced, Sevier County slave owner Thomas Buckingham offered a reward for the return of a runaway slave named Ned— "about 25 years of age, of a black complexion, a very sensible fellow when spoken to." A few months later, Knox County resident Benjamin White offered $20 for the return of Henry—"an artful fellow" who could be easily recognized because he "has had both his ears cropped," the ad explained. In December, a Jefferson County slave owner named Alexander Outlaw ran an ad in search of a runaway named London.

Runaway slave ads would continue to be published in the *Knoxville Gazette* in 1797 for slaves named Derry (Blount County), Dick (Knox County), Jack (Knox County), Isaac (Harrison County, Kentucky), Aaron (Knox County) and Sampson (Washington County).

RAN-AWAY, or stolen from the subscriber, in November 1796, a negro fellow named London, about 35 years of age, 5 feet 6 or 7 inches high, rather slim built and bow legged, one of his fore teeth out Any person who will secure the said negro, in any jail, or deliver him to me, in Jefferson county, State of Tennessee, shall receive 20 Dollars reward, and all reasonable expences : and if stolen, 100 dollars for the thief, delivered to me.
    ALEXANDER OUTLAW.
January 4. 1797.                    11 3t.

*Knoxville Gazette*, December 19, 1796

## Five Dollars Reward.

RAN away from the subscriber, on the 7th inftant, February, a Negro man, named Derry, about twenty feven years old, this country born, of a black complexion, about five feet eight or ten inches high, he hath a place on the upper part of his head a little to the rightfide, a fize larger than a dollar, that has no wool on, and appears white and fcaly, he commonly wears a handkerchief on his head to hide faid place, he took fundry cloaths with him, but cane be deferibed, as he is often trading. Who ever will take up faid negro, and deliver him, if taken in the ftate of Tennefiee, to Mjr James Lackev in Blount County, t, put him in ja.l, fo as he may be go tha'l have the above reward and all refonable chaar ges paid by Maj. Lackev for

William Meha e.

*Knoxville Gazette*, March 20, 1797

Suffice it to say that slavery was very much part of Tennessee's culture when it became a state. All of this was juxtaposed with a society still fighting Cherokee and Creek Indians and still recovering from the American Revolution.

An item in the October 12, 1793, *Knoxville Gazette* proves just how complex the relationship was between the American Revolution and slavery. The ad was purchased by John Sharp, a Revolutionary War veteran from Georgia. In it, Sharp claims that several East Tennessee slaveholders—including James Mahen of Greene County, William Owen of Hawkins County and John Chisolm of Knoxville— were keeping slaves that did not rightfully belong to them. Sharp claimed that the slaves legally belonged to the late John Thompson of Georgia and that they were stolen from Thompson sometime during the war (ostensibly by Cherokee Indians). "I hereby forwarn the above-named persons from parting with the above-mentioned negroes, and all persons from trading with them, as I am determined to bring suit for the recovery of said negroes," Sharp said.

Sharp's ad is a reminder of two points about the American Revolution and the southern frontier that many modern Americans have forgotten. First, most Native Americans were allied with the British; all battles with American Indians that took place during the war were considered part of the American Revolution. Second, Indian attackers often took black slaves away from white settlers and kept them as slaves, and white settlers were known to do the same from Indians. So it was very possible that a slave in Georgia could have been stolen in a battle with the Cherokee and then stolen again in a battle against settlers from Tennessee.

John Sharp may have been right in his accusatory letter. However, at least one Knoxville slave owner refused to allow his name to be besmirched. In a response published in the *Knoxville Gazette* a week later, John Chisolm of Knoxville said Sharp was quite wrong.

"I therefore take this public method of desiring Mr. Sharp to prove his property and take them away; at the same time request the public to take notice that he has published a lie; for they never belonged to John Thompson or any other person except John Chisolm"[2]

*Note: For details about sources cited in this and all chapters, see "Sources Cited" section, which begins on page 305.*

---

[2]Chisolm's home, also known as Chisolm's Tavern, may have been one of the first places in which the Tennessee General Assembly met during Knoxville's stint as the state capital in the early 1800s. It was still standing in the 1960s and was razed as part of an urban renewal project.

We learn that the French troops had met with no obstacles to their progress, and that Christophe and Dessalines, the two chiefs, subordinate to Toussaint, had been taken prisoners.

On the 17th of February, a cessation of hostilities was announced, which was to last four days, when a general attack of the blacks was to take place throughout the whole extent the Island, unless the blacks submitted.

## Nashville, May 12.

———:o:———

We are informed by a gentleman just from Eddyville, that the indians have killed several families on the Ohio and Mississippi, and that the people have generally retired into forts.

We are also informed the inhabitants are forted up about Fort blount, on account of the whites having killed an indian.

The last Mails have brought no papers.

———

ERRATTA, For No 95.

In the 2d column, & 2d paragraph, 10th line from the top, for *has*, read *had*. In the same page, 3d line above the table, for *suspecting*, read, *representing*.

CHAPTER TWO

# SLAVES ACROSS THE PLATEAU

In the 1780s and 1790s, settlers who had made their way to Middle Tennessee were surrounded by Native American tribes that didn't want them there. With Chickasaws to the west, Creeks to the south and Cherokees to the east, hundreds of early settlers were killed in raids. The bloodiest era was between 1791 and 1795.

Slaves were sometimes just as likely to fall victim or be taken prisoner in these attacks as the white settlers. The best documented incident in this regard was the raid on Zeigler's Station, in present-day Sumner County, on July 20, 1788. In this notorious raid, four people were killed—two of them slaves. Among the dozen people taken prisoner was a slave named Cador, who was never heard from again.

After Tennessee became a state in 1796, the flow of settlers over the Cumberland Plateau picked up. According to the 1801 census, the Mero District (present-day Middle Tennessee) had 32,000 inhabitants, and more than 8,000 of them were slaves.

How did these slaves get there? Some were brought to Middle Tennessee as part of these early migrations. Others were brought by men who first came to Tennessee with their families and then made buying trips to Virginia. We can also assume that some slaves were

**TO BE SOLD,**

**FOR CASH & LIKELY NEGROES,**

THAT elegant situation on Red river, known by the name of

**MOUNT GALLANT,**

on which there is an excellent dwelling house &c. with a fine Peach and Apple orchard, with about 300 acres of the richest low grounds,— also about 1100 acres land, near Big Harpeth, for low terms, apply to the subscriber,

**JOHN NELSON.**

Dec. 25th, 1800.

*Tennessee Gazette,* January 14, 1801

sold to traders in the east, then brought by those slave traders across the mountains and sold in places such as Knoxville, Kingston and Nashville.

Unfortunately, the westward migration of these slaves is not well documented in newspapers. A thorough search yields no mention of migrants bringing slaves with them from the east or articles about traders who brought slaves from Virginia to sell in places like Nashville.

There are a couple of possible reasons for this gap in the record. One is that there were no newspapers in Middle Tennessee until 1800; the earliest copy of the (Nashville) *Tennessee Gazette* on microfilm at the Tennessee State Library and Archives is from November 1800. A second is that newspapers of that era consisted almost entirely of national and international news and paid advertisements. Truth be known, quite a few important events occurred in Middle Tennessee in the generation after the American Revolution which aren't well documented in newspapers.

In her 1989 book on the early history of Middle Tennessee, Anita Goodstein researched the topic of slave trades in Davidson County. Using deeds, she found that between 1784 and 1803, "the overwhelming number" of slave sales were of a single slave. Apparently, few big slave transactions were occuring in Middle Tennessee. Most of the slaves migrating to Middle Tennessee were bought by their eventual holder in Virginia or Maryland and brought west by that person.

Here are three other non-newspaper sources that mention the presence and migration of slaves across the Cumberland Plateau:

In 1797, a French aristocrat traveling under the name "Mr. Orleans" crossed the plateau heading toward Nashville and stopped at several households. He saw so many slaves along the way that it made a distinctly negative impression upon him. "These immigrants are far from admirable," he wrote in his diary. "With their Negroes they bring the obduracy and laziness of slaveholders. These slaves will settle here and by normal increase maintain the ratio, and under such

WILL be hired for one year, on the laſt day of December next, in the town of Springfield, Robertſon county. Five or Six likely NEGROES, the property of Henry Hart, minor. Thoſe who hire muſt give bond with approved ſecurity.

　　　　THOs. JOHNSON, guardian.
Nov. 1801.　　　　　　　　　 *2

*Tennessee Gazette*, **November 9, 1801**

a system I doubt that the region will ever attain the level of culture and prosperity which it certainly favors otherwise."[1]

Five years later, another Frenchman (botanist Francois Andre Michaux) also crossed the plateau heading west. "Forty miles from Nashville," he wrote, "we met some wealthy emigrants, travelling in a carriage, followed by their negroes on foot, who had passed it [the route] without any accident."

Through most of the 19th century, the largest slave plantation in Robertson County was Wessyngton. In 1915, the grandson of Wessyngton founder Joseph Washington gave a speech about the history of the plantation. After first acquiring land in 1796, "Joseph made several trips back to his home [in Virginia] and brought out a number of Negroes and other property." By 1812, there were 25 slaves at Wessyngton, practically all of whom had walked from

---

[1] "Mr. Orleans," the son of King Louis XVI of France, later became the king of France from 1830 until 1848, and ruled under the name Louis Phillipe I.

## Five Dollars reward

WILL be given to any person who shall apprehend and to confine A Negro Fellow, that I get him again : His name is

## N E D,

Of a yellow complexion. a slim meagre looking fellow, upon close inspection he has a mark on one of his cheeks, plays well on the Violin it there should be any extraordinary trouble, or distance should require it, I will give a generous additional reward.

JOHN M'NAIRY.

February 16, 1801.

*Tennessee Gazette*, **February 18, 1801**

Virginia to Sumner County. Through acquisition and procreation, that number would grow more than 10 times by the Civil War.

Early issues of Nashville's newspapers (the *Tennessee Gazette* and the *Impartial Review and Cumberland Repository*) may not have long articles about slave migrations from Virginia and Maryland. They do, however, contain evidence that slaves were already changing hands, running away, and being hired out. In December 1800, property owner John Nelson advertised the sale of his house and 300 acres on the Red River and 1,100 acres on the Big Harpeth River in exchange for cash or slaves—not an unusual arrangement for the time. A few weeks later, slave holder John McNairy offered a reward for the return of a runaway named Ned, who was of "a yellow complexion, a slim meagre looking fellow. . . [who] plays well on the violin." In November of that year, guardian Thomas Johnson of Springfield ran an ad in an attempt to "hire out" half a dozen slaves who belonged to Henry Hart, a minor. "Those who hire must give bond with approved security," the ad explained.

There was a similar level of slave activity in 1802. In the May 12 *Gazette*, slave owner Benjamin Philips offered $10 for the return of "a negro man named Jim," who was in his early 20s. Six months later, an advertisement appeared in the *Gazette* offering $20 for the return of a slave named George, who "is knock kneed, and is extremely awkward, both in make and manners," Knoxville resident Thomas McClung said in the ad. Meanwhile, Davidson County Sheriff J. Boyd arrested two "negro fellows" named Charles and Stephen, suspected of being runaway slaves, as reported in November 20, 1802.

In 1803 there were at least four separate ads in the *Gazette* about runaway slaves. The first was for Barlett, who had run away while on a forced march through Nashville a few months earlier and was being sought by his owner in Natchez, Mississippi. The second was for Spencer, who ran away from Mill Creek area resident James Wilson in March. The third was for Anthony, who had run away from J. Beauvice of Natchez months earlier. Among other things, Anthony "speaks French and English tolerably well" and "is artful at telling stories," the advertisement claimed. The fourth was for Tom, who ran away from J. Ozburn of Nashville on Christmas Day.

---

WILL be fold in the town of Nafh-
ville, on the fecond day of the
Superior court in May,

7 or 8 Likely Negroes,

on a credit until the firft day of January eighteen hundred and four, the
purchafer giving bond with approved
fecurity, if any chufe to pay the cafh
in hand a deduction of fix per cent
will be made them by,

*T. Hardeman*

*Tennessee Gazette*, **February 3, 1803**

Middle Tennessee was also already seeing slaves change hands because of unpaid debts. In April 1803, the *Tennessee Gazette* announced that some of the assets belonging to Joseph Neville, including three horses, twenty cattle and two slaves (a man and a woman) would be sold to satisfy his debts.

By this time, Nashville's first generation of slaveholders was beginning to pass away, leaving slaves to be sold at auction after they died. In September 1802, "a number of very likely negroes" were sold at the Sumner County house of John Morgan, deceased. "Several likely negroes" belonging to the estate of Williamson County's late Matcalfe Degraffenread were sold in January 1805. The "chattel estate of Benjamin Knox, deceased, consisting of fourteen or fifteen NEGROES" was auctioned about a year later.

As the population of Middle Tennessee increased, so did the number of runaway slaves. In one of the first ads purchased by a slaveholding woman in Nashville history, Elizabeth Evans offered $10 for the return of Andrew in March 1804. In June, Michael Dickson of Dickson County offered $26 for the return of Cato, who was "six feet high, spare built, thin bearded, about 28 years of age." A female slave named Sarah, "about common size and now pregnant with child," ran away from Thomas Britton of Davidson County in June.

Barham Newson of Davidson County offered $20 in September for the return of Lucy, a female slave about 20 years old. Slaveholder H.L. White, who lived near Knoxville, ran an ad in search of a slave named Joe in August. John Instone of Frankfort, Kentucky, ran an ad in search of another slave named Joe in September. Joe, Instone's ad pointed out, ran away at the Chickasaw Bluffs of the Mississippi River.

At least two issues of the October and November 1804 *Tennessee Gazette* contain advertisements for the return of "a mulatto man slave" who was about 30 years old, "stout made and active, talks sensible, stoops in his walk, and has a remarkable large foot." The ad was purchased and signed by a man who had already made a name for himself as a lawyer, judge, farmer and as Tennessee's first representative in Congress: Andrew Jackson.

It was right about this time that a man named Montgomery Bell purchased the Cumberland Furnace iron works from Middle Tennessee political leader James Robertson. Bell immediately set to work to run it with slave labor. "WANTED, On hire at the Cumberland Furnace, a number of good Negro fellows, for which generous wages will be given by me," read the February 1804 ad.

> ONE HUNDRED DOLLARS
> ## REWARD.
>
> RUN-AWAY from the subscriber, on the 26th inst. a Negro Man Named
>
> ### PHILIP,
>
> About 28 years of age; about 5 feet 9 inches high; well made, holds his head high when walking, of a dark mulatto colour, his hair very thin on the crown of his head, has a small scar over his left eye, and a scar on one of his thighs near the groin, when he looks up has large wrinkles in his forehead; is a house carpenter by trade—no doubt will attempt to pass as a free man, & I suspect he has procured forged papers for that purpose—he took with him a small bay horse branded on one of his shoulders, as well as I recollect, S W,—he took with him a variety of clothing, among which were two superfine cloth coats a blue and green, black velvet pantaloons, swansdown waistcoat and fur hat. Whoever will deliver the said Negro to me near Port-Royal, Tennessee, shall receive the above Reward, or Fifty Dollars if lodged in any Jail, so that I get him again.
>
> #### John Baker
> Robertson county, (T.) 29 Oct. 1806.

*Nashville Impartial Review and Cumberland Repository*, **November 8, 1806**

The number of runaway ads picked up as the decade went on; several issues of the *Impartial Review and Cumberland Repository* had as many as four per issue in 1806 and 1807. Returning to the matter of how slaves had gotten to Middle Tennessee in the first place, sometimes a detailed reading of a runaway slave ad revealed the information.

"They [runaway slaves Bob and Tom] will probably make for Amelia County, Virginia," wrote slaveholder Thomas Ryan Butler in 1806.

"I brought him [John] from Norfolk, Virginia," wrote Nathaniel McNairy in an 1807 ad. "I suppose he will attempt to return hither."

The fact that most of these slaves made the journey from Virginia to Middle Tennessee would also work its way down through generations of slaves. In 1929, a researcher from Fisk University named Ophelia Egypt interviewed former slaves as part

# Scheme of a Lottery

*Proposed by Daniel Alexander, for the disposal of eight thousand dollars worth of valuable property, including six hundred dollars in cash.*

## 2,500 Dollars for four ! ! !

THE highest prize consists of that valuable and highly improved plantation known by the name of Kavenaugh's Old Store, lying near the head of Hickman's creek in Smith county, on the main road leading from Knoxville to Jefferson, Nashville, Franklin, &c. The plantation consists of 199 acres of land; 50 acres of which are under good fence and well improved in plough land, grass lots, orchards, &c. There is on the premises a handsome two story cedar log house well finished, with two good stone chimneys and divided into six apartments; there is likewise a store house, still house, cotton machine house, stable, kitchen, corn house, &c.

All valued at     -        -        -    2,500

1 prize, 284 acres of first rate land in White county   1200

1 prize, 50 acres of land, with valuable improvements thereon at the new stand on the wilderness road, where Ephraim Alexander now lives, 4 1-2 miles east of Obey's river   -        -      -    500

1 prize, a likely negro woman   -    -    400

1 prize, 120 acres of land on the Falling water, with an excellent mill seat, and about ten acres cleared   -  400

1 prize 60 acres of first rate land on Falling water, 50

*Carthage Gazette*, **August 17, 1809**

of a research project. The slaves were quite old by that time and in some cases unable to remember clear details from their childhood. But, describing the process under which her grandparents had been brought to Tennessee in the early 1800s, one elderly lady explained it in this manner:

"When white folks got a notion to move to Tennessee or anywhere, they just taken the colored folks up, and of course my grandmother had to go, too.

"They [the slaveholders] brought her from old Virginny to Tennessee when she was a child," she said. "They settled in Gallatin."

By 1809, enslaved people were being routinely sold at estate sales, traded for land, and swapped for supplies. Slaves were so much a part of the normal exchange process that, just like in Greeneville years earlier, a slave was given away as a prize in a private lottery. "A likely negro woman" was one of the main prizes in a lottery that was heavily promoted by the *Carthage Gazette* in August 1809. The woman's name and age were not revealed by the newspaper. However, her estimated value was ($400), as was the estimated value of 284 acres of "first rate land" in White County ($1,100) and the estimated value of a horse ($300), both of which were also being given away.

Middle Tennessee was the frontier. But people who lived there knew the value of land, slaves and horses.

## Sale of Lots,

IN THE

# Town of Sommerville.

ON *Wednesday the 14th day of September* next, we will offer for sale, the LOTS in the town of Sommerville, in the county of Fayette, and state of Tennessee, on a credit of twelve months, and continue from day to day until all are sold. ☞Bond with approved security will be required.

This town is beautifully situated on Loos Hatchie river, near never-failing water, and also near the centre of a county affording large bodies of excellent land, well adapted to the culture of COTTON, and all the varieties of produce common in this country; and it is found by experience to be one of the healthiest counties in the Western District; and, no doubt, in a few years, will be as thickly inhabited as any county West of Tennessee river. We deem a further description needless, as those, we presume, wishing to purchase Lots in this town, will make themselves acquainted with the situation previous to the day of sale.

    HENRY KIRK,
    DAN'L JOHNSON,
    HAMILTON THORNTON,
    WILLIAM OWEN,
    JNO. T. PATTERSON,

} Comm'rs.

June 25, 1825—tds

# Runaway

FROM the subscriber, on the 12th inst. a negro man, named

## BEN,

About six feet high, of very dark complexion rather spare made, his feet are about twelve inches long, the big toes considerably longer than those next to them. He has a wife at Parson Haralson's, in Haywood county, and may be lurking in that neighborhood. Any person apprehending said negro, and delivering him to me, four miles East of Jackson, Madison county, or confining him in jail, so I get him again, shall be well rewarded.

July 21—tf      GEORGE TODD.

# Land Agency.

THE subscriber, as agent for others, offers for sale, a few thousand acres of LAND, in the counties of Haywood and Dyer. He is authorized to give Twenty or Thirty Leases, on the usual terms, in Gibson, and the aforesaid counties. ☞He will also attend to the selling and leasing of any Lands lying in Haywood County, which may be committed to his care. ☞Letters directed to him, in Haywood county, will be attended to.

    WM. H. HENDERSON.
    REFERENCES:
John C. M'Lemore, Esq. *Nashville.*

*Jackson Gazette,* August 20, 1825

CHAPTER THREE

# SLAVES ACROSS THE RIVER

After the Chickasaw Purchase of 1818, slavery moved across the Tennessee River into West Tennessee with remarkable speed. The best proof of this may be found in two newspaper items published nearly a generation apart.

In a September 1804 (Nashville) *Tennessee Gazette*, John Instone offered $20 for the return of a slave named Joe. According to the ad, Instone was "at the Chickasaw Bluffs on the Mississippi" when Joe ran away.

Students of Tennessee history recognize the name of the Chickasaw Bluffs. In seeking his freedom, Joe may have become the first slave to run away at the future site of Memphis.

Sixteen years later, a man announced in the (September 1820) *Nashville Whig* that he had "in his possession since the month of August last, a negro man named ROBERT" whose rightful owner he was trying to track down. The details of the ad are not all that important. But what is interesting is how it was signed: "Will Irvine, Memphis, T."

This was, to the best of my knowledge, the first time the word "Memphis" ever appeared in a Nashville newspaper. In other words,

## A Runaway Negro,

APPREHENDED, on the old Natchez trace, by William Boyd, on the 1st inst. and committed to the Jail of Madison county on the 7th inst. who calls himself SOLOMON, and says he belongs to John Green, who lives on or near the Mississippi. Solomon is six feet one inch high, knock-kneed, has a large foot, wears a blue sailor jacket, round-a-bout considerably worn, stitch down shoes, an old fur hat purporting to have been made by R. Wright, & Sons, Dublin. He says his master married Miss Betsy Crawford, of Virginia,

The owner of said Negro is requested to come and prove his property, pay charges and take him away.

THOS. SHANNON, Shff.

Sept. 11, 1824—3t.

☞On further examination, Solomon confesses that he belongs to Col. Wm. Berry, of Lewis county, Va.

*Jackson Gazette*, September 11, 1824

the first time Memphis was mentioned in print in a Tennessee newspaper was in a runaway slave ad!

Most of East and Middle Tennessee was organized, settled, and divided into counties by the 1820s. But the same could not be said for West Tennessee, which remained Chickasaw Indian territory until it was purchased by the federal government in 1818. What followed the Chickasaw Purchase was a rush to claim land grants, organize towns, build roads, and begin the process of harvesting natural resources (lumber being first on the list).

The earliest West Tennessee newspaper to which we have access is the *Jackson Gazette*, which debuted in 1824. In September of that year, the new Jackson newspaper contained an item headlined "Runaway Negro" about a slave named Solomon who had been nabbed by Madison County Sheriff Thomas Shannon. A few weeks later, Thomas Woodward offered a "liberal reward" for the return of five slaves named Reuben, Jim, Jerry, Jinny and Sucky—whom he said had been "stolen." In October, the *Jackson Gazette* announced that "a few likely NEGROES" would be sold by Madison County auctioneer A.L. Martin as part of the sale of the estate of Major Jason Wilson. In December, Madison County resident John Maness offered $50 for the return of three runaways named Ezekiel, Isaac and Shadrach.

In 1825 and 1826, there are other items in search of runaway slaves named, in order of appearance, Peter, Henry, Ben, Grace, Henry (unrelated to the first Henry), Mary (alias Polly), Rachel, Jacob, Daniel, and Ben (unrelated to the first Ben). And, in July 1826, there were at least two more items about slaves being sold—one of them advertising the sale of a "likely young NEGRO WOMAN and CHILD" to be sold at the courthouse.

What makes the immediacy of slavery so notable is what else was going on in West Tennessee at the time. In February 1825, the *Jackson Gazette* announced the creation of a new town called Covington. Brownsville and Dresden were also announced that month, and in the summer of 1825 were published items introducing the towns of Dyersburg,

## Fifty Dollars Reward.

RAN AWAY on Saturday night last, three Negro Men, the property of William Steele, of the following names and descriptions, viz—

### Ezekiel,

About forty years of age, nearly six feet high, yellow complexion, his fore-teeth out, heavy beard; said to be part Indian, his clothing not recollected.

### Isaac,

About thirty years of age, five feet five or 6 inches high, stout and well made, large whiskers, remarkably white teeth, which he shews very plain, bold look; had on a round-about jacket of striped yarn, pantaloons nearly of the same kind; an old hat, small brim.

### Shadrach,

About twenty-eight or thirty years of age, spare made, about five feet high, knock kneed; had on a roundabout jacket of white cloth, not recollected whether of cotton or yarn—a wool hat. They have a GREY HORSE with them: also two new Axes. It is supposed that there is another negro in company with them, and that they will aim to go to Illinois or some other free state.

The owner of these negroes removed to this part of the country, from Montgomery county, North-Carolina, but they were raised, it is believed, on the Eastern Shore of Maryland.

☞ The above reward, and all reasonable expenses, will be paid for said negroes, if delivered to the owner, or secured in any jail so they are got again.

JOHN B. MANESS.
Madison county, Tennessee, Nov. 29—3tcS

*Jackson Gazette,* December 11, 1824

Somerville and "Gibson Port" (later Trenton). In 1826 came announcements about Fulton, Estanaula and Raleigh.

Slaves were running away; slaves were being rounded up; slaves were being sold before many important West Tennessee towns were being laid out and formed— and long before most of them had real jails.

Further west, the earliest newspaper we have from Memphis was the *Memphis Advocate and Western District Intelligencer*. This newspaper published at least four runaway slave ads during the last three months of 1827 (all of them printed several times). By the end of 1827, Shelby County residents were on the lookout for slaves named Emery, Adam,

**Twenty Dollars Reward.**

RAN-AWAY from the subscriber, about the middle of June, at the Chickasaw Bluffs, on the Mississippi, a likely Young Negro Fellow, named

**J O E,**

about 20 years of age, 5 feet 9 or 10 inches high, very black, a smooth face, and a smiling countenance, particularly when spoken to—on one of his shoulders has a lump about the size of a marble, and the little finger of one of his hands very much bent, having been formerly broken.

As the particular route he may have taken is unknown, should any person observe a negro of the above description either in Tennessee, the Indiana Territory, or in the lower parts of Kentucky, they would confer a favor on the subscriber by communicating the information to him, through the medium of the Post-Office, or by some speedy private conveyance, and should it lead to a recovery of the slave, a reasonable compensation shall be made for their trouble. The above reward of 20 dollars will be paid to any person who will deliver the said negro to me, or lodge him in any gaol in this state, so that I may recover him.

JOHN INSTONE.

*Frankfort, (Kentucky)*
*August 28th, 1804.*

*Tennessee Gazette,* September 19, 1804

Crese, Pleasant and Ned. And, on December 8, 1827, readers of the newspaper could find an advertisement about the sale of "TWO Likely Negro Plough Boys: one thirteen and the other ten years of age. Both of good character and qualifications. For terms apply to the editors of the *Memphis Advocate*."

By the late 1830s, West Tennessee had rapidly organized. It had counties, courthouses, and sheriffs who were already busy rounding up runaway slaves and putting them in brand-new jails. However, West Tennessee actually wasn't Tennessee's last frontier. The southeast part of Tennessee remained in American Indian hands until 1838, when the Cherokees were forced to leave their homeland in the journey known today as the "Trail of Tears." Much like the black slaves who crossed the Tennessee River into East Tennessee, the Cherokee Indians would soon be forced to cross the Mississippi River, to places further west.

A few points about the Cherokee nation and slavery.

First of all, many Cherokee Indians owned slaves. In 1832, the 15,060 Cherokee Indians living in present-day Tennessee, Georgia and North Carolina owned more than 1,200 slaves.

Secondly, the *Cherokee Phoenix*—a newspaper printed by Cherokees and in the Cherokee language—ran runaway slave ads. "RUNAWAY from the subscriber on the 4th of December 1831, a negro man named JACK," ran an item in the January 28, 1832, *Phoenix*. "[He is of] black complexion about twenty four years of age well set stooped forward about five feet eight inches high weighs about 165 or 170."

Showing a remarkable similarity with other Southern newspapers, on October 4, 1830, the *Phoenix* reported that a "likely negro boy" named George would be sold later that month at the Ahmohee

---

## Runaway

FROM the subscriber, living 8 miles South West of Jackson, Tennessee, on Sunday night, the 6th inst. a Negro Man, named HENRY, about 22 years of age, yellow complexion, good countenance, about 5 feet 5 inches high, several scars on his face, had on a round-about homespun coat and pantaloons, much worn, and patched, wool hat, good shoes one of them patched. Any person delivering said negro to me, or securing him in jail so that I get him again, shall be liberally rewarded.

JAMES BAXTER.

March 12, 1825.—4w*

*Jackson Gazette*, **March 26, 1825**

# Notice.

THE Superintendent of Cherokee Removal will commence enrolling Five Horse Wagons for hauling baggage, &c. of Cherokee Emigrants, on Wednesday the 20th of June next. About three hundred Teams will be needed. Five dollars per day will be given while in the Cherokee country, the Teamster finding himself and Team; and $4 50 per day and found by the Government, when on the route West.

No man will be permitted to enroll any but his own Teams, and when enrolled, must come into service when called for, from which time pay will commence. The Drivers must be steady and sober men.

NAT. SMITH.
*Superintendent.*

CHEROKEE AGENCY, EAST, }
May 28, 1838. }

# $30 REWARD.

RANAWAY from the subscriber, living in Jacksonville on Saturday last, 19th inst. a mulatto boy named CY, belonging to Thomas Crutchfield of Athens, Tennessee. Said boy is a bright mulatto, about twenty-five years of age, 5 feet 9 or 10 inches high, has but one hand; all the fingers of his right hand was burnt off when young and also the thumb except a small part, but he still uses it nearly as well as the other, his voice is somewhat fine, and when spoken to he has rather a down countenance. There is reason to believe he will seek shelter in in the Cherokee Nation, and aim to make his escape in that way.

The above reward will be given to any person who will apprehend and deliver the above described boy, either to me in this place, or to Thomas Crutchfield, of Athens East Tennessee, or secure him in any Jail so that I get him.

JOHN CRUTCHFIELD.
Jacksonville, Ala, May 24, 1838.—tf,

(Athens) *Tennessee Journal*, June 8, 1838

courthouse "levied on as the property of AMBROSE HARNAGE, to satisfy a judgment . . . in favor of William Richardson."

Since Chattanooga didn't exist until 1839, the oldest newspaper published by white settlers in southeast Tennessee was the *Hiwassee Reporter*. It was printed in Calhoun, which is presently located on the border of McMinn and Hamilton Counties. The *Hiwassee Reporter* was publishing advertisements related to slavery as early as February 1827. "Ranaway from the subscriber, living ten miles north of Athens . . . a dark MULATTO FELLOW called LAWSON," stated one such item.

The *Hiwassee Reporter* changed its name several times in the decades prior to the Civil War. By 1838, the publication was known as the *Tennessee Journal*, and it was teeming with news about the imminent removal of the Cherokee Indians. In fact, perhaps the best evidence of how Indian Removal and slavery co-existed can be found in the June 8, 1838, edition.

On page 4, one finds an item offering $30 for the return of a runaway slave named Cy, who belonged to Thomas Crutchfield of Athens. "There is reason to believe he [Cy] will seek shelter in the Cherokee Nation, and will aim to make his escape in that way."

Right above that ad, an item indicating that Cy might have trouble if he were trying to escape with the help of a Cherokee. "Notice," began the item, in boldfaced print. "The Superintendent of Cherokee Removal will commence enrolling Five Horse Wagons for hauling baggage of Cherokee Emigrants on Wednesday the 20th of June next.

"About three hundred Teams will be needed."

# Knoxville Register.

## KNOXVILLE. TUESDAY MORNING, FEBRUARY 9, 1819.

fered for sale in regular numeri
order, commencing with the lowest
ber of section, township & range,
continue three weeks and no lon-

Given under my hand, at the city
of Washington, the 24th of
November, 1818.
JAMES MONROE.
the President:
JOSIAH MEIGS.
Comm'r of the Gen Land Office.
Printers who are authorised to
lish the laws of the United States,
publish the above once a week till
1st of May next.

### THE PRESIDENT OF THE UNITED STATES.

WHEREAS, by an act of Congress
sed on the 17th of February, 1818.
itled "an act making provision for
establishment of additional Land
ices in the Territory of Missouri,"
President of the United States is
thorised to direct the public lands
ich have been surveyed in the said
ritory, to be offered for sale.
Therefore I, JAMES MONROE, Presi
nt of the United States, do hereby
lare and make known, that public
es for the disposal (agreeably to
v) of certain lands in the territory of
ssonri, shall be held as follows, viz
Louis At, in the said territory, on
first Monday in August, October,
cember, February and April next,
d three weeks after each of the said
ys, for the sale of lands in the dis-
ct of St Louis. Thirty township
all be offered at each sale, commenc
g with the most eastern ranges wess
the fifth principal meridian line, and
oceeding westerly.

### BANK AGENCY.

THE undersigned will transact business at the Bank at Knoxville.
His terms are as follows, viz: all sum
under five hundred dollars, fifty cents,
500, and under 1.000 75 c'ts, 1.000
and under 2,000 $1, 2,000 and up-
wards $2 persons confiding their bu-
siness to him will be careful to have
their papers in good order and forward-
ed in time.

The postage on all letters addressed
to me must be paid or they will not be
attended to.
WM. H. STOCKTON.
Knoxville. Jan. 19, 1819.        3t.

### A RUN-A-WAY.

RAN AWAY from the subscriber,
in Jefferson county, a black fellow named

## JERRY,

about 40 years of age, tho' from his
appearance would not be taken to be
more than 25 black complexion, about
five feet nine inches high ; he rode a-
way a small bay horse, saddle and sad
dle bags ; he got a pass on the 24th
Dec. last, for twelve days, and was not
suspected for running away for sevrs!
days after the expiration of the term
for which his pass was given. Jerry
was seen on the road to the state of
Ohio, for which state he is no doubt
aiming. A reasonable reward will be
given for apprehending and securing
the above runaway, so that I get him
again, and all reasonable charges paid
if brought home.
CHA'S HODGE, senr.
Jefferson county Tenn. ?
January 12, 1819.    5    6t.

dians in the same light, it was a
no less incumbent upon her b
laws of na ions, than by treaty, to
repressed their lawless depredat
and, in her agents' failing to do
through neglect, they made them
parties in the war or if through
ness, they forfeited the right of
eignty in that territory where
failed to maintain it. But if Sp
gards the Indians as communitie
solutely independent, then they to
ry, by right of occupancy, belong
the Indians, and not to Spain, a
invasion was of the enemy's terr
Had the commandant of the S
post at St. Marks done his du
withholding from the enemy, su
and in denying them a refuge
the reach of his own fort, the nec
of interrupting his garrison wou
have existed ; nor is it presume
any attempt would have been m
Gen. Jackson to possess himself
post. And it is also presumed
his orders to respect the Spanish
were predicated upon this su
state of things. But, as the en
into Florida, was the reduction
Indian force—to bring the Se
war to a speedy and successful
nation, which was exhaustin
blood and the treasure of the nat
was a duty which he owed to his
try to effect that object. Any
short of this would have only i
ed the evils which it was his d
correct ; and this could not be e
while Spanish fortifications we
propriated to their defence, and
garded as sacred by him. To h
tired with his forces, under such
bination of circumstances, which
have confirmed the erroneous i

*Knoxville Register*, February 9, 1819

CHAPTER FOUR

# LAWS AND PATTYROLLERS

To understand slavery as it existed in Tennessee, one needs to become familiar with how it was addressed in state law. In short, the law not only tolerated slavery but required all officials to enforce the institution and punished people who acted in opposition to it.

Slavery was not prohibited by Tennessee's first Constitution, which was written in 1796. (In fact, the word "slave" only appears once in Tennessee's first Constitution, and that is in a context of taxation.) There was some talk of banning slavery at Tennessee's Constitutional Convention in 1834. That proposal didn't get very far. In fact, authorities in Tennessee were so worried about a repeat of Virginia's Nat Turner Rebellion that they passed a series of measures in the 1830s that made life far more difficult and restrictive for slaves.

Tennessee did not codify its laws until 1858. This makes it difficult to find out what the laws related to slavery were at any single point prior to that time. However, Tennessee's laws related to slavery in 1858 were clear and, from the point of view of the slave, harsh.

Slaves were not citizens and had practically no rights. Slaves did not have the right to file lawsuits or to bring charges against slaveholders. Slaves did not have the right to claim they were being abused, underfed

## COMMITTED

TO the jail of Knox county, on the 10th inst. a negro fellow, who says his name is

## LEWIS,

and that he belongs to a Mr. Thompson, a negro trader from whom he ranaway in the Cherokee Nation. The fellow says he was bought by Mr. Thompson, from a gentleman in Baltimore. He is a good looking fellow of common size. The owner is requested to come and prove property, pay charges and take him away.
JOHN R. NELSON, jailor K. C.
June 20, 1823.                                    3t.

*Knoxville Register,* June 20, 1823

or overworked. Furthermore, a free person who believed a slave owner was abusing, underfeeding or overworking his or her slave had no right to press charges or file a lawsuit against that person.

There were, practically, no laws that restricted what a slaveholder could do to his or her slaves. Slave owners could work slaves as much as they wanted and force them to do whatever type of work they wanted. Slaveholders could, legally, rape their slaves. They could beat their slaves. They could not, however, "wantonly and without sufficient cause beat or abuse the slave of *another* person."

In other words, it was legal for a slaveholder to beat his or her own slave "wantonly and without sufficient cause." It was also legal to beat someone else's slave, so long as it was not "wantonly and without sufficient cause." It just wasn't legal to randomly and without cause beat a slave that belonged to someone else.

It was, at least, illegal for a person to kill a slave. But there were two corollaries built into that law. For instance, it wasn't considered murder if a slaveholder killed a slave who was "in the act of resistance to his master." It also wasn't considered murder if a slave died "under moderate correction"—a clause that was not amplified in the law.

Slaves had no right to privacy. "Negro-houses," as the law referred to slave residences, could be searched at any time. If slaves were found roaming the streets by sheriffs or by special "slave patrols," which the slaves referred to as "pattyrollers," they had to have a written pass from their slaveholders. If they did not, they could be whipped and jailed.

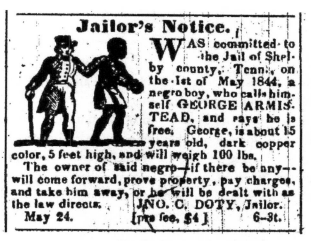

**Jailor's Notice.**

WAS committed to the Jail of Shelby county, Tenn., on the 1st of May 1844, a negro boy, who calls himself GEORGE ARMISTEAD, and says he is free. George, is about 15 years old, dark copper color, 5 feet high, and will weigh 100 lbs. The owner of said negro—if there be any—will come forward, prove property, pay charges, and take him away, or he will be dealt with as the law directs. JNO. C. DOTY, Jailor.
May 24. [fee, $4.]   6–3t.

*Memphis Commercial Appeal*, May 17, 1844

If struck by a slaveholder, it was illegal for a slave to strike back. It was illegal for a slave to marry without the permission of his or her slaveholder. It was against the law for a slave to "hire out" himself or herself; only the slaveholder had that right.

It was against the law for a slave to carry a weapon (unless he or she was hunting with his or her slaveholder and, of course, had the permission of his or her slaveholder to carry a weapon). It was illegal for a slave to sell alcohol. It was against the law for a slave to own livestock.

It was illegal for a slave to assemble with other slaves unless each of them had written passes from their slaveholders "setting forth such slave's business and time of absence."

In recent years, there has been increasing talk about Tennessee's abolitionist movement and about the state's involvement in the underground railroad. It is also true that there were some white

## KIDNAPPING.

A man who calls himself Dillingham, was arrested in this city on Tuesday night by Constable Maddux, in the act of kidnapping a number of slaves. He had them in a hack and was about crossing the bridge. This is a curious transaction for this latitude, as he could hardly expect one would suppose to get them off to a free State unmolested. He is in custody.

*Republican Banner,* **December 8, 1848**

Tennesseans who were against slavery and who aided runaway slaves. However, it needs to be emphasized that the vast majority of white Tennesseans were not abolitionists and would not aid runaway slaves. It also needs to be pointed out that there was an entire series of laws in Tennessee that restricted the actions of free people in relation to slaves.

For instance, it was against the law for a slave to visit a free black person at night (even if that free black person was their spouse or parent). It was illegal to harbor a runaway slave or give a slave a forged pass. It was against the law for a stagecoach contractor or ship's captain to carry a slave on board their carriers without the written permission of the slaveholder.

## CHOLERA.

We regret to learn that the Cholera is rather on the increase in this vicinity. On Sunday there were some sixty cases of cholera and diarrhœa at the Penitentiary and one death, the deceased, a man named Dillingham, (put in for attempting to run off negroes,) having been attacked about breakfast time, died, and was buried at half past three P. M. The malignity of the disease appears without precedent. We learn that a large number have been attacked on the opposite side of the river, many cases of which have proved fatal. This is a sad condition of things.

*Republican Banner,* **July 2, 1850**

There were many instances in which people were convicted of breaking these laws. Perhaps the best publicized was Richard Dillingham of Cincinnati, who was arrested when authorities found three slaves in his carriage as he tried to drive it out of Nashville in 1848. Dillingham confessed to his crime and was sentenced to three years in the state penitentiary, where he died of cholera in August 1850.

NEGRO STEALING.—The city of Memphis seems to be peculiarly afflicted with gentlemen negro stealers. Professor J. Milton Saunders, formerly occupying a chair in a Medical College in that city, was several weeks since arrested and is now in jail for harboring a negro woman. The other day Dr. Landon, another Esculapian Professor, was placed in the same institution.

*Athens Post*, August 11, 1854

I also found two instances in 1854 where convictions for violating the state's slave harboring law were publicized. The first was in Memphis, in which Memphis Medical Institute Professor J. Milton Saunders was sentenced to two years in the state penitentiary for "harboring a negro woman." The second was in Nashville, where four men (whose last names were Williams, Graham, Taylor and Wright) were convicted of harboring slaves. "Crime will be checked," the *Nashville Union and American* said, praising the U.S. Postal Service for its assistance in helping to prosecute the case. "Villains will select some other field for their operations than the Sixth Solicitorial District."

It was also illegal to persuade a slave to disobey or rebel against his or her slaveholder. In fact, Tennessee's law related to enticing slaves to rebel was one of the most detailed laws in the state, and written in a way to avoid loopholes:

"No person shall, in this State, write, print, paint, draw, engrave or aid or abet in writing, printing, painting, drawing or engraving on paper, parchment, linen, metal, or other substance with a view to its circulation, any paper, essay, verses, pamphlet, book, painting, drawing or engraving, calculated to excite discontent, insurrection or rebellion amongst the slaves or free persons of color." This law, by the way, was passed after the 1820s, when there were two anti-slavery newspapers in East Tennessee.

**MAIL DEPREDATIONS.**

On Saturday last, in the Criminal Court, the jury, under the charge of Judge Turner, found and returned a verdict of guilty against Jno. Williams, Graham, Taylor, and Wright, for negro-harboring.

We had seen from day to day, during the progress of this trial, in and about the Court-house, the Special Agent of the Post Office Department, B. Martin. His presence had created some little inquiry. The question was frequently asked, what interest the "old Indian" had in this trial of negro harboring? After the verdict, it was ascertained that the Special Agent had discovered that the Post office had been frequently visited by this John Wil-

*Nashville Union and American*, **December 19, 1854**

Here are more laws related to slavery and African Americans:

- A slave could not testify against a white person. Even if it *were* illegal for slaveholders to beat their slaves (which it wasn't), then it probably would have been impossible to convict someone of the crime, since the testimony of a slave would have been inadmissible.

- It was illegal for a "white person to marry a negro, mulatto, or other person of mixed negro blood to the third generation inclusive." Ministers who performed such marriages and county clerks who issued such marriage licenses were guilty of a misdemeanor and liable for fines of up to $500.

- There was a series of laws regulating the process under which "a free person of color" could intentionally become a slave. The process required the free person to sign a petition, file it with the chancery court and choose an owner. It required the petition be published in the local newspaper or (if no newspaper was published in the said town) "be posted at the front door of the courthouse, for at least a month." It required a judge to examine the petition, and for the chosen slaveholder to pay a $10 fee.[1]

ELOPEMENT.—A loving couple—
an Irishman and a negro girl belonging to Mrs. Eakin of Shelbyville,
eloped together a few days ago.—
The parties came to this place, and
took stage for Chattanooga. They
were pursued and overhauled on the
Cumberland Mountains, bro't back
to this place, and sent over to Shelbyville. Shakespeare says "the
course of true love never did run
smooth."——*Murfreesborough Telegraph.*

*Fayetteville Observer,* **January 29, 1852**

- Tennessee had detailed laws setting out procedures and public notice under which sheriffs sold runaway slaves that they had apprehended (after a year waiting period). It also set out procedures in which chancery and circuit courts sold slaves.

Speaking of slave sales, Tennessee law did not address whether it was illegal for slaves to be sold away from their families. We can therefore assume it was not only legal for slaveholders and professional auctioneers to sell mothers away from infant children, it

---

[1]This was actually done several times, although the reasons why it was done in each case are not clear. In 1861 a free black woman who lived in Hawkins County named Cindy Bayley went through the process to voluntarily become a slave. Gordon Belt, director of public services for the Tennessee State Library and Archives, has researched her case and believes that she did it so that she could be close to her family. (Keep in mind that laws restricted how much time a free black person could spend with an enslaved person.)

> ☞ A negro named Kennedy was Monday on trial before the recorder, charged with violating one of the commandments with an abandoned white woman, who lives in gallows hollow. Corrections intended to bring him to a sense of the enormity of his conduct, and the difference between white and black, were ordered to be administered. •

*Clarksville Jeffersonian*, November 26, 1856

was legal for the Davidson County sheriff and the Lincoln County chancery clerk and master to do so (more on this in later chapters).

Tennessee law regarding the slave trade in 1858 differed greatly from what had been the law in the state for much of the three decades prior to that time. From 1827 until 1855, it was illegal to "import into this state [Tennessee] any slave or slaves, either for life or for a shorter period, for the purpose of selling or disposing of them or any of them as articles of merchandise in this state."

What did this law allow, and what did it theoretically ban?

Under Tennessee's interstate slave ban, it was illegal for a person to buy slaves in Virginia and bring them to Tennessee and sell them.

It was legal, however, for a person to go to Virginia, buy slaves in Virginia and bring them to Tennessee for their own use (which was very common). If that slaveholder was forced by circumstances to sell slaves at a later time (to pay debt, for instance), they could argue that they had not brought slaves into Tennessee "for the purpose of selling or disposing of them."

It was legal for a person or organization to commission and pay someone else to go to Virginia and bring back slaves on their behalf. This is what the city of Nashville did in 1830, when it paid William Ramsey $12,000 to go to Virginia and buy 24 slaves on the city's behalf.

It was legal for a person to buy slaves at an estate sale in Knoxville, take them across the state and sell them in Memphis.

It was legal for a professional slave trader to buy slaves in Virginia or Maryland and transport them through Tennessee to be sold in Louisiana or Mississippi.

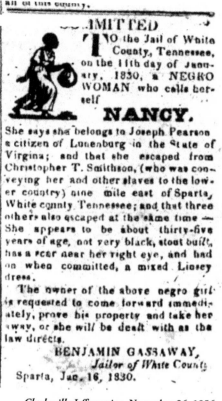

COMMITTED

TO the Jail of White County, Tennessee, on the 11th day of January, 1830, a NEGRO WOMAN who calls herself

**NANCY.**

She says she belongs to Joseph Pearson a citizen of Lunenburg in the State of Virginia; and that she escaped from Christopher T. Smithson, (who was conveying her and other slaves to the lower country) nine mile east of Sparta, White county Tennessee; and that three others also escaped at the same time — She appears to be about thirty-five years of age, not very black, stout built, has a scar near her right eye, and had on when committed, a mixed Linsey dress.

The owner of the above negro girl is requested to come forward immediately, prove his property and take her away, or she will be dealt with as the law directs.

BENJAMIN GASSAWAY,
*Jailor of White County*

Sparta, Jan. 16, 1830.

*Clarksville Jeffersonian*, **November 26, 1856**

It was legal for a Tennessee slaveholder to sell his or her slaves to a professional slave trader to be taken across the state line and sold in Mississippi, Louisiana or Texas.

Not only was Tennessee's "ban" on the interstate slave trade full of loopholes, books on the subject also raise questions about how seriously it was enforced. As one very knowledgeable author wrote in 1957, "Interstate trading again became legal [in Tennessee] in 1855, and those who had been carrying on the trade under cover now came out into the open where they could reap much more substantial rewards."

## $50 REWARD

WAS missing from the neighborhood of the chickasaw Bluff, about the middle of December last.

### CLARA.

a negro girl about 19 years of age, middle size, African face, heavy built with toes somewhat turned inwards & scattering—she is talkative when indulged and was originally purchased of Mr. Richard B. Tunstal of Louisville Ky. At the same time

### LOUISA.

a black girl about twelve years of age, small for her years, with slender feet for a negro,—bad face, and bad expression of countenance—she was purchased from Thomas Hargrave and J. W. Crockett, living in the Green river county, on the Nashville road. Louisa may possibly be recognized by speaking of her brother George, a small boy, who is also owned by her mistress ; and either of them, of their former masters.

About the time these negroes disappeared from the Bluffs, two horses were also missing, which have not since been heard of, one a LIGHT SORRELL, raw-boned, slim, with a switch ta l and one white hind foot. The other a BROWN BAY MARE, small round and well made, with a heavy switch tail. No other marks, nor any brands recollected.

The negroes are the property of Mrs Henrietta Jacobs, a helpless widow with three little children. They comprise the chief part of their estate and that portion of it upon which they relied much for immediate support. It is supposed they were decoyed from the Bluffs by one M'Clennan, who lately escaped from the jail at the Bluffs and his accomplices. That they were carried off on horses, either to Alabama or Missouri, and there sold. There is most reason to suspect they were carried to the former state.

The above reward will be paid for the apprehension and delivery of the negroes, or half that price for securing either of them. A liberal reward will also be given for the return of the horses, and any information relative to them thankfully received, & generously rewarded if required.

Should this advertisement meet the eye of those in whose hands the negroes now are, it is to be hoped, that they will communicate the circumstance and unite their endeavors in bringing the offenders to JUSTICE.

He will continue to practice MEDICINE, SURGERY &c. in Madison and the adjacent countres. Jackson Aug. 14, 1823.        87—5

# LANDS

### For Sale in the Western District of Tennessee.

THE Trustees of the University o N. Carolina, offer for sale 25,000 acres of Land, lying in the Western District of Tennessee. Their lands are situate in different parts of the District ; and purchasers can be accommodated with large or small tracts, on the Obion, Forked deer, Hatchee, Loosatchy or Wolf Rivers, as they shall prefer. Titles will be made, with general warranty against all adverse claims, and sales will be made upon a liberal credit. The subscriber living on Forked deer river is duly authorised to make sales and conveyances.        SAM'L. DICKENS.
July 15 —tf.

## MONEY IS WANTED!!

THOSE indebted to the PIONEER OFFICE for JOB-WORK, &c whose accounts have been some time standing will please settle the same immediately, for the Proprietors stand in need of money.

## NOTICE.

BY VIRTUE of a fieri facias to me directed from the late Superior court of Law for the District of Mero, on Saturday the 4th of October next, I will proceed to sell at the court-house in the Town of Memphis, all the right title and interest that Joel Rice, Nathan Rice, William H. Rice, heirs of John Rice dec'd—and that Joel Rice, Harriet Rice, Elizabeth Rice and Nancy Rice Heirs of Elisha Rice, dec'd, who rias also one of the Heirs of said John wice, ded'd. hath in and to a certain tract or parcel of Land containing

### 5000 Acres,

in the 11th Surveyors district 2nd range of the 8th and 9th sections, on the north side of Big Hatchie river. Taken to satisfy an execution obtained by Philemon Thomas, against the heirs of said John Rice dec'd.    Sale at the hours prescribed by law.
SAMUEL R BROWN.
Aug. 19. 1823.        Sdff. Shelby county,

JOEL RICE, Nathan Rice, William H. Rice, Heirs of John Rice, dec'd. Joel Rice, John Rice, Harriet Rice, Elizabeth Rice, and Nancy Rice, heirs of Elisha Rice, who was also me of

*Jackson Pioneer*, **September 9, 1823**

PART TWO
# RUNAWAYS

## Forty Dollars' Reward.

Ranaway from the Turnpike Gate
on the Cumberland Mountain,

### Allen,

a dark mulatto man of portly stature
and elegant appearance, his address
is soft, smooth and without hesitation
though not fluent. He is near 6 feet
high and is inclined to corpulency,
the contour of his face is bold, but
his eyes are mild. He plays on the
fiddle, understands boating, has been
upon sea, and talks much of naval
affairs. He is a native of Maryland.
A mr Walton who moved last fall
from North Carolina to some part
of this state, (I believe) formerly
owned him, and now owns his wife;
four days after said Walton passed
the Turnpike Gate, Allen run off,
which gives good reason to presume
that he skulked after his wife, no
doubt unknown to mr Walton. However his aim is to obtain his freedom,
and he may have taken passage in a
boat down the river towards New
Orleans, or passed over to the state
of Ohio on his way to Baltimore. I
will give forty dollars for the apprehension and safe incarceration of
the said Negro if found out of this state,
and twenty taken within it.

### Thomas H. Holland

Maury county, Jan 27

*Impartial Review and Cumberland Repository*, February 11, 1808

CHAPTER FIVE

# BLACKSMITHS AND FIDDLERS

In the course of researching this book, I found around 1,200 runaway slave ads that appeared in Tennessee's newspapers. More than 900 of them were purchased by slaveholders in Tennessee (as opposed to slaveholders in Mississippi or Alabama, who advertised in Tennessee newspapers anticipating that their slaves might have fled north). Those advertisements appear in Appendix One, and these are the ads usually referred to in this book.

About the format of the ads: In antebellum Tennessee, newspapers were usually four pages and published weekly. There wasn't much room for local news. Papers generally consisted of national and international stories (sometimes weeks after they occurred), along with local advertisements. Runaway slave ads were usually found on pages 3 or 4, although sometimes they would run on page 1, especially the first time they were published.

A runaway slave ad was typically 10-30 lines long, usually enough room for between 100 and 300 words. They were often illustrated with a silhouette of a runaway slave, and almost always concluded with the name of the slaveholder who purchased the ad. Runaway slave ads were typically published for 4 to 8 consecutive issues. An ad first appearing in late October might still be running at Christmas.

## 50 Dollars Reward

Ran away from the subscriber, two negro fellows named Adam and Cato Adam is about 23 or 24 years of age of a yellow complexion, about 5 feet 8 or 9 inches high, has a white hat a & surout of snuff colour. camurraed & white a little, has a pass, is a Shoemaker, and can work a little at the Carpenter's Business.—Cato is a well set fellow, about 20 or 21 years of age about 5 feet 7 or 8 inches high, was apprehended on westside of Cumberland mountain about two miles from the foot, was taken and broke custody, had on a pair of handcuffs, when he escaped, his clothing were an old blue stright coat, an old black worn, and a pair of pattaloons of dark mixed broad cloth broke at the knees. The above named fellows have run from South Carolina out of York District their master's name is William Edward Hayne. They are making for the Black Fox Camp, or the Indiana Territory. Any person apprehending said negroes is requested to lodge them in Carthage jail, so that the said master gets them again, shall be entitled to the above reward, or twenty dollars for either of them.

Alexander Ardrey, for
William Edward Hayne.
Nov. 28, 1810.

*Impartial Review and Cumberland Repository*, January 11, 1811

Ads usually started with the name of the slave (slaves typically didn't have last names) and an estimate of the slave's age (slaveholders apparently almost never knew the exact age of their slaves). They included a general description of the slave's appearance, such as height, age, build, length of hair, color of skin and—since most slaves only had one set of clothes—a description of the clothes the slave was wearing when he or she ran away.

Slaves who were multiracial were described as "yellow," "copper" or "mulatto"—common descriptions at the time. Regardless of age, a male slave in a runaway slave ad was typically referred to as "boy"; a female slave was almost always referred to as a "girl." The slaveholder would often predict the general direction he thought the slave was heading—usually either toward a free state or in the direction of some of the slave's family members.

## RUNAWAY

FROM the subscriber, on Monday, the 21th instant, a yellow negro man slave named

### JOSHUA,

about 5 feet 6 or 8 inches high,—has a scar on one side of his face, aged about 50 years, has been a Baptist preacher a number of years, had on when he went away a suit of blue mixt jeans, and white fur hat, he rode away, a bay mare of his own, and will probably make for a free State. A liberal reward will be given if he is delivered to the subscriber or secured that he can be got.          SERENE J. HULME,
    March 29--21*                           near Franklin, T.

*Nashville Republican*, **March 29, 1834**

When a slaveholder referred to a runaway slave's wife, he almost always referred to her as "a" wife rather than as "the" wife—I suppose to imply that slave spouses were different than white spouses, or that slaves weren't monogamous.

If more than one slave had run away, several slaves would be described in the same ad, and the ad might be a lot longer. I found ads for as many as seven slaves who had run away from the same slaveholder at the same time—a family of seven, ranging in ages from 45 to infant, who ran away from Samuel Clampett of Limestone County, Alabama, in 1820.

The reward for the return of a slave ranged from as low as $3 to as high as $500. That award usually varied based on whether the slave was apprehended in Tennessee or in a different state.

Some slaveholders included the slave's job or skill in the description of the slave. Since the majority of runaway slave ads did not include this detail, this information doesn't necessarily prove anything about what percentage of slaves did agricultural work versus how many did skilled work. But it does remind us that not all slaves worked on farms. For instance:

## $100 REWARD.

RANAWAY from the subscriber, living 6 miles North of Dandridge, Jefferson county, East Tennessee, 2 NEGRO MEN—one named GEORGE aged about 28 years, of a tawny color, six feet high, straight and handsomely built, inclining to Roman nose, assuming consequential airs when spoken to; by trade a brick-layer, plasterer and painter—has pretensions as a barber.

The other, named LIGE, aged 26 years, of a black color, six feet high, and thickness corresponding with his height. It is believed that they will aim for Nashville, or some point on the Ohio river. I will give $50 for each, if taken out of the State, or $25 each, if taken in the State, and secured in jail so I get them.

WILLIAM MASSENGILL.

Dandridge, Sept 23, 1840—3t.

*Republican Banner*, September 26, 1840

- In 25 of the ads, the slave was described as a blacksmith. "He [Isaac] is a blacksmith, which can be discovered I expect by some scars on the arms from the burning of the sparks," according to slaveholder John S. Willis of Maury County in 1830.

- In 18 of the ads, the slave was described as a carpenter. "He [Elijah] has been employed for several years as a house carpenter and will probably endeavor to get employment in that line," wrote slaveholder W. Chilton of Overton County in 1821. "He took with him some plain bits and probably other tools."

- In 13 of the ads, the slave was said to be a shoemaker.

Other professions include cooper, seamstress, stonemason, bricklayer, flatboat maker, ostler, tanner, weaver, barber, plasterer, painter, millwright, turner and tin-plate workman, cook, waiter, race horse trainer and minister.

"[Ben] can work at the Mill-wright business, and is well acquainted with attending a mill,"[1] wrote slaveholder Francis Newsom of Nashville in 1807.

Four runaway slaves were even described as engineers. "Runaway from the Worly Furnace, Dickson County . . . TOM, an engineer, about 21 years old, well formed, middle size and intelligent," wrote Montgomery Bell in an 1845 ad.

Other slaveholders mentioned outside work experience, likely to increase the number of readers who might recognize the slave from having seen him on the job. A slave named Billy "drove a hack between Nashville and Louisville [for] about three months," according to slaveholder Edward Jones of Sumner County. A slave named David, who ran away from Henry C. Bell of Obion County in 1833, "has served as a cook for two or three seasons on different steamboats."

Some slaves were said to have more than one profession. "[Sam is a] good cook, an excellent waiter in the house, and carriage driver," said slaveholder Michael Campbell of Nashville in 1813. "He understands all kinds of farming work and the distillery."

According to Charles W. Metcalfe of Springfield in 1833, the runaway slave named Major was "a stone-cutter, stone mason and brick mason, and a very superior workman at either branch."

---

[1] The mill which Francis Newsom and his slave Ben ran together was undoubtedly at Newsom's Station, now part of the Harpeth River State Park.

## REWARD.
### $25! $25!! $25!!!

**R**ANAWAY on Wednesday, 10th inst., ALBERT, a dark mulatto, about 22 years of age, a Carpenter by trade, about 5 feet 8 inches in height. Said boy can read and write, is also something of an Engineer, having served in a cotton factory. Any person securing said boy in any jail in the State, shall receive the above reward by applying to Thomas K. Handy, Franklin, Tenn., or H. & J. Kirkman, Nashville, Tenn.

Nashville, Jan. 17, 1844.—tf

*Republican Banner,* July 31, 1844

Fanny was "a good seamstress, milliner and mantua," wrote Elizabeth Cox of Nashville in an 1835 ad.

Squire, who ran away from Miles M. Temple of Tipton County in 1839, had been "a house servant, bar-keeper, ostler and gardener."

George, who ran away from William Massengill of Jefferson County in 1840, was "by trade a brick-layer, plasterer and painter— has pretensions as a barber."

Albert, who ran away from Thomas K. Handy of Franklin in 1844, was "a carpenter by trade" and "also something of an engineer, having served in a cotton factory."

Anderson, who ran away from William P. Cannon of Franklin in 1847, was "a carpenter by trade" who "has been preaching for some time past."

There were also special skills occasionally mentioned in runaway slave ads—the most common being the ability to read and write, which I found in 33 ads.

"He [Allen] plays on the fiddle, understands boating, has been upon sea, and talks much of naval affairs," slaveholder Thomas H. Holland of Maury County said in an 1808 ad.

$100 REWARD.

RANAWAY from Worly Furnace, Dickson County, on the 3d instant, two likely light colored Mulatto Boys, TOM, an engineer, about 21 years old, well formed, middle size and intelligent. JIM, a Blacksmith, about 18 years old, one leg shorter than the other, perceivable when he walks. It is supposed that two low white women left the neighborhood about the same time, and that the boys may be in Company with them. I will pay the above reward to any person who will deliver the boys to James L. Bell, at the Patterson Iron Works, Davidson County, Tennessee.

MONTGOMERY BELL.

August 6; 1845.—3t          W&U

*Republican Banner*, **August 15, 1845**

**$500 Reward.**

RANAWAY from the subscriber, on the 25th May, a very bright Mulatto Boy, about 21 or 22 years old, named WASH. Said Boy, without close observation, might pass himself for a white man, as he is very bright—has sandy hair, blue eyes and a fine set of teeth. He is an excellent bricklayer; but I have no idea that he will pursue his trade for fear of detection. Although he is like a white man in appearance, he has the disposition of a negro, and delights in comic songs and witty expressions.—He is an excellent house servant, very handy about a hotel—tall, slender, and has rather a down look, especially when spoken to, and is sometimes inclined to be sulky. I have no doubt but he has been decoyed off by some scoundrel, and I will give the above reward for the apprehension of the Boy and thief, if delivered in Chattanooga; or I will give $200 for the Boy alone, or $100 if confined in any jail in the United States, so that I can get him.     GEORGE O. RAGLAND.
Chattanooga, June 3, 1852—je16

*Memphis Eagle and Enquirer,* June 30, 1852

Clem "is a remarkable fellow" who "has wrestled a great many times and was never thrown down by black or white, and but seldom beat at running or jumping," according to slaveholder William B. Robertson (1820).

Willis "professes to be a conjurer or fortune teller," wrote slaveholder John G. Easley of Hickman County (1825).

"[Joshua] has been a Baptist preacher a number of years," wrote slaveholder Serene J. Hulme of Williamson County (1834).

Margaret "speaks some Cherokee and likely a little French," according to slaveholder George W. Murphy of Memphis (1846).

Jacob Crockett (one of the few runaway slaves in Tennessee who apparently had a last name) was "a first-rate wagoner and an excellent fiddler," according to slaveholder Montgomery Irvin of Washington County (1840).

There was no set format to runaway slave ads. Purchasers of such ads were apparently not asked to fill out a form, nor asked a standard set of questions by newspaper staff. Instead, the slaveholders wrote these ads by hand. As a result, the order of information and detail in runaway slave ads varies wildly. Some ads hardly say anything

**$50 REWARD.**

I WILL give the above reward for the apprehension and safe keeping (until I get him) of my man NAT, if taken out of the State, and $25 if taken in the State. Nat is about 27 or 28 years old, smooth black skin, 5 feet 6 or 8 inches high; wears a goatee, has an intellectual appearance, would weigh about 185 lbs., had on when he left a black sack Coat, striped Pants, Boots and black Hat; had a fiddle under his arm and is a carpenter by trade.

My address is Chesnut Grove P. O., Davidson County, Tennessee. JAMES L. BELL.

mar10 '54—tf

*Nashville Union and American*, **March 21, 1854**

about the slave's mannerisms. But here are examples of ads that not only discuss the slave's behavior, but give an idea of how well some slaveholders knew their slaves:

- Oston has "an effeminate voice" and "when he looks at any person is in the habit of shutting his left eye," wrote slaveholder Andrew Jackson of Nashville (1809).

- Abraham "is extremely proud; smokes segars, and walks with a considerable air," according to slaveholder Captain Sample of Davidson County (1813).

- Davy is "cringing and sycophantic in his manners," wrote Alexander McMillan of Knox County (1830).

- Jacob "possesses a good countenance and easy address, well calculated to impose on the unsuspecting," according to James W. Wily of Greene County (1831).

- Lilburn "looks earnestly at you when spoken to," wrote Albert Ward of Nashville (1835).

- Shack "is very much addicted to whittling and singing," according to George T. Taylor of Haywood County (1835).

- "When walking, [Green] steps very long, and inclines to bend forward," wrote Daniel Dansbee of Maury County. "He is a very artful fellow, and well calculated to deceive."

- "[John] is fond of telling extravagant tales for the amusement of those that are present," according to William Winfrey of Germantown (1843).

- "[Wash] delights in comic song and witty expressions," wrote George O. Ragland of Chattanooga (1852).

Slaveholders were generally annoyed and angry when slaves ran away, and this tone is often made very clear in the ad. "Abram is a boy about 19 or 20 years of age," the Bedford County jailer wrote in an 1842 *Shelbyville Intelligencer* ad. "No scars recollected, only on one occasion by a rifle ball shot through one of his thighs when he was taken this summer."

## $100 Reward.

RANAWAY from the subscriber, on the night of the 24th of July, a mulatto fellow, named CYRUS, a Tanner by trade, and a first rate Mechanic.

Cyrus is copper-colored, with a very heavy suit of hair (wavy); is forty-two years of age, but does not look nearly so old. He is very intelligent, but speaks in a slow, undertone, and has a habit of clearing his throat frequently during his conversation. He may be known easily by having a stiff finger on the right hand, I think. The bone of the third finger was broken and indented, and the finger presents the appearance of a stick cut half in two.

Cyrus was well dressed, and carried off a large wardrobe and plenty of money. He is very likely off for a Free State. I will give a reward of $50 for his apprehension and confinement in jail so that I can get him, if caught in this State, and $100 if caught out of the State.

Dr. JAMES B. STONE, White House,
Aug2—tf        Williamson county, Tenn.

*Nashville Union and American,* **August 6, 1856**

In an 1857 ad in Clarksville, slaveholder James Radford wrote that a runaway slave named William "has a very sulky appearance when spoken to, and is quite bushy headed. He may have a wound from a pistol shot as he was shot at twice."

However, this was not always the case. In 1816, Wilson County resident Baker Wrather offered $10 for the return of a slave named Major, who he had only recently purchased from the estate of Thomas Masterson. Major took with him a horse and a good saddle "with plated stirrup irons." However, Wrather said that Major had "absconded without the least provocation" and that, if he returned, "he shall be forgiven."

Finally, one more important point about antebellum newspapers in Tennessee: They never reported whether runaway slaves were ever caught and returned to their slaveholders. There wasn't much local news in newspapers of that era, including reports on the apprehension of slaves. Slaveholders had no reason to buy ads announcing that they had captured a runaway.

Of course, whenever sheriffs apprehended runaway slaves, they ran a notice in the newspaper with a short description of the slave, the name of the slave and the person to whom the slave said they belonged (if the slave had revealed this information). Despite these notices, it is very difficult to link runaway slave ads with notices about captured runaways (which were often from other states such as Georgia, Alabama or Mississippi).

So, in general, we know that a slave ran away. We usually know the name that they went by, what they were wearing, about how old they were, whether they had any special skills, whether they had a nervous tic, whether they had scars, and in what direction they probably headed.

For the most part, what became of them remains a mystery.

CHAPTER SIX

# NAMESAKES AND LEADERS

Today, wealthy and important people generally use agents to do their unpleasant work. They have lawyers and personal assistants to perform tasks with which they don't want to soil their hands.

That's not the way it was done in the early 1800s. In fact, many of the runaway slave ads in this book were purchased by people I have encountered elsewhere in historical research.

Abraham Maury was a prominent state senator who, in the 1790s, had a plantation near Franklin. Today he is best known as the uncle of Matthew Fontaine Maury, who is now known as the "Pathfinder of the Seas" because of his contributions to oceanography. In September 1798, Abraham Maury ran an ad in the *Knoxville Gazette* offering a $10 reward for a runaway slave named Godfry. "It is probable he [Godfry] has changed his name, having before eloped and called himself Robert Wilson," the ad stated.

During Nashville's first decade, John McNairy was one of its most important residents. Having migrated to Middle Tennessee in 1788, McNairy was appointed by President George Washington to be the first judge of the U.S. District Court in the state of Tennessee. In February 1801, McNairy ran an ad in the *Tennessee Gazette* hoping for the return of one of his runaway slaves. "Five Dollars reward WILL be given to any person who shall apprehend and confine a Negro Fellow that I get him again," McNairy wrote. "His name is NED."

RUNAWAY from my farm on Mill creek, in Davidson county, on the 26th of May last, a negro man named

JACOB,

a little upwards of 20 years of age, is 6 feet high or upwards, rather slender made, has rather a down look when spoken to, his eyes are generally very red, he is generally humble in the presence of white people, he carried away his working clothes though it is presumed he has changed them. Any person who will secure the said slave in jail so that I get him, or delivers him to me at my farm, shall receive a handsome reward.

JOHN OVERTON,
By his agent,
William Dickerson.

July 29th, 1806.    15.    3w ortf.

*Tennessee Gazette*, August 19, 1806

John Overton was one of the founders of Memphis; Overton Park is named for him. Overton was also a prominent judge, banker and the original owner of the Traveller's Rest plantation in Nashville. In August 1806, Overton ran an ad in Nashville's *Impartial Review and Cumberland Repository* newspaper in hopes of retrieving a slave named Jacob. The runaway was "a little upwards of 20 years of age, is 6 feet or upwards high, rather slender made, has a rather down look when spoken to, his eyes are generally very red; he is generally humble in the presence of white people." Anyone who found, secured and returned the young man would receive a "handsome reward," the ad assured.

Thomas Hardeman was already prominent in Williamson County when he offered $20 for the return of a slave named Bob. "It is supposed that he [Bob] will aim for the Cherokee nation or state of Ohio," Hardeman speculated in his 1807 ad. Hardeman would later fight in the War of 1812 and then move to Texas, where he became a leader in the fight for independence.

Twenty Dollars Reward.

On the 18th inst. runaway from the subscriber a negro man called *BOB*, of yellow complexion, about 23 years of age, five feet seven or eight inches high; he took with him a new rifle gun engraved on the barrel M. Buil, she was stocked with walnut, had on iron guard and silver thumb piece, and star on the breach—Also he took a three point blanket, a blue cloth coat turned up with red, a straw hat, yarn hunting shirt and other clothing of cotton and toe manufacture. It is supposed that he will aim for the Cherokee nation or state of Ohio—Any person delivering him to me, in Williamson county, state of Tennessee, or secure him any Jail in the U. States, so that I get him, shall receive the above reward.

Thomas Hardeman.

27th sept.

*Impartial Review and Cumberland Repository*, September 24, 1807

Felix Grundy was a U.S. Representative, Senator and the 13th Attorney General of the United States. The November 11, 1812, *Nashville Whig* newspaper contains an ad in which he offered $50 to the person who returned to him a slave named Jim. Jim, the ad said, was "about nineteen or twenty years of age, 5 feet 6 or 7 inches high, and remarkably stout made—He had on, when taken, a coarse linen shirt and pantaloons." Grundy theorized that Jim had been "stolen by a certain JAMES SMITH, who was convicted of horse stealing at the last September term of the Davidson circuit court."

William Carroll was one of the heroes of the Battle of New Orleans, and the longest-serving governor in Tennessee history. On January 30, 1822, the *Whig* ran an ad that offered $10 for the reward of Ellick, a slave held by a business known as R&W Armstrong but who had formerly been held by Carroll.

Besides buying ads for runaway slaves, Abraham Maury, John McNairy, Thomas Hardeman, Felix Grundy, John Overton and William Carroll have something else in common: Today there are Tennessee counties named for all six.

In 1805, Joel Childress offered $30 for the return of a 22-year-old slave named Aaron who, like so many runaways in Tennessee history, was believed to be heading in the direction of Virginia. Today, not a lot of people recognize Joel Childress' name. But many have heard of his daughter Sarah Childress Polk, wife of President James K. Polk.

The city of Hendersonville is named for William T. Henderson. On August 23, 1806, he ran an ad for the sale of his farm, which he referred to as "Farmer's Delight." The sale included 640 acres, beef cattle and "two negroes"—a woman and a child (age not disclosed).

Giles Harding Sr. was one of the first members of the Harding family to migrate from Virginia to Tennessee. Like so many of Middle Tennessee's early migrants, he brought slaves from Virginia. In 1816, six years after Giles Sr. died, one of the slaves tried to run away. "The above reward [$10] will be given to any person who will deliver said Frank to me, or secure him so that I can get him again," Giles Harding Jr. wrote in an ad that appeared in the *Nashville Whig*. Giles Jr.'s brother John would later start the Belle Meade plantation, which eventually stretched over 5,000 acres and became nationally famous.

Murfreesboro was named for Hardy Murfree, a colonel in the Revolutionary War. In 1808, Murfree offered $20 for the return of a slave named Toby. "I do expect he is on his way to South Carolina," Murfree said. "Any person apprehending said negro and delivering him to me, or confining him in any jail in this state, so that I [can] get him, shall have the above reward."

George Colbert was one of the most famous Chickasaw Indians of his time. He commanded 350 Chickasaws who fought for Andrew Jackson at the Battle of Horseshoe Bend. Colbert also ran the ferry along the Natchez Trace that crossed the Tennessee River, near present-day Florence, Alabama. (The county south of Florence is named for him.) In April 1823, Colbert ran a *Nashville Whig* ad in hopes of tracking down three runaway slaves named Trouble, Phillip and July. "I am disposed to think they will push for some of the free states and may probably attempt to get to the western side of the Mississippi," Colbert wrote in his ad.[1]

## $100 REWARD.

RANAWAY from the subscriber, living near Old Town, in the Chickasaw Nation, three negroes named TROUBLE, PHILIP and JULY. Trouble, an African, is about 55 years old, very black, coarse featured, about 5 feet 8 or 9 inches high - all that is recollected of his clothing is a 3½ point blanket capo coat. Philip is about twenty years old, and about 6 feet high, a very dark mulatto, rather a good looking fellow, and had on, when he started, the Indian garb, with a 3½ point blanket capo coat, he is an excellent hunter, and took with him a rifle, long and heavy, small bore and plain walnut stock, stained black. July, is about 5 feet 10 or 11 inches high, dark complexion, and about 18 years old ; and had on when he left here the Indian garb, but also took with him pantaloons, hat, &c. I cannot describe any marks on either of them as none are recollected. The two youngest are likely and well made, and were raised by me, they all speak English as well as the Chickasaw language. It is very probable when they reach the white settlement they will change their dress. I am disposed to think they will push for some of the free states and may probably attempt to get to the western side of the Mississippi. I will give the above reward of one hundred dollars for the three, and in proportion for each, if taken and secured so that I can get them—or one hundred dollars and all reasonable expences paid if delivered to me at my place of residence.

GEORGE COLBERT.

Chickasaw Nation, }
April 9, 1823. }        3m.

*Nashville Whig*, April 30, 1823

Lysander McGavock's home still stands, and is used as part of the Brentwood Country Club. On November 22, 1824, McGavock offered $10 for the return of a slave named Thornton. "He had a pair of handcuffs on when he broke away," the ad said. "It is probable he will endeavor to get to Kentucky."

Henry Crabb was the father of Henry A. Crabb, one of many Tennesseans who would eventually migrate west and play a role in the early history of California. In October 1825, the older Crabb offered $50 for the return of a slave named Elijah.

Patrick Meagher was one of the first prominent citizens of Memphis. In December

[1] Ironically, Colbert died in 1839 during his forced journey west as part of the Indian Removal (also known as the Trail of Tears).

1827 (about a year after the city was incorporated), he purchased an ad in the *Memphis Advocate* offering a $25 reward for the return of a female slave named Crese—"a likely negro girl, about sixteen years, with nose inclined to Roman. . . [she] is extremely forward and pert when spoken to."

## $100 REWARD.

RUNAWAY from the Narrows of Harpeth on the last of February: came to White's Bend, where he spent Sunday, the 1st of March, without manifesting himself to me: that night crossed the river at Hillsboro'. JACOB is a round smooth faced fellow, about 22 years old, low of stature, but stout and strongly formed. He is a tolerable blacksmith. He may have got in company with a runaway negro Jesse, formerly the property of Mr. Rape of Harpeth, and for which negro there is a high reward offered, or he may have got into a boat under some pretence. I will give the above reward to any person that will lodge him in Nashville Jail, or deliver him to me in White's bend. M. BELL.

March 23--eo1&w3t

*Daily Republican Banner*, **March 23, 1840**

Montgomery Bell was one of Tennessee's wealthiest men of his era. Today there is a state park and a private school named for him. To read some material written by the man, consult the August 27, 1807 *Tennessee Gazette*, the August 9, 1814 *Nashville Whig*, the June 2, 1816 *Nashville Whig*, the March 23, 1840 *Republican Banner*, the September 20, 1843 *Republican Banner*, the August 15, 1845 *Republican Banner*, and the December 14, 1854 *Nashville Union and American*. My favorite of those ads is the sixth one, in which Bell theorized what happened to two runaways named Tom and Jim. "It is supposed that two low white women left the neighborhood about the same time, and that the boys may be in Company with them," Bell wrote. "I will pay the above reward [$100] to any person who will deliver the boys to James L. Bell at the Patterson Iron Works, Davidson County."

> *A negro boy named ABRAHAM,*
> RANAWAY from the house of cap-
> tain Sample, in the county of Da-
> vidson, about the first of April. He is
> 18 or 19 years of age, about 5 feet 6 or
> 7 inches high, and will weigh probably
> 135 or 40. He has a very broad flat foot,
> speaks rather quick, and (in commen-
> cing) somewhat stammers.
>
> Information has been had of his cross-
> ing Cumberland at Haysborough about 3
> weeks ago ; and of his having a letter in
> his possession, a free pass perhaps that he
> has procured from some white man.
>
> I will reward liberally any person that
> will deliver him to me, or secure him in
> some gaol.        JOHN H. EATON.
> Franklin, T. May 5, 1813.

*Nashville Whig,* **May 19, 1813**

John Henry Eaton of Franklin would eventually become a U.S. Senator and U.S. Secretary of War. Today, American history students learn about "Eaton's Affair," a Washington saga that played a major role in Martin Van Buren's ascent to the presidency. Eaton's name appeared twice in Tennessee runaway slave ads: In 1813, when a slave named Abraham ran away, and in 1837, when a slave named Claiborne ran away.

Remember John Overton? His son, John Overton Jr. was the developer of Nashville's Maxwell House Hotel, which may have been the nicest place to stay in the South for a time. John Jr.'s name appears on a runaway slave ad in 1847. "Ranaway from the subscriber, living about five miles from Nashville, on the Franklin Turnpike, two likely young men, FOSTER and HAYWOOD," the ad said.

Cave Johnson was a member of the U.S. House of Representatives for 14 years and the Postmaster General of the United States during the presidency of James K. Polk. We have a wonderful photograph of the man visiting the White House, pictured with President and Mrs. Polk, James Buchanan and Dolly Madison. In September 1847, an 18-year-old slave that Johnson held title to named Henry tried

> ## $40 Reward.
>
> **R**ANAWAY from the subscriber, living about five miles from Nashville, on the Franklin Turnpike, two likely young negro men, FOSTER and HAYWOOD. The former is of dark complexion, about five feet nine or ten inches high, rather slender, and has a thin face—he is a quick-spoken and very smart and active boy, aged about nineteen years. The latter, Haywood, is of dark yellow complexion, about five feet eight or nine inches high, rather slow to speak, has a full face, and is aged about eighteen years. I will give $20 for the apprehension of either of them.
> June 11—t2w.            · · JOHN OVERTON.

*Republican Banner*, June 23, 1847

to escape. John Hiter, acting on Johnson's behalf, ran an ad in the *Clarksville Weekly Chronicle* offering to "suitably reward the person" who apprehended Henry.

Finally, there is Andrew Jackson—farmer, attorney, judge, general and seventh president of the United States. Jackson published at least three runaway slave ads. In 1809, he offered $20 for the return of a slave named Oston (who, according to the ad, had run away before and made it all the way to the Ohio River). A few months after he got back from the Battle of New Orleans, Jackson ran an ad offering $25 for the return of Ned—"of a yellow complexion, about 5 feet 8 inches high, long face walks very sprightly."

Jackson's most famous runaway slave ad was published in October 1804, about the time he first bought the property that later became the Hermitage. The item, in the *Tennessee Gazette,* offered $50 for the return of a runaway slave about 30 years old, six feet and one inch tall, "stout made and active, talks sensible, stoops in his walk," and other descriptions. The ad goes on to say that Jackson will pay "ten dollars extra, for every hundred lashes any person will give him, to the amount of three hundred."

In the more than 1,200 runaway slave ads I found in Tennessee newspapers for this book, this is the only one in which the slaveholder offered a financial incentive for the beating of the slave.

## Stop the Runaway.

### FIFTY DOLLARS REWARD.

ELOPED from the subscriber, living near Nashville, on the 25th of June last, a Mulatto Man Slave, about thirty years old, six feet and an inch high, stout made and active, talks sensible, stoops in his walk, and has a remarkable large foot, broad across the root of the toes—will pass for a free man, as I am informed he has obtained by some means, certificates as such—took with him a drab great-coat, dark mixed body coat, a ruffled shirt, cotton home-spun shirts and overalls. He will make for Detroit, through the states of Kentucky and Ohio, or the upper part of Louisiana. The above reward will be given any person that will take him, and deliver him to me, or secure him in jail, so that I can get him. If taken out of the state, the above reward, and all reasonable expences paid—and ten dollars extra, for every hundred lashes any person will give him, to the amount of three hundred.

ANDREW JACKSON,
Near Nashville, State
of Tennessee.

*Tennessee Gazette*, October 3, 1804

And what of James K. Polk, Jackson's devoted follower and the president known affectionately during his lifetime as "Young Hickory?" I did not find his name in a single runaway slave ad published in the state of Tennessee. However, Polk did own slaves and he did have problems with runaways, as it turns out. According to researcher and author William Dusinberre, a slave known as Chunky Jack tried unsuccessfully to run away from James K. Polk's two plantations (in Hardeman County and in Mississippi) twice in the 1830s. Polk sold Chunky Jack to a slave trader after his second attempted escape. "Jack never saw his wife, Cloe, and their children again," Dusinberre wrote.

CHAPTER SEVEN

# THE LETTER "L"

At the same time Andrew Jackson's army was preparing to whip the British at New Orleans, George Smith of Nashville offered a $10 reward for the return of a slave named Charles. The January 1815 ad sounded fairly routine. George was "a yellow negro man" who spoke "bold and sensible," according to the ad. He "was brought up in the plastering business," the slaveholder said. However, there was one phrase in the ad that left the image of George indelibly on the mind.

"His right foot," the ad stated, "is deformed and nearly half off."

In runaway ads, slaves were usually described by their sex, color of skin, height, weight and build. Many were also characterized by a physical trait that makes them clearly identifiable. This trait—sometimes a deformity, missing finger or scar, leads to several possible conclusions: One, that the lack of access to decent health care left many people marred in the early 19th century. Two, that the nature of slave work was so dangerous and demanding that slaves often ended up deformed or scarred. Three, that the reliance on fire for warmth caused many people to be burnt. Four, that slave owners sometimes punished their slaves by burning them, stabbing them or whipping them. Five, that some slave owners intentionally scarred or deformed slaves so they would be easier to track down if they escaped.

My best guess is that all five reasons contributed to the large number of slaves who had these identifiable traits.

---

### TEN DOLLARS REWARD.

RUNAWAY from the subscriber in Nashville some time in November last, a yellow negro man, called
CHARLES,
spare made, his right foot is deformed and nearly half off, walks limping, has large white eyes,
speaks bold and sensible, by some means may
have procured a pass. He was brought up to
the plastering business.

Any person delivering him to me, or securing
him in some jail within the state, shall have the
above reward, and if without the state, TWEN-
TY dollars reward, and all reasonable expences
paid.
GEORGE SMITH.
December 27. 1814.—23.

---

*Nashville Whig*, January 3, 1815

## MISSING LIMBS OR DIGITS

In the novel *Roots*, the slave Kunta Kinte has his foot cut off as punishment for persistently running away. After the broadcast of the *Roots* mini-series in 1977, there was debate in America about whether slaveholders would actually have done such a thing.

I thought of this when I read the following ad from an 1836 *Nashville Republican*. "RANAWAY from the subscriber in Nashville . . . a Negro fellow named WILLIAM, about 35 years old, upwards of 5 feet high, with his right hand cut off before the elbow—He can read and write."

The fact that William was missing his right hand when he was, apparently, left handed (how else could he write?) made me wonder whether the loss of William's right hand was accidental.

I was relieved that this is the only time (at least that I could find) in which a runaway slave in Tennessee was described as missing a hand or part of a limb. However, there were many instances of missing fingers or toes.

In 1797, for example, Abner Witt of Knox County offered $10 for the return of a runaway slave named Jack. "Some of the toes on both his feet have been cut off," the ad said.

In 1815, Thomas Napier ran an ad in search of a slave named Bristol, who had his "middle finger off on his right hand."

Solomon, who ran away from Thomas Washington of Rutherford County, had six fingers on each hand when he was born. They "were cut off," Washington explained in 1815, "but the appearance is yet to be seen."

In an 1821 ad offering a reward for the return of Levi, Austin Coats of Davidson County described the slave as having "the first and second fingers of one . . . hand bit off at the first joint."

Crese, a 16-year-old female slave who ran away from Patrick Meagher of Shelby County in 1827, had "the end from the third and fourth fingers of the right hand taken off by a burn."

In 1830, slaveholder Edward Chambers of Tipton County said that his slave Toney had "lost some of his toes and one of his forefingers when he was a child." Two years later, another Tipton County slaveholder said his runaway slave Archer had "lost several toes from frostbite."

---

## LOOK OUT FOR THE RUNAWAY.

**R**ANAWAY from the subscriber in Nashville, Tennessee, on the night of the 14th of January, a Negro fellow named *WILLIAM*, about 35 years old, upwards of 5 feet high, with his right *Hand cut off below the elbow.*—He can read and write; he will make for a free State and will attempt to pass for a free Man, as he ran off once before and made to Canada.—It is supposed he left here on the Steam Boat Native. I will give thirty dollars for him, delivered to me, or twenty dollars, if secured in any jail so that I get him again.

PHILIP CALLAGHAN.

Nashville, Jan. 18—3t, *

*Nashville Republican* **January 19, 1836**

Hulda, a slave who ran away from Thomas Talbot of Nashville in 1835, was missing one of her "thimble fingers" at the first joint.

Thomas Crutchfield of McMinn County revealed in an 1838 ad that Cy, a runaway slave whose title he owned, "had all of the fingers of his right hand burnt off when young." Only a year later, the very same slaveholder stated that runaway slave Pleasant wore a glove on one hand because one of his fingers was missing.

John Henry, who ran away from S.M. May of Shelby County in 1861, had the ends of two of his fingers "mashed off."

In addition to these ads, there were about a dozen other slaves described as having deformed, unusable or stiff fingers. "[Hannibal] "bears an unmistakable mark in the leaders of one or two fingers of his right hand which are contracted so that they cannot be extended," wrote G.P. Smith of Davidson County in 1851.

## WHIP MARKS

Tennessee law authorized the whipping of slaves who were caught without written passes from their slaveholders. Therefore, it is an undeniable fact that many Tennessee slaves were whipped.

Evidence of whippings is found in these runaway slave ads:

## BLOUNT COLLEGE

WILL be ready for the reception of STUDENTS, on the first Monday in April next.

SAMUEL CARRICK, President.

Knoxville, December 16, 1797. 41.

RUN AWAY from the subscriber, living in Washington county, Nolichucky river, some time in September, 1797, a negro man, named Sampson, about five feet eight inches high, about five or six and twenty years of age, a small scar in the forehead, a good deal marked with the whip on the back, a strong, well set fellow, with a surly look, can work some at the smith trade. A handsome reward will be given, and all reasonable charges paid to any person that will secure him so that I can get him again.

THOMAS BROWN.

*Knoxville Gazette, February 2, 1798*

Sampson, who ran away in 1797, was "a good deal marked by the whip on the back," according to slaveholder Thomas Brown of Washington County. Slaveholder Michael Campbell of Davidson County would use almost identical language in describing a runaway slave named Sam 16 years later.

Joseph Morton of Rutherford County noted in 1814 that the runaway slave named Dennis had a back "very much cut with the cow-hide."

Major, a runaway slave from South Carolina who had previously been apprehended in Tennessee's Sequatchie Valley, "has been whipped," according to his slaveholder David Sloan, in an 1821 ad.

The slave known as Gabriel, who ran away from Joseph Miller of Nashville in 1830, had a back "much marked with the whip." Will Polk of Hardeman County used similar language four years later in an ad concerning a slave named Jim.

Nancy, who grew up in Greeneville and who ran away from William Bardin of Columbus, Georgia, had "whip marks on her back, arms and thighs," according to the 1853 ad in the *Loudon Free Press*. "Some on her back," the ad continued, "are fresh."

## $20 REWARD.

RANAWAY from the subscriber, a negro woman, NANCY, 22 years old stout square built, copper color—Whip marks on her back, arms and thighs—some on her back are fresh. I think she has been enticed off by some young White man, or has been given a pass; she was raised about Greenville Tennessee, and was owned by a Mr. Craigmiles of Dalton. All persons are respecfully requested to look out for the Runaway and thief.

WM. Y. BARDIN.

Columbus Ga., July 16 1853.

*Loudon Free Press*, August 5, 1853

H.C. Stark of Shelby County said that the slave known as Morgan, who ran away from him in 1856, was "probably marked with the whip."

Henry, who in 1860 ran away from John Taylor of Sumner County, had "some marks on his back or hips."

---

## 20 DOLLARS REWARD.

**R**ANAWAY from the sub-
scriber, on the 3d day of
July last, a negro man named
JESSE ; about 27 or 28 years
of age ; formerly belonged to Dr.
Ward. The half of his right ear
is cut off, and a large scar on his
left cheek. Any person who will
apprehend said negro and secure
him, so that I get him again, shall
receive the above reward.
GEO. W SANDERS.
*Big Bone Cave, White*
*county, Aug.* 10, 1813. 52–4w.

---

*Nashville Whig*, **August 31, 1813**

### CUTS ON THE EAR

Some of the slaves who ran away in Tennessee could be identified
by an irregularity to one or both of their ears.

Slave owner George Sanders of present-day Van Buren County
ran an ad in 1813 which offered a reward of $20 for the return of a
slave named Jesse. "Half of his right ear is cut off," said the ad.

About a year later, slave owner Thomas Eastland of Stone Fort
(present-day Coffee County) offered a reward for a runaway slave
named Anthony, who had "a small piece out of his right ear."

Bob, who ran away from James Reese of Jefferson County in
1822, had "a piece bit out of one of his ears." The verb "bit" was also
used by Madison County slaveholder John McClellan in 1826 and
Davidson County slaveholder James Newsom in 1859 to describe the
origins of an ear deformity.

Then there was Bob, a slave who ran away from John Y. Perry of
Robertson County. Bob was said to have "a small piece out of the
top of one of his ears, resembling a small swallow-fork." He was also

said to have "a large scar on the abdomen, extending from the nipple down, caused by a burn," "a small scar on his right leg just above the ankle" and "a small scar in his forehead over one of his eyes."

## SCARS

Speaking of scars, nearly 200 of the runaway slave ads which appear in the appendix contain mention of at least one.

The simple presence of a scar does not prove that a slave received it intentionally from his or her slaveholder. Many slaves did not wear shoes as children, which may account for why so many of them are said to have a scar "caused by an axe" on their foot or ankle. It is also plausible that a slave might have been scarred by an accident while doing their normal jobs. "[Isaac] had scars on his arms from being a blacksmith," stated slaveholder John S. Willis in 1830. "[Robin] has on one of his hands some severe scars, having been torn by a cotton gin," said slaveholder Lewis Dinhins of Knox County in an 1839 ad.

> ## · $40 Reward!!
>
> **R**ANAWAY from the subscriber, living on Buzzard Creek, seven miles north-west of Springfield, Robertson county, Tenn., on the 24th March, 1842, a negro man named BOB, 31 or 32 years old, 5 feet 8 or 9 inches high, weighs about 160 lbs., of dark complexion, and rather bold countenance; has a scar in his forehead over one of his eyes, and a small piece out of the top of one of his ears, resembling a small swallow-fork, a large scar on the abdomen, extending from the nipple down, caused by a burn; a scar on his right leg just above the ancle, running up the bone. I have no doubt but he will deny his name and owner. I will give the above reward if delivered to me at my residence, or $10 if lodged in jail so that I can get him. Address the subscriber at Barren Plains, Robertson county, Tenn.
>
> JOHN Y. PERRY, Executor
> of Joseph Perry, dec.
>
> Dec. 14—w2t*

Nashville *Republican Banner*, December 14, 1842

It does appear, however, that some of these scars might not have been by chance. One of the reasons I believe this is because of the number of times slaves were described as having scars on their foreheads or on their chests. Both seem like unlikely places to have been accidentally scarred.

Some examples of notable scars:

In 1796, in one of the first runaway slave ads to appear in a Tennessee newspaper, a runaway slave named Elice was described by her Virginia slaveholder as having "a mark on her right cheek, a scar on her breast." (The use of the word "mark" rather than the word scar or birthmark struck me as odd.)

Ned, who ran away from Frederick Stump of Nashville in 1813, had "a small scar in his face, a scar on his thigh and neck, made by a rope."

Isaac, who ran away from Charles Bosley of Nashville in 1825, had a scar "in the center of his forehead resembling a cross."

Lawson, who ran away from James Thomas of McMinn County in 1827, had "a very bad scar on his head, running with the mold thereof, and then down toward the ear, as to form an angle."

Jack, who ran away from Thomas Clark of Roane County in 1830, had "a scar across his nose, extending on each cheek, made with a knife."

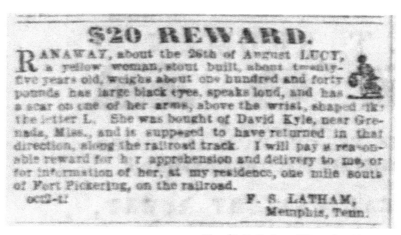

*Memphis Daily Appeal,* **December 23, 1857**

Lucy, who ran away from F.S. Latham of Shelby County in 1857, was said to have "a scar on one of her arms, above the wrist, shaped like the letter L."

The presence of a scar in the shape of the letter "L" on the arm of a slave owned by a man named Latham raises the matter of how many runaway slaves were branded with the symbol or initial of their slaveholders. Besides Lucy, I could only find one—Jack, who ran away from Orville Shelby of Tipton County in 1835 and who, according to the ad, had run away before. "No particular marks recollected," wrote Shelby, who lived near the now abandoned community of Randolph, "except a burn under the right ear in the shape of the letter O."

The frequent presence of scars raises another question: If only about 200 or so of the more than 900 runaway slave advertisements in Tennessee mention scars, that means that the vast majority of slaveholders mentioned no scars. Why were scars not even more common?

I have two theories. The preferred one is that many slaveholders were merciful people who didn't want to harm their slaves. The other reason is resale value—a concept best explained by Henry Watson, a former slave who published his story in 1848. Describing his experiences of being inspected for sale at a Richmond slave auction, and doing so in the present tense, Watson wrote that "if they discover any scars they will not buy, saying that the nigger is a bad one."

PART THREE

# BUYING AND SELLING

Pumps and Shoes of all kinds, which he will sell wholesale or retail for cash.

He has a nice DEARBORN WAGON. with a falling top and good HARNESS, and two or three HORSES for the Saddle or Harness, which he will sell on a credit.

Nashville, May 1, 1819.—2m.

## SAM. HOUSTON,
### Attorney & Counsellor at Law,

HAS taken as an office, a part of the house occupied by DR. J. L. WYNNE, and will be found there at all times, unless absent on professional business.— All business confided to his management, in this or the adjoining counties, will be promptly attended to.

Lebanon, March 12, 1819.—32-t

## AUCTION SALES.

WILL BE SOLD,
On Thursday, June 17, 1819,
AT 20'CLOCK, AT THE
NASHVILLE INN,
THE FOLLOWING VERY VALUABLE

## REAL PROPERTY.

The ELK TAVERN, College st. This large and commodious house has a Well of excellent water, Stables, &c. 50 feet unimproved ground on College st. and the use of an alley to Market street.

A two story BRICK HOUSE, on Market st. adjoining Mr. John Folwell.

The DWELLING HOUSE lately owned by Capt. Kingsley, now occupied by Col. Butler; this is an elegant family residence and is situated on the top of College Hill; it is unrivalled by any site in or near Nashville.

THIRTY unimproved LOTS adjoining the above, these lots are beautifully situated, and to each lot will be deeded, the use of a Well of good water, every lot fronts on two streets, and an alley; the lots are laid off about 40 feet front, running 176 feet back, except the fractional Lots, which are smaller; the purchaser of one lot will have the privilege of taking as many adjoining lots as he pleases.

Plans may be seen at the Nashville Inn and at the Auction Store. Terms of payment, 6, 12, 18 and 24 months, payable in Bank, with approved endorsers.

MONTGOMERY BELL.
ROBERTSON & CURREY, Auc.

---

adjoining Mr. Joseph Park, at the lower end of Market Street

Where he will execute *Deeds, Bonds, Conveyances, &c.* or do writing of any description. He hopes by the neatness of execution, accuracy, care and *strict attention to legal forms*, to give entire satisfaction to those who may favor him with their patronage and support.

J. K. KANE.
Nashville, Oct. 31, 1818.—tf

## SALE

THE undersigned, having obtained letters of administration, on the estate of Jos. Colman, deceased, will on the 9th day of June next, proceed to sell, (at the late dwelling house, of the deceased.) the chattel estate of said deceased. Terms will be made known on the day of sale.

ANNA M. COLEMAN, adm'x.
B. COLEMAN, adm'r.
May 15, 1819.—4

## WOOL! WOOL!!

THE FULLING MILL formerly owned by McCorkle and Anderson, two miles south of Gallatin, is now conducted by the subscriber. The Wool Carding Engines, formerly owned by Mr. Wilson, and run at the above Mill, have likewise fallen into the hands of the subscriber; and are now ready for

## CARDING WOOL.

Customers would do well to bring in their wool early, the warm season being the proper time for carding: Wool must be greased with one pound of Hog's lard to ten of wool, before sent to the machine. Wool should be washed clean, though not handled or rubed so much as to make it grow, or stick together, (this is one way you spoil your Merino wool, and cause it to nap in carding.) All burs and trash must be carefully picked out of the wool, they are destructive to the cards, and cannot be suffered to go into them.

An industrious and accommodating young man is employed to card the present season.

WM. H. ANDERSON.
Sumner county, May 8.—50-8t

## TENNESSEE
## BOOK STORE,
### NASHVILLE.

THE subscribers inform the public, that they have just opened, at their

---

Nashville, May 15, 1819.

## 10 DOLLARS REWARD.

RUN away from the subscriber, living six miles south of Nashville, on the 22d instant, a negro man named HARRY. Harry is about 5 feet, 6 or 7 inches high, very bowlegged. Had on when he run off, a dark coloured Roundabout, and brown homespun Pantaloons, and a wool Hat. He was lately brought from Virginia, by John Criddle.— Whoever will deliver to me the said boy, shall receive the above reward, and all reasonable charges paid.

WASHINGTON PULLIAM.
April 24, 1819.—tf

## Commission Business
### AT WHEELING, Va.
### S. SCOVIL & Co.

ARE prepared to receive and forward, with the least possible delay, all goods consigned to their care—They also transact any other business in their line on the usual terms.

Arrangements are making to freight goods from this place at all seasons of the year. Merchants are informed, that owing to the advantages of the U. States' road, goods from Philadelphia or Baltimore, can be shipped at this place as soon or sooner than the same goods could have reached Pittsburg or any other point on the Ohio.

April 3.—33-3m

## On Consignment,
AND FOR SALE BY
TH: HILL, College st.
900 Bags Allum Salt.
Nashville, May 1, 1819.

## THE SUBSCRIBERS,

WISH to contract for a quantity of LYNN BARK, for which they will give the highest current price in CASH.

FRANCIS H. LE COQ,
THOS. WESTON.
Nashville, May 8.—39-tf

## NEGROES FOR SALE.

THE subscriber would sell five likely young NEGROES—two boys, one 18, the other 20 years old—three girls, 10, 15 and 18 years old. Apply to the subscriber living on Richland Creek, five miles west of Nashville.

Z. W. WATERS.
March 27 1819.—tf

COFFEE, by the barrel or tierce,

---

CHAPTER EIGHT

# LIKELY NEGRO

The most common slave ad was the simplest slave ad. "For sale," stated the ad in the July 1804 *Tennessee Gazette*, "a likely negro woman, which will be sold at a reduced price for cash. Any person wishing to purchase may know the terms by applying at Capt. John Gordon's, near Nashville, where the said negro may be seen."

Ads such as this one appeared in almost every newspaper published in Tennessee from 1791 until 1863. With one notable alteration, they read like modern-day ads for used cars and old furniture. And, much like modern-day ads for used cars and old furniture, they were usually terse, their wording often similar.

### Negro Girl for Sale.

I WILL sell on Saturday the 20th inst. at the upper end of the Market House, a like Negro Girl, ten or eleven years old, on a credit of nine months. The girl is perfectly healthy and sold for no fault—the owner having no use for her.

L. E. TEMPLE, Auct.

April 19—2t.

Nashville *Republican Banner*, April 20, 1839

"Negroes for Sale," stated the ad in the 1849 issue of *Brownlow's Whig and Independent Journal.* "A likely young Negro woman and Child, and a girl 14 years of age, are offered for sale on terms reasonable, for cash. Persons willing to purchase would do well to call and examine."

As one delves into the world of newspaper advertisements related to the sale of slaves, it is best to start with these short ones and to make a few points along the way. In the early 19th century, "likely" meant "having the appearance of being strong and capable." A "likely negro"—a phrase which appeared quite commonly in slave sale ads— implied a healthy, versatile slave.

Slaveholders were also more likely to emphasize the positive attributes of a slave when they were trying to sell that slave than when they were trying to track down a runaway. A female slave being marketed in an 1814 *Nashville Whig* ad was said to be "a very strong, handy, active woman who falls behind no negro man at field work & can also do house business as well as common." A sales pitch in the 1828 *Knoxville Register* said a female slave "has been accustomed to house work such as cooking, washing, ironing" and "is a first rate spinner." A man being sold through an 1857 *Clarksville Weekly Chronicle* ad was a "splendid hewer, sawyer and barn builder, and a negro of good character." Other descriptions frequently used in such ads were "valuable," "healthy," "reliable," "active," "experienced" and "sound."

Advertisements rarely offered the reason that a family might have been selling slaves. Perhaps the family was short of cash. Perhaps their lifestyle had changed and they no longer needed as many slaves. Perhaps a member

CORN.

I wish to purchase 500 Barrels of Corn, for which cash will be given.

I have for sale a likely negro girl, about fifteen or sixteen years of age.

JNO. GARNER.
June 6th, 1814.      9 - tf.

*Nashville Whig,* June 7, 1814

NEGROES
FOR SALE.

One Negro boy named Tom, about 20 years of age, and a Negro girl aged 17 years, named Esther. Both healthy and well grown. They will be sold on reasonable terms for cash. Apply to
LEWIS ROSS.
Cherokee Agency, Jan. 29      61¶

*Knoxville Register*, **January 29, 1822**

of the family had died and his or her personal servant was being sold. Perhaps there was a personality conflict.

In any case, here a few of the "small time" slave sales advertised in Tennessee's newspapers that caught my eye:

- "For Sale: A NEGROE WENCH, with children. She is about 19 years old—the Children are smart and active. She will be exchanged for a YOUNG FELLOW or a BOY, taken at their valuation."—*Carthage Gazette*, February 1813

- "NEGROES FOR SALE. The subscriber would sell five likely young NEGROES—two boys, one 18, the other 20 years old, three girls, 10, 15 and 18 years old. Apply to the subscriber, living on Richland Creek, five miles west of Nashville. Z.W. Waters"—*Nashville Whig*, May 1819

- "FOR SALE, A LIKELY NEGRO MAN, who is a first rate SHOEMAKER and a tolerably good BLACKSMITH. For terms apply to this office."—*Knoxville Register*, May 1833

- "FOR SALE—A likely negro BOY, 23 years of age. Also, 2 mules and 2 horses. Enquire at JO. W. HORTON, at Horton & Macy's"—*Republican Banner and Nashville Whig*, May 1852

LAND.

FOR sale a valuable tract of land, containing two hundred and seventy acres; lying four miles north of Nashville and two miles from Page's Ferry. Negroes will be taken in payment.

C. Y. HOOPER.

June 16, 1822 ——tf

*Nashville Whig,* **June 19, 1822**

- "FOR SALE, A NEGRO MAN, tall and sensible . . . Has lately become rather independent of his master or manager—a few nights since the watchman put him in jail, where he may now be seen by traders. I wish to sell him. I never gave him but one whipping. He was born mine and raised by me."—*Republican Banner and Nashville Whig,* December 1853

Simple slave sale ads such as these would remain prevalent in Tennessee newspapers through the Civil War. In a similar category (though harder to translate) are ads which I classify as "deed of trust" ads, which I found in newspapers starting in 1820.

In a standard "slave for sale" ad, the slaveholder took on the responsibility of showing the slave, haggling over the price of the slave, and filing the legal paperwork when a slave was sold. In a deed of trust sale, slaveholders transferred the responsibility of doing all that to someone else, who would announce the sale in the newspaper.

To make a modern-day analogy, a slaveholder running a simple "slave for sale" ad was akin to a person selling their house "for sale by owner." A "deed of trust" ad was more along the lines of a person using a real estate agent.

The wording of this July 1820 *Nashville Whig* ad was, therefore, fairly complicated. "By virtue of a deed of trust, executive to the subscribers by Tho. B. Jones, dated the 18th April last, recorded in the county seat of Giles . . ." The bottom line was that "One Negro Woman" (along with two horses, two cows and a lot of kitchen furniture) would be sold on July 29 in the town of Elkton.

The wording used in a June 1821 *Knoxville Register* ad was similar, again starting off with the phrase "by virtue of a deed of trust." It resulted in the sale of seven slaves owned by William Johnston of Knox County—Moses, Joseph, Phillis and "4 children, the eldest is about 8 or 9 years old."

Often these "deed of trust" ads were silent about exactly what caused the owner of the slaves to sell their property. But some "deed of trust" ads cite the need to liquidate assets to "secure a debt." Such verbiage was present when John McNairy Robertson of Nashville sold 6 slaves (including 3 children) in February 1830; when John and Charles Robertson of Madison County sold 6 slaves (4 children) in March 1839; when J.G. Gooch of Murfreesboro sold "ten or twelve likely Negroes, consisting principally of boys and girls" in July 1844; and when M.F. Baldwin of Davidson County sold 7 slaves (2 children) in February 1847. For a slaveholder to get out of debt, slaves had to be sold.

In fact, sometimes "deed of trust" ads went so far as to imply that, depending on the price, only some of the slaves might be sold. In February 1823, a *Knoxville Register* ad announced the sale of many of

## Trust Sale.
### 23 Likely Negroes For Cash!!

BY virtue of a Deed of Trust to me executed, by Dr. James Wheatley, bearing date the 20th day of May, 1842, and recorded in the Register's office for Montgomery County, in Book S, pages 514, 515, 516, and 517, I will on Monday the 6th day of November next, at the court house door in the town of Clarksville, sell to the highest bidder for cash,

Twenty Three Likely and Valuable Negroes, consisting of 10 Men, 3 Boys, 4 Women and 6 Children. Sale between the hours of 11 o'clock, A. M. and 5 P. M.

M. A. MARTIN, *Trustee.*

Sep 19, 1843—tds

*Clarksville Weekly Chronicle*, September 19, 1843

the assets of a man named Edwin Wiatt. The sale was set to include 11 slaves—eight of whom were children named Richmond (11), Mary (9), Stella (9), Alexander (7), Lucy (6), Titus (5), Ben (4) and an infant child. The sale would be continued until as "much of the aforeseen property as shall be sufficient to make the sums due and provide for by the said deed."

In other words, only some of the 3 adult slaves and 8 child slaves might have been sold in Knoxville "on the 24th day of August 1823."

Newspapers contained far more ads for people wanting to sell slaves than for people wanting to buy slaves. However, they were a few of the latter. In fact, in the early 1830s, the *National Banner and Nashville Whig* published a regular list of slave types for which certain prospective purchasers were looking. In the November 9, 1832, issue, for instance, there were at least six ads from prospective buyers. One of them said he would pay cash for "4 likely boys from 14 to 18 years of age." Another said he was looking for a bright "mulatto" boy, about 23 years old, who is a first-rate house servant, and for several years has acted as a gentleman's servant." However, the slave also had to have a "good" disposition, and no "bad habits."

CHAPTER NINE

# ESTATE SALE

Today, when people die, assets must be liquidated. In modern times, this generally results in the sale of houses, cars, shares of stock and businesses.

Things worked the same way in 1820. The difference between then and now is that these assets often included slaves.

Today, as then, people often designate "executors" or "trustees" to carry out their wishes after they have died. Today, as then, courts appoint "administrators" to handle situations when a person dies without a will.

No sooner were newspapers created in Tennessee than executors, trustees and administrators started buying ads advertising the sale of slaves as part of the probate process. When James Gallaher died in 1792, his home in Washington County was part of the Southwest Territory. After his death, his executor saw to it that his estate was sold. It included, among other things, "two negroes, cattle, sheep and hogs; farming utensils, household furniture."

Two hundred miles west of Gallaher's home place, Morgan's Station was one of the places where settlers would find refuge during the Indian raids of the early 1790s. In 1802, Nicholas Bray ran an ad

To be Sold by Public Vendue,

ON the tenth day of November next, in Washington county, on the south side of Nolichucky river, the following property of James Gallaher deceased, to wit.——One Plantation, containing four hundred acres, ninety acres cleared, fifty of which his bottom; two Negroes, Horses, Cattle; Sheep and Hogs; Farming Utensils Houshold Furniture, &c. One year's credit will be allowed, the purchasers giving sufficient security. Attendance will be given by
John Gallaher, Executor.
July 25, 1795. 18 3.

*Knoxville Gazette*, October 23, 1795

NOTICE,

WILL be sold for cash, on Friday the 24th of September next, at the house of John Morgan. esq. on Dry creek, Sumner county, a number of very likely negroes, some horses and other articles—the property not to be altered until the money is paid.
Nicholas A. Bray,
Att'y in fact for the Ex'rs. of
Wm. Dennis, dec.
Sumner county, August 20, 1802.

*Tennessee Gazette*, August 25, 1802

in the *Tennessee Gazette* announcing that the estate of William Dennis (deceased) would be liquidated at Morgan's Station. Among the assets: "a number of very likely negroes, some horses, and other articles."

In 1812, "attorney in fact" A. Potter ran an ad in the *Nashville Whig* advertising the liquidation of the estate of Thomas Masterson. Among the assets to be auctioned: "Negroes, Horses &c.; An elegant Gig and Harness; A quantity of Iron and Castings; Whiskey; Two desks, and a variety of other things."

Sometimes the person who handled the liquidation of an estate was an actual lawyer. Sometimes it was a private citizen designated in a will to be the executor of an estate. Sometimes it was an "administrator" designated by the court to handle the liquidation of an estate.

To summarize, slaves were routinely sold—and sometimes quite a few of them—when slaveholders died. The number of slaves sold in these estate sales varied from one slave to more than a hundred.

Here are a few examples:

- In November 1816, under the direction of "J. Wharton, administrator," between 30 and 40 slaves that were part of the estate of William Wharton (deceased) were sold at the Davidson County Courthouse. Among them, according to the newspaper announcement, were men, women and children. "From my own knowledge of them [the slaves], I can with truth say that such a parcel of negroes, both for their good qualities and appearances, have never been sold in this part of the country since I lived in it," Wharton wrote in the ad.

- In March 1819, "upwards of 20" slaves were sold at the plantation of James Miller of Knox County, along with the horses, mules, cattle, hogs, sheep, wagons, etc. that were part of his estate.

## 30 or 40 Negroes for Sale.

PURSUANT to an order of the Court of Davidson county, I will expose to public sale at the Court-House in Nashville, on Tuesday the 19th day of November next, between 30 and 40 likely NEGROES, consisting of Men, Women, Boys and Girls, the property of the heirs of Wm. Wharton, deceased. These Negroes are all young, and most of them raised by said Wharton, and from my own knowledge of them, I can with truth say, that such a parcel of negroes, both for their good qualities and appearances, never have been sold in this part of the country since I lived in it. On this score I am very desirous that those persons only who wish to procure negroes for their own use, should purchase them; and that too in families; and for that purpose a credit of twelve months will be given the purchasers, upon bonds and approved security being given, bearing interest after six months.— Sale will be opened at 12 o'clock, and continue from day to day until all are sold.

J. WHARTON, Adm'r.

October 29, 1816.---10-5t

*Nashville Whig*, **November 5, 1816**

- In March 1825, "11 or 12 likely" slaves belonging to the late Governor Joseph McMinn were sold at his plantation in Hawkins County.

- In January 1829, 26 slaves were sold at the plantation of the late Andrew Blair, in Maury County, along with horses, pigs, cattle, mules and other property.

- On Christmas Eve 1834, "about" 35 slaves were sold as part of the estate of Dickson County's R.C. Napier, one of the important iron industrialists in that part of the state.

*Knoxville Enquirer,*
**January 12, 1825**

## SALE OF VALUABLE LAND AND NEGROES!

BY virtue of the last will and testament of Wm. W. Miller, deceased, and the authority conferred upon me by regular power of Attorney, from the heirs and devisees of Wm. W. Miller, deceased, I will proceed and sell on

### Friday, the 4th of January, 1856,

The very valuable and highly improved farm upon which Miller resided at the time of his death, containing 411 acres of the finest quality, and convenient to Schools and Churches. This land lies within half a mile of Bellbuckle depot, in Bedford county, on the Nashville and Chattanooga Railroad, and cannot be surpassed for fertility. Also, the following slaves:

| | |
|---|---|
| Adeline, aged 35 years; | Morgan, aged 10 years; |
| Victoria, aged 5 years; | Sylia, aged 3 years; |
| Julia, aged 10 years; | Clement, aged 6 years; |
| Samuel, aged 4 years; | Ned, aged 20 years. |
| Lawyer, aged 18 years; | Clay, aged 11 years. |

TERMS.—The land will be sold on a credit of one, two and three years, except $500 to be paid in cash. The negroes will be sold on a credit of twelve months. Bond and security will be required from the purchaser, and a lien retained on the land until the purchase money is paid.

All persons indebted to said estate are requested to come forward and make payment, and those having claims are requested to present them for payment in the time prescribed by law.                J. M. MILLER,
dec8—w8t                                        Executor, &c.

*Daily Nashville Patriot,*
**December 22, 1855**

- In January 1856, 10 slaves were sold as part of the estate of the late William W. Miller of Bedford County. Among the liquidated on that day were Clay (age 11); Morgan (10); Clement (6), Victoria (5), Samuel (4); and Sylia (3).

- In January 1857, "about twenty Negroes of various ages, consisting of men, women and children," were sold at the Hamilton County residence of the late Lewis Shepherd.

With lists and statistics, it is important to remember how traumatic these events were to slaves and their families. On January 1, 1854, an Ohio native named William Fletcher King was visiting Murfreesboro, Tennessee, with his brother. They heard that a slave auction was taking place at the courthouse and so they went over to watch. Although King's account of the event, published in his memoirs half a century later, does not explain the legal circumstances for the auction, I believe, based on his account, that it was an estate sale.

"The first person that was put up for sale was a boy about twelve years old. He was put on the wall which surrounded the courthouse grounds, a brick wall about six to eight feet high.

### Negroes for Sale.

WILL be sold to the highest bidder for cash, at the Court house door, in the Town of Shelbyville, on Monday the 29th inst., five likely negroes, (to wit:) **One Woman 20 years old, one Boy 12 years old, one Girl 9 years old, one Boy 7 years old, one Girl 5 years old, one Horse and one Carryall,** the property of Mrs Elizabeth Williams dec'd. By mutual consent of the heirs.

JESSE TAYLOR,
ELIZA W. HARRISON.
Shelbyville, June 19, 1835–n24–2w.

Shelbyville *Western Freeman,* June 19, 1835

He was barefoot and otherwise scantily clad. When they began to bid he became very nervous, and took a kind of semidancing attitude, as though he were on springs. As the bidding progressed he showed evident interest, glancing his eyes from one bidder to another with great alertness. The bidding continued for about a quarter of an hour and he was finally sold.

"Another case was that of a decrepit old man, who was very much cramped up by rheumatism or hard labor. Before the bidding began he was asked whom he would like to serve, and he replied, 'I will be

# CHANCERY SALE.

IN virtue of a decree of the Court of Chancery of the Western Division of Tennessee, the undersigned commisioner appointed by said Court, will expose to public sale, on *Thursday the 2nd day of Oct. next,* all the property, real personal and mixed, of Yeatman, Woods & Co, in Stewart county, State of Tennessee.

The real property consists of about 18,000 acres of LAND, on both sides of Cumberland river, on which is erected one large ROLLING MILL, immediately on the south bank of said river, with a steam engine estimated at 120 horse power. The Rolling Mill is now in complete operation, making iron of every description, on a large scale. Attached to said mill is a NAILERY with five machines for making nails.

Also—one STEAM BLAST FURNACE, about one mile from the Rolling mill called "Bear Spring Furnace," now in complete opperation, manufacturing Pig metal. A FORGE attached, with a nobling hammer for the manufacture of Bloon Iron.

Also—one other STEAM BLAST FURNACE, about 4 miles from the Rolling mill, called 'Dover Furnace," now in complete operation, manufacturing Pig metal and castings of all kind. There is attached to the Rolling mill and Furnaces, all the necessary dwelling houses, negroe houses, work shops, and stabling for such establishments.

There will also be included in said sale, TWO HUNDRED SLAVES, among which are Engineers Forgemen, Hammermen, and Workmen of almost every description required at such establishments.—Also, all the stock of horses, mules, oxens, wagons and gears, carts, implements and tools for digging ore for coaling, &c. &c. Also—all the household and kitchen furniture, milch cows, &c. &c. on hand on the day of sale, at Said Rolling mill and Furnace. Also, one keel boat, and two Tow boats.

The sale will take place on the day above named, at the "Rolling mill." The terms, as prescribed by the Chancellor, CASH.

The death of Thomas Yeatman having rendered the sale of the foregoing property necessary to make a proper distribution between his heirs and surviving partners, the sale will therefore be peremptory; and upon the ratification thereof by the Chancellor and payment of the purchase money, titles will be made

E. S. HALL, *Commissioner.*

The property will be shown, and all necessary information given, upon application to the manager at the 'Rolling mill "             June 26 ———td

Nashville *Daily Republican,* July 15, 1834

glad to serve anybody who will treat me well.' He seemed to show loyalty to himself and his present owner by trying to act as spry as he possibly could. As the bidding progressed he also showed great interest as to where his lot should be cast. Finally the bidding closed and his countenance fell."

Two of the estate sales of slaves in Tennessee history took place in the iron-rich area northwest of Nashville. On October 2, 1834, more than 200 slaves were sold as part of the liquidation of the estate of Thomas Yeatman and his business, Yeatman, Woods & Co. This event included the sale of 18,000 acres, a mill, several steam blast furnaces, mules, oxen, wagons, tools and hundreds of other assets—a huge event for a part of the state which was, and remains, sparsely populated.

A generation later, on February 19, 1856, an estimated 140 slaves—including men, women and children—were sold as part of the liquidation of the estate of the late Montgomery Bell. This event occurred near Dickson's Valley Forge, an early 19th century industrial site which only the most devout local history buffs could locate today. Ironically, Montgomery Bell himself would have disapproved of the event, since he made it clear in his will that he wanted his slaves relocated to Liberia.

The rules of that day's auction were also very interesting:

"The said slaves will be sold on 12 months credit, and in families, as far as practicable," stated all of the newspaper ads that led up to the event. "Negro traders and non-residents of the State of Tennessee (except the legatees of the Testators, who will be permitted to purchase and carry out of the State) are prohibited by the will from purchasing any of said slaves."

In other words, at one of the biggest slave sales in Tennessee history, the act of professionally buying and selling slaves was spurned from beyond the grave.

## Spalding and Rogers
### NORTH AMERICAN CIRCUS,

WILL exhibit at PULASKI, on Friday December 12, 1851. Doors open at 1½ and 6½ o'clock. Performances to commence at 2 and 7 o'clock.

ADMISSION—Boxes 50 cts. Children and Servants 25 cents.

THE characteristics of this establishment consist in the largest collection of

EQUESTRIAN, GYMNASTIC AND DRAMATIC Talent ever collected in one travelling company.

MUSIC, DRAMA & HORSEMANSHIP!
Being here concentrated into one grand threefold combination, in which
*Mirth Music, Magic, Melo Drama Equitation, Spectacle, Pantomine, Farce and Tragedy,*
Mingle, bubble, effervesce, and bursts upon the eye and ear, alternately bewildering and delighting the spectator. The wonderful

## APOLONICON.

Drawn in procession by forty horses—four in abreast, containing the
RENOWNED NEW YORK CORNET BAND.
Which will execute several popular marches, overtures, &c., while moving through the streets. P. A. CLARKE, Ag't.

WILL exhibit at Lynnville, Thurday Dec. 11. Elkton Dec. 15. [Nov. 28.

## Land and Negroes for Sale.

PURSUANT to a Decree of the Chancery Court at Pulaski, in the cause pending therein of Robert S. Higgins and others, *Ex Parte*, I will, on the 30th day of December—

---

C. E. GRENVILLE & Co.
Chattanooga, Oct. 31, 1851–26–1w

## Real Estate and Slaves
## For Sale.

PURSUANT to Decrees of the Chancery Court at Pulaski, to wit: On the 28th day of Nov. 1851, at the late residence of James T. Fogg, deceased, 5 miles South west of Pulaski, the two negro slaves, Lucy and Easter, upon a credit of one year with interest from date.

### Also,

On the 30th of December next, at the late residence of James Higgins, deceased, on the South side of Elk River, on Kelley's creek, the lands upon which he resided, and including all the lands of which he died seized and possessed, supposed to contain about 200 acres, upon a credit of one and two years with interest from date—also, at the same time and place, 11 negro slaves, upon a credit of one year with like interest.

JAMES McCALLUM, C. & M.
Nov. 21, 1851–26–4w

### Taxes.

PERSONS owing TAXES for the present year are requested to call at the office of the Clerk of the Circuit Court, where my Tax Book is deposited, and C. C. Abernathy authorized to receive and receipt for Taxes in my name, during my inability to attend in person.

THO'S. S. WEBB.
Nov 14, 1851–25–1f

A. W. JOHNSON.     G. F. SMITH.

## Johnson & Smith,
*Commission, Receiving and Forwarding*
### MERCHANTS ;
*Wholesale Grocers and Dealers in*
## Cotton and Tobacco,

HAVING made arrangements with W. H. JOHNSON and E. A. HORNE to take charge of our large and spacious fire-proof TOBACCO WAREHOUSE AND COTTON SHEDS, to which latter we are now making extensive additions, they will give the Storage of Produce their undivided attention.

This arrangement will enable the undersigned to pay more attention to the purchase of COTTON AND TOBACCO than heretofore, and for which they expect to pay lib-

---

CHAPTER TEN

# LAWYERS, CLERKS AND COURTS

On June 3, 1844, Periander Priestly stood at the steps of the Montgomery County Courthouse and sold slaves. Some were adults and some children; we aren't certain about the breakdown. According to the newspaper notice which preceded the event, the slaves' names were Isaac, Honson, Joshua, Lewis, Jack, Jess, Bob, Web, James, John, Madison, Major, Tom, Winston, Sancho, Ralph, Peter, George, Dick, Bill, Mariah, Nancy, (a second) Nancy, Fanny, Abbey, Lucinda, Bickley, Jenny, Martha, Margaret, Harry, Mary, Patsey, Betsey, Billy, Jorich and Silas—37 in all.

However, Priestly wasn't a full-time slave trader. He was the chancery court clerk and master for Montgomery County—a position that still exists in every Tennessee county.

Selling 37 human beings was all in a day's work for Periander Priestly, just like any other clerk and master.

The Tennessee Constitution of 1834 better organized the judicial branch of state government and authorized the creation of a position known as clerk and master. Since that time, it has been the clerk and master's job to sell assets mandated by chancery court cases. Today, those valuables usually consist of real estate, stock and motor vehicles. But in antebellum Tennessee, they often included slaves.

**Chancery Sale,**
**OF 38 NEGROES and 4 TRACTS**
**OF LAND.**

Albert G. Wheatley, Administrator of James Wheatley,
*vs.*
The Bank of Tennessee, et. als.

BY virtue of an interlocutory decree made in the
above cause, I will on the 3d day of June next,
at the court house door in Clarksville, offer for sale
to the highest bidder for *cash*, the following Negroes,
as named in the deed of trust; filed in said cause, to
wit:—Isaac, Honson, Joshua, Lewis, Jack, Jess, Bob,
Web, James, John, Madison, Major, Tom, Winston,
Sancho, Ralph, Peter, George, Dick, Bill, Mariah,
Nancy, Nancy, Fanny and Child, Abbey, Lucinda,
Bickley, Jenny, Martha, Margaret, Harry, Mary,
Patsey, Betsey, Billy Jorich, Silas.
I will also at the same time and place, offer for
sale Four Tracts of Land, as set out in said trust
deed—One Tract of about 740 acres—One of three
acres and 56 poles—One of sixty acres; and the other
containing about 4¾ acres, and lies adjoining the
town of Clarksville. The lands herein mentioned
will be sold on a credit of one and two years—the
purchaser will be required to execute notes, with at
least two good securities, and a lien will be retained
on the land till the purchase money is paid. A particular description of the lands can be seen by calling
at my office; or by reference to Book S, pages 514,
515, 516, and 517, in the Register's office of Montgomery county.
☞ If the sale is not completed in one day, it will
be continued from day to day until all the Negroes
and lands are sold.
P. PRIESTLEY, C. & M.
april 16, 1844—4w—pf 10.

*Clarksville Weekly Chronicle*, **April 23, 1844**

Without the complete records of a case, it is hard to know what caused the sale of slaves in a case eventually disposed of by a clerk and master. We can assume, however, that in early 19th century Tennessee, people used slaves as collateral whenever they borrowed money. When bad times occurred; when people got overextended; when people got divorced; and when people lost lawsuits, the courts often ordered slaves to be sold to generate cash to settle disputes. "Extravagance, carelessness, misfortune and death brought thousands of slaves into the market, for they were the chief security, the most salable and the major part of all agricultural property," wrote author Frederic Bancroft.

We can also suppose that by its very nature, the sale of a slave could cause myriad disputes between buyer and seller. What if the slave's title wasn't clear, as the seller claimed? What if the slave had an ailment or disability that was not revealed at the time of sale? What if the slave immediately ran away? What if the buyer and seller had a verbal agreement at the time of sale which one person later claimed was violated? There was, no doubt, an entire world of legal cases that could be classified into a series of volumes. All cases of this nature could result in the court-mandated sale of slaves.

Because of these factors, Tennessee's antebellum newspapers are littered with slave sales conducted by chancery court clerk and masters.

For instance, due to the financial fallout from an 1836 case involving David Cartwright and William B. Ament, it was part of Williamson County Clerk and Master Benjamin Litton's job to sell "a NEGRO WOMAN named Martha and her child or children" as well as "a negro woman named Kissey."

The next year, Litton wrote the following ad, which appeared in the March 24, 1838, *Daily Republican Banner*. "I will on the 31st day of March next offer for sale at the Market House in Nashville the following negro slaves or so much as will be sufficient to pay the amount directed by the decree: Jack, Tom, Sam, John, Maria, Violet, Martha, Louisa, Patsey, Flora and her two children. Terms of sale cash."

## Chancery Sale---Land and Negroes!!

IN PURSUANCE of an Interlocutory Decree made at the December Term, 1846, of the Chancery Court at Paris, in the case of Craige, Holmes &Co., vs James Cowan, I, Eldridge G. Atkins, Clerk & Master of said Court, will, on *Wednesday the 2nd day* of June next, at the residence of James Cowan, proceed to sell to the highest bidder for *Cash in hand*, all the right, title, claim and interest which said James Cowan has in and to

**700 Acres of Land,**

Known as the *Mount Holy-Oke Farm*, together with the improvements thereon, being the same on which said Cowan now resides, and about

**20 LIKELY NEGROES,**

of various ages, consisting of *Men, Women and Children.*—The boundaries of the land and the ages & descriptions of the negroes can be seen by reference to me. The above property will be sold to satisfy a decree which Craige, Holmes &Co. obtained against the said Cowan at the December Term last of the Chancery Court at Paris, for Ten thousand one hundred and forty six dollars and seventeen cents, $10,146 17.—Sale to commence at 11 o'clock.

ELDRIDGE G. ATKINS, C. & M.
April 9, '47.—tds—Pr's fee $9.

*Paris Anaysis,* April 9, 1847

Two years later, Litton auctioned a "negro girl named MARIA" because of another chancery court decree. On January 25, 1847, Litton sold 14 more slaves.

Davidson County Clerk and Master Jackson B. White sold many children during his tenure. On December 4, 1847, White sold four slaves named Caroline (24), Tom (12), Henry (7) and Bob (2). Three months later he sold Deaderick (13), Emily (11), Mary (9) and Fanny (3). In May 1848 White sold a 9-year-old girl named Frances. Six months later he sold four slaves, including a 52-year-old woman named Anne and her 9-year-old daughter Mary. In January 1851, White sold 12 more slaves, two of whom were children named Laura and Jenny. In August of that year he sold a 7-year-old boy named John. In April 1852 he sold a 12-year-old girl named Eliza and a 5-year-old boy named William. Two months later he sold a 17-year-old girl named Jane.

White's successor, T.R. Cheatham, sold seven slaves in December 1853 named Abner, Mary, Martha, Albert, Priscella, Louisa and Maria (their ages were not published). Only a few days later, Cheatham sold eight more slaves, including Mahala (50), Hartly (25), Nathan (23), Wiley (18), Jenny (14), Lotty (11), Andrew (11) and Jim (8). He sold 12 slaves in December 1855, including Louisa (12), Henry (11), Nancy (9), George (7), Martha (5), Solomon (4) Alley

## Chancery Sale of Negroes.

BY virtue of a decree of the Chancery Court at Nashville, at the Nov. term 1846, in the case of Elizabeth P. Burton, executrix, &c. vs. the creditors of George H. Burton, dec'd., I shall on the 30th day of December 1846, at the residence of the late George H. Burton, sell at public sale the following negroes: Stephen aged 40 years, Dock aged 25, Matilda 38, Lydia 70, Margaret 14, Ann 11 and Ellen 3 years old; upon a credit of six months, bond and good security will be required.

J. B. WHITE, C. &. M.

December 10, 1846—td.

*Republican Banner*, **December 28, 1846**

**Chancery Sale of 22 Negroes.**

BY virtue of a decree of the Chancery Court at Cleveland, Tennessee, made at its February term, 1850, in the case of John D. Traynor, and his wife Mary Ann Traynor, and others against William B. Cozby, William McDonald, and David Ragsdale, Administrators of John Cozby, deceased, and others, I will on Tuesday, the 20th day of August next, expose to public sale at Smith's cross Roads, in Rhea County, Tennessee, twenty two Negroes, belonging to the estate of said John Cozby, deceased.

The above Negroes will be sold on a credit of six months, the purchaser giving bond with two or more sufficient securities for the price of the slave or slaves purchased.

JAMES BERRY, C. & M.
July 12, 1850—4t    Pr's fee $3,50    94.

*Athens Post*, **August 2, 1850**

(3), Josiah (1 ½) and Harriet (1 ½). In December 1856 Cheatham sold six slaves named Judith (50), Anderson (23), Thomas (15), William (4), Mary (2) and Judith (6 months).

White and Cheatham sold all these slaves—and many more—on the steps of the stately Davidson County Courthouse.

Elsewhere in Tennessee, court officials were also routinely selling slaves:

- In May 1835, Sumner County Clerk and Master S.H. Turner sold two female slaves named Lucy and Clarissa, a male slave named Jess and an unnamed child.

- In August 1850, Bradley County Chancery Clerk and Master James Berry auctioned 22 slaves at a place known as "Smith's Crossroads"—present-day Dayton. He would sell four slaves at the Bradley County Courthouse in November of that year; three more in January 1851; and two more in April 1852.

**NEGROES FOR SALE.**

BY vertue of a decree of the County Court of Polk county, Tennessee, at the January term, 1857, I will sell to the highest bidder, at the Court-house door in the town of Benton, Polk county, Tenn., on Friday, the 20th day of February, 1857, the following named NEGROES, to wit:—Cynthia, a woman aged about forty; Lafayette, a boy aged about twenty one; Robert, a boy aged about twelve; Elizabeth, a girl, aged about nine; Queen, a girl, aged about seven; Joseph, a boy, aged about five; Lewis, a boy aged about three—belonging to the heirs of Richard Kird, deceased, late of McMinn county, and sold by petition of the heirs, for distribution among them.

TERMS:—One-third of the purchase money will be required on the day of sale—the balance on a credit of twelve months, with bond and approved security, and a lien retained on the slaves until the final payments are made.

E. P. DOUGLASS, *Clerk.*

Jan 9, 1857–td–prs fee $5,60–433

*Athens Post,* February 20, 1857

- In February 1854, Monroe County Clerk and Master Elisha E. Griffith auctioned seven slaves at a private residence. Ten days later, Griffith auctioned two slaves at a different private residence. In March 1855, he auctioned five slaves at a third private residence.

- On January 1, 1859, Stewart County Chancery Clerk and Master C.M. Roberts sold 18 slaves "consisting of men, women and children, of all ages and all sizes" at the courthouse in Dover. On September 6, 1861, his successor A.B. Ross sold "a negro boy named Lafayette, about 7 or 8 years old."

- On January 13, 1859, Shelby County Clerk and Master John Trezevant sold seven slaves, including Hannah (28), Ann (8), Stephen (7), Cindy (6), Frank (3), Flora (3) and an infant.

- In September 1859, Coffee County Chancery Clerk and Master S.N. Burger sold four slaves at a private residence. The names of the slaves were Noah, Amanda, Narcissa and a child, unnamed.

Two of the biggest sales of slaves by a clerk and master in Tennessee history were in Fayetteville. On January 4, 1858, Robert Farquharson of Lincoln County auctioned more than 60 slaves at the Lincoln County Courthouse. Fifty-four of them were "house servants and field hands" previously owned by a man referred to as Colonel Fulton. Four months later, Farquharson sold 49 slaves to settle the separate estates of four individuals who died and owned between 5 and 15 slaves each.

Cases appealed to the Tennessee Supreme

**Chancery Sale of Slaves.**

ON the first Monday in January, 1858, that being the 4th day of the month, in pursuance of a decree of the Chancery Court for Lincoln county, Tennessee, pronounced at the August term, 1857, in the case of John S. Fulton and others against James M. Davidson and wife and others, I will offer for sale to the highest bidder, at the court-house in Fayetteville, SIXTY LIKELY NEGROES, consisting of house servants and field hands.

Also, at the same time and place, in the case of A. G. Smith, Adm'r, &c., vs. James T. Davis and others, I will offer for sale to the highest bidder, TWO LIKELY YOUNG NEGROES, viz:—Mary, about 15 years, and Joana, about 6 years of age.

And also, at the same time and place, in the matter of Theophilus Harris, Adm'r, &c. —Bill for sale of Slaves—I will offer for sale to the highest bidder, TWO LIKELY NEGRO WOMEN, Sally and Elizabeth.

TERMS:—All the above Negroes will be sold on a credit of one year from the day of sale. Notes with two or more good securities will be required of purchasers in all cases, and titles made only when the purchase money is paid.

N. B.--Persons having Negroes in possession belonging to Col. Fulton's estate, will please deliver them to the Executors in Fayetteville, or to the undersigned, between the 25th and 28th days of December next.

R. FARQUHARSON, C. & M.

Nov. 26, 1857--[4t-$6]

*Fayetteville Observer*, **November 26, 1857**

Court occasionally resulted in the sales of slaves, and I found seven instances of such between 1842 and 1853. The largest such case, *Planters Bank v. S.S. Mayfield*, resulted in the sale of 10 slaves by Davidson County Clerk and Master James P. Clark at the courthouse on March 14, 1853. The slaves were Leah, Bob, Mary, Lili and Lili's six children (Maria, Mary Ann, Jackson, Henrietta, Betsy and Eliza).

In all, I located 163 instances in which chancery or circuit clerk and masters sold slaves between 1836 and 1863. These auctions occurred in every part of the state and resulted in the sale of 1,199 slaves. (All of this data can be found in Appendix Two.) These numbers represent only the sales I noticed, working alone, with limited time, and looking at a limited number of newspapers. A team of researchers could find many more, and even then not have a complete number, since there are many parts of the state whose early newspapers have been lost.

In more than half of the cases I found, the clerk listed the ages of the slaves that were being sold as part of the proceedings. In cases where the ages of the slaves were revealed, children under the age of 18 made up more than half of the slaves being sold. In only five out of 163 auctions did the clerk express any intention of trying to keep families together (and all of those sales took place after 1860). I believe we can assume that in other cases, little or no effort was made to keep families together.

---

## Sale of Slaves.

**Planters' Bank vs. S. S. Mayfield et als.**

IN pursuance of the decree made by the Supreme Court at its late December Term, 1852, in said cause, I shall sell at the Court House in the town of Franklin, on Monday the 14th of March inst., on a credit of four months—bond and undoubted security, payable in bank—the following slaves, Lili and her children. (Maria, Mary Ann, Jackson, Henrietta, Betsey and Eliza,) and Leah, Bob and Mary.

March 1—td—$4     J. P. CLARK, C & M.

---

*Republican Banner and Nashville Whig*, March 1, 1853

**774**        *Mercantile Miscellanies.*

### PRICE OF NEGROES.

The great prosperity of the South has had its influence in advancing the price of hands, and the rates at which some sales have been made were remarkable. At a chancery sale at Lebanon, Tennessee, the results were as follows :—

The negroes belonged to the heirs of INGRAM and DELOACH, and were recently recovered against HENRY SMITH and others of Wilson County, after eleven years' litigation.

The terms of the sale were one-third cash and the balance in twelve months. JERRY, 16 years old, one arm defective, $1,125 ; HARRIET, 19 years old, and a little child, $1,675 ; JUDY, 30 years old, $905 ; LEWIS, 15 years old, $1,406 ; JACOB, 34 years old, $1,305 ; JANE, 26 years old, and two small children, $2,050 ; SALLY, 8 years old, $1,051 ; EMELINE, 7 years old, $1,051 ; JOHN, 14 years old, $1,575 ; PARALEE, 22 years old, and two small children, $2,280 ; TOM, 21 years old, $1,656 ; HANNAH, 19 years old, suckling child, $1,687 ; TABBY, 15 years old, $1,501 ; EMELINE, 25 years old, unsound, $700 ; PRINCE, 10 years old, $860 ; BOBB, 7 years old, $800 ; HASTY, 60 years old, $100.

*Hunt's Merchants' Marine and Commercial Review,* July-December 1859 issue

In fact, in one case (a clerk and master sale in Lebanon in 1859), we know beyond a doubt that children were sold separately because the prices fetched by the 23 slaves sold were published in a national publication called *Hunt's Merchants' Magazine and Commercial Review.* At the Wilson County Courthouse that day, a 15-year-old boy named Lewis was sold for $1,406; a 15-year-old girl named Tabby went for $1,501; a 14-year-old boy named John fetched $1,575; a 10-year-old boy named Prince sold for $860; an 8-year-old girl named Sally went for $1,051; a 7-year-old boy named Bobb fetched $800; and a 7-year-old girl named Emeline sold for $1,051. The children were sold in separate "lots," as goes the vernacular of the auction world.

## NASHVILLE LIBRARY.

BE it ordained, that all persons who are share-holders in the Nashville Library Company, or who claim to be owners of shares who have not paid the money and assessments due on their shares since the first day of July July, 1822, shall have the liberty of paying up all the dues on their shares in Books, to be approved of by one of the Directors, or money, on or before the first day of September next; and on their failure so to do, the share or shares of such persons, shall be forfeited; and he, she, or they, shall cease to be members of the company.

Per order,      JERVIS CUTLER,
August 5. 1825.      *Librarian.*

\*.\*The Library in future will be kept open for receiving and delivering Books, only on the regular Library days, Wednesdays and Saturdays, from 10 o'clock, A. M. to 2 P. M.
     J. C.

## TIN-WARE, &c.

THE undersigned, in consequence of bad health, is under the necessity of quitting his present occupation; and being desirous to close his business as soon as practicable, he will sell his present stock of TIN-WARE, and other articles in the Hard-ware line, lower than the usual prices in this market The assortment of Tin-ware is large and complete. Those who wish to purchase will find it to their interest to give him a call. He respectfully requests those indebted to him to make payment.

     S. M'MANUS.
August 6.———y

## CARRIAGE FOR SALE.

A LIGHT Barouche carriage, second hand, calculated for one or two horses, and peculiarly well constructed for the convenience of three or four persons, is offered for sale Apply to

     S. V. D. STOUT, or
     JOHN R. BURK.

August 6.

PHILIP BOULTNEY

## NOTICE.

THE Agency of J. H. LAMBDIN for me, whether arising from his late general superintendence of my concerns, or from any power specially given by me, has ceased.—All accounts to be settled by me alone.
     HENRY HOLDSHIP.
Pittsburgh, July 22, 1825.—(A 6—3t)

## 500 DOLLARS REWARD

RANAWAY from the subscriber, living on Station-camp creek, Sumner county, on the night of the 31st July, the following Slaves, to wit: BRADLEY, about thirty or thirty-five years of age, six feet high, rather spare made, complexion yellow for a negro, high forehead, when spoken to is very deliberate, and has a pleasant countenance. SHEDRICK, about the same complexion, about five feet six or seven inches high, stout made, rather a homely and bad countenance. his wool grows close to his eyebrows. BILL, about 35 years of age, five feet eight or nine inches high, rather spare made, very black. high forehead, large beard, and wears his whiskers; open countenance. ELIAS, about twenty-five years of age, also black, 5 feet 8 inches high; very well made, brisk active walk, smiles when spoken to, a very pleasant countenance. ALFRED, about 19 years of age, black smooth face, regular handsome features, slim made, and has a pleasant countenance. If taken in Sumner, Smith, David son or Robertson county, twenty-five dollars will be given for each; if in Kentucky, fifty dollars; if in the state of Ohio or Illinois, the above reward, and all reasonable charges paid if brought home. Letters of information to be addressed to the subscriber at Gallatin, Tennessee.

     ISAAC FRANKLIN.
Station Camp, Sumner cty. T. Aug. 5, 1825.
☞The Lexington Reporter, Louisville Morning Post, and Knoxville Register, will insert the above three times, and forward their accounts to this office.      A 6, 3t\*

## Wertemburg Academy.

THE Trustees of this institution wish to employ a Principal Teacher, to com-

*Nashville Whig*, August 6, 1825

98

CHAPTER ELEVEN

# MANACLED
# AND CHAINED

Newspapers are replete with ads indicating the sale of a slave from one Tennessee slaveholder to another. They do not, however, reveal much about how slaves got from places such as Virginia and North Carolina to Tennessee, nor do they tell us much about how slaves were forced to migrate to places even further south and west such as Mississippi and Louisiana.

The saga of a Tennessee-born slave trader named Isaac Franklin does, however, tell us about this larger story.

James Franklin was a long hunter who first came to Middle Tennessee in the 1770s. By the early 1800s, he had a burgeoning plantation in the Station Camp Creek area, north of the Cumberland River. James Franklin had 10 children, five of whom were sons. As a teenager, Isaac probably went with his father and his brothers on the annual river trips to New Orleans, where products from the farm were sold and traded. Isaac thus became familiar with rafting on the Cumberland and the Mississippi, trading in New Orleans and traveling the Natchez Trace.

Between 1770 and 1810, East and Middle Tennessee were, in a sense, the western frontier of the American South. But after about 1820, Americans migrated further south and west into present-day West Tennessee, Arkansas, Mississippi and Louisiana. At the time, this region of

**20 Dollars Reward.**

RUNAWAY from Maj. Chotard, near
Natchez, a Negro man named HARRY :
he is low square built, about five feet five inches high, a scar below one of his eyes.—
Said boy was purchased from Isaac Franklin
of Tennessee, where it is presumed he will
aim for. The undersigned will give the a
bove reward, and reasonable expenses, for
the delivery of said boy in Nashville jail.
                                R. & W. ARMSTRONG
April 10, 1822 · 3t.

*Nashville Whig,* April 17, 1822

the country was an unbroken forest inhabited by bears and other beasts of
prey, as described by early settlers such as David Crockett.

As Americans moved into these areas, they began to clear the land and
plant cotton and sugar. This took manpower, which meant slaves. However,
the large slave populations were in states such as Virginia, North Carolina
and Maryland. These Atlantic states had a glut of slaves because tobacco
had declined as a cash crop and because slave populations had gone up due
to natural increases (birth rates exceeding death rates).

By around 1800, slaves cost twice as much in New Orleans as in
Richmond. Virginia planters were quite aware of what this meant to
their long-term financial security. This was the main reason that Thomas
Jefferson and other Virginia leaders were in favor of the ban on the
importation of slaves to the United States (which went into effect in 1808).

We know Isaac Franklin was selling slaves in Natchez in 1819—
probably ones he bought in Tennessee and took down there on log rafts. In
1828, he started a long-distance slave trading firm with his nephew John
Armfield. With business associates throughout Virginia and Maryland,
Franklin & Armfield bought slaves from tobacco plantations in the east
and transported them to New Orleans and Natchez, where they were
sold at great profit. According to 1828 advertisements in the (Alexandria)
*Phenix Gazette* and the *Washington Daily National Intelligencer*, Franklin
& Armfield was in the market for 150 slaves. Thanks to increasing lines of
credit from various banks, that number soon grew to 500.

As plantations owners sold slaves to Franklin & Armfield, they at first housed them in so-called "slave pens," the best known of which was adjacent to the firm's building in Alexandria. Slaves might live there for days or even weeks, milling around the slave pen during the day and sleeping in a two-story adjacent building while chained up at night. Once enough slaves had been accumulated, the company would usually transport them to New Orleans by ship. Early on, Franklin & Armfield sent slaves via third party liners. As the business got bigger, it eventually made more sense for the firm to purchase its own ship, then another, then another, until by 1832 the company owned at least four (the *United States*, the *Tribune*, the *Uncas* and the *Isaac Franklin*).

Because of the legal requirement that ship manifests contain detailed passenger lists, we have a lot of information about how many slaves Franklin & Armfield moved to New Orleans. The shipping season for slave transport ran from October through May. At its peak, the firm sent 75 to 100 slaves per trip and as many as two boats per month on the long journey around the Florida panhandle. On the return voyage to Virginia, the ships carried sugar, molasses, whiskey and cotton.

In the summer, the company would move slaves by land, herding as many as 300 slaves per trip in slave coffles. These overland trips

## Cash in Market.

THE subscribers having leased for a term of years the large three story brick house on Duke street, in the town of Alexandria, D. C. formerly occupied by Gen. Young, we wish to purchase one hundred and fifty likely young negroes of both sexes between the ages of 8 and 25 years. *Persons who wish to sell* will do well to give us a call, as we are determined to give more than any other purchasers that are in market, or that may hereafter come into market.

Any letters addressed to the subscribers through the Post Office at Alexandria, will be promptly attended to. For information, enquire at the above described house, as we can at all times be found there.
may 15                    FRANKLIN & ARMFIELD,

(Alexandria) *Phenix Gazette*, May 17, 1828

came right across Tennessee, through Blountville, Knoxville and Kingston, then over the Cumberland Plateau to Nashville. From there, the slaves would either be loaded onto boats and floated down river or marched down the Natchez Trace and sold at the Mississippi slave market known as the Forks in the Road.

Slave coffles were a somewhat common sight in the South—so common, in fact, that it wasn't even news when they passed through towns. (I have been unable to find a single mention of one of them in a Tennessee newspaper.) However, Northerners and Europeans who visited the South were often shocked when they stumbled upon these forced marches.

One was G.W. Featherstonhaugh, an English geologist who encountered a Franklin & Armfield coffle in southwest Virginia in September 1834. "It was a camp of negro slave-drivers, just packing up to start; they had about three hundred slaves with them, who had bivouacked the preceding night in chains in the woods," he wrote. Feathersonhaugh noted that the caravan included nine wagons to carry supplies and to transport any slaves who could not walk. Describing what he saw, he said "the female slaves were, some of them, sitting on logs of wood, whilst others were standing, and a great many little black children were warming themselves at the fires of the bivouac. In front of them all, and prepared for the march, stood, in double files, about two hundred male slaves, manacled and chained to each other."

Perhaps the most dreadful account of a slave coffle came from a northerner named William Seward, who was visiting a country tavern in Virginia when he saw something he never forgot. "Ten naked little boys, between six and twelve years old, tied together, two and two, by their wrists, were all fastened to a long rope," Seward wrote. They were "followed by a tall, gaunt white man who, with his long lash, whipped up the sad and weary procession, drove it to the horse-trough to drink, and thence to a shed, where they lay down on the ground and sobbed and moaned themselves to sleep.

"These were children gathered up at different plantations by the 'trader,' and were to be driven down to Richmond to be sold at auction, and taken South."

Seward never knew which firm's employee or agent he saw driving the naked children that day. But the sight of the sad procession was one of many things that turned him against slavery. Seward later became New York governor, senator and U.S. secretary of state in the Lincoln and Johnson administrations.

Why Franklin & Armfield transported slaves via both land and sea, rather than just via one method, is something we aren't sure of today. A 1938 biography of Isaac Franklin maintains that the sea route was quicker, but more dangerous because it didn't give the slaves time to acclimate themselves to the climate of Louisiana.

Another idea of why slave traders such as Franklin & Armfield might have chosen the overland route over the sea route can be derived from the *Narrative of Henry Watson*, a first-person account of a former slave published in 1848. Watson recalled being sold to a Richmond trader named Denton, who chained his slaves together and forced the coffle to march all the way to Natchez. "I will not weary my readers with the particulars of our march to Tennessee, where we stopped several days for the purpose of arranging our clothes," Watson recalled. "While stopping, the men were hired out to pick cotton." Watson's recollection raises the possibility that Isaac Franklin might have used his Sumner County plantation as a stop-over on the journey. This would have allowed him the added benefit of using the slaves he was transporting to harvest his own crops.

Because it was so large, because it involved the movement of so many people and because we have so many records of it, Franklin & Armfield is probably the best-documented slave trading firm in American history. It also may have been the largest. From 1828 until 1836, the firm bought, moved, and sold an estimated 1,000 to 1,200 slaves per year, making it responsible for the forced migration of more than 10,000 people. Isaac Franklin earned so much money from the slave trade that he eventually owned six plantations and 600 slaves in Louisiana and several thousand acres in Texas—plus sizable stock holdings in a Mississippi bank, the Nashville and Gallatin Turnpike Company and a horse track in Nashville.

Franklin retired from the slave trading business in the late 1830s. In 1839 he married Adelicia Acklen, a Nashville woman 30 years his

## $50 REWARD.

RANAWAY from the Walnut Ridge Plantation, in Washington county, Mississippi, on the 25th April last, a negro man named ISAAC HATCHET, 20 years old, 5 feet 5 inches high, rather of a copper color, very full and red eyed, slow to answer when spoken to; had on when he went away, red jeans coat and pantaloons, and a common fur hat; he was brought to this State by Mr Isaac Franklin from Virginia, in April last.—The above reward will be paid to any person who will secure him in jail, either in or out of this State, and inform me of it, so that I may get him again.

JOSEPH NEIBERT.

Natchez, July 31, 1835 —sept. 5 —3tẘ, Prs fee $3

*Nashville Republican* **December 17, 1835**

junior. She would long outlive him and spend much of his fortune building a Nashville mansion and estate called Belmont.

Despite the size of his enterprise, Isaac Franklin's name appeared only a few times in Tennessee's newspapers during his life. In August 1825—three years before he co-founded Franklin & Armfield—five slaves named Bradley, Shedrick, Bill, Elias and Alfred ran away from Franklin's plantation in Sumner County. The ad offered $500 for the return of the five—a hefty sum by standards of runaway slave ads.

Also, in 1822, 1833 and in 1835, Isaac Franklin's name was mentioned in ads published in Tennessee newspapers—each time as the person from whom the slave had been acquired. "He [a runaway slave named Isaac Hatchet] was brought to this State by Mr. Isaac Franklin from Virginia, in April last," a Mississippi slaveholder named Joseph Neibert wrote in a runaway slave ad published in the *Nashville Republican* in December 1835.

Franklin died in 1846. Although we will never know how many of his contemporaries looked askance at him for the manner in which he made his fortune, we know wonderful things were written about him when he died. "We knew Isaac Franklin," the *New Orleans Weekly Delta* said after his death. "He was a man of discerning mind, sound judgment, great worth, indomitable spirit and vast enterprise. . . By his industry and enterprise he had succeeded in amassing a princely estate, had become a millionaire, and from our knowledge of his character we have no doubt that he often contemplated with delight the character and usefulness of his immortal name-sake, Benjamin Franklin, and resolved in his own mind to imitate his bright example in an effort to scatter good among his fellow men."

John Armfield also moved back to Tennessee after he left the slave trading business. He developed the Beersheeba Springs resort in Grundy County and was a major benefactor of the University of the South in Franklin County. Armfield is buried at Beersheba Springs, and there is a bluff in Sewanee named for him.

Franklin & Armfield may be the best example of a long-distance slave trading business in America. However, it wasn't the only company that bought slaves, moved them far, and then sold them. Throughout the antebellum period, many firms bought slaves in Virginia and Maryland and sold them in Natchez, New Orleans and other locations in the South. "[Harry] was lately brought from Virginia, by John Criddle," slaveholder Washington Pulliam of Davidson County wrote in May 1819, invoking the name of a slave trader who never reached Isaac Franklin's level of fame.

## $300 REWARD!

RANAWAY from the subscriber near Memphis, on the 28th September last, three negro men, JIM, a stout black, about thirty years old, purchased by me of Mr. Porter of Giles county Ten, who purchased him of Samuel Grigsby near Kingston, Ten. SIMSON likewise a stout black about 23 years old, purchased by me from the same individual, who purchased him in or near Columbia; MICHAL, a tall black about 30 years old, (arm much cut from frequent bleeding) was purchased from Isaac Franklin, and by him brought from Virginia. Jim and Simson have probably gone to their old neighborhood and Michal is with one or the other.—The above reward will be given, or in proportion for either.

WM. T. GHOLSON.

May 1—6t.

The Nashville Banner and Knoxville Register will please give the above advertisement six weekly insertions and forward their accounts to this office for payment.

*Memphis Times.*

*Knoxville Register*, May 8, 1833

As I mentioned in a previous chapter, between 1827 and 1855, it was illegal for a trader to sell a slave in Tennessee which he had purchased in another state. But there are many pieces of evidence that the law may have been violated.

In May 1833, for instance, a Shelby County slaveholder named William Gholson offered $300 for the return of three runaway slaves. One of them was named Michal, described as "a tall black about 30 years old . . . [who] was purchased from Isaac Franklin, and by him brought from Virginia."

Five years later, several slaves ran away from the Gwin & Love Iron Works in Perry County. According to the runaway slave ad, four of the five slaves had been purchased from "some negro traders, who brought them from Virginia or South Carolina."

Both of these runaway slave ads may have referenced illegal slave sales.

More evidence that Tennessee's "ban" on the interstate slave trade was ignored comes from the example of Joseph Meek. Meek was a Davidson County resident who in the 1820s bought slaves in Virginia and sold them in Mississippi. In 1835 Meek formed a partnership with three Virginia men whose last names were Logan, Haynes and Magee. According to a series of letters between the four, the partnership raised money, purchased 98 slaves and herded them via coffle to Nashville in the summer of 1836. Somehow the partners managed to sell most (or all) of the slaves. But it isn't clear how much money they made or whether the partnership was successful.[1]

We do know, at least, that one of the slaves didn't want to leave Virginia. After learning he had been sold, the slave cut off his hand, forcing the partners to try to exchange him for a slave with two hands. After all, Haynes wrote in one of his letters, a one-handed slave could be "counted as nothing."

---

[1] In April 1839, Nashville resident Robert Moore offered a $25 reward for the return of a runaway slave named Joe. The ad claimed that Joe had been purchased from Joseph Meek.

CHAPTER TWELVE
# AUCTIONEERS THROUGHOUT THE STATE

According to census data, Tennessee had about 44,000 slaves in 1810 and 80,000 slaves in 1820. In researching this book, I have come to believe that the vast majority of those slaves were purchased by their eventual slaveholders in Virginia, North Carolina or Maryland and brought to Tennessee rather than brought across the mountains and sold by slave traders in Tennessee. One reason for this conclusion is that there were very few advertisements bought by professional slave traders in Tennessee's newspapers before about 1820. There are slaves being bought and sold in newspaper ads, and sold in quantity when someone died. But if there was a regular slave market in Nashville which sold slaves that had been imported from Virginia, it doesn't appear to have advertised.

The interstate slave trade was (technically, at least) illegal in Tennessee from 1827 until 1855, which means that it was against the law to buy slaves in Virginia and sell them in Tennessee. For more than a quarter century, therefore, Tennessee's professional slave traders who sold in Tennessee had to content themselves buying slaves who were already in Tennessee to begin with (assuming they wanted to obey the law).

In spite of this legal restriction, one starts to find hints of professional slave trading throughout Tennessee after about 1820. Rather than talk about Tennessee's slave traders at once, I've decided to talk first about smaller markets throughout the state. Up front I need to admit that my data is spotty. Unable to read every newspaper on file at the Tennessee State Library and Archives, I could only look at some issues here and there. It also needs to be pointed out that we simply do not have many of the earliest newspapers.

Nevertheless, the following discoveries hint at the nature of the slave trade in some of the smaller markets of the state.

## KNOXVILLE/KINGSTON

In 1820, Benjamin W.S. Cabell announced in the *Knoxville Register* that he had moved "his NEGROES from Knoxville to Kingston where they will remain until Friday or Saturday next." Cabell said his slaves consisted of men, women, boys and girls and boasted that "a more healthy and likely set of Slaves has never before been offered for sale in this country."

I searched for more information about Cabell, but found no mention of his name in any other Tennessee newspaper. However, the wording of his ad indicates he was a regular slave trader and not selling slaves as part of an estate or on behalf an individual slaveholder. I also think the ad proves there was at least a semi-regular slave trade in both Knoxville and Kingston by that time and that residents of both places knew exactly where Cabell would be selling slaves, since the ad did not give a specific location. We can assume, based on the ad, that sometime prior to its publication, he and his men had herded a coffle of slaves

**NEGROES.**

I HAVE removed my NEGROES from Knoxville to Kingston where they will remain until Friday or Saturday next. Persons wishing to purchase will do well to apply soon. I have no hesitation in saying that a more healthy and likely set of Slaves has never before been offered for sale in this country. They consist of men, women, boys and girls of different ages. They will be sold very low.
BENJ. W. S. CABELL.
Jan. 25.

*Knoxville Register*, **February 1, 1820**

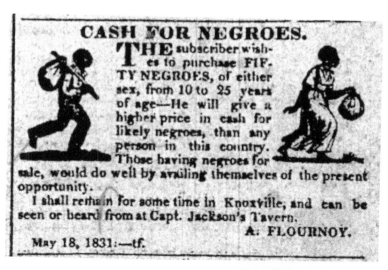

*Knoxville Register*, May 25, 1831

on the main road from Knoxville to Kingston (present-day route of Highway 70).

Speaking of Kingston and its slave trade: In 1824 the *Knoxville Enquirer* published a runaway slave ad that had been purchased by William Whiteman of Knox County. In the ad, Whiteman stated he expected the runaway slave Hugh to migrate toward Kingston, "as I purchased him of Blackwell and Martin"—probably in reference to another slave trader who operated there around 1820.

In 1831, a man named A. Flournoy announced in the *Knoxville Register* that he wished to purchase 50 slaves "of either sex, from 10 to 25 years of age." Using language very similar to that being used by other long distance slave traders of that era, he said he would pay a "higher price in cash for likely negroes than any person in the country." He also said that he would be staying at "Capt. Jackson's Tavern."

I never found Flournoy's name in a Tennessee newspaper again, nor did I find his name among the names of national slave traders in books or websites. However, I believe the ad indicates that he was making rounds through East Tennessee, buying enough slaves to form a coffle he could deliver to a larger market such as Nashville, Memphis or New Orleans.

Jumping ahead to the Civil War, a close examination of newspapers reveals the names of several slave traders who did business in Knoxville

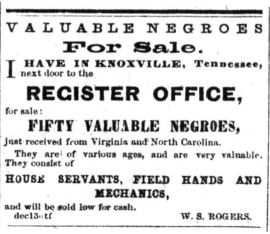

**VALUABLE NEGROES**
**For Sale.**

I HAVE IN KNOXVILLE, Tennessee, next door to the

**REGISTER OFFICE,**

for sale:

**FIFTY VALUABLE NEGROES,**

just received from Virginia and North Carolina.

They are of various ages, and are very valuable. They consist of

**HOUSE SERVANTS, FIELD HANDS AND MECHANICS,**

and will be sold low for cash.

dec13.tf                    W. S. ROGERS.

*Knoxville Daily Register*, December 14, 1862

in 1862 and 1863. In a sale that does not appear to have been associated with a legal case or an estate, J.M. Horton sold two women and two children at the Knox County Courthouse on December 20, 1862. That very week, a man named W.S. Rogers advertised that he had no less than 50 "VALUABLE NEGROES just received from Virginia and North Carolina" for sale at a location next to the register office in downtown Knoxville.

## ELIZABETHTON/MORRISTOWN

Between April 30 and October 8, 1835, every issue of the *Nashville Republican* newspaper contained an ad for Dr. Joseph Powell, a slave trader who lived in Elizabethton, but who apparently bought and sold slaves all over Tennessee. "Having been engaged to some extent in this kind of traffic for two or three years past, he [Powell] believes himself fully competent to judge the worth of such property," the ad said. Powell charged two percent

**NEGROES.**

DR. JOSEPH POWELL, of Elizabethton, Carter county, Tenn., is disposed to engage, on commission, in the purchasing of negroes to the orders of all such persons as may be willing to entrust their interest with him. Having been engaged to some extent in this kind of traffic for two or three years past, he believes himself fully competent to judge the worth of such property. He will charge, as a commission for his services, two per cent. on all sums invested, and would, if requested, deliver the negroes so purchased, at any place designated, for reasonable wages, including expenses.

Such as may wish his services, are referred to Co Ephraim H. Foster, Nashville; Dr. T. G. Greenfield near Columbia, Maury county; Adam Huntsman Esq Jackson, Madison county Tenn; and Washingto Keys Esq. cashier of the bank at Decatur, Ala.

P. S. If those making remittances would forward drafts on Baltimore or Philadelphia, they could be cashed conveniently.                    April 16-6m.

*Nashville Republican*, June 2, 1835

commission for his services and said he would deliver slaves to any location, so long as his expenses were reimbursed. The ad listed several references, including Colonel Ephraim Foster of Nashville.

What makes this ad interesting is that Joseph Powell was not an unknown slave trader or slaveholder like so many of the men mentioned throughout this book. Powell was prominent East Tennessean whose son Robert would later be a Tennessee state senator and whose daughter Eleanor would later be the wife of Tennessee House of Representatives speaker Landon Haynes. The presence of this ad—and the fact that it ran more than 70 times in Nashville—proves that Dr. Joseph Powell at least dabbled in the cross-state slave trade.

Morristown was an important stop on the East Tennessee and Virginia Railroad which, like other railroads in the South, was frequently used by slave traders. In December 1862 Jonesboro slaveholder Z.L. Burson offered $50 for the return of a runaway slave named Mollie. "I bought her last February at Morristown, at the sale of Blevins & Franklin," Burson wrote in the ad, revealing the name and location in which another slave trader operated.

## Fifty Dollars Reward

RUNAWAY FROM THE SUBSCRIBER at Jonesboro', Washington county, Tenn., on Monday morning, Dec. 8th, a girl named MOLLIE, 16 years old, about 5 feet high, weighs about 120 pounds, and is rather copper color. I bought her last February at Morristown, at the sale of Blevins & Franklin. Her mother belongs to Dr. Drake, at Bull's Gap. She may be lurking around his premises. I will pay the above reward if confined in jail so I can get her, or delivered to me. If she is caught in the county, I will pay $20.

dec12dtf                                 Z. L. BURSON.

*Knoxville Daily Register*, December 4, 1862

## SWEETWATER/ATHENS/CLEVELAND

Speaking of railroad stops in East Tennessee, here are three more that had slave traders, at least occasionally: In March 1863, a firm called Neil & Wright advertised that it had 25 slaves to sell at the Sweetwater Depot. Only a few weeks later, Jason Chiborne & Co.

said it had 11 slaves "consisting of one woman and child, two men and two girls and five good plow boys"—all available to be seen at Sweetwater.

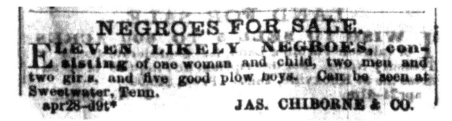

*Knoxville Daily Register*, April 29, 1863

Just a short train ride away, many advertisements indicate that slave traders operated in Athens with regularity. In 1862, a partnership called Latham & Farrell said it would attempt to sell 20 slaves at nearby Mouse Creek Depot (present day Niota) on December 19. Under the name Latham & Howard, similar ads were published throughout the spring of 1863, with wording that indicates that regular slave trades were nothing new to the area. "LATHAM & HOWARD ARE JUST IN receipt of another lot of prime Negroes—twenty in number," said the ad in June 1863. "Among them a likely family—a man, his wife and three children—two or three good cooks, and several first rate plough boys— At their old stand at Mouse Creek Depot."

We also know from advertisements that a professional slave trader named J.M. Horton lived in Cleveland. In one ad, from 1862, Horton indicated that he would be selling slaves at the Knox County Courthouse. "Anyone desiring further information can address me at Cleveland, Tenn.," he wrote.

Like so many of the advertisements discussed in this book, the items about sales in Sweetwater and Athens raise as many questions as they answer. We do not know, for instance, how long regular slave trades had been occurring in these areas. We also don't know whether the opening of the railroad increased the importation of slaves from Virginia (although I strongly suspect that it did).

The ads, do, however, prove that rural East Tennessee had regular slave traders. They also prove that coffles of slaves were a regular sight on the East Tennessee and Virginia Railroad.

## CLARKSVILLE

Hundreds of slaves worked in the iron furnaces of Montgomery, Stewart, Dickson and Cheatham Counties in the early 19th century. Some were owned by the various iron foundries; others were hired out to work on an annual basis. That being the case, we can rightfully assume that there was a slave market in Clarksville. However, the best information I can find about regular slave trades came much later, in the 1850s, with advertisements for an auctioneer named T.D. Leonard.

An item in the April 1860 *Clarksville Chronicle* makes it sounds as if Leonard had been around for some time. "He [Leonard] has sold hundreds of thousands of dollars worth of property in the city and neighborhood, and has, we believe always given satisfaction. He is prepared, at all times, to undertake the sale of Lands, Houses, Negroes, Horses, Cattle, Furniture or Merchandise on fair terms."

We also have proof of Clarksville's slave mart from a former slave who said her sister was sold there. "There used to be a nigger trading yard right there where the Clarksville National Bank is," a former slave and resident of Clarksville said in the late 1920s. "They sold my sister right in this nigger trading yard. She had a baby, and at first they didn't want to buy her because of the baby, but finally a man from Arkansas bought them, and we heard nothing of her for 12 years."

# AUCTION SALE
OF NEGROES, MULES AND HORSES.

I will offer, at the Market House in Clarksville, on the 1st Monday in March next, 10 likely negroes, men, women and children; one of the men is a good boot and shoemaker, the others are farm and Iron-works hands. Among the women are several first rate cooks, washers and ironers. Also 20 Mules and 10 Horses—and any other property that my friends may wish me to sell on that day.          T. D. LEONARD, Auctioneer.
Feb 6, '57—4w

*Clarksville Chronicle*, **February 20, 1857**

FOR SALE

BY the subscribers at Jefferson, between 20 and 30 likely NEGROES, of which there are men, women, boys and girls.
PHELPS & THORNHILL.
December 26.—1t

*Nashville Whig,* **December 26, 1825**

## SOUTHERN MIDDLE TENNESSEE

The year 1830 is about half way between Tennessee's creation and the Civil War. In 1830, Tennessee's top five counties ranked by population were (in order) Bedford, Davidson, Maury, Williamson and Rutherford. All five of these counties had between about 25,000 and 30,000 people in 1830. Meanwhile, Knox County only had a population of about 15,000; Shelby County less than 6,000; and Hamilton County only about 2,500.

Given the relative size of these counties, plus the fact that they all had large slave populations, I feel certain that communities such as Murfreesboro, Shelbyville, Columbia and Pulaski would have had slave trades above and beyond estate sales and clerk and master sales. But because there are so few old newspapers from these communities, I didn't find very much. Here are a few hints:

- In 1825, a firm known as Phelps & Thornhill announced it was selling between 20 and 30 slaves in the Rutherford County community of Jefferson.[1]

- A runaway slave "bounty hunter" named William Rose bought ads in several issues of the 1835 *Nashville Republican.* "Having spent the last 7 or 8 months in the state of Illinois, and made considerable excursions through the state to search for some runaway negroes, in my travels and enquiries I took a description of a considerable number of runaways," he explained. "As I expect to return in a

---

[1]Jefferson, once the Rutherford County seat, is now abandoned.

## LOOK AT THIS.

TO the citizens of Tennessee—gentlemen, having spent the last 7 or 8 months in the State of Illinois, and made considerable excursions through the State to search for some runaway negroes, in my travels and enquiries I took a description of a considerable number of runaways; and as I expect to return in a few months to Illinois, and spend several months there, gentlemen having negroes runaway and suspecting them to be in a free State, if they will direct a few lines to me, post paid, living in Pulaski, Giles county, Tennessee, giving a minute description of their negroes—the time they run off, and the promise of such a reward as will justify me for my trouble, it is more than probable that they may recover their negroes.

Dec 24.—2t.                    WILLIAM ROSE.

*Nashville Republican*, **December 31, 1835**

few months to Illinois, and spend several months there, gentlemen having negroes runaway and suspecting them to be in a free state, if they will direct a few lines to me, post paid, living in Pulaski, Giles County, Tennessee, giving a description of their negroes . . . it is more than probable that they may recover their negroes." Given Rose's description of his profession, it seems likely that he also sold slaves.

- William Fletcher King taught at the Unionville Male Academy in Bedford County for a semester in 1854. In his memoirs, he said that there were five trustees, "one of whom, William Little, was a prominent slave trader." Unfortunately, very few antebellum newspapers from Bedford County have survived. It's possible he was associated with a prominent slave trading firm known as Hill & Little, which operated in Memphis in 1852 and 1853.

- In October 1851, the *Pulaski Gazette* announced that William C. Mayfield would be selling "22 or 23" slaves "consisting of boys and girls from 9 to 18 years old." In

### Negroes for Sale.

I HAVE a lot of **22** or **23** LIKELY YOUNG NEGROES for sale, consisting of Boys and Girls from 9 to 18 years old.

I expect to be in Pulaski or vicinity till after the Circuit Court in December. I invite my friends to give me a call and I will do the very best I can for them.

WM. C. MAYFIELD.

Oct. 29, 1851.    23—2w.

*Pulaski Gazette*, **October 31, 1851**

the ad, Mayfield said that he expected "to be in Pulaski or vicinity 'till after the Circuit Court in December" and that he invited his "friends to give him a call and I will do the very best I can for them." Mayfield did not say exactly where his slaves would be or when he would be selling them, which indicates that prospective buyers knew where to find him.

- In 1854, William Cowan ran an ad in the *Bedford Weekly Yeoman* announcing that someone had "left with me to sell, a Negro Woman, 49 or 50 years of age; a good cook and washer. If not sold before the first Monday in March," he continued, "I will then sell her at the courthouse in Shelbyville." It seems strange for Cowan to have run this ad and made these public statements were he not an auctioneer who sold slaves with some regularity.

Since slavery was such an important part of the Tennessee economy, one might ask why it is that mentions of slave traders aren't easier to find. One possible clue comes from the 1931 book *Slave Trading in the Old South*, when author Frederic Bancroft recalled a letter he had received around 1890 from a Southern judge who had been a slaveholder before the Civil War. "In the South the calling of a slave-trader was always hateful, odious, even among slaveholders themselves," the old judge wrote. "This is curious, but it is so. A trader's children recovered, to some extent, but there was ever a thin cloud resting on them, which they could not get rid of. We had two or three slave-traders in this section, and although their children were taken into society, it was no uncommon thing to hear the sly remark—'his or her father was a slave driver.'"

One reads such assessments about the social status of slave traders in many books and articles. This may explain why some slave traders didn't run newspaper ads, or might live in one place and operate in another, or operate in one market for a few years and then move away. However, being a slave trader didn't stop Isaac Franklin from marrying into one of Nashville's most elite families. It also didn't stop a semi-literate slave trader from Memphis from being elected alderman and eventually rising in status so high that a statue of him is still displayed prominently in the state Capitol.

CHAPTER THIRTEEN

# FANCY GIRLS IN NASHVILLE

The two largest slave markets in Tennessee, the ones with the largest numbers of professional slave traders, were Nashville and Memphis. Even in these large markets, though, it is not easy to trace the early development of professional slave traders.

At first, most professional slave traders sold other things besides slaves. In the early 1800s, Tennessee's retail world had not advanced to the point where there were separate grocery, drug and furniture stores. Customers routinely bought all types of products from auctioneers, who might have furniture one week, blankets the second and slaves the third.

## AUCTION.

ON TUESDAY, 27th September, 1814, at the Court-House, the following valuable property, to wit:—

Several *NEGROES*;
An elegant GIG;
A plantation *WAGGON*.
Terms made known on the day of sale.
　One Negro WOMAN and two CHIL-
　　DREN—Cash
　100 pieces FLOWERED PAPER;
　　50 Groce STEEL ROLLER BUCKLES, at
　　　90 days;
　　2 Hhds. SUGAR, at 90 days;
　　1 box TEA;
　　14 boxes Cotton Ball THREAD;
　A quantity of *SHAWLS*;
　1 Lady's *SADDLE*;
　Several Tea-boards and Waiters.
PATENT CORN SHELLERS.
This useful machine is not sufficiently known
—it can be seen at Geo. Poyzer's, or at
my store. It will save the labor of one
man to Distillers and Millers.
*Cotton, Whiskey, &c. taken in payment.*
　D. ROBERTSON, Auctioneer.

*Nashville Whig*, September 20, 1814

After about 1830, slave traders came and went. Based on advertisements, it appears as if the average life expectancy of a Nashville slave trading business was between two and four years. One wonders whether slave traders regularly worked in the business for a few years and then, like Isaac Franklin, retired to life as a wealthy farmer.

The first generation of Nashville's slave auctioneers were men such as Alpha Kingsley, Stephen Cantrell, Duncan Robertson and Robert Currey, who often conducted the estate auctions described in chapter nine. A prominent firm in Nashville between 1810 and 1825, Robertson & Currey sold real estate, furniture from estate sales and whatever oddities might have floated to town on the latest steamboat. The partners also sold slaves when they could. On September 27, 1814, Robertson & Currey sold a hodgepodge that included a wagon, some tea, a lady's saddle, some flowered paper and "several NEGROES." Advertising in most issues of the *Nashville Whig* between 1818 and 1826, Robertson & Currey might report that they had just received a shipment of candles, several boxes of books, three barrels of fish oil or a few kegs of ground ginger. In this mix might appear the occasional slave sale.

## AUCTION.

ON SATURDAY, February 15, at twelve o'clock, will be sold at the court-house in Nashville, TEN likely young NEGROES. Terms made known on the day of sale.
  ROBERTSON & CURREY, Auct's.
February 5——2w

## LOST OR MISLAID.

I Have lost out of my Library the 4th *volume of Tucker's Blackstone*, besides several other Books, with my name written in the title page. Any person who may have those books in their possession, will please return them as soon as possible.
  JNO. W. OVERTON.
Nashville, February 5——3t

*Nashville Whig,* February 5, 1823

By the mid 1830s, Nashville's main slave auctioneer appears to have been L.E. Temple, who specialized in the sale of horses, mules and slaves. "NEGRO FOR SALE," said a March 1838 ad. "A LIKELY negro boy nine years of age, for sale for cash." A few months later, Temple was in a buying mode, offering to purchase "six or eight young negro fellows sound and of good character, from 18 to 25 years of age." In April 1839, Temple was trying to sell "a likely Negro Girl, ten or eleven years old, on a credit of nine months. The girl is perfectly healthy and sold for no fault—the owner having no use for her." Temple's advertisements ran through 1842.

Former slaves later described slave auction yards as deplorable places. Nashville's auction houses described themselves in more flattering terms. The February 1847 *Republican Banner* contained ads for a new slave trading firm called Maddux and Dawson. "Our establishment is on College Street, below the Planters Bank, and so walled in that Negroes cannot escape from the yard during the day," the ad stated. "And we have a strong and comfortable house in the yard for safe keeping during the night."

Maddux and Dawson must not have been the success that its owners hoped, since I can't find a single ad for the business after this introduction. The big slave trader in the first part of the 1850s appears to have been A.A. McLean, a real estate agent with an office and auction yard on Cherry Street, "two doors south of Deaderick."[1] McLean ran a "one-stop shop" for any transaction involving slaves— he bought slaves, sold slaves, hired out slaves, and found slaves for businesses looking to lease them. A January 1850 newspaper contains two ads for McLean. In one, he claimed that he had businesses ready and waiting to hire slaves who were cooks, washers, ironers, house girls, farm hands and railroad workers. In the other ad, he said he had three different female slaves for sale, ages 20, 15 and 14.

McLean had slaves coming and going at a constant clip. He also bounced between real estate and slaves, depending on the season and what happened to be coming his way. In February 1850 McLean said he had 16 slaves to sell and wanted to buy 15. In July of that year, he listed 33 houses and farms that he had for sale and rent. Just

---

[1]Cherry Street later became Fourth Avenue.

below there, he said that he had a family of five slaves, "valued at $2,000, which will be exchanged for a family residence in town." In December McLean wanted to purchase 100 slaves between the ages of 12 and 25 years. In May 1851, he announced that he had 29 slaves to sell ranging in ages from 10 months to 46 years.

> **Wanted immediately,**
> *FOR THE YEAR 1850, THE FOLLOWING:*
>
> FOR HIRE—A superior man servant for house work.
>
> Also, Cooks, Washers and Ironers, House Girls and Boys—Also 50 good working hands, for out door business, Farming and Railroads—in fact every description of servants wanted at my office.
> **A. A. McLEAN, Genl. Agent.**
> Office on Cherry street, 2 doors south of Deaderick.
> Jan. 3, 1850.
>
> FOR SALE—Two Negro Girls, 14 and 15 years old, and a Woman 20 years old: all good servants, Also, for sale, a good Dwelling House, pleasantly situated.
> FOR RENT—Good Dwelling Houses, fiom $75 to $225 per year.
> **A. A. McLEAN Genl. Agent**
> Office on Cherry street, 2 doors south of Deaderick.
> n. 3.

*Republican Banner and Nashville Whig,* January 12, 1850

McLean either died, went out of business, or left town after 1852. In his wake came a firm called Glover & Boyd, which also did both real estate and slaves at its office at Number 50 Cherry Street. In a single issue of the *Nashville Union* in February 1853, Glover & Boyd had six separate ads. One publicized the sale of numerous pieces of real estate, including 2,000 acres on Mansker Creek. A second stated that the firm had six slaves for sale—including a 10-year-old boy. A third ad for Glover & Boyd listed several prominent references, including the governor of Tennessee, half a dozen bankers, several court clerks and the founder of the Nashville and Chattanooga Railroad. Glover & Boyd advertised as far away as Shelbyville, which indicates that the firm reached far across the countryside.

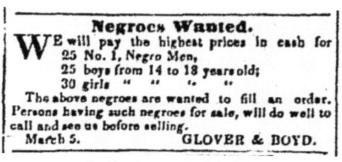

*Republican Banner and Nashville Whig,* **March 11, 1853**

Glover & Boyd also "filled orders" for large clients, who may have been slave traders in other parts of the South. In April 1853 the company said it wanted to purchase 80 slaves—30 men over the age of 18; 25 boys between 14 and 18 years old; and 25 girls between 14 and 18 years old.

But by 1855, the only mention of Glover & Boyd that I can find in Nashville's newspapers involves lawsuits.

In terms of newspaper advertisements, the best documented slave trading firm in Nashville was started by James Dabbs and Rees W. Porter, both of whom had previously worked for Glover & Boyd. Dabbs and Porter announced their business with a big ad describing their luxurious slave pen. "We can at all times be found at our office at 33 Cedar Street . . . where we have erected safe and comfortable quarters for keeping all number of Negroes," said an 1853 ad. "Those wishing to sell may be assured of getting the highest market price, as we will either buy on our own account or sell on commission for others."

*Nashville Union,* **April 25, 1853**

Dabbs and Porter broke up their partnership about a year later. Porter stayed in the business for about three more years and, during that period, did more advertising than any other slave trader in Nashville history. Porter's advertisements indicate that he constantly had slaves of all ages and skill levels locked up in his slave pen. In the December 1854 *Nashville Union and American*, Porter claimed to have "an excellent shoe and boot maker and several good cooks." In April 1856, he advertised that he had 55 slaves ready to sell, "consisting of men women and children, amongst them several good Blacksmiths" and "several House Girls." In October 1856, Porter claimed to have 32 slaves in his pen, including "6 or 8 likely girls, from 12 to 14 years old, an extra house servant, seamstress, washer and ironer, likely and intelligent, and several stout men. Also, an extra blacksmith. Call while the excitement is up." In February 1857, Porter had 69 slaves to sell, including carpenters, blacksmiths, seamstresses, cooks and washers.

## 55 Negroes for Sale.

I HAVE on hand 55 NEGROES for sale, consisting of men women and children, amongst them several good Blacksmiths, a No. 1 Fancy Girl. Also several House Girls. These Negroes are bound to go; call immediately.
March 7. REES W. PORTER.

*Republican Banner*, December 1856

Porter was the only slave trader in Nashville whose advertisements mentioned the sale of "fancy girls" and "fancy boys" which raises the question of what the terms meant. A "fancy boy" was a young, multiracial slave who was generally sold to be a doorman or personal servant. A "fancy girl" was a physically attractive slave, usually multiracial, who was sold to be a concubine. "Fancy girl" slaves were more commonly associated with the New Orleans slave market, where they were often leased out as bar maids in riverboats or brothels. As many books on slavery point out, "fancy girls" were typically very young and often of such a mixed race that they almost looked white. "Many of these children [from 12 to 20 years old] were fair mulattoes, and some of them very pretty," author Frederika Bremer wrote after a tour of the slave markets of New Orleans in the 1850s. "One girl of twelve was so white that I should have supposed her to belong to the white race . . . These white children of slavery become, for the most part, victims of crime, and sink to the deepest degradation."

Rees W. Porter's frequent mentions of "fancy girls" prove that children were publicly and regularly sold for the sex trade—two blocks west of the Davidson County Courthouse and two blocks east of the Tennessee State Capitol.

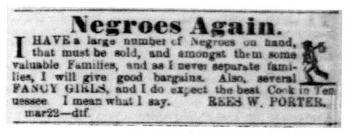

*Nashville Union and American,* **April 1 1856**

His enthusiastic advertisements for "fancy girls" and "fancy boys" resulted in the publication of some of the more disturbing newspaper advertisements in Tennessee history.

- "FOR SALE—An excellent Blacksmith, warranted . . . 1 Woman and Child, 21 years old, good Cook; 1 very pretty Girl, 13 years old; 1 No. 1 fancy Boy 12."—February 1853

> **HERE IS THAT FANCY BOY.**
> I HAVE for sale an extra No. 1, Fancy Boy, 10 years old. Some 4 or 5 women, several of whom are warranted *good cooks.* Some small boys from 9 to 12 years old; 6 or 8 good men from 18 to 35; and several valuable body servants. Be in a hurry or Christmas will come and find you without a negro and you will have to hire again at higher prices than ever. REES W. PORTER.
> I also want to hire 25 or 30 negroes for the Ironworks.
> dec21—tf R. W. P.

*Nashville Union and American,* **December 23, 1854**

- "I have for sale an extra No. 1 Fancy Boy, 10 years old. Some 4 or 5 women, several of whom are warranted good cooks. Some small boys from 9 to 12 years old . . . Be in a hurry or Christmas will come and find you without a negro."—December 1854

---

**THE RIVER IS UP!**
I HAVE 29 negroes to sell, amongst them several good Mechanics, two or three extra fancy Girls. I will give good bargains to persons living in the city.
Dec. 2. REE?   W. PORTER.

---

*Republican Banner,* December 1856

- "THE RIVER IS UP! I HAVE 29 negroes to sell, amongst them several mechanics, two or three extra fancy Girls."—December 1856

---

**HERE IT IS.**
AMONG a lot of about forty Negroes, I have the finest Fancy Boy, fifteen years old, in Tennessee.
April 8. REE? W PORTER.

---

*Republican Banner,* April 1857

In 1857, like so many of his predecessors in the slave trading business, Porter's name vanishes from Nashville's newspapers. By then, the firm of James & Harrison dominated the market. Led by Thomas G. James, who had been a slave trader in Natchez, Mississippi, only a few years earlier, James & Harrison advertised that its operation at 18 Cedar Street bought slaves, sold slaves and took care of slaves left in its keep. In items that appeared throughout that year, James & Harrison frequently said it would buy up to 100 slaves, to be resold at events occurring "every Saturday morning at 10 o'clock." But—again—within a year or two, James & Harrison appears to have gone out of business.

H.H. Haynes, a former clerk for Porter, took over his former employer's spot at 33 Cedar Street. The next year the location was

## 100 Negroes Wanted.

THE undersigued will pay the cash for one hundred likely young Negroes, delivered to them at their Sale House at No. 18, Cedar Street Nashville, Tenn They will board Negroes and sell for other persons on commission, will keep a large number on hand for sale at all times will be responsible for Negroes left in their charge, and will have regular Auction Sales of Negroes every Saturday morning at 10 o'clock. Call and see.

JAMES & HARRISON.

Dec. 16—1y.

*Republican Banner*, May 13, 1857

taken over by R.J. Lyles, who advertised heavily. By 1860, Nashville's main slave traders appear to have been Lyles & Hitchings, E.S. Hawkins (18 Cedar Street); and Webb, Merrill & Co. (8 South Market Street). The latter claimed in advertisements that it "will, at all times, purchase NEGROES suited to the New Orleans market," which indicates that the slaves it bought were loaded onto rafts for the long ride to Louisiana. These appear to have been the three main slave yards that the U.S. Army found when it marched into Nashville a week after the Battle of Fort Donelson.

## JAMES C. JONES.

I HAVE on hand 32 negroes for sale. Among them 6 or 8 likely girls, from 12 to 14 years old, an extra house servant, Seamstress, washer and ironer, likely and intelligent, and several stout men. Also, an extra black smith. Call while the excitement is up.

oct22—tf

REES W. PORTER.

*Nashville Union and American*, October 22, 1856

This list of some of Nashville's leading slave traders is not complete. In addition to these firms, which stayed around enough to become regular newspaper advertisers, there were slave traders who pop up in only one or two issues. In 1825, a man named William Compton ran an ad declaring he would pay cash for "a few Negro men and women of good character," adding his pledge that "they will not be taken out of the country" and "be treated with more than

## $100 Reward.

RANAWAY, my boy, **Joe**, about twenty-two years old, black, likely, smart, and dresses well, and weighs about 140 pounds, some unsoundness about his teeth, is a painter, paper hanger and barber, tries to show off in conversation, and his pronunciation somewhat peculiar, about 5½ feet high. I think he is lurking about Nashville. I will pay twenty-five dollars for his delivery to me near Nashville, or the above reward if taken out of the State and secured so that I can get him again.

May1—tf. L. B. McCONNICO.

## For Sale.

I HAVE a good lot of Negroes for sale, consisting of men and women, boys and girls, at No. 83 Cedar St.
may25—tf R. J LYLES.

## 40 Negroes.

I HAVE just received about forty negroes, including several good families, and a few well qualefied house servants, some very likely girls and a lot of No. 1 young men, all for sale cheap for cash. R. J. LYLES,
may27—tf. 83 Cedar Street.

## For Sale.

A NEGRO MAN thirty seven years old that is well recommended—cheap for cash. R. J. LYLES,
june3—tf 83 Cedar Street.

## Now is the Time to Buy Negroes.

JUST received, at No. 18 Cedar Street, a very likely lo of **young Negro Girls**, which will be sold low
Apr26—tf E. S. HAWKINS, Ag't.

## For Sale.

A GOOD farm hand, thirty years old, on a credit of six or twelve months, if desired. R. J. LYLES,
may31—tf. No. 83 Cedar Street.

## For Hire.

A GOOD Blacksmith that is under a first rate character at 83 Cedar street. R. J. LYLES.
June 1—tf

*Republican Banner*, June 7, 1859

usual humanity." In 1850, Samuel H. Davis bought ads offering "the highest price" in cash for slaves between the ages of 14 and 30. Neither one of these men bought newspaper ads in Nashville (that I could find) again, raising the possibility that they floated the slaves down river to another market where they could sell them for more.

A footnote about Nashville's professional slave traders: As far as historical preservation is concerned, they might as well never have existed. As of this date, there are no historical markers in downtown Nashville that acknowledge the fact that thousands of slaves were sold there, most them in the small area between the courthouse and the corner of Fourth and Cedar (now Charlotte).

*Memphis Daily Eagle and Enquirer*, May 2, 1857

CHAPTER FOURTEEN
# BOLTON, DICKINS AND FORREST

You only have to look at a map to see how the slave trade favored Memphis over all other Tennessee cities.

As people began moving into states such as Mississippi, Louisiana, Arkansas and Texas, they wanted slaves to clear the land and help them grow crops such as sugar and cotton. Almost all of these slaves had to come from Maryland, Virginia, North Carolina, Kentucky and Tennessee—states that were all exporting slaves by the 1840s. Memphis is at the southwest tip of Tennessee, alongside a river that flows south like a moving sidewalk, straight to Vicksburg, Baton Rouge and New Orleans.

As mentioned in chapter 3, there were slaves in Memphis long before it even had that name; a slave ran away from her slaveholder at the Chickasaw Bluffs of the Mississippi River in 1804. We also know that slaves were in all parts of West Tennessee, were running away in West Tennessee, and were being apprehended in West Tennessee as soon as white settlers moved in. So we can assume that slaves were being bought and sold in Memphis, and probably by professionals, from the start. However, since newspapers from Memphis' early years are hard to come by, we have little to go on until the 1840s.

Advertisement for various slave traders who operated in and around Memphis appeared in the *Memphis Commercial Appeal* during the 1840s. Ads purchased by W.F. Hughes, J.E. Phillips and G.B. Locke indicate that they did their buying and selling in front of the Exchange in downtown Memphis. An 1844 ad for John Anderson states that he was about to offer for sale between 12 and 15 slaves in La Grange; six weeks later he was selling 15 slaves in Somerville. In 1846, Henry M. Clay said that he was going to be selling about 40 slaves—"most of them superior cotton pickers and all acclimated to the Arkansas River"—at the ferry landing across the Mississippi River from Memphis.

*Memphis Daily Eagle and Enquirer*, January 8, 1853

The volume of sales by these slave traders paled in comparison to Bolton, Dickins & Company. One of the largest slave trading firms in American history, Bolton, Dickins & Co. was led by brothers Isaac, Jefferson, Wade and Washington Bolton and Thomas Dickins, who was the son-in-law of Isaac Bolton. At its height, it had buying offices and slave marts in Memphis, New Orleans, Vicksburg, Mobile, Lexington (Kentucky), Richmond, St. Louis and Charleston. Like Franklin & Armfield had done a few years earlier, Bolton, Dickins & Co. sent agents to places where slaves were in less demand, bought them, herded them in coffles to one of their various slave-pens, and eventually transported them to markets where they could be sold.

Ads for the Bolton, Dickins & Co. "SLAVE MARKET" on Adams Street in Memphis were running in newspapers such as the *Memphis Daily Eagle and Enquirer* by 1847. These ads claimed that the partners "have now, and will continue to keep on hand throughout the season, a large supply of CHOICE NEGROES, suited to every capacity, which they offer at the lowest market rates. They have agents abroad engaged in purchasing for them, which enables them to bid defiance to competition."

Bolton, Dickins & Co. bought and sold slaves in large quantities and in multiple markets. They might buy 20 slaves from someone in St. Louis and sell them to someone in New Orleans; or buy 40 in Memphis and sell them in Vicksburg; or buy 40 in Vicksburg and deliver them to Texas. (Prior to 1855, however, they could not legally buy slaves in another state and sell them in Tennessee.) Bolton, Dickins & Co. was, in some ways, a superstore for slaves, with agents, slave-pens and auctioneers anywhere there was supply and demand near the Mississippi River or one of its tributaries. Starting around 1852, the firm proudly advertised that it had a jail "as safe as the county jail, to secure all negroes left with us to sell." From 1853 onward, its ads were almost always headlined with the words "500 NEGROES WANTED"—a reflection of how large a line of credit that the company carried with various banks.

**SOME FORTY OR FIFTY ACCLIMATED COTTON NEGROES FOR SALE.**

FROM the State of Georgia, consisting of men, women, boys and girls. Among them are some very likely families In a few days we intend to concentrate our purchases from Kentucky and Virginia to this point, and give the buyers of this country an opportunity of investing their money in good Negroes. Give us a call before making your purchases.

mar22-3m      BOLTON, DICKINS & CO.

*Memphis Daily Appeal,* **April 8, 1857**

Bolton, Dickins & Co. remained in business for a long time—more than a decade. It went out with a bang, literally. Sometime around 1856, a slave trader named James McMillan sold a slave to Bolton, Dickins & Co. who turned out to be a free black man. Bolton, Dickins & Co. sold the black man. (Whether they knew the black man was legally free was a matter of later dispute.) Somehow, the black man eventually got a lawyer and obtained his freedom. The matter was publicized, resulting in financial loss and embarrassment to the firm.

Then, in May 1857, at the Memphis office of Bolton, Dickins & Co., Isaac Bolton shot James McMillan. People who heard the gunshots carried McMillan's body to the nearby office of another slave trader. He died a few hours later, and Bolton was arrested for the murder.

At least seven criminal lawyers were hired in the defense of Isaac Bolton, and he was somehow found not guilty of murdering McMillan.[1] (It was rumored that members of the jury were bribed.) However, the crime and the publicity surrounding it resulted in the immediate decline of Bolton, Dickins & Co.'s business and the rise of business of a competing slave trader—the man to whose office McMillan had been brought after he was shot. That slave trader's last name was Forrest.

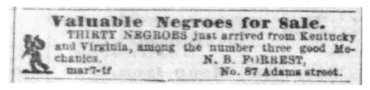

*Memphis Daily Appeal,* May 9, 1857

Nathan Bedford Forrest was born in 1821 in Bedford County, Tennessee, near the community of Chapel Hill. His father was a blacksmith and he was the oldest of 11 children (8 sons and 3 daughters). Like many families in Tennessee during that era, the Forrests moved west and south to northern Mississippi in the 1830s, in search of greener pastures. Nathan's father died when he was 16, which left him to help support the family. Five of Nathan's siblings, including all three of his sisters, died of typhoid fever. Bed, as he was often known, eventually went into horse trading with his uncle in Hernando, Mississippi. Horse trading led to slave trading.

Many anecdotes (accurate or exaggerated) surround Forrest. One maintains that in 1852 he was on a steamboat from Houston

---

[1] One of Bolton's defense lawyers was Henry S. Foote, a former governor of Mississippi. Foote later moved to Nashville and became one of Tennessee's representatives in the Confederate Congress. A former residence of Foote's still stands at Vanderbilt University and is known as Old Central.

to Galveston when the captain began racing another boat. Forrest complained to the captain, saying he was risking the lives of everyone on board. The captain ignored him, whereupon Forrest found a place to sit as far away from the engines as possible. A few hours later, when the boiler exploded, Forrest helped save the lives of several other passengers.

This story reveals much about Forrest's common sense and courage. What none of his biographers has ever explained, however, is why Forrest was in Houston in the first place. There is a very good chance that he was on his way home after having delivered a coffle of slaves. A big part of the business of any Mississippi River area slave trader was the acquisition and delivery of slaves to Texas. In fact, the Lone Star State imported a staggering 99,000 slaves in the 1850s.

The steamboat incident happened the same year Forrest moved to Memphis and became a regular participant in the slave trade there. Like many in the industry, Forrest would change partners over the years. At various times, he did business as a "lone wolf" slave trader, while other businesses to which he attached his name at various times were Forrest & Jones, Hill & Forrest, Forrest & Maples and then, in 1859, Forrest, Jones & Co.

*Memphis Daily Appeal,* **August 3, 1858**

Regardless of the business arrangement, Forrest was a long-distance trader who would travel through places such as Kentucky, Missouri and West Tennessee, buying slaves from plantation owners and transporting them to Memphis. After Tennessee lifted its ban on the interstate slave trade in 1855, slave traders could openly advertise the sale of slaves from other states for the first time in a generation. One ad for Forrest & Maples in the 1855 Memphis City Directory claimed that the business received "daily" from Virginia, Kentucky and Missouri "fresh supplies of likely young Negroes."

The language of the ads for firms associated with Forrest lacked the detail of some of the Nashville slave traders who boasted about the specific number of carpenters, blacksmiths and fancy girls they had for sale.[2] Forrest's ads sounded more like the ones commonly published in big markets such as New Orleans and Charleston. "FIVE HUNDRED NEGROES WANTED," stated an 1854 ad for Hill & Forrest. "WE will pay the highest cash price for all good Negroes offered. We invite all those having Negroes for sale, to call on us, at our Mart, opposite Hill's old stand, on Adams Street. We will have a good lot of Virginia Negroes on hand, for sale, in the fall. Negroes bought and sold on commission." Over the years, Forrest would change the tone of his ads, depending on market conditions and whether he had too many, or not enough, slaves on hand. At one point, for instance, he aggressively advertised that he was in the market to buy "250 Negroes, from 12 to 25 years old."

*Memphis Daily Appeal,* **October 31, 1858**

A small item that appeared in the 1856 *Nashville Union and American* gave even more details about how far-reaching Forrest's business had become. The item pointed out that a runaway slave named Frank had been caught and was in the Dickson County jail in Charlotte. Frank, the ad said, had once lived in Nicholas County, Kentucky—which is east of Louisville—and had run away from Aaron Forrest, a brother and business partner of Nathan's.

By the mid-1850s, the growth of the Memphis slave trade was greatly aided by the arrival of railroads. The Memphis and Charleston Railroad was completed in 1857, connecting with the Nashville and Chattanooga Railroad at Stevenson, Alabama. As the Memphis and

---

[2]According to my research, Rees W. Porter is the only slave trader in Tennessee who used the phrase "fancy girls" in his ads.

Charleston line opened bit by bit, slaves could be brought by rail to Memphis from Charleston, Nashville and Atlanta—adding efficiency and speed to long-distance slave trading. Forrest even advertised in the *Charleston Courier*.

In 1856, a slave named Richard ran away from the Forrest & Maples slave yard. Richard, the ad said, was a Charleston-bred carpenter, which probably accounts for the high reward price for his return ($500). The next year, Memphis slaveholder B.B. Mitchell ran a runaway ad in search of a slave named Bent. The slave was raised in Charleston "and brought from there some four months since by Mr. N.B. Forrest, from whom I bought him; he will probably attempt to get back there."

Unlike the generations of slaves who had walked every mile of the trip west, Richard and Bent made parts of their journey by rail, chained to other slaves.

Forrest brought five of his brothers—John, William, Aaron, Jesse and Jeffrey—into business with him at one time or another. He built great wealth, buying a house on Adams Street in Memphis in 1854 and 1,900 acres in Mississippi and 1,300 acres in Arkansas in 1858. His businesses thrived and grew even more after the murder of James McMillan destroyed the reputation of Bolton, Dickins & Co. From that point onward, Forrest was not only a wealthy slave trader—it is estimated that his firms sold more than 1,000 slaves per year in good years—but also a civic leader: he was elected a Memphis alderman in 1858.

And what sort of slave trader was he? His 600-page biography *That Devil Forrest* by John Allan Wyeth devotes less than one page of text to Forrest's career as a slave trader. Wyeth never names any of Forrest's business partners; never mentions any first-person accounts of his slave trades; never describes Forrest's business operations; never quotes or refers to a single advertisement. The only treatment he gives to Forrest's career as a slave trader is a lengthy quote about Forrest from fellow Confederate officer Colonel George Adair. "Forrest was kind, humane, and extremely considerate of his slaves," the quote begins. "He was overwhelmed with applications from a great many of this class, who begged him to purchase them. He seemed to exercise the same influence over these creatures that in a greater degree he exercised over the soldiers who in later years served him as devotedly as if there was between them a strong personal attachment."

In truth, many slaves would later say that they were fed and clothed fairly well while kept in slave pens in places such as Richmond, Nashville and Memphis. After all, well-fed, healthy slaves fetched a higher price than starving slaves wearing rags. Slave traders also knew that contented slaves were less likely to run away than mistreated ones. There is, meanwhile, one first-person account from a former slave (Horatio J. Eden) who said that Forrest took care to see that their family remained together, while another account from former slave Louis Hughes claimed that his family was broken apart when sold there.

As a professional trader, it would have been part of Forrest's job to occasionally (or frequently) break up families and force-march people for hundreds of miles. Slaves were loathe to be taken from their families and homes and turned over to men such as Forrest, Rees W. Porter, Isaac Bolton and Isaac Franklin. That's why slaves had to be handcuffed at gunpoint; that's why they were forced into coffles and herded like cattle; that's why they were kept locked up; and that's why they ran away and risked being whipped. It may have been true that Forrest treated his slaves decently by slave trading standards of the times. But slaves did run away from the man, since he purchased runaway slave ads at least three times—in 1853, 1856 and 1859.

In regards to Forrest the trader, one other published tidbit tells us something about both him and the Southern slave trade. In April 1859, a *Memphis Appeal* article noted that Forrest had, among the slaves in his pen, seven African slaves "directly from Congo." The article went on to describe these seven slaves in detail, pointing out that they were in many ways different "from the generality of our homebred and hometrained negroes." These slaves were "of short stature," very dark in color, had very slender ankles and wrists and had slender fingers. Also, "one or two of them can say a few English words, but all can use some pretty expressive pantomime."

This article may have struck its readers as amusing, and it may have resulted in many of them going to Forrest's slave pen to see what real Africans in a cage looked like. But the direct import of slaves into

## A Rare Importation.

Persons feeling any interest to see the genuine native African can be gratified by calling at the negro yard of our friend Forrest, on Adams street. He has for sale, among other negroes, seven direct from Congo. We saw them yesterday, and found them in appearance very lively and contented, a very slight thing moving them to laughter. They differ materially in conformation and expression of countenatce from the generality of our homebread and hometrained negroes. They are of short stature, very dark color, and generally slight in the make of the limbs, the ancle and wrist being very slender, and the hand small, with slender fingers, more like a woman's hand than a man's. One or two of them exhibit some corpulency, but the tendency of the fat is principally to the abdomen. They are all youths but one, and he is a full grown man, and exhibits some peculiarities distinct from the rest; his hands are shorter and broader, and his forehead is of a formation somewhat singular. One or two of them can say a very few English words, but all can use some pretty expressive pantomime, not difficult to understand. The principal peculiarity observed in their behavior, since they were at Mr. Forrest's yard, is their strong manifestations of preference for the pure blooded black females; they view the mulatto girls with feelings evidently very different, the mixture of white does not please their eye.—*Memphis Appeal.*

*Nashville Union and American,* **December 18, 1859**

# If You Want Negroes,
## COME TO MEMPHIS.

HAVING permanently located myself in this Bluff City, with the advantage of many years' experience and close observation as to the wants of the people, and how those wants may be best supplied, I have therefore established a NEGRO MART, upon a basis more liberal and accommodating in its character than heretofore introduced in the South. I propose to keep always on hand an assortment of the

### VERY BEST NEGROES

that several markets afford, consisting of MEN, WOMEN, BOYS and GIRLS, to-wit: Field Hands, Mechanics, Body Servants, Cooks, Washers, Seamstresses, Nurses, etc., all of which I will sell at

## PRIVATE SALE AND AT AUCTION.

*Memphis Daily Appeal,* **March 17, 1859**

the United States had been banned since 1808. The fact that Forrest was selling seven slaves "direct from Congo" proves that he was knowingly breaking the law. The fact that the newspaper printed the article proves there was no danger in publicizing violations of the law, which makes you wonder if the law was routinely ignored in places like Charleston, New Orleans and Memphis.[3]

Forrest retired from slave trading sometime in 1860. He spent about a year living the life of a Southern planter and plantation owner before enlisting as a private in the Confederate cavalry. There he would rise to the rank of general and become such a thorn in the side of the U.S. Army that, by the end of the war, General William Tecumseh Sherman said Forrest "must be hunted down and killed if it costs ten thousand lives and bankrupts the federal treasury."

---

[3]The obvious question is how seven slaves, freshly kidnapped from Africa, made it all the way to Memphis. My best guess is that they were smuggled into Charleston and brought by train to Tennessee.

The drama associated with James McMillan's murder and the rise of Nathan Bedford Forrest might obscure mention of other Memphis slave trading firms. But there were others—some quite large—with names such as Delap & Witherspoon, Neville & Cunningham, John Wilkerson and M.C. Cayce & Son. Simply put, Memphis had a huge slave industry—by the eve of the Civil War perhaps the largest in the country.

Byrd Hill, a former partner of Forrest's, may have captured the spirit more than anyone else. Throughout the 1850s, Hill continued to buy and sell slaves at his "negro mart" on Adams Street. At various times, he boasted that he had "field hands, mechanics, body servants, cooks, washers, seamstresses, nurses, etc." on hand to sell. The success of his business, he stated, would "obviate the necessity of our countrymen going to Virginia or elsewhere to buy negroes."

Hill's advertising headline really summed it up. "If You Want Negroes, COME TO MEMPHIS."

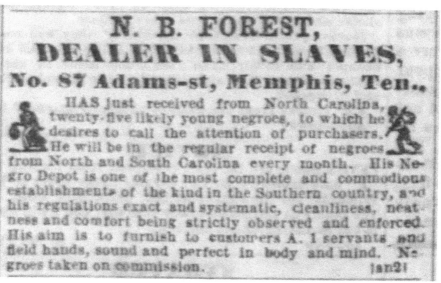

*Memphis Daily Appeal*, **May 28, 1857**

## Legislation on Slavery.

The Governor of Alabama, in a message to the Legislature, suggests the enactment of a law to prevent the separation of husband and wife, and parent from children, in the sale of slaves.

A bill in relation to the sale of slave mothers and their children is now before the legislature of Georgia. It provides that no slave children under 6 years of age shall be separated from their mother, by any kind of sale whatever, legal or otherwise, unless, in legally dividing an estate, it shall be found impossible to effect a division without such a separation

The Richmond Enquirer disapproves of legislation on this subject. Referring to the recommendation of the Governor of Alabama, that paper says.

There is no necessity for any such law in restraint of the right of the master, as is suggested by the Governor of Alabama. The suggestion implies the prevalence of an evil which does not exist to any extent, and thus does injustice to the moral sentiment of the slaveholding community. The proper remedy for this, as for every other evil incident to the condition of slavery, is not to be found in compulsory legislation, but in the voluntary action of an enlightened public sentiment. Excessive cruelty is as rare in the South as crime of a far more heinous character, and is as fatal to the social position of the master. And in a few years the violent disregard of the family relations of the slave would be as uncommon as the more outrageous occurrencies of physical cruelty and oppression. It is as unnecessary as it is perilous, to tamper with the relation of master and slave.

## Public Lands.

It is calculated that the bills introduced in the first three weeks of the session contemplate a cession to the States or to railroad companies of over one hundred and twenty millions of acres of public land. The antagonism between these schemes and the equitable division proposed by Mr. Bennet is evident. The entire amount of the grants proposed in his bill is 59,400,000 acres. It is the only project by which the old States which have paid for the original acquisition of the lands, and now pay more than their proportion for managing them, can expect to secure any part of that magnificent public property which is about to be distributed.

---

**FRIDAY, Jan 6, 1854.**

Mr Wheeler presented a petition which was, without being read, referred to the Committee on County Lines.

Mr Cowart: a petition from citizens of Chattanooga on the subject of establishing a Criminal Court at Chattanooga. Referred to the Judiciary Committee.

Mr Pope, Chairman of the Committee on Public Buildings reported back sundry resolutions &c., and asked the discharge of the Committee from their further consideration Discharged.

Mr. Richardson, Chairman of the Committee on Enrolled Bills, reported sundry bills as correctly enrolled.

Mr Hebb offered a resolution to adjourn *sine die* on the 6th Feb. next.

Mr Morris, of Cocke: a resolution directing the Speaker of the House not to sign the bill providing the extension and completion of the Lunatic Asylum, which has passed both Houses, for the reason that its provisions were not understood by a large portion of the members of the House when they voted for it.

On motion of Mr Clemons the rule was suspended and the resolution taken up, whereupon

Mr Cooper moved to postpone it indefinitely; which motion failed.

After some discussion in regard to the power of the House to instruct the Speaker as contemplated by the resolution, in which Messrs. Buford Brown, of Monroe, Baily, Steele, and Sykes participated.

Mr Tibbs moved to make the resolution the Special Order for the 2d of March next, which motion failed.

The Previous question was then demanded, and having been ordered, the resolution was rejected—ayes 32, noes 39

*Bills passed on First Reading*

Introduced by Mr. Wheeler: a bill to change the line between the counties of Anderson and Scott.

Mr. Lane: a bill to appoint J. Shultz to settle with Wm Smith and Alexander Campbell.

Mr. Cowart: a bill to authorize the extension of the N E & S W Railroad or the Will's Valley Railroad to Chattanooga or elsewhere in this State.

Mr Hubbard: a bill without a title.

Mr Smith, of H.: a bill to amend the tippling laws.

Mr. Dortch: a bill to establish an Agricultural Bureau, &c.

Mr. Wood, of C.: a bill to amend the act of Feb. 19th, 1850, to increase the jurisdiction of Justices of the Peace.

Mr. Wisener: a bill to incorporate the Annual Conference of the Methodist Church for the District of Tennessee.

Mr Brown, of McNairy: a bill to increase the Common School Fund, &c.

Mr. Brown, of Monroe: a bill to prevent Hawking and Peddling by persons who have not been citizens of the State twelve months

## CHAPTER FIFTEEN

# MOTHERS AND CHILDREN

In November 1792, the Washington County Sheriff apprehended a runaway slave named Natt. According to the item in the *Knoxville Gazette*, Natt admitted to Sheriff George Gillespie that he belonged "to a certain Joseph Phillips of Cumberland, Mero district." Natt said "he was going to see his wife and children near Tarborough, in North Carolina, and that he formerly belonged to Joseph Burden near Tarborough."

Assuming he was telling the truth, Natt had journeyed more than 300 miles, on foot, crossing the Cumberland Plateau and numerous rivers. He had made it most of the way across the state, slept out at night, procured food and water, and managed not to be killed by wild animals. He had avoided not only law enforcement authorities along the way but—at a time when the settlers were in a state of war against Native American tribes—military units and hostile Indians as well.

Despite his incredible effort, Natt didn't make it back to his family. Natt's long journey landed him in jail in Jonesboro.

It is undeniable that the institution of slavery was devastating to the family unit. Mother, father, sister and brother were frequently separated through slavery, causing unhappiness, distress and depression among slaves.

Runaway slave ads prove that slaveholders were very aware of this. In many ads, the slave owner predicted that the runaway slave would not head in the direction of a free state, but toward family members.

In 1801, slaveholder Charles McClung of Knoxville speculated that Abraham, who ran away from him, would head "toward the Mero District [Nashville]" because his brother had already been taken there. In 1808, slaveholder David Peeples of Montgomery County said runaway slave Jesse would head east, in the direction of Sullivan County and his previous slaveholder Thomas Titsworth, rather than head north across Kentucky. In 1814, slaveholder John Zollicofer of Maury County said that runaway slave Betty, who was six months pregnant, may "attempt to get to Rhea County, Tennessee valley, where she was brought from."

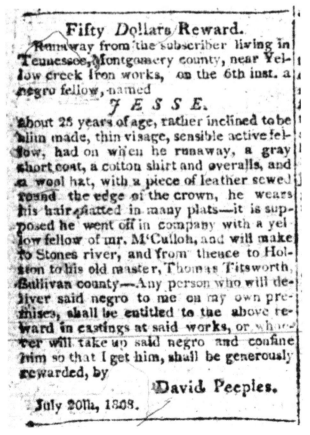

*Nashville Impartial Review and Cumberland Repository*, July 28, 1808

In 1833, Elisha Clampitt of Claysville (present-day Cumberland County) predicted that runaway slave John would "probably aim to Nashville" because his mother lived there and because John was raised in the household of Nashville resident Joseph Elliston. In 1834, Booker Nevels of Maury County opined that runaway slave Levi was "aiming for Norfolk, Virginia." Three years later, John Peck of Weakley County predicted that runaway slave Sip would head east because "I purchased him several years ago of Mr. Gardener of Robertson County, where his father now lives, and he may attempt to go back there."

### RANAWAY—REWARD.

RANAWAY from the subscriber on the first of October my Negro Man Ben. Ben is about 40 years old, though no grey hairs,—very dark color—weighs about 140—fore teeth considerably gone—scar across his fingers, left hand I think—has a scar about the middle of his back, wore off a deep blue sack coat, and trowsers Janes.

His wife belongs to E. M. Dunn, of Benton, Polk county, Tenn. He will either make for Polk co., or Kentucky. If taken and secured I will give a reasonable reward.

H. G. REDMAN.

Huntsville, Scott, Co., Tenn., Nov. 18,—tf.

\*\* Somerset, (Ky.) *Democrat* please copy three weeks, and send bill to this Office.

*Kingston Gazette* **December 2, 1854**

Tilford, who ran away from Nashville in 1854, was said to be heading for Wilson County, since "his wife lives about 6 miles from Statesville." Mary, who ran away from Henderson County in 1854, "might likely make her way back to Sumner county, where she was raised . . . and where she has some children now living." When a slave named Bent ran away from Shelby County in 1857, his slaveholder suspected he would head toward South Carolina since he was "raised in Charleston" and brought to Tennessee by trader Nathan Bedford Forrest.

When a slave named Manuel ran away from Clarksville in 1859, it was predicted that he would flee in the direction of his former home in Jonesboro. That same year, when a slave named Huston ran away from Christian County, Kentucky, it might have seemed logical that he would go north, toward the Ohio River. But slaveholder J.G. Foster speculated that Huston would head toward Nashville, since he was "raised near Buena Vista Ferry on the Cumberland River and has a wife at Mr. Anderson's in the same neighborhood."

In fact, in some cases, slaves had families in so many different places that their slaveholders weren't sure which ones they would gravitate toward. "It is probable he [Granderson] will be lurking about Jackson, or the neighborhood of that, as he has a good many acquaintances in that place and county," William Harris of Haywood County wrote in an 1834 ad. However, he added that Granderson also "has a good many relations about Columbia . . . and it is probable he will aim for that place."

### $200 REWARD.

I WILL give the abc e reward for the apprehension and confinement in any jail, so that I get him, of my man WILSON who ran off from my place in Rutherford county on the 17th day of April, 1857.

Wilson is of copper color, about 30 years of age, 5 feet 5 or 6 inches high, black hair, slightly inclined to be wavy; good teeth, he is slightly round shouldered, was raised in Williamson county, Tenn., his mother belonged to the widow Maxwell, of Davidson county, his father is a free man of black color, and named Alfred, and I am informed lives in the neighborhood of Mrs Maxwell. He also has some children in the neighborhood of Huntsville, Ala., and I have reasons to believe he has been harboring Wilson for the last years in the neighborhood Nashville and Huntsville.

GEO. SANFORD,
nov6 d&w1w  Murfreesboro', Tenn.

*Republican Banner*, November 12, 1859

In 1859, slaveholder George Sanford of Murfreesboro wrote that a slave named Wilson "was raised in Williamson County," but his mother lived as a slave in Davidson County, his father was a free man in Nashville, and his children lived in slavery near Huntsville, Alabama.

The list goes on and on. In fact, in about one-fourth of the runaway ads I found, the slaveholder specifically mentions the location of that slave's relatives or previous homes. "I purchased John in Maryland, and Sam high up in Virginia," wrote slaveholder David Harding of

Davidson County in 1822. "There is no doubt that they are aiming to get back again."

This recurring theme in runaway slave ads proves that many slaveholders were aware of how much distress they had caused by moving slaves away from their families. It also proves that slaveholders understood that, despite being chattel, slaves were human.

Though "runaway" conjures the image of single slave heading off across the countryside, a surprising number of families ran away together. In 1816, a husband, wife and infant daughter ran away from William Porter of Smith County. In 1818, a woman took her two small daughters and ran away from Joseph Cotton of Fayette County. In 1830, a husband, wife and child ran away from John Patterson of Rhea County. In 1836, a family of five ran away from J.W. Wright of Tipton County. In 1845, a family of three (which had been split up by sale) ran away from Thomas Figures of Williamson County and T.B. Dawson of Davidson County. In 1858, a family of three ran away from Mitchel Trotter of Benton County.

I also found at least 14 instances of a husband and wife (but no children) running away together — six in Davidson County.

The idea that runaway slaves were trying to reach other family members raises the matter of how families got split up in the first place. They often got separated, of course, by slave sales by government officials, private sellers or professional auctioneers. In fact, a close examination of advertisements reveals a lot of evidence that families were routinely split apart—along with evidence that, on occasion, an effort was made to keep them together.

*Jackson Gazette*, May 2, 1829

In previous chapters, I categorized slave sales into "small-time" sales, estate sales, "deed of trust" sales, clerk and master sales, and sales by professional auctioneers. In more than 700 newspaper ads reflecting all types of these transactions, I found evidence that an effort was being made to keep family members together less than five percent of the time. Here are three such examples:

- In 1818, when Sarah McLean of Nashville announced her intention to hire out two slaves who were man and wife, she said that "the man and wife [will] go together."

- In 1851 Nashville auctioneer A.A. McLean took the unusual step of listing 29 slaves for sale in 14 separate "lots," which may have meant that he intended to try to keep family units together.[1]

---

[1] I do not know whether Sarah and A.A. McLean were related.

## NOTICE.

IN pursuance, to an order of the Circuit Court for Claiborne County sitting at Tazwell upon the second Monday in Janua ry, 1840; I shall offer for sale, to the highest bidder, at the door of the Court House in Tazwell, upon the 7th day of March next, five slaves, namely, Esther, aged about 35 years and her four children to wit: Jacob, aged about 8 years, Calvin aged 4 or 5 years, Mary Ann aged 2 or 3 years. and a young child aged 8 or 9 months. Terms,—Such sums as will be necessary to defray the costs and expenses of sale, &c., will be required down, the balance will be required to be se-cured, by bond with approved securities, pay-able in twelve months.

ALEXANDER MOORE, Administrator, of John Moore, decd. with the will annexed.

Tazwell, Te Jannn., 25, 1840,

*Rogersville East Tennessean*, May 7, **1840**

- In 1852, J. Halstead of Memphis advertised the sale of an 18-year-old slave woman with experience as a house servant. The ad stated that the woman would be sold "with her child, a likely healthy boy, 18 months old."

These are exceptions to the rule. In the vast majority of newspaper ads about upcoming slave sales, the purchaser of the ad expressed no intention or desire to keep family units together. In 1819, trustee Robert Gardner of Knox County announced that he would, on February 8 of that year, sell four slaves—"a likely Negro woman, 22 years old, and three likely children." There was no hint that the slaves would be sold together. In 1829, the *Jackson Gazette* had an ad publicizing the sale of six slaves at a "deed of trust" sale at the Madison County Courthouse. Based on their ages—Tom (30), Nancy (30), Anthony (8), Peter (16), Maria (17) and a small child—it seems very likely that family members were being separated. However, trustees Rob Lake and William Stoddert expressed no interest in doing anything other than just selling the six so that "certain debts" could be paid. In 1835, five slaves were sold at the Bedford County Courthouse—a woman (39), a boy (12), a girl (9), a boy (7) and a girl (5). Despite the likelihood that this sale consisted of a woman and her four children, the heirs of Mrs. Elizabeth Williams gave no hint in the *Shelbyville Western Freeman* ad that they would try to sell the slaves together.

In the many clerk and master sales announced between 1853 and 1856 by the Chancery Court of Davidson County, clerk and master F.R. Cheatham announced the sales of at least 27 children. None of the announcements indicate which adults at auction were the parents of the children he was selling. Furthermore, in one well-documented 1859 event, seven children under the age of 16—including three eight years old or younger—were sold separately, under the approving eye of the Wilson County clerk and master.

As noted in previous chapters, we have few eyewitness accounts of these sales. However, Ohio native William Fletcher King attended a Murfreesboro slave auction in on January 1, 1854, and wrote about it in his memoirs:

The most remarkable case was that of a woman about thirty years old, who was put on a block outside the courthouse wall, with a crowd of two or three hundred men standing around, and a red-faced, burly auctioneer standing by her side. She held a young babe in her arms. The auctioneer made various comments as to her appearance and showed her off in very unbecoming style, making her show her teeth, and in other ways treated her as though she were a horse. Coarse men came up and felt her limbs to test what kind of muscles she had. It was the most disgusting performance we had ever witnessed. . . The auctioneer seemed to pride himself in his rough language and unbecoming treatment of the woman. She bore the indignities with a certain air of dignity.

Her husband was in the crowd near where my brother and I stood and near him was his owner. There were two bidders actively bidding for her, one the owner of her husband and the other a slave-driver who shipped slaves to the cotton fields of the South. As the bidding progressed the husband of the woman pleaded with his owner in a most plaintive way to buy his wife. As we stood by we heard him say, 'I have been faithful in my serving you, and if I had my wife and children with me, you know that I could serve you even better.' His owner seemed to bid carelessly, while the slave-trader on the other side of the crowd seemed to bid with more interest. As the bidding progressed the husband kept pleading with his owner in a most touching manner to bid more. My brother and I standing together got so wrought up that we thought it prudent to step apart, lest we should utterly break down and show our sympathies and get into serious trouble. The bidding went on for a half hour, all the time the owner of the husband bidding with little interest and making only slight advances over to the other man and the other bidding with apparent purpose of securing the woman. Finally the mother and child were sold to the slave-trader.

Although no Tennessee law required slave sellers make an effort to keep slave families together, I found discussion in the 1854 *Republican Banner and Nashville Whig* about proposed laws in Alabama and Georgia that would have affected the separation of slave families. The

Alabama proposal would have prevented the sale of husband from wife and parent from children. The Georgia proposal would have banned the sale of children under eight years old from their mothers.

The Nashville newspaper didn't offer its opinion about the two ideas. It did, however, point out that the *Richmond Enquirer* had opined against both. "The proper remedy for this, as for every other evil incident to the condition of slavery, is not to be found in compulsory legislation, but in the volunteer action of an enlightened public sentiment," the *Richmond Whig* had editorialized.

"Excessive cruelty is as rare in the South as crime of a far more heinous character, and it is as fatal to the social position of the master . . It is as unnecessary as it is perilous to tamper with the relation of master and slave."

In terms of the frequency with which slave children were separated from their families, one final example is the 11th president of the United States. Unlike Andrew Jackson, James K. Polk's career as a slaveholder has been little discussed over the years. Thanks to author William Dusinberre, we now know that Polk regularly bought slaves during his adult life. Polk bought 26 slaves between 1831 and 1839, then 19 more during his four-year term as president, between

**NEGRO SALE.**

AGREEABLE to a Deed of Trust dated the 27th October, 1840, from Calvin Thompson, of Madison County, Tenn. to myself, and duly Registered in the Registers office of Gibson County, in Book G Pages 371 and 372, and in the Registers office of Madison County, Tenn. in Book No. 7 Pages 290 and 291, I will sell at the Court House Door in the town of Trenton on Saturday 22d May inst. to the highest bidder, for cash, the following Negro Slaves to wit:—
Cambridge, a man, about 50 years of age.
Humphrey, a man about 30 years of age.
Judy, a woman, about 26 years of age.
Bill, a boy, about 11 years of age.
Ann, a girl, about 3 years of age.
And apply the proceeds of said sale as expressed in said Deed of Trust, giving a good title to the purchasers.
LEWIS LEVY, Trustee.
May 6th 1841,—2w.

*Trenton Journal*, May 13, 1841

1841 and 1845. Almost all these slaves were sent to work on his two plantations, the first of which was in Hardeman County and the second in Mississippi. Since nearly all were young males, Polk was ignoring family ties by the very act of these purchases. "Of the nineteen slaves Polk bought during his presidency, one was ten years old, two were eleven, two were twelve, two were thirteen, two were fifteen, two were sixteen and two were seventeen," Dusinberre wrote. "Each of these children was bought apart from his or her parents and from every sibling."

*Fayetteville Observer*, April 12, 1859

PART FOUR

# SLAVES AND THE ECONOMY

## FOR SALE.

A TRACT OF LAND, on Parney's (alias) Turner's creek, one mile from Newsom's mill on big Harpeth river, in a good range; containing 3 or 400 acres: 70 in cultivation, with 3 sugar orchards. On the premises are a two story house, with two fire places of brick, newly built, with necessary out houses—A seat for a saw and grist mill, and distillery, with excellent water: fifteen miles from Nashville and Franklin, on the road leading from Nashville to Hickman and Dickson court houses, and an eligible stand for a tavern. I will take for the above, $800; one third in hand, or cotton at cash price, the balance in two years.

**JESSE SHELTON.**

October 13, 1817.—3t*

---

## NOTICE.

THE undersigned wish to hire twenty or thirty strong NEGRO MEN, for twelve months, to work at the Cumberland Saline, Jackson county. They also inform the public that their works are in complete operation, and will be able to supply that and the adjacent counties with SALT. Application made to C. Stump or Stump & Cox, Nashville.

**STUMP, TILFORD, & Co.**

Cumberland Saline, Sept. 23, 1817.—4tf

---

## NEW & CHEAP GOODS,
### For Cash.

### THOMAS EDWARDS, & Co.

HAVE just received from Philadelphia, and are now opening in LEBANON, in the house formerly occupied by John M. Tilford, a large assortment of

## MERCHANDIZE;

*Consisting of the following articles:*

Superfine Broad cloths and Cassimeres:
Fine     do     do.
Coarse Cloths of all descriptions:
Flannels and Blankets;
Irish Linens;
Cotton Cambricks;
Calicoes;
Ginghams;
Fancy Muslins;
Lady's Beaver hats;

---

...in & Mason, Franklin, or to James Stewart, Nashville.

## FREIGHT WANTED;
### AND
### STONE WARE FOR SALE.

THE subscriber respectfully informs the merchants & planters of Nashville and its vicinity, that he now has three excellent KEEL BOATS, and intends having two or three very strong flat ones built; in which he proposes freighting produce to New-Orleans this fall; they will be steered by sober, careful and experienced captains—and as a full cargo down, and part of one up, is engaged for one of the keels, it is intended she shall make an early return. With those who are pleased to confer on him their favors, he is desirous to make contracts; and they may depend on punctuality, care and dispatch.

He also shortly expects (from his manufactory near Pittsburgh) a complete assortment of first quality STONE WARE, which to early applicants will be disposed of on liberal terms—It will be stored in the ware-house of Messrs. West & Norvell, College street, and during his absence, the sale and package of which will be attended to by his son.

**S. R. BAKEWELL.**

Nashville, Oct. 13, 1817.—4t

P. S. A box containing twelve dozen Porter bottles, was either stolen or taken through mistake (probably by some waggoner) from my door on Market street, about a month since; the words "Bridgport Glass," was branded on the end of it. Whoever gives information so that I get it again, shall be handsomely rewarded for their trouble.

---

## CORDAGE, &c.

10,000 lbs. best Bale Rope, of a good quality; bed-cords; plough lines; cables, and every kind of rigging suitable for barges and boats; seine, sewing and baling twine; also seven hundred gallons of Tar, for sale, wholesale or retail, by the subscriber, near the middle ferry, Water street, Nashville.

**WM. BOSWORTH.**

Sept. 22, 1817.—tf

---

*Nashville Whig,* November 10, 1817

CHAPTER SIXTEEN

# HIRING OUT

It is a simple statistic—easy to quote, easy to remember and in many textbooks. In Tennessee, in 1860, only one in four white Tennessee families owned slaves. That means 75 percent of white Tennessee families did not own slaves. Therefore, slavery wasn't nearly as embedded in Tennessee as in other parts of the South, right?

Then again, maybe it was.

Although only one in four white Tennessee families *owned* slaves, many people and companies *leased* slaves. Though not the same as owning, families and companies that leased slaves participated in the institution of slavery without having to invest money in buying and maintaining slaves. They were also avoiding the higher wages of a free person who might otherwise do the same job.

"Slave wanted" ads appeared in Tennessee's first newspaper. "Wanted to hire," said an ad in the April 1797 *Knoxville Gazette*, "a negro man who understands plantation work, and is honest. For such a one generous wages will be given."

There would be many, many more such items in Tennessee's antebellum newspapers.

The best way to understand the world of "slaves for hire" is to forget that slaves were human beings and just think of them as assets to be used to produce dividends. In early 19th-century Tennessee, one way to make money was to acquire a farm and buy slaves to work it. Another was to acquire a farm and hire someone else's slaves to work it.

A third way was to buy slaves, then hire them out to other people to work in their homes, on their plantations and in their factories. Under this set-up, the slaveholder would receive the pay for the labor the slaves performed from the person who leased them. As long as you didn't pay too much for the slaves, as long as you hired them out wisely, and as long as the slaves didn't successfully run away, it was a manner in which many southerners made money in the early 1800s.

**Knoxville Gazette, September 4, 1798**

Slaves were typically hired out on January 1 for a year at a time. A contract was signed between slaveholder and slave "leaser" specifically spelling out the length of the contract, the amount of money being paid and the various responsibilities of each party (such as who paid for clothing and medical attention during the course of the agreement).

I've already mentioned several cases of slaves being hired out throughout Tennessee, but there are a few specific "slave wanted" advertisements in newspapers prior to 1835 that I would like to highlight in this chapter. These examples demonstrate how common it was for slaveholders to hire out their slaves.

In 1801, the *Tennessee Gazette* had an item proclaiming that "five or six" slaves, the property of Henry Hart, minor, would be hired out for one year in Springfield. Apparently, the father of a boy named Henry Hart had died, leaving about half a dozen slaves to his son. Since his son was not yet an adult, Hart's guardian, Thomas Johnson, was seeing to it that the slaves were hired out to bring in money. Ostensibly, when he came of age, Henry Hart would receive both the slaves and the money that they had earned while he was a minor.

**WANTED,**
ON hire at the Cumberland Furnace, a number of good Negro fellows, for which generous wages will be given by me,
MONTGOMERY BELL.
February 10th, 1804.

*Tennessee Gazette*, **February 29, 1804**

In February 1804, Montgomery Bell ran an ad in the *Tennessee Gazette* offering to hire "a number of good Negro fellows, for which generous wages will be given by me" to work at the Cumberland Furnace. Four years later, Bell said he wanted to hire "eight or ten negro fellows by the year for which I will give a generous price." By 1850, Bell owned 332 slaves, making him one of the largest slaveholders in the state. These ads prove that in the first decade of the 19th century, he was hiring other people's slaves.

In 1806, the owners of Winn's Inn, one of Nashville's first overnight lodges, ran an ad seeking to hire a female slave. Nashville hotels such as the Bell Tavern and Nashville Inn would continue this practice. In fact, a slave named Sally (who was owned by Davidson County resident Clayton Talbot) ran away from her job at the Nashville Inn in September 1816.

In 1810, George Poyzer of Nashville said he wanted to hire eight or nine slaves "of the age of ten or twelve years" to work in his cotton factory.

In 1814, a man identified as T. Overton ran an ad expressing his desire to hire several

**WANTED TO HIRE**
EIGHT or nine Negro Boys, of the age of ten or twelve years—to work in the Cotton Factory, for a term of 3 or 4 years—Apply to
GEO. POYZER.
Nashville, Nov — 816

*Nashville Impartial Review and Cumberland Repository*, **December 21, 1810**

slaves including a blacksmith and stone mason for 12 months.

In 1815, the executor of the estate of the late Peter Jones of Nashville announced his intention to "offer for hire for 12 months, a number of negroes, men, women, boys and girls." In other words, instead of selling the slaves in Peter Jones' estate, the decision was made to hire them out and receive an ongoing stream of revenue from them instead of a one-time sum. A few years later, thirty slaves belonging to the estate of the late Benjamin Philips were also hired out rather than sold.

## PUBLIC SALE.

ON Friday the 6th of December next, will be sold to the highest bidder on a credit of twelve months, at the late dwelling house of Batsy Harding, deceased, all the remaining part of the perishable property belonging to the estate of the dec'd consisting of a balance of household & kitchen furniture, the crop of corn, one horse, one cow, one first rate yoke of oxen, and sundry other articles. Also four NEGROES to be hired out for the next year—Terms made known on the day of hiring.

E. MADDOX, Admr.

November 12, 1816.—12–4t

## Wanted to Hire,

THREE or four active BOYS; also, immediately, a decent Black Woman, who gives suck, and without incumbrance, if possible. JOHN B. WEST.

Nashville, November 19, 1816.—13--4t.

*Nashville Whig,* December 4, 1816

In 1817, the owners of a Jackson County operation called Cumberland Saline were looking to hire between 20 and 30 male slaves to work on one-year contracts. This wasn't the only such place where slaves could be employed; a salt mine in Gallatin County, Illinois, known as the United States Saline advertised that it was looking for laborers in 1821. "Negroes will be preferred," the ad said.[1]

In 1822, Robert Nicholas, U.S. agent to the Chickasaw nation, ran a series of ads in the *Nashville Whig* seeking to lease six male

---

[1]Despite the fact that it was a free state, a special clause in Illinois law allowed black slaves to be used at this salt mine until 1825. The site later became associated with the "reverse underground railroad," under which free blacks were kidnapped and taken South to be sold into slavery.

slaves "to work a crop of cotton" in Chickasaw territory. He offered to pick up the slaves at one of three locations: Big Spring (present-day Huntsville, Ala.), Colbert's Ferry (present-day Florence) or the Chickasaw Bluffs (present-day Memphis). "I will give bond and security for six hundred dollars a year, and clothe them [the slaves]," Nicholas promised. "I will also be bound for their safe return, the acts of God only excepted."

In 1823, two slaves named Clara and Louisa ran away from the Chickasaw Bluffs. The ad revealed more about the slaveholder than it did the slaves. "The negroes are the property of Mrs. Henrietta Jacobs, a helpless widow with three children," the ad stated. "They comprise the chief part of their estate, and that portion of it upon which they relied for immediate support." In other words, Jacobs hired out Clara and Louise to make ends meet through their wages. This arrangement, under which families were entirely dependent upon income from hiring out slaves, was quite common in the South.

**NEGROES TO HIRE.**

ON SATURDAY the 25th inst. there will be hired at the court-house door, Nashville, a number of likely NEGROES, Men, Women, Boys and Girls, until the first day of January next.

MATTHEW BARROW,
*Agent for the Branch Bank at Nashville.*
January 22, 1823.——1t

*Nashville Whig,* January 22, 1823

Finally, in several ads, slaveholders refer to runaways with occupations such as carpenter, stonemason and painter. Since there is clearly only so much carpentry, masonry and painting that one slaveholder needed done, we can assume that slaves with such skilled occupations were hired out.

By the late 1820s, the practice of hiring out slaves had grown to the point where there were people who made their living arranging such hirings. In 1826 a Nashville man named Edward Ward advertised he would soon be hiring out "NEGROES, men, women, boys and girls" on year-long work contracts. Four years later, Addison East appeared to have a similar profession, running ads that said he wanted to "hire immediately, by the month, fifteen or twenty able bodied NEGRO MEN, for whom good prices would be given." By 1832, an agency known as Webb & Co. regularly published a list of available jobs for slaves. On June 23 of that year, it posted seven different "slave wanted" ads, mostly for people wanting to hire slaves as domestic servants.

Eventually, so many Tennessee slaveholders hired out their slaves that there were frequent advertisements to insure them. One ubiquitous ad for the Merchant and Planters Municipal Insurance Company stated that slaveholders could purchase life insurance for slaves, "whether employed as house servants, in hotels, in factories or farms, or on steamboats as waiters, firemen or deck hands." An ad for the Tennessee Marine and Fire Insurance Company offered policies ensuring "Negroes against the dangers of the river."

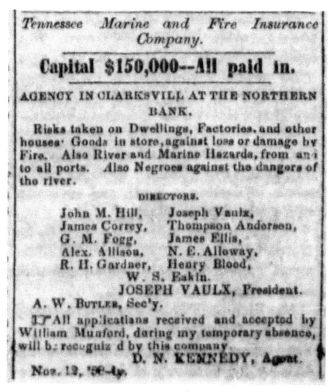

*Clarksville Chronicle*, **November 12, 1858**

The frequency with which slaves were farmed out raises a rather obvious question: Why were slaveholders not worried that their slaves would run away? I'll make several points about this.

The first is that many slaves may have understood that working in a cotton mill or salt mine in Tennessee was preferable to working on a sugar plantation in Mississippi or Louisiana—a fate that probably befell them if they tried to run away and were caught.

Another reason is that some of the slaves who were put to work on outside jobs were literally chained together and constantly watched by armed guards. By the 1830s, slaves throughout Tennessee were hired in large numbers to work on big projects such as roads and railroads. I am fairly certain that slaves on those jobs would have been treated with the same security as prison chain gangs would be in future years.

A third reason is that many male slaves were sent away from their wives and children when they were hired out. In such a situation, the slaveholder would have known that a slave who ran away would have been running away from his family—not something that many slaves would have been inclined to do.

It should also be pointed out that, in rare cases, slaveholders made deals with their "hired out" slaves that allowed the slaves to eventually "purchase" their freedom. Through this process, many Tennessee slaves became free.

The final point is that some slaves did, in fact, try to run away when they were hired out. In 1807, Elijah Hughes of Robertson County ran a runaway ad about a slave named Esther who, he explained, was "the property of John W. Bryan." In 1818, a married couple named Bob and Tilla, whose slaveholder was a "Mrs. Newman of Grainger County," ran away from Matthias Firestone of Knox County. In 1830, a slave named Gabriel, whose slaveholder was Joseph Miller of Davidson County, ran away from his job as a steward on the steamboat *Red Rover*. Three years later, a slave named David, whose slaveholder Henry Bell lived in Obion County, also ran away from his job on a steamboat. In 1836, a family of five slaves (husband, wife and three small daughters), who were owned by the estate of a

North Carolina man named Freeman, ran away from J.W. Wright of Tipton County.

In short, the act of "hiring out" slaves and sending them far away to earn money had its rewards. But it was not without risks.

## STOP THE ROGUES AND RUNAWAYS.

I WILL give a liberal reward for the apprehension and confinement of Tom, Agy, and *three children* who made their escape from my premises on the 30th July, at night, and took with them a horse, about fifteen years old, yellow roan color,—swiab tail and short mane. Tom is a boy about six feet high, dark complexion, and tion visaged; supposed to be about thirty-five years of age: The girl is low, of a yellow complexion, and has long curly hair. The children are all three girls, the largest a very likely yellow girl; the smallest about six months old.

It is expected that there are in company with them one other fellow and woman from the same neighborhood, left on the same night, the fellow supposed to be about forty years of age, black complexion, the girl about sixteen years old, also black complexion, belonging to James D. Moseer. Also one other fellow, the property of A. Hunter, supposed to be about thirty five or forty years of age—black complexion, heavy built, and quite impudent.

The first family belongs to the estate of —— Freeman, N. Carolina, and was hired by J. W. Wright, for the present year. I ai believed that they are conducted off by some infamous scoundrel. We are fearfu

*Randolph Recorder*, **September 9, 1836**

CHAPTER SEVENTEEN

# FACTORIES AND BANKS

In antebellum Tennessee, those who could afford to buy slaves did so. Those who could not afford to buy slaves leased them. Those who could not afford to buy or lease slaves competed in a marketplace where slave labor drove down wages.

This may be a slight oversimplification of pre-Civil War society in the Volunteer State. But these three sentences come closer to explaining the true economic effect of slavery on Tennessee than most realize.

This chapter will explore some of the ways in which slave labor was involved in the economy.

## IRON MANUFACTURING

The first generation of Middle Tennessee's settlers noticed that there was plenty of iron ore in the ground throughout the Highland Rim. James Robertson (sometimes known as the "Father of Middle Tennessee") built a furnace at Barton's Creek in present-day Dickson County. Montgomery Bell purchased it in 1803 and, as mentioned in the previous chapter, hired slaves to cut firewood, haul rock, make charcoal and do other tasks necessary to create pig iron on the site.

Bell expanded his operations, buying more than 15,000 acres and creating numerous mines and furnaces. He is credited with supplying much of the weaponry and ammunition used by Tennessee's troops in the War of 1812. In 1818, Bell's workers (probably consisting largely of slaves) dug a tunnel through a bend in the Harpeth River, creating a permanent waterfall that powered one of his operations. That tunnel is the centerpiece of Harpeth River State Park.

Bell may have been Tennessee's largest single slaveholder in the 1820s and 1830s, and he also leased slaves from other owners. At least eight slaves tried to run away from Bell's industrial operations between 1807 and 1854. Later in his life, Bell freed many of his slaves and paid to send more than 100 of them to resettle in Liberia.

People recognize Bell's name because a private high school and state park are named for him. Fewer people know about Thomas Yeatman, who had a retail business in Nashville, operated one of Tennessee's early steamboat lines, and invested heavily in cotton. Yeatman also built an iron mining and manufacturing operation in present-day Stewart County known as Cumberland Rolling Mill. One of its furnaces, the Bear Creek Furnace, still has his name engraved on it.

## $375 Reward.

RUNAWAY from my Furnace, Wayne county, Tennessee, (*near Tennessee river,*)

HAZZARD, about 21 years of age, rather tall and slender, copper color, speaks slowly when spoken to, and sometimes indistinctly, and was raised in South Carolina.

WESLEY, of yellow complexion, about 22 years of age, smart and likely, medium size, speaks long, was raised near Nashville.

JIM, of bright complexion, about 19 years of age, thick and heavy set, he has been an Engineer, and is free at 21 years of age.

GEORGE, about 28 years of age, black and heavy built, speaks quick when spoken to (very smart) was raised near Columbia.

HENDERSON, about 20 years of age, rather low, speaks slowly, and is dark yellow, or nearly black, rather bow legged, was raised in Nashville.

I think it more than probable they have been stolen, or induced to leave my Furnace by white men, with the expectation of getting to a free State. The two first mentioned, Hazzard and Wesley, will be more apt to keep together. It is quite likely they will make down the Tennessee river, either in flat or steamboat.

I will give $50 reward each, if lodged in any jail in the State, so I can get them; or $75 each, if taken and lodged in any jail out of the State.

For information respecting them, address me at Nashville, Tenn., or Waynesboro', Wayne county.

JOHN W. WALKER.

July 9, 1847.—w&tr

*Republican Banner,* July 12, 1847

When Yeatman died in 1834, his business was sold, including mill, steam engine, furnace, horses, mules, wagons, workshops, worker housing and about 200 slaves. According to the ad, the slaves consisted of "engineers, forgemen, hammermen, and workmen of almost every description required at such establishments."

There was also a large iron manufacturing operation in present-day Wayne County. Built in 1839 along Forty Eight Creek, John Walker purchased it out of bankruptcy in 1841. Like Bell and Yeatman, Walker ran his operations with slave labor and had more than a hundred slaves working there. Like Bell, Walker had problems with runaways. At least five slaves ran away from him in 1847; three in 1848; and three more in 1851.

The number of operating iron foundries varied because of demand and the general health of the economy. One researcher estimates that in the late 1850s there were more than 30 blast furnaces employing more than 3,000 slaves along the Cumberland and Tennessee Rivers.

## OTHER MANUFACTURING WORK

Because of the better availability, condition and searchability of Nashville's early newspapers, a disproportionate number of the following examples are from Middle Tennessee. But I have no reason to think that factories in Middle Tennessee were more inclined to hire slave labor than those in East and West Tennessee.

As mentioned in the previous chapter, a cotton mill in Nashville and a salt-making operation in Jackson County both operated with slave labor in the 1810s.

In 1820, a cotton and shoe manufacturer in Davidson County called Sanders & Chandler hired about 40 slaves, including "men, women, boys and girls."

In 1835, the partnership of Baxter, Hicks & Ewing bought the Tennessee Rolling Works, a Nashville business that turned pig

**NEGROES WANTED.**
WE wish to hire 30 NEGRO MEN AND BOYS for the ensuing year; a fair price will be given, BAXTER, HICKS & EWING.
Nov 22, 834—B

**Negroes Wanted.**
WE wish to hire 10 or 12 Negro men and boys, to be employed in a bagging factory— a liberal price will be given for them, for the present and ensuing year. Apply to DAVID WILLIAMS,
June 11,—1m or WILLIAM BOSWORTH.

*Nashville Republican*, September 25, 1835

iron into products such as axes, nails and wagon wheels. The firm immediately began running ads stating that "we wish to hire 30 NEGRO MEN AND BOYS for the ensuing year." That same year, Bosworth's Rope and Bagging Factory (located near the former site of the Metro General Hospital) ran advertisements announcing it wished to hire 10 to 12 slaves.

In 1850, a steam-operated corn, wheat and rye milling factory called B.F. Foster & Co. advertised it was hiring six "stout young" slaves. Three years later, the Agricultural Manufacturing Company said it wanted "eight or ten" teenage slaves to work as blacksmiths for a wagon and plow company. And in 1857, Nashville businessman W. Meredith ran regular ads in Nashville's newspapers asking to hire "20 negro men and 15 boys from 11 to 18 years old" to work in a tobacco factory—an item that reminds us that many of the slaves working in Tennessee's factories were children.

## Negro Men and Boys Wanted.

MEREDITH, HALEY & CO., wish to hire for the ensuing year, FIFTY NEGRO MEN AND BOYS from 10 to 80 years old, to work in their Tobacco Factory, No. 44 and 48 College street They prefer 'to hire negroes that are for hire annually, so that they may learn them the business, and not be compelled to learn *new* hands every year. Dec25—till Jan3.                            c.

Nashville *Republican Banner,* January 4, 1859

In addition to the "slave wanted" ads, there is proof from runaway ads of slaves working in various forms of manufacturing:

In an 1837 ad, slaveholder Geraldus Buntyn of Shelby County explained that an arm of a runaway slave named Dick "was torn from about half way from the elbow to the wrist very badly from the teeth of a cotton gin." Two years later, slaveholder Lewis Dinhins of Knox County said runaway slave Robin "has on one of his hands some severe scars, having been torn by a cotton gin."

In 1838, a 15-year-old slave named Sam ran away from a Nashville chair factory. Sam, the ad explained, was owned by Robert Lusk and had been hired out to work at S.C. Earl's factory.

In 1848, two slaves ran away from a Nashville candle-making

operation called Smith & Hobbs.

In 1857, a slave ran away from his job at the Nashville brickyard of David Hicks. "Henry," the ad explained, "is the property of Mrs. Jane W. Campbell, living in the South Field." That same year, a slave named Logan ran away from his job at J. Lumsden's tanning yard.

## RAILROADS AND BRIDGES

The first two Tennessee cities to be connected via railroad were Nashville and Chattanooga. A major impediment stood between the two—that being the Cumberland Plateau. To get from one city to the other, the railroad hired workers to blast a 2,200-foot tunnel through the mountain near Cowan, in Franklin County.

We know slaves worked on this tunnel because the firm of Hugh Stuart and Company ran advertisements in 1849 and 1850 in an effort to hire 100 of them. "To correct an erroneous impression in regard to danger from laboring in rock work, it is proper to say the hands have nothing whatever to do with blasting," the ad ensured. "This is altogether done by blasters of experience immediately under the direction of the Superintendent."

About a year later, the Nashville and Chattanooga Railroad needed more men to build the line itself—work which would have required blasting, moving thousands of tons of limestone, putting down cross ties, and laying tracks. General contractor Murdoch & Townsend bought ads saying they needed 2,000 workers—"1,000 Irish Laborers, 500 Native born Laborers and 500 Negroes."

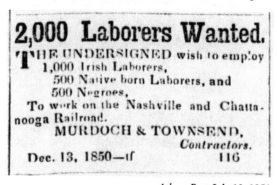

*Athens Post*, July 18, 1851

There is a very good chance that one of those 500 slaves was owned by a slaveholder named Matthew Barrow, who lived near where Vanderbilt University is today. In 1853, Barrow advertised that he intended to sell a male slave, about 26 years old. Barrow said that the slave "has been working on the railroad for four years, most of the time foreman in drilling [and] blasting." The slaveholder said that he wanted to sell the slave because he had "lately become rather independent of his master or manager."

The role of slavery in East Tennessee is often downplayed because of the lower percentage of slaves there compared to the other two Grand Divisions. However, slaves helped build several railroads and bridges in the eastern part of the state. When the East Tennessee and Virginia Railroad (connecting Knoxville to Bristol) was under construction in 1851, contractor Samuel Ferguson ran ads in Knoxville's newspapers asking for 100 slaves to work on it. "Persons having a slave to hire will have an opportunity to have them well taken care of," assured the ads.

Six years later, contractor John D. Gray & Co. ran ads offering to hire and lease 100 slaves to work on the Cleveland and Chattanooga Railroad. "We will pay $180 per year, clothe and lose all lost time, except run away time."

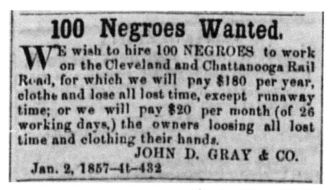

*Athens Post*, **February 20, 1857**

Two other items: in the early 1850s, general contractor James Gettys & Co. hired 25 slaves to help build a bridge across the Tennessee River in Loudon. Shortly thereafter, George Saulpaw hired 12 slaves to work on the railroad near Lenoir City.

# TRANSPORTATION

Before steamboats and railroads came to Tennessee, stagecoaches were the most popular method of transportation in and out of the state. Common sense would indicate that the last place a slaveholder would want their slaves working would be on these long-distance transportation routes. However, in an 1822 runaway slave ad, Sumner County slaveholder Edward Jones said that Billy (the runaway) "drove a hack between Nashville & Louisville about three months last winter."

After steamboats came to the South, the use of slave labor to operate their engines, serve as deck hands, and work as porters and cooks became very common. In 1840, according to Nashville newspaper advertisements, the *Constellation* hired between 25 and 30 slaves and the *Red Rover* hired between 20 and 25 slaves. In 1845, the *Old Hickory* advertised that it wanted 15 slaves and, five years later, the *Carroll* hired 20 slaves.

**NEGROES.**

WANTED to hire, 20 to 25 stout, able-bodied, healthy negro men, to be employed as fire-men and deck hands, on the new steamboat Red Rover, M. S. Pilcher, master, to be run in the New Orleans trade the ensuing season. The hands will be wanted between the 15th October and 1st of November. Enquire of

SIMON BRADFORD & CO.

Sept. 25, 1840.—3w        W&U

Nashville *Daily Republican Banner*, September 26, 1840

Within runaway slave ads, there are many references to slaves working on steamboats. "[Runaway slave] Jim has been hired on the steamboat *Nashville* the last three years," wrote slaveholder Peyton Robertson in 1833. "It is supposed that he will endeavor to escape to Canada, where he has a brother who ran away 12 years since."

# CONSTRUCTION

Many Tennessee houses built before the Civil War were constructed with the help of slave labor. We know this from the descriptions of slaves in runaway ads. Slaveholders frequently describe their slaves as masons, bricklayers, carpenters, plasterers or painters, and they often make direct reference to such skilled workers being hired out.

Here are two examples:

"[Elijah] has been employed for several years as a house carpenter," wrote Overton County slaveholder W. Chilton in 1821.

"The boy [Daniel]," said slaveholder J.L. Bayne of Davidson County in 1856, "is a good Stone Mason, has been hired about Nashville to work at the trade."

In 1859, a Memphis general contractor named Greenlaw went out of business and "made sale of their negroes, stock, etc.," according to an item in the *Memphis Daily Appeal*. Thirteen slaves were sold that day for between $850 and $1,515. The highest price was paid for a 23-year-old named John. The lowest price was for a 40-year-old man named Julias.

One interesting example of a high profile construction project in Tennessee that used slave labor is the University of the South at Sewanee. Began in 1857, many white masonry workers and carpenters were used to build the campus, located on top of the Cumberland Plateau in Franklin County. However, "the bulk manual labor was performed by 'negroes,'" according to author and professor emeritus Gerald L. Smith. Many of these slaves were still being logged in university records only by their first names even after the Civil War. "The culture and effects of slavery did not end sharply in 1865," Smith says.

# MISCELLANEOUS

Speaking of educational institutions, the Nashville Female Academy was a prominent and respected educational institution that operated from 1817 until 1878. The academy had a slave named Billy who escaped in October 1824. "He would be easily recognized by any person who has been much in the habit of visiting there," the advertisement in the *Nashville Whig* stated. The University of Nashville also had at least two slaves working on its campus in the 1830s.

SERVANTS WANTED.

TWO negro men, of good character, may have constant employment and liberal wages at the University of Nashville. Apply to the
PRESIDENT.

January 8, 1837—2t

*Nashville Republican,* January 3, 1837

Nashville's first hotel, the Nashville Inn, had at least one slave working in it from the month it opened. The same was apparently true of other hotels. "Wanted immediately," said an 1817 ad. "At the Bell Tavern, a negro man, suitable for a house servant; and two boys."

In 1838, deep in East Tennessee, a restaurant in Athens was looking for a waiter. Not wanting to hire a free person, it advertised that it wanted to buy a slave to do the job. "WANTED TO PURCHASE," read the ad in the (Athens) *Tennessee Journal.* "An intelligent likely BLACK OR MULATTO BOY AS A WAITER, from 12 to 20 years of age . . . Enquire at Mr. Mountcastle's Store, at the Agency."

Johnson, Horne & Co. was a wholesale and retail grocery business at the corner of Market and Broad in Nashville. In 1857, a slave named Tom ran away from his job there.

Finally, this one from the March 30, 1854, *Nashville Union and American*: "Wanted to hire or buy: a likely Negro girl, from nine to twelve years of age—for such, a good cash price will be given."

The business? Robertson's Confection—a candy store at 21 Broad Street.

## BANKING

Although we can safely say that there weren't many slaves working as bank tellers, a case can be made that no sector of Tennessee's economy was as dependent on slaves as banking.

Today, people finance the purchase of cars through bank loans and almost no one pays cash when they buy a house. After all, most

**GLOVER & BOYD,**
[Successors to Williams & Glover,]

WILL attend promptly to Buying, Selling, Leasing, and Renting Real Estate, *Buying, Selling. and Hiring Negroes,* ( ☞ we have comfortable Rooms and Cells for taking care of 100 Negroes, 🖘 ) negotiating Loans, Buying and Selling Stocks of every description; Collecting Debts in any part of the United States, &c. &c. Orders for Negroes attended to promptly, and instructions faithfully obeyed.

REFERENCES.—Gov. W. B. Campbell, Ex-Gov. A. V. Brown, Dr. John Shelby Wheless & Hobson, Bankers; Dyer Pearl & Co., Bankers; W. B. Shapard & Co., Bankers; Col. V. K. Stevenson; Gen. S. R. Anderson, Cashier Bank of Tennessee; O. Ewing, Cashier, Planters' Bank; J. B. White, Clerk and Master Chancery Court; T. T. Smiley, Clerk Circuit Court; F. R. Cheatham, Clerk County Court; D. T. Scott, Nashville Inn; S. M. Scott, City Hotel; H. Bridges, Sewanee; D. Y. Winston, Union Hall; C. H. Bachus, Verandah.                    feb 23.

*Republican Banner,* March 23, 1853

people can't afford to make such major acquisitions with a lump sum payment. For much the same reason, people in antebellum Tennessee bought slaves on the installment plan. "Terms one third cash, the balance on one and two years credit," explained a typical ad (from 1839) about the sale of 30 slaves in Nashville. "Notes payable in the Bank of Tennessee, and satisfactorily endorsed will be required."

Banks were also deeply connected to slavery because they loaned money to slaveholders who used slaves as collateral. That, of course, is one reason so many slaves were sold at "deed of trust" and "clerk and master" sales. Banks also extended lines of credit to professional slave traders such as Rees W. Porter of Nashville and Nathan Bedford Forrest of Memphis. In fact, in an 1853 ad, the Nashville slave trading firm of Glover & Boyd listed several banks as references, including Cashier Bank of Tennessee, Planter's Bank and Wheless & Hobson. (It also listed as references Tennessee Governor William B. Campbell and former Governor Aaron V. Brown.)

It would be impossible to determine the exact percentage of the assets listed on the books of various Tennessee banks in 1860 that were slaves. At an average value of $800, we can estimate the book value of the 275,000 of the slaves living in Tennessee in 1860 at $220 million. A sizeable portion of that amount was claimed on the balance sheets of Southern banks.

So it is plausible that a bank employee in slavery-era Tennessee might have personally been against the idea of slavery. But as far as institutions were concerned, Tennessee's antebellum banks would have viewed the emancipation of slaves with the same enthusiasm that a modern-day bank would view a stock market crash or real estate collapse.

*Description of Negroes*                                          Spring of 1831

*Purchased by Wm Ramsey Jr for the Corporation of Nashville in the month of*

Ben — (heretofore called Boatsman) 5 feet 7½ inches high — dark complexion upper lip thick — a small scar across the upper edge of the right wrist — speaks deliberately when spoken to, purchased of Wm OHara, Ann Arundel County Maryland ✝25 — ✕ 39 years of age — cost $450.

Emanuel — 5 feet 3 inches high — dark yellow complexion — a small scar in his left eye brow — stout and muscular — Purchased of Wm Finch, Chesterfield County Va. Raised in Petersburg Va by Edward Stokes ✝25 — 35 ✕ years of age. Cost $420

Peter — 5 feet 2 inches high — dark brown complexion — a scar on the inside of the right knee joint occasioned by a burn — also two scars on the right arm, one below, and one above the elbow — Purchased of Thos Hill Stafford County Va — Raised by Robt Ratliff in Fairfax County Va ✝26 — 30 ✕ years of age — Cost $390

Franks — 5 feet 7 inches high — black complexion — two of his upper, & all his under front teeth out, Purchased of German Jordan Campbell County Va — Raised by Charles Slaughter of the same County ✝34 — 45 ✕ years of age

Lewis — 5 feet 9½ inches high — black complexion — his upper left eye tooth out — a scar across his breast, occasioned by a burn, about three inches long, purchased of German Jordan Campbell County Va — Raised by John Strange in the same County — ✝32 — 46 ✕ years of age.

Moses — 4 feet 7¾ inches high — brown complexion — thick prominent under lip — considerable space between his front teeth — a small scar on his right arm below the elbow occasioned by a burn — purchased of German Jordan Campbell County Va — Raised by Richard Shelton same County 16 years old

Salem — 5 feet 9 inches high — Yellow complexion — small scar on his right eye brow — rather slender made — a scar on his left arm above the elbow occasioned by a burn — purchased of Isaac Lawson Isle of Night County Va — Raised by Thos Applewhite, Southampton County Va 22 years old — cost $425

Anthony — 5 feet 10 inches high — complexion black — a small scar under the left eye thick lips — apt to smile when spoken to — purchased of Abednigo Hornick, Isle of Night County Va — Raised by Robt Honeycut, Surry County Va 21 years old — cost $450

Descriptions of the slaves bought by the government of Nashville can be found in the log book *City of Nashville, Agreements, Loans and Slaves, November 2, 1830 to September 20, 1851.*

CHAPTER EIGHTEEN

# TAXPAYER DOLLARS

The year 1831 was an active one for runaway slaves in Nashville. The *National Banner and Nashville Whig* published at least 25 different runaway ads, some of them as many as 15 times each, as was the custom of the time. These were purchased by slaveholders such as James Bosley, Peter Vaughan, Elizabeth Moore and Amsel Epperson—names unrecognizable to even the most devout history buff.

But of all of the runaway slave ads published in Nashville in 1831, the one that debuted on June 25 stands out. Why? Because it was about two slaves (a man and a wife) who tried to run away from the government of Nashville, Tennessee.

"Ranaway from the Corporation of Nashville," stated the ad, "a Negro Man named DANIEL, about 25 years of age, of black complexion, stout, active and likely, and has a good countenance." The ad went on to say that Daniel ran away with his wife Betsey. Daniel and Betsey, it explained, had once been the property of a Mississippi man named Joseph Dunbar. The city had only recently purchased the two of them out of the Williamson County jail. (The ad doesn't say, but one assumes that Daniel and Betsey had been picked up as runaways by the Williamson County sheriff.)

**$65 REWARD.**

RANAWAY from the Corporation of Nashville on yesterday, 24th June, a Negro Man named DANIEL, about 25 years of age, of black complexion, stout, active, and likely, and has a good countenance. He speaks mildly when spoken to, and appears to be good natured. The Corporation purchased him of Mr Jos Dunbar, of the state of Mississippi, from whom he ran off and was lodged in jail of Williamson county, Tenn. out of which he was purchased two or three weeks since. The Corporation at the same time purchased out of jail his wife, who also eloped with him from Mr Dunbar, who states that he spoke of going to Canada frequently, through Hopkinsville, Ky.—Daniel, when he went off, had an old fur hat, dark mixt cassinet coatee, tow linen trowsers, and no shoes on. A reward of Fifty Dollars will be given if taken out of the state, and Twenty Dollars if taken within the state,—and brought to Nashville and delivered to the Corporation authorities, or put in jail so that they can get him.      SAM. V. D. STOUT, *Mayor pro tem.*
    Nashville, June 25, 1831.
    N. B.—On yesterday morning, 26th instant, Daniel's wife, BETSEY, also eloped, and there is but little doubt they are both together. She is also about twenty-five years old, complexion black, and had with her in a bundle, it is thought, a dark purple silk dress, which she borrowed the day before, on pretence of going to church.—Sixty-five Dollars will be given for the delivery of Daniel and Betsey, or if put in any jail so we can get them, if taken out of the state; or Twenty-five Dollars if taken within the state; and all reasonable expenses paid.     SAM. V. D. STOUT, *Mayor pro tem.*
    Nashville, June 27, 1831.          j4—6

*National Banner and Nashville Whig,* June 25, 1831

"A reward of Fifty Dollars will be given if taken out of the state, and Twenty Dollars if taken within the state—and brought to Nashville and delivered to the Corporation authorities, or put in jail so that they can get him," stated the ad, which was signed by "Sam V.D. Stout—Mayor pro tem."

This wasn't the only time that a slave owned by the city of Nashville tried to run away. In August 1834, Mayor John M. Bass offered a $30 reward for the return of a slave named Emanuel. "He [Emanuel] is about 35 years old, is five feet three inches high, dark yellow complexion, rather a sulky countenance, a small scar on left eyebrow," read the ad, which would have been paid for by the taxpayers of the city of Nashville.

Slavery was legal in Tennessee. In terms of explaining the state's relationship to the institution, this is the first point to be made. Looking closely at newspapers prior to the 1860s, it becomes clear that the relationship between the state and slavery was more complex than that.

First of all, law enforcement authorities were constantly arresting African Americans suspected of being runaway slaves. With each arrest—and every sheriff in Tennessee was required to do this as part of his job—sheriffs ran newspaper ads advising the public and asking the slave owners to come forward. Here is one such item in the March 27, 1797 *Knoxville Gazette*:

> "Received into the district jail . . . in Knoxville, two negro men slaves named William and Dick, who saith they are belonging to William Robertson and his son, living in Powell's Valley, in the state of Virginia. The said slaves are in irons. Their masters are desired to come, prove their property, pay charges, and take them away." –Abner Witt, keeper of the public jail

These "apprehended" or "runaway committed" ads were present in practically every newspaper in the state, from the first issues published until 1863. (In fact, in some cases, authorities were apprehending runaway slaves before they had jails in which to put them.) Tennessee newspapers contain many such notices, all of them ending with this sentence: "The owner is requested to come forward, prove property, pay charges and take him [or her] away, or he [or she] will be sold as the law directs."

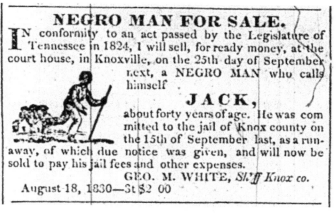

**NEGRO MAN FOR SALE.**

IN conformity to an act passed by the Legislature of Tennessee in 1824, I will sell, for ready money, at the court house, in Knoxville, on the 25th day of September next, a NEGRO MAN who calls himself

**JACK,**

about forty years of age. He was committed to the jail of Knox county on the 15th of September last, as a runaway, of which due notice was given, and will now be sold to pay his jail fees and other expenses.

GEO. M. WHITE, *Sh'ff Knox co.*

August 18, 1830—3t $2 00

*Knoxville Register,* **August 18, 1830**

Unfortunately for historans, news that the "rightful owner" later came forward was never published. On those occasions when the rightful owner did not come forward, Tennessee law allowed the sheriff to sell the slave a year and a day after they were apprehended. These "unclaimed slave" sales became routine by the 1830s. On May 2, 1836, Shelby County Sheriff John Balch sold a slave named Isaac Thompson at the courthouse in Raleigh.[1] The Shelby County sheriff followed this up by selling a slave named Charles in November 1836; a slave named John Gray in April 1837; a slave named Mary in May 1837; a slave named David in June 1837; a slave named Ned in June 1844; slaves named George, William and George Green in December 1844; a slave named Barrot in March 1845; slaves named Jack and Bill in June 1847; and a slave named Susan in October 1847.

---

[1]Raleigh was the original county seat of Shelby County.

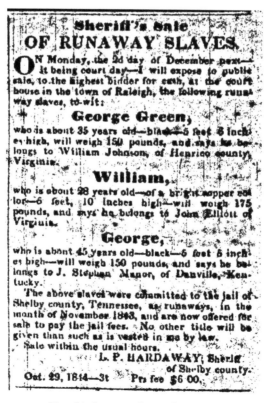

*Memphis Commercial Appeal*, **November 1, 1844**

Of course, these are only some of the sheriff slave sales in one county. There would have been similar sales by sheriffs all over Tennessee. In these cases, Tennessee sheriffs sold slaves that they had caught and jailed for one year. And in all these cases, local governments kept the money from the sale of these slaves.

Tennessee law also allowed sheriffs to put these apprehended slaves to work, which all of them probably did. But that wasn't the only way local governments used slave labor to keep labor costs down. In 1830, Nashville sent slave trader William Ramsey to Virginia on a $12,000 buying trip. Ramsey's purchase of 24 slaves on behalf of the government is documented in log books that are still on file at the Metro Nashville Archives. According to the July 1831 *National Banner and Nashville Whig*, the board of the Nashville corporation (precursor to the city council) ordered that the city's slaves work on improvements to the public square and then on the "water works"—which would have meant a reservoir, pump and engine house then under construction on the hill in downtown Nashville now known as Rolling Mill Hill.

We don't know why the city bought slaves instead of leasing them, or why Nashville subsequently bought two more slaves (Daniel and Betsey). However, we do know the name, age, height and physical description of each slave, along with how much each cost, the names of the prior owners, and the county in which they previously lived. (Isaac, who was 26, had a scar on his left knee "about the size of a half dollar," the log book states.)

Nashville appears to have sold all but two of the slaves it owned after the water works project was completed. From that point onward, the city continued to own two slaves on a semi-permanent basis, while hiring

---

**Wanted,**

FOR the present year, fifteen or twenty stout and healthy negro men, and five or six boys, for the use of the Corporation. Liberal wages will be given if immediate application be made to the undersigned in Nashville.

H. HOLLINGSWORTH, Mayor
of the Town of Nashville.

Jan. 4th, 1838—tf.

---

*Daily Republican Banner*, January 10, 1838

---

**WANTED TO HIRE.**

**T**EN or twelve able NEGROES by the month, or
for the balance cf the year, to work on the streets.
mar12                    I. H. HARRIS, Mayor.

---

*Clarksville Weekly Chronicle*, April 2, 1844

between 15 and 20 additional slaves when the city had a special project requiring labor.

At least one other Tennessee city used slave labor. From April through July 1844, Mayor I.H. Harris ran ads declaring that the city of Clarksville would hire "TEN or twelve able NEGROES by the month, or for the balance of the year, to work on the streets."

The state of Tennessee also used slave labor, at least indirectly. In the 1830s, the state funded a series of internal improvements (mainly road construction and river clearance). Each part of the state got to use its portion of internal improvement funds to work on its own project, and in the case of Davidson, Rutherford and Bedford Counties, that project was a turnpike that led from Nashville to Murfreesboro to Shelbyville. In the spring of 1832, the turnpike company advertised its intention to hire 100 (ostensibly white) "laborers" and an additional "50 to 100 NEGROES" to work on the road.

But how did the state raise money for these internal improvements? That would be through a lottery. Lotteries were legal in Tennessee in the early 1800s. During an era in which the state had few ways of raising money and serious infrastructure challenges—many roads were hardly passable at that time—the state often held lotteries to raise revenue.

Today, cash is given as a lottery prize. But in those days, the state gave away assets which it probably accumulated when people died without wills.

Two slaves were given away as prizes in a private lottery organized in Greeneville in 1794. Slaves were also given away in a 1799 lottery in Knoxville and in an 1809 lottery in Carthage.

The prizes given away in the state lottery of 1836 included 1,070 acres in Dyer County; a 320-acre farm, house and orchards in

*Tennessee Internal Improvement*
## LOTTERY,
### EXTRA CLASS, NO. 1 FOR 1836.
### To be drawn in the City of Nashville.
#### SPLENDID SCHEME.
#### *TWENTY LARGE PRIZES.*

1 Prize; a FARM on Mill Creek, 320 acres, with a fine frame dwelling, out houses, stables &c. young apple and peach orchards, and saw and grist Mills, all in complete order, nearly 8 miles from Nashville. Also 1070 acres land in Dyer county, on Obion River. **$14,000**

1 do. The brick house and 40 feet ground on Summer street, lot No 92, opposite T. J. Read's Esq; a new building roomy and comfortable, together with 1000 acres of land, part of the tract adjoining Centreville, granted to Daniel Shaw, being such portion unsold, to be laid off in the north-east corner of the tract. **5,500**

1 do 150 acres land adjoining the Robertson Springs, with all the improvements thereon, including a large frame house, &c. **3,000**

1 do. The Barren Farm, lying about 4 miles from the Springs, containing 300 acres. **1,000**

1 do. A tract of 216 acres of land in Dickson county, on Barton's creek, within about 3 miles of three furnaces; well timbered, and some good soil. **80**

1 do. Lot in the Southfield, 80 feet front & 160 ft. deep, fronting on Vine street, No 43. **850**

1 do. do. adjoining the same on the south side. part of lot No 43--same size. **750**

1 do. Steam Boat HARRY HILL, in complete repair. **8,000**

1 do. Steam Boat TOM YEATMAN, now undergoing a thorough repair under the superintendance of Capt Garrison. **5,000**

1 do. Bay colt, 4 years old this spring, by Pacific, dam by Timoleon, g. dam John Lowry's dam by old Pacolet, fine size and form. **2,000**

1 do. Baltic, by Pacific 5 years old, **1,500**

1 do. Bay filly Panama, by Crusader, 3 years old; **1,000**

1 do. Carolinian filly Medora Howard, 4 years old, **750**

1 do Bay mare by Cook's Whip, dam imp Knowsley, now with foal by Havock, 8 years old and near 16 hands high. **800**

1 do Sorrel filly, by Havoc, 3 years old dam by Conqueror. **550**

1 do Negro man CHARLES, aged 45, **1,100**

1 do Yellow girl MATILDA, aged 12. a first rate house servant, **1,050**

1 do Negro girl REBECCA, very likely, aged 11 years, **1,000**

1 do. Negro woman NANCY, aged 43 years, a first rate cook and washer. **800**

1 do Negro girl MARIA, very likely, aged 6 years. **700**

*Nashville Republican,* **March 8, 1836**

Davidson County; various houses and smaller farms; two steamboats and several horses. At the bottom of the list of prizes were listed a 45–year-old negro man named Charles, a 43-year-old negro woman named Nancy, and three girls named Matilda (12), Rebecca (11) and Maria (6). There was no indication that any of the slaves would be given away together.

So, to summarize: In 1836, the state raised money by raffling off five slaves—individually. In the process, the state probably broke up at least one slave family.

The state of Tennessee also endorsed the institution of slavery in the construction of its state Capitol. Commissioned in the 1840s, the Capitol

---

## State Capitol.

TEN or twelve stout, able-bodied NEGROES are required, for quarrying and hoisting stone for the building. They will be hired by the month or building season. Apply at the office of the Architect, on the hill.        W. STRICKLAND,
April 21, 1847—3w                                    Architect.

---

*Republican Banner*, April 23, 1847

was a massive undertaking—the biggest building in Nashville at that time. From the start, the commissioner of the project (Sam Morgan) and the architect of the building (William Strickland) knew it would be impossible to keep the project on budget.

To obtain some of the limestone needed for the Capitol, the state bought and dug a quarry west of the construction site. In 1846 and 1847, the state ran regular ads in Nashville's newspapers seeking slave labor to operate the quarry. "Ten or twelve stout, able bodied NEGROES are required for quarrying and hoisting stone for the building," one of the ads claimed. "They will be hired by the month or building season. Apply at the office of the Architect, on the hill. W. STRICKLAND, Architect."

On October 21, 1848, one of these slaves died working at this quarry. "We learn that a sad accident happened on Saturday, about noon, at the Capitol quarry. A negro man belonging to Mr. Baldwin, whilst at work there, received a blow from a lever, by some mismanagement, which broke his spine."

The slave's name was never published, has never been revealed, and almost certainly will never be known.

---

SAD ACCIDENT.—We learn that a sad accident happened on Saturday, about noon, at the Capitol quarry. A negro man belonging to Mr. Baldwin, whilst at work there, received a blow from a lever, by some mismanagement, which broke his spine.

---

*Republican Banner*, October 23, 1848

CHAPTER NINETEEN

# APPLY TO THE PRINTER

Search the Internet with the words "newspaper, Tennessee, slavery," and you will find information about an anti-slavery publication called *The Emancipator*. A man named Elihu Embree published *The Emancipator* in Jonesboro between April and October 1820. According to its masthead, the purpose of *The Emancipator* was "to advocate the abolition of slavery

GENIUS OF UNIVERSAL EMANCIPATION.

EDITED AND PUBLISHED BY BENJAMIN LUNDY, GREENEVILLE, TENNESSEE.

"We hold these truths to be self-evident; that all men are created equal, and endowed by their Creator with certain unalienable rights; that among these are life, liberty, and the pursuit of happiness." — *Declaration Independence U. S.*

No. 1. Vol. III.       *SEVENTH MONTH,* 4th, 1823.       Whole No. 29

## ANNIVERSARY
### OF
### FREEDOM'S BIRTH DAY,
#### IN THE
#### NORTH AMERICAN UNION.

The morning dawns on ten millions of free men! exclaimed the Colonel, as he was roused, at break of day, by the shrill note of Chanticleer, from the tree beside his stately mansion.—This is the anniversary of the glorious birth-day of American Liberty— the day on which the people of the United States spurned the yoke of oppression, and declared to the world that "FREEDOM IS THE NATURAL RIGHT OF ALL MEN."——Jack! you lazy dog, are you up

Liberty mus be good ting,—but poor negur, why he no feel it?
*James.*—Why every body knows that the negroes are not fit to enjoy their liberty; they are so debased and degraded, that they never could get a living without somebody to oversee them.
*Caesar.*—Wat de reason negur so debase? —How come wite man make slabe ob him? Who gib him de pribilege do dis?
*James.*—The negroes are so *barbarous,* in their own country, that they are always at war; and they sell their prisoners for slaves. It is a blessing to be brought to this free Christian country, [*Caesar—*(aside) Curious *blessin,* indeed; me wonder dey

and to be a repository of tracts on that interesting and important subject." Once an obscure and forgotten publication in Tennessee history, all seven issues of *The Emancipator* were reprinted by B.H. Murphy of Nashville in 1932 as well as in a paperback book published in 1995.

Publication of *The Emancipator* ceased after Embree's death in December 1820. Two years later, another abolitionist named Benjamin Lundy moved his newspaper called the *Genius of Universal Emancipation* to Greeneville. It also lasted for a short time, until Lundy moved to Baltimore in 1824.

I suppose we Tennesseans can all be proud of Elihu Embree. Accurately or not, *The Emancipator* has been dubbed the first newspaper solely devoted to the cause of abolition, which is why a lot of school kids in Tennessee learn about him.

A paper has been established at Jonesburg, Tennessee, by *Elihu Embree*, styled "THE EMANCIPATOR" the object of which is to bring about the abolition of Slavery. It is a holy cause, God prosper him.

*Susquehanna Democrat,* June 2, 1820

However, a couple of points need to be emphasized about this fascinating footnote in Tennessee history. First of all, both *The Emancipator* and the *Genius of Universal Emancipation* had very short lives. Neither of them had much of an impact on Tennessee. In fact, no Tennessee newspaper outside of Jonesboro appears to have even mentioned the existence of *The Emancipator*, although at least one newspaper outside of Tennessee mentioned it. "A paper has been established at Jonesburg [sic], Tennessee, by Elihu Embree, styled 'The Emancipator,' the object of which is to bring about the abolition of slavery," the *Susquehanna Democrat* of Wilkes-Barre, Pennsylvania, noted. "It is a holy cause, God prosper him."

The truth is that not only were the vast majority of Tennessee's newspapers in favor of slavery, but they promoted the institution by habitually running advertisements associated with slavery. By publishing these items and accepting money for them, newspapers were "in on it" (at least the profitable ones).

If you look at newspapers from Tennessee's first seven decades, it becomes obvious that ads for runaway slaves, upcoming slave sales and slave wanted ads were among the newspaper industry's most consistent sources of income (about as prevalent as real estate ads and missing horse ads). In fact, these ads were so routine that by the 1830s, Tennessee's newspapers had art specially created to accompany them. The ubiquitous silhouette of a slave heading down the road with his meager possessions tied to a stick slung over his shoulder appears to have been one of the very first pieces of design work created in the offices of newspapers across the state.

Lotteries were discussed in the last chapter. There are at least four examples in Tennessee history in which slaves were given away by lottery. In 1794, the *Knoxville Gazette* helped organize, promote and sell tickets to a Greeneville lottery in which two slaves named Joe and Luce were among the prizes. Five years later, the *Knoxville Gazette* promoted another lottery in which a slave was given away, and in 1809 the *Carthage Gazette* promoted a lottery in which a slave was a prize. Finally, in 1836, newspapers across the state helped promote a lottery in which five slaves, including three children, were given away.

Without the promotion of newspapers, these four lotteries would not have made money.

*Knoxville Gazette,* May 23, 1749

The active role that newspapers played in the buying and selling of slaves also needs to be amplified. In practically every newspaper published in Tennessee from 1791 until the Civil War, items which advertised the sale of slaves concluded with a similar phrase referencing "the printer":

- "FOR SALE, FOR CASH, a stout active NEGRO FELLOW about thirty years old. The only reason his master has for selling him is that he has no employment for him. Apply to the printer." *–Knoxville Gazette*, August 6, 1806

- "NEGROES FOR SALE. A girl 20 years old, used chiefly to work out, but often in the house; and a very strong active woman, who falls behind no negro man at field work. . . Enquire at the printers."—*Nashville Whig*, July 12, 1814

- "WANTED to purchase, for cash, two or three young NEGRO WOMEN, of good character and constitutions, and raised in the country. Enquire at the Printer."— *Nashville Whig*, July 12, 1820

*Memphis Advocate*, **December 8, 1827**

**THIRTY DOLLARS REWARD**

RANAWAY from the subscriber living at Rotherwood, Hawkins county, Te.,
on the 15th inst., a negro boy named GEORGE.
Said boy is about 24 years of age; 5 feet 6 or 7
inches high; heavy set; dark complected; high
forehead; a good countenance, and weighs
about 160 pounds; had on when he left a fine
pair of boots and a fine cloth frock coat. It is
probable that he will attempt to get to a free
state. I will give the above reward for his
apprehension and delivery to me or confinement in jail, so that I can get him. Or I will
give twenty dollars if taken out of the State,
may 29t                         JOSHUA PHIPPS.

*Rogersville Times*, **June 12, 1851**

- "For Sale. Two Likely Negro Plough Boys, one thirteen
and the other ten years of age. Both of good character
and qualifications. For terms apply to the editors of the
*Memphis Advocate*"—*Memphis Advocate*, Dec. 9, 1827

The frequent presence of the phrase "apply to the printer" indicates
that newspapers provided an additional service beyond just printing
these ads. A person selling slaves could hide his or her identity from the
public by using this clause, which required prospective buyers or sellers
to come to the newspaper office to find out more. A person selling
slaves might have done this to avoid the public appearance of financial
difficulty, since the sale of a slave was often a sign of insolvency. They
might have done this to hide the fact that they were breaking up a
family of slaves. We really don't know. But we do know that, regardless
of the reason, almost every newspaper in Tennessee regularly acted as an
agent in the slave trade.

By the 1840s, slavery was more prevalent in West and Middle
Tennessee than it was in East Tennessee. Parts of East Tennessee would
eventually become so "anti-slavery" that the region would eventually
reject the Confederacy in both of Tennessee's 1862 referendums. That
being the case, I half expected to find a newspaper, or even several
newspapers, that chose not to run runaway slave ads.

Besides the *Emancipator* and the *Genius of Universal Emancipation*, I found only one: the *Rogersville Railroad Advocate* (a short-lived publication in Hawkins County). Meanwhile, *The Knoxville Gazette* ran runaway slave ads and slave sale ads. So did the *Athens Post*, Athens *Tennessee Journal, Chattanooga Advertiser, Chattanooga Daily Rebel, Chattanooga Gazette,* (Elizabethton) *Tennessee Whig, Greeneville Democrat, Greeneville Mountaineer, Hiwassee Reporter, Kingston Gazetteer, Knoxville Argus and Commercial Herald, Knoxville Enquirer, Knoxville Register, Jonesboro Whig, Loudon Free Press* and *Rogersville Times.*

Granted, East Tennessee newspapers didn't publish as many runaway slave ads and slave sale ads as those in Nashville, Clarksville, Fayetteville, Jackson and Memphis because there weren't as many slaves in East Tennessee as in the other two Grand Divisions. But the vast majority of East Tennessee newspapers were happy to take money in the cause of catching runaway slaves and selling slaves. Effectively, therefore, they were part of the institution of slavery.

Starting in the 1840s, William Brownlow was the most famous newspaper editor in the South. First in Jonesboro and later in

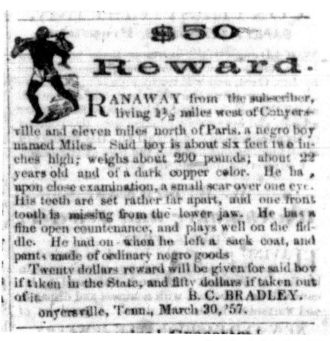

*Paris Sentinel,* **April 3, 1857**

ted and consummated. Fearful and terrible examples should be made, and if need
be, the fagot and the flame should be
brought into requisition to show these deluded maniacs the fierceness and the vigor,
the swiftness and completeness of the white
man's vengeance. Let a terrible example
be made in every neighborhood where the
crime can be established, and if necessary,
let every tree in the country bend with negro meat. Temporizing in such cases as
this, is utter madness. We must strike
terror, and make a lasting impression, for
only in such a course can we find the guar-
anties of future security.

*Clarksville Jeffersonian,* **December 3, 1856**

Knoxville, "Parson" Brownlow's newspapers were wildly popular, in part because of his vitriolic editorials. Appointed military governor of Tennessee during the Civil War, Brownlow's hard-nosed attitude toward Confederates made him wildly popular in the North. "A rebel has two rights," Brownlow once said, "a right to be damned, and a right to be hung."

Given his anti-secessionist attitude and the location of his target market, I didn't expect to find slavery ads in *Brownlow's Knoxville Whig.* But there are plenty, dating from 1849 until 1860. In October 1859, Brownlow's newspaper published a runaway ad for slaveholder Guilford Cannon, who (in what sounds like a chapter out of *Huckleberry Finn*), suspected that the runaway Dennis was being "piloted" by a 16-year-old white boy. In May 1860, readers of Brownlow's newspaper could see one item offering $150 for the return of Gipson (a slave held by William McClellan of Knox County) and another offering $50 for the return of Sol (who was held by William Lackey of Knox County).

While researching this book, I focused on ads about slavery rather than on editorial content about slavery. Editorials I did read made it clear that Tennessee newspapers not only defended slavery, but they also mocked people who were critical of it and even accused them of being traitors. Tennessee's antebellum papers consistently stood up for slaveholders against the rights of slaves and even, at times, promoted brutal violence against slaves.

The best example of this was the so-called slave insurrection of 1856. In the fall of 1856, rumors of an armed slave rebellion among ironworkers swirled around Montgomery and Stewart Counties. The events were said to have occurred because of publicity associated with Republican John Fremont, the first openly anti-slavery candidate nominated to a major ticket (the Republican Party). In November, the *Clarksville Jeffersonian* reported that at least eight slaves and an English carpenter (who allegedly encouraged slaves to rebel) had been arrested over a plot to blow up a white church near the Louisa Furnace in Montgomery County. The account of the plot turned out to be false, but that didn't stop a slave named Britton from being killed in the hysteria.

A few weeks later there was news of a plot in Stewart County in which slaves were reportedly planning to "kill the white men and children at the forge, seize the white women as wives, and then link up with the slaves from the Cumberland rolling mill for a joint rush on Dover." As a result of this second panic, many slaves were interrogated and whipped, and some number of them killed. Again, however, there does not appear to have ever been massive, organized slave insurrection, contrary to reports by many newspapers at the time.

In spite of published accounts that as many as 65 slaves were tortured and 28 executed as a result of these two incidents, we aren't sure today how many slaves were tortured or killed. (It does appear to be true that several slaves belonging to Tennessee Senator John Bell were among those killed). We do know that several newspapers published vitriolic editorials threatening mass executions of slaves. "Fearful and terrible examples should be made, and if need be, the faggot and flame should be brought into requisition to show these deluded maniacs the fierceness and the vigor, the swiftness and completeness of the white man's vengeance," the *Jeffersonian* said. "Let a terrible example be made in every neighborhood where the crime can be established, and if necessary, let every tree in the country bend with negro meat."

## CHAPTER TWENTY

# MONUMENTS AND GHOST TOWNS

Very few antebellum buildings or structures are still standing in Tennessee. Those that are left are generally celebrated for what happened there, who lived there, and because of how unusual it is that they are still standing. To the degree that the histories of these antebellum structures are still told, those stories are usually connected to the Civil War. But you don't hear much about how slaves helped build these old structures. One reason for this, I suspect, is that the degree to which slave labor was involved has been murky.

Old newspaper items clear up some of the murkiness. They provide clear evidence that slaves were involved in the creation of roads and railroads we still use. They give us details about the slaves who worked at and around iron foundries in Middle Tennessee, some of which are still standing. Newspaper clippings make us realize that it is possible, even likely, that slaves built many of the homes and stone walls that pre-date the Civil War. They also make it clear that a slave died in the construction of the state's most famous building.

We take roads for granted today. We forget about how much trial and error went into creating the best path from point A to point B— not to mention how difficult it was for generations of road builders to create a dry road through West Tennessee lowlands and a passable road up the Cumberland Plateau. The U.S. government (in the Southwest Territory days) and the state government (after 1796) "bid out" roads to private contractors. It is probable, even likely, that these contractors owned or hired out slaves as part of their normal operation.

In a previous chapter I mentioned the use of slave labor in the creation of the Nashville, Murfreesboro and Shelbyville Turnpike. I should mention three other examples of Tennessee newspapers running ads for slave labor in road construction. In 1835, road contractor Wellman & Dean said it needed up to 200 workers for two roads to be built near Huntsville, Alabama. "Gentlemen owning slaves, wishing to hire them on this road, will receive Thirteen dollars per year," the ad stated.

Two years later, the U.S. Army Corps of Engineers leased slaves for the construction of a road leading from Memphis north to a point across from the St. Francis River. "Abundant and wholesome food, good quarters, and the best medical attention are provided by the United States," the ad claimed. Slaveholders were referred to Spiral Hale, a slave owner in Dyersburg, whose slaves had worked on the road previously.

**Negroes Wanted.**

ANY number of able bodied negro men and women will find constant employment on the U. States Military Road, leading from Memphis to the St. Francis River. Twenty-two dollars will be given per month for men, and from ten to twelve for women. The negroes on this work, for the last two years, have been as healthy as any in the Western District of Tennessee. Abundant and wholesome food, good quarters and the best medical attendance are provided by the United States. Masters desirous of hiring their slaves are referred to Dr. Wyatt Christian, of Memphis, who has attended those on the work for two years past, for information on all subjects relating to their health, food and treatment; or to Spiral Hale, Esq., of Dyersburgh, Tennessee, whose negroes for the same period, have been hired upon the Road.
A. H. BOWMAN,
July 22—21-tf.  *Lt. Corps of Engineers.*

☞The Somerville Reporter, La Grange Whig, and Jackson Telegraph, will publish the above for one month and forward their accounts to the subscriber.

*Memphis Enquirer*, **August 12, 1837**

Also, in 1857, Fayette County slaveholder H.C. Stark ran an ad in search of two runaways. The slaves, Morgan and Isaac, ran away "while at work on the Germantown Plank Road."

Proof that four road projects used slave labor does not mean slaves were used to build every road in Tennessee prior to 1860. However, it does mean there is a good chance slaves were used to build other roads.

We also have proof that slaves worked on at least three railroads—the Nashville and Chattanooga Railroad, the East Tennessee and Virginia Railroad, and the Cleveland and Chattanooga Railroad.

The connection between the iron foundries of the Highland Rim and slavery is clear. Montgomery, Stewart, Dickson and Cheatham Counties retain remnants of this early 19th century industry—in particular, the Bear Spring Furnace, the Great Western Furnace and the Bellwood Furnace.

In a previous chapter there was mention of the Tennessee State Capitol, one of the most beautiful state government buildings in the United States and one of the oldest such buildings that still actively houses its legislature. Numerous advertisements from 1846 and 1847 prove that slaves were hired to work on the Capitol, especially in digging out limestone from the nearby quarry. We now know that on October 21, 1848, a slave died while working in that quarry.

Every year, thousands of tourists and schoolchildren take a guided tour of the Tennessee State Capitol. They learn all sorts of interesting tidbits about the building—the fact that the architect is buried in its walls and that there used to be an escape hatch under the governor's office, for instance. To the best of my knowledge, the fact that a slave died in the construction of the State Capitol has never been included on the tour.[1]

Throughout Tennessee are old mansions that were once centerpieces of larger estates or plantations where slaves lived. Some of the best known are the Hermitage and the Belle Meade Mansion in Nashville; the Carnton Plantation in Franklin; the Ames Plantation in Hardeman County; and the James White Mansion in Knoxville. For many years, slaves were hardly mentioned on the tours of these historic homes. That has changed in

---

[1] I don't believe this information was ever intentionally neglected, just that it was unknown following a minor notice in a Nashville newspaper.

recent years. Not only are staff members, historians and even archaeologists researching the lives of slaves who lived in or on these places, tour guides are now much more likely to mention stories about slaves.

Some mention should also be made about Middle Tennessee's beautiful stone walls. Many of these walls were built before the Civil War, some in urban places such as the Metro Government owned Howard Office Building in downtown Nashville, but far more in rural settings of Sumner and Williamson Counties. In runaway slave ads, many slaves are described as stonemasons. We can therefore conclude that many of these stone walls were made by slaves.

And what about the places where slaves were auctioned? The auction yards used by slave traders in cities such as Nashville and Memphis are long built over, in some cases several times. Nashville's best-known private slave trading block was the one at 33 Cedar Street. It was run by various business owners in the 1840s and 1850s, the most notorious of whom was Rees W. Porter. Today that address is the location of the National Baptist Convention's Morris Memorial Building at 330 Charlotte Avenue. This is not a secret; the connection between slave trading and that address has been noted many times in interviews and local history books. However, there is no historical marker on the site mentioning the land's slave trading legacy.

## $50 Reward

RANAWAY from the St. Cloud Hotel on Saturday last, a negro girl named EVA, of copper color and about seventeen years of age—about medium height, and will weigh 142 pounds; hair black and inclined to be waivy; very pleasant countenance and extra fine teeth. She had on when she left gold cross ear rings and a number of finger rings, brown merino dress and checked gingham sun bonnet—was raised in Coffee county and brought to this city on Saturday morning last for the first time

I will give the above reward for her delivery at the sale yard of W. L. Boyd, of Nashville, Tenn., or her confinement in any jail so that I can get her.
                                        GEO S. BOLLING,
                                        St. Cloud Hotel,
oct25-1w                                Nashville, Tenn.

*Nashville Daily Patriot*, **October 26, 1859**

As for Memphis, the best-known slave auction house was the one run by various business owners at 87 Adams Street—the best known of whom was Nathan B. Forrest. In 1955, the Tennessee Historical Commission placed a marker on the site which mentions Forrest's "business enterprises." Not until April 2018 did someone finally place a marker on the site that explained those "business enterprises."

There are at least a few structures still standing in Tennessee where slaves were regularly auctioned. Those structures are called courthouses. According to the Tennessee Historical Commission, six of Tennessee's working courthouses pre-date the Civil War: those for the counties of Carter (built in 1852), Dickson (1833), Hawkins (1837), Jefferson (1845), Rutherford (1861) and Williamson (1858). There are also at least two remaining buildings which were previously used as courthouses—the old Roane County Courthouse and the old Hardeman County Courthouse.

### Negroes for Sale.

BY virtue of a decree of the Chancery Court at Charlotte, on the petition of R. Batton administrator, with the will annexed of Spencer T. Hunt dec'd. I will sell to the highest bidder at the Court House in Charlotte, on the first day of January next, the following slaves, belonging to the Estate of said Hunt, to wit: Charles, Nancy, June, John, Isham, and an infant Girl, on a credit of four months, the purchaser giving bond with good security. Sold for the purpose of effecting the objects of the will.
JOHN C. COLLIER, C. & M.
Dec. 2d 1848.—tdPr's. fee $5,00

*Republican Banner*, December 20, 1848

Many estate and chancery sales in antebellum Tennessee occurred at private residences, so it would take a lot of research and shoe leather to determine the number of those structures still standing. However, at least one place in Tennessee is still there and looks similar to the way it did 163 years ago. Once known as the Mouse Creek Landing Depot, the Niota Train Depot is where the slave trading firm Latham & Howard sold slaves as late as April 1863.

Despite these examples of existing structures with connections to slavery, the truth of the matter is that most of the places and buildings

## More Likely Negroes for Sale.

LATHAM & HOWARD ARE JUST IN RE-
ceipt of another lot of prime Negroes—twenty in number. Among them a likely family—a
man, his wife and three children—two or three
good cooks, and several first rate plough boys.—
At their old stand, at Mouse Creek Depot.
April 10, 1863—tf—759

## Ten Cents Reward!

RANAWAY FROM THE SUBSCRIBER,
living in the 1st Civil District, McMinn
county, on the 3d of April, 1863, a bound boy
named WM. UNDERWOOD. The above reward
will be paid for the apprehension and return of
said boy to me; and all persons are hereby cautioned against harboring him.
                                    JAMES CARTER.
   April 10, 1863—3t*—759

## NEGROES FOR SALE.

THE SUBSCRIBER HAS FOR SALE, AT
his residence near Mouse Creek Depot, a lot
of Likely Young Negroes.     L. R. HURST.
April 10, 1863—tf—759

*Athens Post*, April 17, 1863

connected with the institution are long gone. Old newspapers remind
us that place names have changed, people have migrated, and that the
Tennessee Valley Authority and U.S. Army Corps of Engineers has
flooded a lot of land. Newspapers also remind us that some history
is, for lack of a better word, lost. I found many runaway slave ads in a
newspaper printed in the 1830s called the *Randolph Recorder*—which
is interesting, because the town of Randolph doesn't exist anymore.
I found at least four county seats where slaves were sold that aren't
even county seats anymore—Jefferson in Rutherford County, Raleigh
in Shelby County, Harrison in Hamilton County and Washington
in Rhea County. I found several references in runaway slave ads to
a now-abandoned community at the Robertson and Montgomery
County border called Port Royal. I found references to a Williamsport
in Maury County and a Williamsburg in Jackson County—both of
which are obscure places today.

Here is a partial list of obscure, unknown and forgotten Tennessee place names that I encountered in old runaway slave ads, listed with the county in which (I believe) they were located:

**East Tennessee:** Camp Creek (Greene County); Grape Springs (Hamilton County); McBee's Ferry (Jefferson County); Montvale Springs (Blount County); Morganton (Loudon County); Mossy Creek (Jefferson County); New Canton (Hawkins County); Post Oak Springs (Roane County); Powder Spring Gap (Grainger County); Rotherwood (Hawkins County); Smith's Cross Roads (Rhea County); Stoney Point (Bradley County); Tampico (Grainger County); Washington College (Washington County).

## $100 Reward!!

RUNAWAY from the subscriber on the 19th inst., his NEGRO BOY GEORGE. He is about 24 years old, weighs about 175 or 180 lbs; lisps when talking, has a sneaking, down-cast look, and has a large scar on his left fore-finger, caused by a straw cutter, no other marks recollected. He is 5 feet 4 inches high, and had on when he left a pair of linsey pants, a shirt, an old pair of shoes, and a black wool hat. When I last heard of him he was near Jenning's Iron Works, and going in that direction, and I think he is apt to be concealed or harbored about there, in the mountains.

I will give fifty dollars reward for said boy, if he is taken in Virginia or Kentucky, or twenty-five dollars if he is taken in this State, and confined in jail so that I can get him. I will give one hundred dollars reward for the conviction of the white man that conceals or harbors him.

My address is Camp Creek, Greene county, Tennessee, or Greeneville, Tennessee.

April 25, 1859.                    SAMUEL W. DAVIS.

*Greeneville Democrat,* **May 4, 1859**

**$10 Reward.**

Ranaway from me, last Sunday night, a likely Negro Boy about 19 years old—dressed in black pants, snuff-colored hat and brown coat. The said Boy is very dark, and about 5 feet high, thick lips and down countenance, I will give the above reward for the arrest of said Boy, deposited in jail or where I can get him. My address is
JAS. BABB,
Black Jack, Tenn.

April 3, 1857—tf.

*Clarksville Weekly Chronicle*, **April 17, 1857**

**Middle Tennessee**: Abbott's Mill (Rutherford County); Black Jack (Robertson); Cainsville (Wilson County); Cairo (Sumner County); Caleb's Valley (Stewart County); Chestnut Grove (Davidson County); Claysville (Cumberland County); Clinton College (Smith County); Cumberland Saline (Jackson County); Dixon Springs, (Smith County); Fort Blount (Jackson County); Fredonia (Montgomery County); Gallows Hollow (Montgomery County); Good Spring (Williamson County); Graysville (Montgomery County); Harpeth Forge (Cheatham County); Haysborough (Davidson County);

**$20 REWARD.**

RANAWAY from the subscriber on the 30th January, a negro man by the name of JESSE, about 26 years old; he is about six feet high, a knot on one of his ankles, occasioned by a cut with an axe,—some of his fore teeth out. I will give the above reward and all reasonable expenses paid, if delivered to me or secured in any jail so that I get him again. Any information given to me at Van Buren, Ten., will be thankfully received.
WALTER L. MASK.

Feb. 18, 1837—47 3t.

*Memphis Enquirer*, **February 18, 1837**

Liberty (DeKalb County); Little Bigby (Maury County); Mount Carmel (Wilson County); New Providence (Montgomery County); Pleasant Plains (Lincoln County); Rally Hill (Maury County); Ready's Mill (Rutherford County); Round Lick (Wilson County); Salisbury (Wilson County); Shelby's Mill (Davidson County); Spring Creek (Rutherford County); Stone's Lick (Davidson County); Three Forks (DeKalb County); Tobacco Port (Stewart County); Turnersville (Robertson County); Valley Forge (Dickson County); Vernon (Hickman County); Walnut Valley (Sequatchie); Woodville (Warren County).

**West Tennessee**: Canton (Lauderdale County); Cherryville (Crockett County); Conyersville (Henry County); Egypt (Fayette County); Fisherville (Fayette County); Harrisburg (Haywood County); Hazel Flat (Shelby County); Macon (Fayette County); Middleburg (Hardeman County); Morning Sun (Shelby County); Mount Pinson (Madison County); Perryville (Decatur County); Portersville (Tipton County); Randolph (Tipton County); Trotters Landing (Benton County); Van Buren (Hardeman County).

# National Banner,
## AND NASHVILLE WHIG.

Volume XVII...Number 1180

Thursday, Novembe

SPLENDID FURNITURE.

THE HERALD.

FIRST CONVEYANCE
FOR NEW ORLEANS.

COMMISSION AND SHIPPING BUSINESS.

FOR SALE,

LAND FOR SALE.

DOCTOR YANDELL.

LAW NOTICE.

STOP THE THIEF AND RUNAWAY.

$50 REWARD.

$100 REWARD.

TRANSYLVANIA UNIVERSITY.
MEDICAL DEPARTMENT.

FOR SALE OR RENT

DISSOLUTION.

UNIVERSITY OF NASHVILLE.

WILSON & ROBERTSON,
Dry Goods and Commission Merchants,
PLAQUEMINE, LOUISIANA.

WILSON & ROBERTSON,

MISCELLANY

*National Banner*, November 4, 1830

# PART FIVE

# THE END OF SLAVERY

# LIFE OF REV. JERMAIN W. LOGUEN.

THE BIOGRAPHY OF REV. JERMAIN W. LOGUEN is already written by an able pen, and would be at once published but for the pecuniary responsibilities incident to its publication.

The undersigned therefore issue this Circular to the friends of Mr. Loguen and of the Underground Railroad, of which he has been, and still is, a faithful superintendent, to donate or subscribe for the publication. The amount of money to be raised to ensure its publication is $1,500—a sum quite too large for Mr. Loguen to assume consistent with his duties to the fugitive and to his family. We therefore invite the friends of Mr. Loguen and of the Slave, by way of donation or subscription, to make up the sum of one thousand dollars.

When $1,000 is thus subscribed, the Book will be immediately published, and the subscribers will receive the amount of their subscriptions in Books, if they wish. All over that sum Mr. Loguen will himself assume.

There are few men whose history is so marked with stirring incidents, instructive lessons, and encouraging examples, as Mr. Loguen's. It contains the peculiarities of Mr Loguen's childhood, his daring escape from bondage, the perils and hardships he endured in his passage to freedom, and the acts of subsequent manhood, which have honorably connected his name with the moral and political causes of the last twenty years, which, to a large extent, have made the subject of African Freedom the living topic of private and public circles, of the press, the pulpit, and the State and National Legislatures.

The Book will be about the size of the life of Frederick Douglass, in one volume, illustrated by a Steel Plate likeness of Mr. Loguen, and will be delivered to subscribers at the price of One Dollar. Subscriptions paid on delivery.

|  |  |
|---|---|
| Hon. A. P. GRANGER, | H. PUTNAM, |
| IRA H. COBB, | ABNER BATES, |
| ANSON G. CHESTER, | C. PRINDLE, |
| MOSES SUMMERS, | J. B. FOOTE, |
| WM. E. ABBOTT. | |

mh22 d1w

*Syracuse Daily Courier and Union*, March 24, 1859

CHAPTER TWENTY-ONE

# FIRST-PERSON ACCOUNTS

A person who can't read or write can't keep a diary or write memoirs. Because of this, we don't have nearly as many first-person accounts of life in slavery in Tennessee as we would like.

But there are some.

J.W. Loguen, who had been a slave in Tennessee from 1813 until 1834, published his memoirs in 1859. "Jarm," as J.W. was called in his slave days, was a typical "mulatto." His mother was a slave and his father was his slaveholder (David Logue, who lived near Mansker Creek in Davidson County).

When Jarm was about eight years old, David Logue sold about twenty of his slaves to his brother Mansasseth, who owned a plantation in southern Tennessee. The slaves didn't know this until they were shackled, handcuffed, and forced into a coffle. In his memoirs, J.W. Loguen described how it was that the slave traders were able to get the slaves into this coffle. "In the dead of night, when they were locked in sleep, the negro quarters were surrounded by stout men, armed with revolvers and shackles," Loguen wrote. "The strongest and bravest of the negroes were manacled in their slumbers--and because of the prospect of frantic agony, and desperate bravery, and strength of Cherry [Loguen's mother], they put the irons on her also, as the best means of managing her. The other women and children were easily secured."

Jarm was sent on the forced march along with the other slaves, through Nashville and Williamson County and to a plantation near the Maury County community of Bigbyville. He would remain a slave until he was 21, when he and another slave took two horses, ran away and made it to Canada. Later a minister in the American Methodist Episcopal Church, he published his autobiography in 1859.[1]

Shortly after his autobiography was published, J.W. Loguen received a remarkable letter from Sarah Logue, the widow of his former slaveholder. In the letter, Sarah Logue reported that Cherry [Loguen's mother] was still there, still a slave and "as well as common." However, Sarah said her family had fallen on hard times, in part because he had run away and taken their horses with him, and that they had sold J.W.'s brother Abe and sister Ann as a result. In the letter, Sarah Logue asked her former slave for a thousand dollars so that she would "give up all claim I have to you."

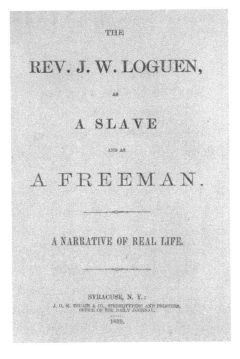

Here is an excerpt from Loguen's return letter:

"You say you have offers to buy me, and that you shall sell me if I do not send you $1,000, and in the same breath and almost in the same sentence, you say, 'you know we raised you as we did our own children.' Woman, did you raise your own children for the market? Did you raise them for the whipping-post? Did you raise them to be drove off in a coffle in chains?"

---

[1]He added an "N" to the end of the name Logue when he was in Canada, which is how he ended up with the name Loguen.

THIRTY YEARS A SLAVE.

From Bondage to Freedom.

THE INSTITUTION OF SLAVERY
AS SEEN ON THE PLANTATION AND
IN THE HOME OF THE PLANTER.

AUTOBIOGRAPHY OF LOUIS HUGHES.

MILWAUKEE:
SOUTH SIDE PRINTING COMPANY,
1897.

Another nationally read first-person account of life in bondage in Tennessee was Louis Hughes' 1897 autobiography *Thirty Years a Slave*. Hughes was born in Virginia in 1832 and sold twice as a boy—the first time away from his mother and the second time to a Mississippi planter named Edmund McGee. Hughes would remain with McGee through the Civil War, first on a Mississippi plantation, then in a Memphis mansion, then on a Bolivar-area plantation and then at a second Mississippi plantation. A house servant for much of his life as a slave, Hughes lived and worked under better conditions than most enslaved people. But McGee's wife beat her slaves frequently, according to Hughes, which prompted him to try to escape several times.

On his first try, Hughes stowed away on a boat that was hauling sugar and cotton and made it all the way to Indiana before he was caught and turned in (apparently for the reward money). Hughes was not beaten after that attempt. But he was after his second try, in which he hid on a ship that carried mail and cotton.

Describing what happened to him upon his return to the Hardeman County plantation, Hughes wrote:

> I was taken to the barn where stocks had been prepared, beside which were a cowhide and a pail of salt water, all prepared for me. It was terrible, but there was no escape. I was fastened in the stocks, my clothing removed, and the whipping began. Boss whipped me a while, then he sat down and read his paper, after which the whipping was resumed. This continued for two hours. Fastened as I was in the stocks, I could only

stand and take lash after lash, as long as he desired, the terrible rawhide cutting into my flesh at every stroke. Then he used peach tree switches, which cracked the flesh so the blood oozed out. After this came the paddle, two and a half feet long and three inches wide. Salt and water was at once applied to wash the wounds, and the smarting was maddening.

This torture was common among the southern planters. God only knows what I suffered under it all, and He alone gave me strength to endure it. I could hardly move after the terrible ordeal was finished, and could scarcely bear my clothes to touch me at first, so sore was my whole body, and it was weeks before I was myself again."

Hughes tried to escape two more times during the Civil War. Once he was captured by Confederate troops, who threatened to hang him but instead took him back to his slaveholder's plantation. Another time, Hughes tried to escape with several other people including his wife Mathilda. After several days of running through swamps and cotton fields, they were tracked down by a slave-catcher with hunting dogs. Again, he was beaten. Hughes didn't obtain his freedom until three months after the war ended (more on that later).

Years later, Hughes had this to say about his former slaveholder: "He [McGee] was in some respects kinder and more humane than many other slaveholders. He fed us well, and we had enough to wear, such as it was. . . But while my master showed these virtues, similar to those which a provident farmer would show in the care of his dumb brutes, he lacked in that humane feeling which should have kept him from buying and selling human beings and parting kindred - which should have made it impossible for him to have permitted the lashing, beating and lacerating of his slaves, much more the hiring of an irresponsible brute [the overseer], to perform this barbarous service for him."

In terms of first-person accounts of slavery in Tennessee, we also have the interviews conducted by Fisk researcher Ophelia Egypt in the 1920s and by the federal government in the 1930s. These interviews are not, however, easy to comprehend. They carry with them all the accuracy and consistency challenges that occur when elderly people are suddenly, and without a chance to think through their answer, asked about their childhood.

In addition, the federal government interviews in the late 1930s are difficult to read, since the transcribers chose to phonetically imitate the speech of interviewees by spelling words the way they were pronounced rather than the way they were spelled. "I claims I's 109 ye'ars ole en wuz bawn near Winchester, Tennessee," a slave narrative interview of Millie Simpkins of Nashville begins. "Mah marster wus named Judy Ewing en may daddy wuz Moses Stephens en he wuz 'free bawn.' He wuz de marster's stable boy en followed de races. He run 'way en nebber kum back." No American reporter could possibly get away with this in 2017.[2]

Because of this oddity, and because Ophelia Egypt did her interviews when former slaves would have been about ten years younger, I prefer Egypt's interviews. Here are summaries of what I consider to be three of her better ones:

Susanna was born in 1858 to free black parents who lived near Nashville's Public Square. In her interview, Susanna explained how her grandfather purchased not only his freedom, but that of his

---

[2] Former Tennessee Lieutenant Governor John Wilder was raised in rural Fayette County, had a strong accent and a very unusual and confusing way of speaking, exacerbated by the fact that he referred to himself in the third person. As a reporter for the *Tennessean* in the 1990s, I once attempted to quote him phonetically, when he told me that "We be in de sunshine; you be in de shade." My editors changed this quote to "We are in the sunshine, and you are in the shade." The accent and manner of speaking of the slaves interviewed by the federal government in the slave narratives program was not edited in this manner.

wife Catherine and daughter (Susanna's mother) in the 1830s. "His white folks hired him to the Nashville Inn," she said, referring to the long-standing hotel near the Davidson County Courthouse. "Every Saturday he would make about $5 or $10 and he would give to them [his slaveholders].

"He worked and worked, till I guess he paid them about $800 in all for himself. Then one day they sent for him and they said 'Well, Hardy, you are a free man; you can go anywhere you please, but you can't take Catherine.' Well, he was just like any other man, he wanted Catherine with him, so he turned 'round and the white folks made him pay the same for grandma."

Susanna said her grandfather then saved enough money to buy his three-year-old daughter. "Finally they charged him, now mind you, for his own child, they charged him $350."

Cornelia was the first name of another woman who was interviewed as part of the Fisk project. Cornelia said she had been brought up as a slave in "Eden" (the Gibson County community of Eaton) and that she and the rest of her family were the slaves of a man named Jennings. Her mother "cooked, washed, ironed, spun, nursed and labored in the field," while her father worked as a "yardman, houseman, plowman, gardener, blacksmith, carpenter, keysmith and anything else they chose him to be."

Cornelia said that there were times when her father and his slaveholder master acted like old friends, especially when they drank. "It was common to see them together, half drunk, with arms locked, walking around and around the old barn." Her mother, however, was not an ideal slave because she was "high spirited and independent." This trait manifested itself one day when her mother got in a physical fight with Jennings' wife, an event that led the family to send Cornelia's parents away to work in Memphis.

Seven decades after the event, Cornelia remembered vividly the day Mr. Jennings took her parents to Memphis. "I cannot tell in words the feelings I had at that time," she said. "My sorrow knew no bound. My very soul seemed to cry out, 'gone, gone, gone forever.' I cried until my eyes looked like balls of fire. I felt for the first time in my life that I had been abused. How cruel it was to take my mother and father away from me, I thought."

Another man (whose name was never revealed) said he was born in 1843 and had been a slave in Missouri, Mississippi and Tennessee. Like several of the interviewees, the man said his natural father was also his original slaveholder. "I was sold four times in my life," he said. "The first time by my half brother." The interviewee went on to say that at one of the auction houses in which he had been sold, "you could see the women crying about their babies and children they had left."

The elderly man had a remarkable memory when it came to Nashville geography. He recalled the locations of Fort Gilliam (present-day site of Fisk University) and the African-American institution known as Roger Williams University (present-day site of Vanderbilt's Peabody campus.) He also remembered the location of Nashville's main slave auction house—"right where the Morris Memorial Building is," he said referring to the headquarters of the National Baptist Convention at 330 Charlotte Avenue. "There was a sale block where they carried the Negroes there and auctioned them off."

... nice we would rate Bro. I would advise us when that "ginger-bread" arrangement is coming off for the benefit of a *certain old bachelor*. *Quilts* are quite convenient arrangements these *frosty* nights, and especially so when situated as Bro.——.

---

Thou shalt not *carry* off the Editor's exchanges unless thou *art* sure he is done with them, neither shalt thou *talk* to him when he is writing or reading proof, lest he get angry and pinch thee out of the sanctum.

---

☞ We learn from the American Presbyterian, Greeneville, that a negro belonging to Peter Earnest was killed on the 2d inst., while blasting rock on the railroad.

---

☞ Absalom Kyle Esq., of Hawkins county, died on the 27th ult. He was about 65 years of age—an enterprising man and valuable citizen.

---

☞ In the city of New York, it is stated there are some 50,000 children, between the ages of five and six years, attending the public schools, while the register shows an occasional attendance of 150,000 pupils. In other words, for every pupil who attends school there are two who are absent.

---

☞ The number of those who have died since the commencement of the christian era, is estimated at three billions one hundred and forty millions.

Australia. Ten thousand pounds have been subscribed in Australia to be presented to Smith O'Brien in the shape of a gold vase.

Governor Burt, of Nebraska died on the 18th

Collision.—The cars due yesterday morning says the Savannah *Republican* of Wednesday, did not arrive owing to a collision of trains that occured, five miles below Macon on Monday night. Thirteen cars were considerably damaged, but no person was injured. The Telegraph wires were disconnected by this occurence, in three different places, but have been repaired and the connection complete.

---

Moore and Richardson, of Cincinnati, have just completed three new locomotives for the Nashville & Chattanooga Railroad, of 22 tons each, and named, the "J. K. Polk," "John Bell," and "Andrew Jackson."

## MORAL CHARACTER.

There is nothing which adds so much to the beauty and power of a man as a good character. It dignifies him in every station, exalts him in every period of life. Such character is more to be desired than everything else on earth. No servile fool, no crouching sychophant treacherous honor-seeker, ever bore such a character; the pure joys of righteousness never spring in such a person. If young men but knew how much a good chatacter would dignify and exhalt them, how glorious it would make their prospects even in this life; never should we find them yielding to the groveling and base-born purposes of human nature.

---

Number of Slaves in the World.—The African Institution of Paris—an association for the diffusion of civillization and Christain light in Africa—has recently issued a circular which shows that the number of blacks held in slavery in different countries is seven and a half millions of which 3,095,000 are in the United States, 3,250,000 in Brazil, 900,000 in the Spanish colonies, 85,000 in Dutch colonies, 140,000 in the republics of Central America, and 80,000 in European establishments in Africa.

CHAPTER TWENTY-TWO

# SLAVERY IN CONTEXT

This book focuses on revelations about slavery which come from runaway slave advertisements and items that publicized the sale of slaves.

There are points to be drawn about slavery which don't fall into these two categories. Newspapers contain other items, ranging from the unexpected to the informative to the tragic.

Census numbers indicate that about two and a half percent of the 282,000 African Americans who lived in Tennessee by 1860 were free. These free blacks faced a series of economic and social challenges that effectively amounted to permanent harassment. Laws restricted their behavior, required them to carry written proof of their status, and mandated that they register with the county clerk. Free blacks also lived in constant fear that they might be kidnapped and sold as slaves in a far-away place.

One early example of this was documented in a March 1802 *Tennessee Gazette* story about Betsey Lucust, a free black woman living in Robertson County. The story said that her 17-year-old daughter had been kidnapped, taken to Natchez, Mississippi, and sold as a slave. "Any information concerning this unfortunate girl will be thankfully received by me, as I have from an impulse of humanity alone engaged to relieve her from her unjust bondage," said Nenian Edwards, who purchased the ad. "It is supposed an attempt may be made to send off three boys, children of the above-mentioned Betsey Lucust, the one aged about 15, the second 13, the third 11 years—all persons are cautioned against taking them away. It is hoped that after this notice no gentleman being about to descend the river, will receive either of them on board his boat."

Fear of being kidnapped was something slaves had to live with as well—especially those with children. In 1819, a slaveholder named Isaac Brunson offered $100 for the return of a slave named Jordan. "He is about five years old, and tolerably grown for that age; has a stoppage in his speech," the ad said. "He was stolen from the bed between his father and mother."

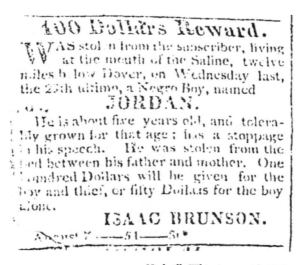

*Nashville Whig*, **August 14, 1819**

In the 1830s, a notorious lawbreaker from Williamson County named John Murrell (sometimes spelled Murel) became the most famous slave thief in the United States. In a book published in 1835, author Virgil Stewart gave a detailed description of Murrell and his group of several hundred lawbreakers, known as the Mystic Clan. The gang, it was said, operated from the Mississippi River all the way to Georgia and was especially active on the Natchez Trace, where it robbed and murdered travelers and mutilated their bodies. Murrell helped slaves to escape from bondage, only to trick them and sell them to another slave owner or trader. The book claimed that Murrell's gang had a "master plan" to organize a slave rebellion which was to have taken place on Christmas Day, 1835.

Books, articles and even movies were made about Murrell. Although many people believed Stewart's account, it was almost certainly a blatant exaggeration that was no more accurate than the fictionalized accounts of David Crockett published at the time. The most serious crime that Murrell was ever convicted of was slave theft, not inciting slaves to rebellion. Present-day historians are inclined to believe that slaveholders and Southern newspapers promoted and exaggerated Murrell's crimes to discourage slaves from being lured away by abolitionist whites.[1]

It should also be pointed out that there was a fine line between slave theft and elopement (even though both would have been regarded legally as slave theft). An interesting example of this was detailed in the April 1836 *Memphis Enquirer*. "My overseer, Bedford Easley, absconded from my plantation ten miles north of Somerville, on the 2d April, taking with him a black girl about 17 or 18 years of age," slaveholder B.W. Patterson of Fayette County wrote. "They both left the same night and

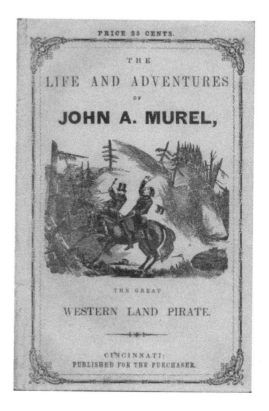

PRICE 25 CENTS.

THE

LIFE AND ADVENTURES

OF

**JOHN A. MUREL,**

THE GREAT

WESTERN LAND PIRATE.

CINCINNATI;
PUBLISHED FOR THE PURCHASER.

[1] The Tennessee State Museum collection includes a human thumb known as "John Murrell's thumb." Once widely believed to be the thumb of the outlaw, more likely explanation is that the thumb was taken from a cadaver by medical school students in the early 1900s and donated to the museum as a joke.

> ## Stop the Kidnapper.
> **$100** REWARD. My overseer, Benford Easley, absconded from my planta-tion ten miles north of Somerville, on the 2d April, taking with him a black girl about 17 or 18 years of age: They both left the same night and no doubt as above. Easley is about 5 feet 6 or 8 inch-es high, 30 years old, has black eyes and is some-what humpbacked; he wore when he left a blue cassinet coat and black broad brimmed hat; the girl took off a large bundle of clothes—she is rather darker than copper-color. I expect he will attempt to get on board a steam boat or cross the Mississip-pi, between Memphis and Randolph. Easley uses very bad language, and can neither read nor write. I will give the above reward for them both, or 50 dollars for the girl, if taken out of the State, with all reasonable expenses paid if delivered to me or con-fined in any jail that I may get her.
> April 5th.—3-tf  B. W. WILLIAMSON.

*Memphis Enquirer, April 5, 1836*

no doubt as above. . . I expect he will attempt to get on board a steam boat or cross the Mississippi, between Memphis and Randolph. Easley uses very bad language, and can neither read nor write. I will give the above reward for them both."

We will never know for sure what Easley's intentions were, but we do know that most white Tennesseans of that era were horrified at the idea of interracial marriage, as reflected in this item in the 1852 *Murfreesborough Telegraph*: "A loving couple—an Irishman and a negro girl belonging to Mrs. Eakin of Shelbyville, eloped together a few days ago. The parties came to this place, and took stage for Chattanooga. They were pursued and overhauled on the Cumberland Mountains, bro't back to this place, and sent over to Shelbyville. Shakespeare says 'the course of true love never did run smooth'."

The *Clarksville Jeffersonian* took a harsher tone regarding such matters. "A negro named Kennedy was Monday on trial before the recorder, charged with violating one of the commandments with an abandoned white woman who lives in gallows hollow," reported the *Jeffersonian* in 1856. "Corrections intended to bring him to a sense of the enormity of his conduct, and the differences between white and black, were ordered to be administered."

In 1858, DeKalb County resident Henry Frazier ran an ad in a Nashville newspaper offering $50 for the apprehension of Jackson Hunt, a free black man who "is accompanied by a white girl, my [15-year-old] daughter, whom he abducted and is running away with; and it is supposed they are aiming to make way for a free state." Frazier said that they left his house a few days earlier and asked readers to sympathize with a "distressed family."

In the 1840s and 1850s, practically all Tennessee newspapers held pro-slavery views. However, items occasionally made the newspaper that indicated there were people in the newsrooms who felt sympathy for the slave.

In 1854, for instance, a case of a man who beat a slave to death made the *Nashville Union and American*. The newspaper reported that Thomas Mathias whipped a slave named Tazewell to death while both were working on the construction of the state lunatic asylum (later the Tennessee Hospital for the Insane). "It appears that Mathias has the contract for making brick to complete the lunatic asylum, and

**$50 REWARD,**

I WILL give a reward of **FIFTY DOLLARS** for the apprehension and confinement in some Jail, so that I can get him, of a certain free negro, named Jackson Hunt, or Hilliard, raised in DeKalb county, Tennessee, having free papers from said county.

Said boy is about 5 feet 10 inches high, dark mulatto color, spare made, weighs about 140 or 150 pounds, good countenance, steps short in walking, aged about 20 years; had on when last seen by me, new black clothing and probably a bluish hat.

Said boy is accompanied by a white girl, my daughter, whom he abducted and is running away with; and it is supposed they are aiming to make their way to a free State.

My daughter, named Harriet, is about 15 years old, well grown for that age, weighs about 130 or 140 pounds, fair complexion, slightly freckled, rather coarse featured, hazel eyes, dark or brown hair; can read print well, and writing, poorly; had on when she left, a black shawl with a flower in one corner of it and a home-made cotton dress, and with her, in a home-made satchel, two worsted dresses alike.

They left my house, seven miles west of Smithville, DeKalb county, Tennessee, about dark, Tuesday evening, November 23, 1858. I also wish my daughter confined so that I can get possession of her.

Papers throughout the country, sympathizing with a distressed family, will please notice. HENRY FRAZER,
nov27—dtw&w3w Smithville, Tennessee.

*Nashville Union and American,* **December 3, 1858**

that the negro, who was in his employ, had neglected or refused to do some work which Mathias had ordered him to do on Sunday, and for which negligence or disobedience he was chastised by Mathias Tuesday morning," the story in the *Union and American* said.

"At dinner time the negro attempted to go off, but was brought back, whereupon Mathias took him into the woods and inflicted the punishment which resulted in his death. . . Mathias has made his escape. We hope he may be arrested and a full measure of justice meted out to him." I could find no stories in later issues of the paper about this crime.

News of slave deaths on the job are rare. In fact, the only times in which I could find slave deaths mentioned in newspapers come after the mid 1840s.

On November 8, 1854, the *Loudon Free Press* reported that a slave belonging to Peter Earnest was killed "while blasting rock on the railroad." As was the case in the accidental death at the state Capitol quarry, the slave's name was not given.

Five years later, the *Fayetteville Observer* reported that "Isaac, a negro man belonging to Mr. G.M. Steele, was so badly injured at the steam saw mill, six miles southeast of this place, by being caught in the machinery, last Saturday, that he died the following day."

Starting in the 1840s, slave suicides occasionally made the newspaper. "A negro woman who was arrested a few nights ago by one of the town watch as a runaway hung herself in jail yesterday morning," the (Nashville) *Republican Banner* reported in 1843. No other details were given.

Eight years later, the *Athens Post* had a small item stating "Nothing of importance since our last issue. A negro, committed to jail as a runaway, cut his throat on Monday evening, and a pair of horses attached to a wood wagon made a break on Tuesday. – No damage done in the latter case, except arousing the captain and first lieutenant of the loafers from their afternoon siesta."

☞ The Literary Societies of the University of Nashville will celebrate their Anniversary on Tuesday, 4th April, at the Baptist Church on Summer street. The Address will be delivered by A. P. Maury, Esq.— Exercises to commence at half past 9 o'clock, A. M.—*Whig.*

☞ A negro woman who was arrested a few nights ago by one of the town watch as a runaway, hung herself in jail yesterday morning.--*Ib.*

*Republican Banner*, March 31, 1843

The *Nashville Daily Patriot* reported in 1855 that "A valuable negro man, belonging to Mr. Chas Porter, residing a few miles west of Franklin, hung himself on Monday night of last week." A few days later, the *Republican Banner* stated that "A negro girl named Louisa, a slave, committed suicide on Thursday by drowning herself in a pool of water near the Reservoir in this city."

Two years later, the *Republican Banner* had a revealing story about the death of an elderly male slave. "An old negro belonging to a citizen of Edgefield fell down in an apolectic fit in the market house Saturday evening," the story said. "He was taken to an office nearby, and was subsequently removed to the workhouse, where medical aid was called in, and every attention was paid to him.

**Republican Banner Steam Press.**

V. F. Bang.    H. K. Walker.    J. Roberts.

**BANG, WALKER & CO.**

HAVING SUPPLIED OUR OFFICE WITH

**A New Adams Power Press,**

AND

**RUGGLES JOB PRESS.**

With all the Late Improvements, and with a Complete Assortment of **New Type,** and having also applied Steam to our Machinery, we are prepared to execute with despatch, all orders for

BOOKS, PAMPHLETS,
ILL-HEADS,    CIRCULARS,
RAILROAD WORK,    STEAMBOAT WORK
BILLS,    CARDS,
FUNERAL TICKETS,

In short, every description of Plain and Fancy Printing that may be desired, at short notice and in the best style of the art.    **Bang, Walker & Co.,**

FOR MAYOR;
**S. N. HOLLINGSWORTH.**

**MONDAY, SEPTEMBER 19, 1859.**

YESTERDAY was a delightful day, and the city as full of "bustle" as a B.-hive in mid summer.

SUICIDE.—A negro girl named *Louisa,* a slave, committed suicide on Thursday by drowning herself in a pool of water near the Reservoir in this city.

*Republican Banner*, **September 19, 1859**

"The negro died during the night and the next day the body was taken to the residence of the owner of the negro, in Edgefield, who refused to receive a 'dead negro.' The parties who carried the body of the negro over the river quietly took it from the vehicle and deposited it in the yard of the owner of the slave.

"The affair became known, and created a little stir in the village of Edgefield—the good citizens over there believing their beautiful village was to be made the Potter's field of Nashville. A coroner's inquest was held, and the examination of the witnesses satisfied all that no such indignity was intended by the workhouse officers, and that it was the duty of the owner of the slave to have his remains decently interred."

## Committed to Jail

OF Davidson county, April 21st, 1862, a negro man, who says his name is LEWIS, and belongs to Josiah McClane, of Lebanon, Tenn. The said man is 5 feet, 10 inches high, about 42 years old, black and heavy sett. The owner is requested to come forward, prove property, and pay charges, as the law directs.
JAMES M. HINTON,
April 23—3t　　Sheriff and Jailor, D. C.

## Committed to Jail

OF Davidson county, April 21st, 1862, a negro woman, who says her name is MAMINDA, and belongs to Wm. C. Brown, of Davidson county, aged about 42 years; 5 feet, 3 inches high, copper color.— The owner is requested to come forward, prove property and pay charges, as the law directs.
JAMES M. HINTON,
April 23—3t　　Sheriff and Jailor, D. C.

## Committed to Jail

OF Davidson county, on the 18th of April, 1862, as a runaway, a negro man who says his name is Jordan, and belongs to W. Talley, of Montgomery county, Tenn. 28 years old, scar in the right corner of the right eye; 5 feet 4 inches high; weighs about 165 pounds. The owner is requested to come forward, prove property and pay charges as the law directs.
J. M. HINTON,
April 29th—3t　　Sheriff and Jailor of D. C.

## Committed to Jail

OF Davidson county, on March the 8th, 1862, as a runaway, a negro man, named Robert; says he belongs to W. Burke, of Jefferson county, Miss.; about 32 years old, weighs about 145 pounds, copper color, 5 feet 8 inches high. The owner is requested to come forward, prove property and pay charges as the law directs.
J. M. HINTON,
April 29th—3t　　Sheriff and Jailor of D. C.

## Committed to Jail

OF Davidson county, on the 6th of April, 1862, a negro man named Willis, says he belongs to Mrs. Marina Cheatham, of Davidson county; 19 years old, dark complexion, 6 feet high, weighs 160 or 170 pounds. The owner is requested to come forward, prove property and pay charges as the law directs.
J. M. HINTON,
April 29th—3t　　Sheriff and Jailor of D. C.

## Committed to Jail

OF Davidson county, April 12, 1862 a negro man who says his name is ALBERT; says he belongs to Henry Heed, of Davidson county; about 29 years old, weighs about 165 pounds, 6 feet high, mulatto color. The owner is requested to come forward, prove property and pay charges as the law directs.
J. M. HINTON,
April 29th—3t　　Sheriff and Jailor of D. C.

## Committed to Jail

OF Davidson county, April 15, 1862, a negro man who says his name is HORACE; says he belongs to A. O. P. Nicholson, of Maury county, weighs about 160 pounds, about 24 years old, dark complexion, 5 feet 6 inches high. The owner is requested to come forward, prove property and pay charges as the law directs.
J. M. HINTON,
April 29th—3t　　Sheriff and Jailor of D. C.

## Committed to Jail

OF Davidson county, March 6, 1862, a negro man who says his name is CLARK; says he belongs to Hugh Kirkpatrick, of Cumberland county, Kentucky; dark copper color, weighs about 190 pounds, 6 feet 3 inches high. The owner is requested to come forward, prove property and pay charges as the law directs.
J. M. HINTON,
April 29th—3t　　Sheriff and Jailor of D. C.

## Committed to Jail

OF Davidson county, April 5, 1862, a negro man, who says his name is BILL; says he belongs to Spencer McHenry of Overton county, Tennessee; he about twenty-one years old, and weighs about 150 pounds; small scar on each eye brow; small scar on the end of his nose; 5 feet 10 inches high; bushy head of hair; dark complexion. The owner is requested to come forward, prove property, and pay charges, as the law directs.
J. M. HINTON,
Ap. 11 (?)　　Sheriff, &c. &c. &c. &c.

## Committed to Jail

OF Davidson county; about 48 years old; weighs about 180 pounds; scar on the nose; also one under the right eye; 5 feet 10 inches high. The owner is requested to come forward, prove property, and pay charges, as the law directs.
J. M. HINTON,
April 20—3t　　Sheriff and Jailor of D. C.

## Committed to Jail

OF Davidson county, April 17, 1862, a negro man, who says his name is NAT, and belongs to Mases Buchanan, of Rutherford county; said boy is about 23 years old; weighs about 140 pounds; mulatto color; 6 feet 2 inches high; two scars, one above and one below the left eye. The owner is requested to come forward, prove property, and pay charges, as the law directs.
J. M. HINTON,
April 20—3t　　Sheriff and Jailor of D. C.

## Committed to Jail

OF Davidson county, March 6, 1862, a negro man, who says his name is GEORGE, and belongs to Hugh Kirkpatrick, of Cumberland county, Ky.; about 18 or 19 years old; dark copper color; weighs about 145 pounds, 5 feet 8 inches high; scar on the left side of neck, from burn. The owner is requested to come forward, prove property, and pay charges, as the law directs.
J. M. HINTON,
April 20—3t　　Sheriff and Jailor of D. C.

## Committed to Jail

OF Davidson county, April 6, 1862, a negro man, who says his name is ALFRED; says he belongs to Mrs. Elizabeth Portee, of Hickman county, Tenn. about 25 years old; weighs about 165 pounds; dark copper color; 5 feet 10 inches high. The owner is requested to come forward, prove property, and pay charges, as the law directs.
J. M. HINTON,
April 20—3t　　Sheriff and Jailor of D. C.

## Committed to Jail

OF Davidson county, April 6, 1862, a negro man, who says that his name is ALBERT; he says that he belongs to Benjamin Halen, of Maury county, Tennessee; about 21 years old; bright mulatto, weighs about 145 or 150 pounds; 5 feet 11 inches high; long, bushy hair. The owner is requested to come forward, prove property, and pay charges, as the law directs.
J. M. HINTON,
April 20—3t　　Sheriff and Jailor of D. C.

## Committed to Jail

OF Davidson county, April 7, 1862, a negro man, who says his name is GEORGE, and belongs to Captain William Kirn, of Warren county, Mississippi; said boy is about 27 years old; weighs about 160 pounds; dark complexion; left hand has been badly burnt; 5 feet 10 inches high. The owner is requested to come forward, prove property, and pay charges, as the law directs.
J. M. HINTON,
Ap. 20—3t　　Sheriff and Jailor of D. C.

## Committed to Jail

OF Davidson county, March 14, 1862, a negro man, who says his name is ALFRED, and belongs to Mrs. Eliza Tay or, of Montgomery county, Tenn.; said boy is about 40 or 45 years old; weighs about 175 pounds; small scar in the center of his forehead, and one in front of his left ear; 5 feet 1 inch high. The owner is requested to come forward, prove property, and pay charges, as the law directs.
J. M. HINTON,
Ap. 20—3t　　Sheriff and Jailor of D. C.

## Committed to Jail

OF Davidson county, April 17, 1862, a negro man, who says his name is GEORGE, and belongs to Henry Heed, of Davidson County; about 35 years of age; weighs about 150 or 160 pounds; copper color; 5 feet 9 inches high. The owner is requested to come forward, prove property, and pay charges, as the law directs.
J. M. HINTON,
Ap. 20—3t　　Sheriff and Jailor of D. C.

## Committed to Jail

OF Davidson county, April 4, 1862, a negro man who says his name is JOE BARTLETT, and who claims to be a free man of color; about 24 years old; says he lives in Henry county, Ky.; light copper color; scar on right side of the neck; weighs about 145 or 150 pounds; 5 feet 1 inch high.
J. M. HINTON,
April 20—3t　　Sheriff and Jailor of D. C.

*Nashville Daily Union*, May 11, 1862

216

## CHAPTER TWENTY-THREE

# SLAVERY IN THE CIVIL WAR (PART ONE)

It was February 1862. The Union Army marched over from Fort Donelson. Once in Nashville, General Don Carlos Buell accepted the surrender of the city. A few hours later a local shopkeeper and unionist named William Driver walked up to the Capitol and presented to Union General William "Bull" Nelson an American flag which he had kept hidden in a quilt for the previous few months. "This is the flag I hope to see hoisted on that flagstaff in place of the [damned] Confederate flag set there by that [damned] rebel governor," Driver told him. Nelson ordered an Ohio regiment to do what Driver asked, and some of the soldiers from Ohio cried for joy when it was raised. A band played the "Battle Hymn of the Republic." Slavery was no more in Tennessee.

It would make for a great movie scene. But a quick glance at Tennessee's newspapers proves that it wasn't this simple. Tennessee was a large state. Emancipation came piecemeal, and no one was sure exactly what was going to happen. Nothing brings this reality to life more than a glance through the papers.

Let's start with Nashville. Throughout 1861, sheriffs remained busy locking up runaway slaves. In Davidson County, Sheriff James M. Hinton caught maybe two or three runaways every week through 1861—a slight

## Proclamation to Free Negroes.

I AM requirsed by the laws of the State to make return to the Governor, of the number of free males of color in the county of Davidson, betwen the ages of fifteen and fifty years.

I am also instructed to make return of all persons of the above descripeion who are willing to volunteer their services in the Army of the State in the capacity of servants or blaorers. All such are, therefore, required to report themselves to me, at my office in the City of Nashville, within the next ten days. Their pay from the Government will be eight dollars per month, rations and clothing furnished. To all who will volunteer, I think I can say that their pay will be increased, and that they will be well protected and cared for while in the service.

J. K. EDMUNDSON, Sheriff.

July 31—10d

*Nashville Daily Patriot,* **August 4, 1861**

increase from before the war, but not much. We know this because Hinton had to run an ad in the newspaper every time he caught one, headed by the ubiquitous headline "Committed to Jail."

Additionally, sheriffs were busy complying with a new law passed by the Confederate government that required all free African-American men between the ages of 15 and 50 to register. Free blacks were also asked to volunteer their services in the army as servants or laborers. "Their pay from the Government will be eight dollars per month, rations and clothing furnished," the ad from Davidson County sheriff J.K. Edmundson stated. "To all who will volunteer, I think I can say that their pay will be increased, and that they will be well protected and cared for while in the service."

## Wanted,

**20** NEGRO Men and 20 Negro Women for nurses for the various Confederate States Hospitals in this city, By order of Dr. D. W. Yandell.  GEO. H. CLARK,

nov20—tf  Office No. 50 College street

*Nashville Union and American,* **December 21, 1861**

Rees W. Porter, Nashville's best-known slave trader in the 1850s, appears to have left town by this time. However, there were still several slave trading firms in Nashville in 1861. One was Webb, Merrill & Co.

at No. 8 South Market Street. In its many newspaper advertisements, the firm promised to "at all times, purchase NEGROES suited to the New Orleans market. Other descriptions sold on consignment." Another Nashville slave trading firm still active was H.H. Haynes & Co. at 15 Cedar Street, between the Public Square and the Commercial Hotel. A typical H.H. Haynes ad advertised a "Negro Girl For Sale. . . Her owner is obliged to have money. A bargain may be had."

Elsewhere in Middle Tennessee there were other signs that, when it came to slavery, nothing had changed. On July 6, 1861, Stewart County Clerk and Master A.B Ross sold a "7 or 8" year old slave boy named Lafayette at the courthouse in Dover. On September 2, Dickson County Clerk and Master H.C. Collier sold two slaves (age unpublished) at the courthouse in Charlotte. On December 21, Davidson County Clerk and Master J.E. Gleaves sold seven slaves at the courthouse—"Rachel, a woman aged 45 to 50 years; Hart, aged 13; Ambrose, 11; Nathan, 8, Arthur, 5; Ben, 3 and Thomas, 1." This Davidson County sale was one of the few times in Tennessee legal history that a clerk and master publicly stated his intention to keep a woman and her children together. "Rachel and Arthur, Ben and Thomas to be sold in one lot," the ad stated. But the ad made no mention of any special consideration for Hart, Ambrose or Nathan, who were probably Rachel's children as well.

### Negro for Sale.

Pursuant to a decree of the Stewart County Circuit Court, made at the November term, 1860, in the cause of A. P. Stilley and others, against Mary Jane Brandon and others, I will, on Saturday, the 6th day of July next, at the Court-house door in Dover, sell, to the highest bidder, a negro boy named Lafayette, about 7 or 8 years old, belonging to the estate of Wm. Brandon, deceased.

TERMS: Cash sufficient to pay expense of sale and the balance on a credit of 12 months, with a note bearing interest from date, with two good securities, and retaining a lien upon the negro until the purchase money shall be paid.

A. B. ROSS, C. & M.

May 31, 1861-4w-pr fee $3 20.

*Clarksville Chronicle,* June 7, 1861

On February 1, 1862, slaveholders John and Hugh Ewing ran an ad in the *Nashville Union and American* offering a $100 reward for return of a female runaway named Tennessee. "[She] has a large nose, one or two front teeth missing, smokes tobacco and drinks whisky, looks young," the ad said, further opining that she was being harbored in Nashville or Edgefield.

"Her husband, Cyrus, lives at Ann Richardson's, in Hartsville. We will pay $50 reward for her, if caught and lodged in Haynes' negro yard; and fifty dollars will be paid for evidence sufficient to convict the free negro or white person who has been harboring her."

The U.S. Army invaded Nashville a week after its victory at Fort Donelson and held the city for the rest of the war. Slavery remained legal, and authorities recognized slaveholders as the rightful owners of their slaves just as before. However, Nashville's newspapers clearly reflect the fact that slaves were leaving their slaveholders in numbers never seen before. In March and April, Davidson County Sheriff J.M. Hinton could hardly keep up with the large number of runaway slaves—let alone with the mandatory reporting requirements inherent when runaway slaves were caught. The four-page issue of the May 11, 1862, *Daily Nashville Union* newspaper contains nearly 40 different "slave apprehended" ads.

In alphabetical order, here are the names and places of origin of the slaves in custody at that time.

1. Albert (Benjamin Halan of Maury County)
2. Albert (Joseph Dodson of Davidson County)
3. Albert and George (Henry Blood of Davidson County)
4. Alfred (Elizabeth Porter of Hickman County)
5. Alfred (Eliza Taylor of Montgomery County)
6. Andrew (R.L. Brown of Davidson County)
7. Bill (Spencer McHenry of Overton County)
8. Charles (Joseph Campbell of Todd County, Kentucky)
9. Clark, George and Martin (Hugh Kirkpatrick of Cumberland County, Kentucky)
10. George (Ann Lanier of Davidson County)
11. George (Lewis Lindsley of Wilson County)
12. George (William Rurm of Warren County, Mississippi)
13. Henry (J. Wilboorn of Marshall County)
14. Henry (Buck Martin of Davidson County)

15. Horace (A.O.P. Nicholson of Maury County)
16. Jackson (Noah Criswell of Davidson County)
17. Jerry (Thomas Henry of Williamson County)
18. John (Fount Mosbey of Rutherford County)
19. John (Flavor Cooper of Maury County)
20. John (Reese Alexander of Maury County)
21. Jordan (W. Talley of Montgomery County)
22. Lewis (Zebulon Baird of Wilson County)
23. Lucinda (William Donelson of Davidson County)
24. Malvina (John Overton of Davidson County)
25. Marinda (William C. Brown of Davidson County)
26. Nat (Moses Buchanan of Rutherford County)
27. Randall, Jim and Lewis (Josiah McClane of Wilson County)
28. Robert (W. Burke of Jefferson County, Miss.)
29. Simon and Sam (Robert Owen of Williamson County)
30. Willis (Marina Cheatham of Davidson County)
31. Winnie and her two children, Adolphus and Charles (Sarah Allen of Rutherford County)

One wonders how Sheriff Hinton found beds for all these people, let alone food to feed them!

# One Hundred Dollars Reward!

IN FEBRUARY LAST I HAD TWO NEGRO MEN to run away on a boat from Clarksville, by the names of FOSTER and EDMUND. Said boys left Clarksville a few days after the Federal troops took possession of the place.

Edmund is about 6 feet, and weighs 160 or 170 pounds, and is 23 or 24 years old, and of dark complexion. Foster is 5½ feet high, and is of yellow complexion, and will weigh 140 or 150 pounds, and is about 22 or 23 years old. When they were heard from last they were in Gen. McCook's division.

I will give the above Reward to any one if they will bring them to me in the City of Nashville.

WM. S. CHEATHAM.

Nashville, Tenn., August 7th, 1862.          aug7-1m

*Nashville Daily Union*, August 8, 1862

In spite of this obvious sign that something had changed, runaway slave ads and slave sale ads continued to run through the end of 1862. On August 8, 1862, the *Nashville Daily Union* published several slave-related ads. One, purchased by Nashville alderman William S. Cheatham, offered a $100 reward for the return of two slaves named Foster and Edmund—both of whom appear to have joined the U.S. Army division of General Alexander McCook. The second, also paid for by Alderman Cheatham, offered to hire out a negro slave. The third, signed by Robert Cato, offered $50 for the return of a slave named Tilmon. All the while, Sheriff Hinton continued to round up runaway slaves, announcing new ones on September 7, 9, 11 and 12.

On September 20, after the Battle of Antietam, President Lincoln signed the Emancipation Proclamation. It was, and remains, one of the most misunderstood documents in American history. The proclamation declared that "any slaves in states not under Union control" as of January 1, 1863, would be free as of that date. In other words, it theoretically freed slaves in states such as Georgia, Alabama and North Carolina – over which the U.S. government had no control at that time. However, it did not free slaves in states such as Maryland, Delaware and Kentucky, where the U.S government did have control.

Secretary of State William Seward—who detested slavery from the moment he saw a slave coffle of children being marched through Virginia—was one of Lincoln's many Cabinet members dissatisfied with the proclamation. "We show our sympathy with slavery by emancipating slaves where we cannot reach them and holding them in bondage where we can set them free," Seward said.

To further add to the confusion, Lincoln specifically exempted Tennessee from the Emancipation Proclamation at the request of Governor Andrew Johnson and other leaders. Why? Because Tennessee was not under Confederate control in the fall of 1862 (at least in the opinion of the Lincoln administration).

Regardless of whether Tennessee was exempt from the Emancipation Proclamation, slave-related ads nearly vanished from Nashville's newspapers after Lincoln's announcement. After September 1862, the "Committed to Jail" items listing runaways ceased being published. This change doesn't, on its own, prove that emancipation came to Nashville. But it does seem to indicate that the authorities in the government were no longer allocating their resources to returning runaways to their slaveholders.

After January 1, 1863, the status of slaves in and around Nashville was a very confusing matter. On February 22, E.A. Herman offered $50 for the return of a "servant" named Bill in a *Nashville Daily Union* advertisement. "Why he left me I know not; he had a good home, and was indulged as much as possible for a servant to be," Herman wrote. This may have been the last runaway slave ad ever published in Nashville.

Meanwhile, news items that ran throughout 1863 hint that the city was being overwhelmed by refugee slaves. They also indicate that authorities weren't exactly sure what to do with them. "The law in regard to runaway slaves cannot now be enforced in every particular, owing to the fact that some slaves are in our city while their owners are in the Southern Confederacy, and the enforcement of said law would come in conflict with Mr. Lincoln's Emancipation Proclamation," the *Daily Union* said in a story about the city council.

length. It was thought that the law in regard to runaway slaves cannot now be enforced in every particular, owing to the fact that some slaves are in our city while their owners are in the Southern Confederacy, and the enforcement of said law would come in conflict with Mr. Lincoln's Emancipation Proclamation.

*Nashville Daily Union*, **Feb. 27, 1863**

In May 1863, President Lincoln declared that black males could enlist in the Union Army. At first, this change in federal policy doesn't appear to have resulted in any major changes in Nashville, because in June, the Nashville City Council passed a resolution asking military authorities to "put" runaway slaves in the army to work "on fortifications, in hospitals, on railroads, or some other public work." (The council, now a body of mainly pro-union men, passed the resolution 6-1). In September, U.S. Army Major George Stearns established a recruiting station for colored troops at 38 Cedar Street—a location within sight of two of Nashville's old slave trading yards.

4th. And whereas, a large, unprecedented collection of runaway slaves, contrabands and free negroes, without profitable occupations, or place of residence, and without means of subsistence, now infest the city and vicinity, in gross violation of the State and Municipal laws, a source of great annoyance to the citizens: Therefore, we earnestly suggest and request the military authorities to take charge of and control said negroes, at least so far as practicable, put them in the army, to work on the fortifications, in hospitals, on railroads, or some other public work for the Government, or suffer and permit the civil and municipal authorities to enforce the law in reference to said negroes; but not in such manner, as to aid or assist rebel owners or claimants in repossessing themselves of said slaves, or their services, or their hire.

The vote by which the foregoing preamble and resolutions were adopted is as follows:

YEAS—Messrs. Brien, Carper, Claiborne, Mayfield, Scovel, and Smith.

NAYS—Mr. Cheatham.

*Nashville Union,* June 25, 1863

By this time, the *Daily Union* had this to say about the status of slavery in Tennessee's capital:

"In a speech in Rockville, Maryland, some days since, ex-Governor Thomas said that slavery is effectively dead in that State . . . What Governor Thomas says of slavery in Maryland is equally true of slavery in Tennessee. No slave here can be compelled to work for his 'owner' against his will, nor can a slave be made to remain with his owner unless he chooses to do so. Whenever the slave is dissatisfied with his home, he walks off, as freely as a black man would in a Northern State, or in Europe. The slave code is dead; and the master has no longer absolute control over the body and limbs of his former bondsman."

Moving 40 miles southeast of Nashville, a Murfreesboro newspaper called the *Daily Rebel Banner* was still being printed as Christmas 1862 approached. On December 23, the *Daily Rebel* ran an ad purchased by a company called S.R. McCaney & Co. "WANTED—FIFTY able bodied negro men needed to work in a pork house, for which two dollars per day and board will be paid," the ad stated. Slaves were still around; slaveholders were still around; and the practice of "hiring out" slaves was still around—at least in the opinion of a Murfreesboro newspaper and slaveholders who read it.

Murfreesboro *Daily Rebel Banner*, January 1, 1863

The U.S. Army was also still around. On December 30, a battle broke out in the fields northwest of Murfreesboro, near the banks of Stones River. The Confederate Army prevailed that day but, as is the case with many Civil War battles, the Union Army would have its way on subsequent days. As a result, the *Daily Rebel* would no longer be printed in Murfreesboro. It, like the Confederate army, moved southeast.

CHAPTER TWENTY-FOUR

# SLAVERY IN THE CIVIL WAR (PART TWO)

Slave-related ads practically vanished from Nashville after President Lincoln issued the Emancipation Proclamation, but they didn't vanish from newspapers in the rest of the state. In small towns throughout Tennessee, in Knoxville, Chattanooga and Memphis, slavery continued as openly and publicly as before. Evidence suggests that emancipation came with the advance of the U.S. Army.

> **RANAWAY**
>
> FROM James M. Wordan, on Friday night last, a NEGRO MAN named GEORGE, full 6 feet high, dark ginger-cake complection, rather quick spoken, a close observer will notice a slight stammering in his speech, had on when left a brown janes coat, smartly worn, brown jane pants, an old fur hat much worn. Said Negro belongs to the estate of Robert Wordan, deceased. A reward of $40 will be paid for the apprehension and delivery of said boy to the subscriber, 4 miles north-east of Fayetteville, or $30 if apprehended in the country, and information directed to the subscriber.
> JOHN H. STEELMAN, *Admr.*
> April 30, 1863—2t
> Said boy will probably attempt to make his way to the Federal lines.

*Fayetteville Observer*, April 30, 1863

Two Middle Tennessee newspapers that clearly reflect this trend were the *Winchester Daily Bulletin* and *Fayetteville Observer*. The *Daily Bulletin* published at least three runaway slave ads in the spring of 1863. One was for an 18-year-old female named Dolly, who ran away from the town of Cowan; the second for 19-year-old Jane, who left from Decherd; the third for two men named Tom and John, who ran away from Winchester.

We also know that Independence Day, although probably not celebrated as the birthday of the United States government, was memorable in Fayetteville. On July 4, 1863, Lincoln County Clerk and Master Daniel J. Whittington stood on the courthouse steps and sold three slaves—a 20-year-old woman named Delia and her two young sons. Three weeks later, Whittington stood there again and sold eight more slaves, six of whom were children.

Meanwhile, two hundred miles east of Fayetteville, the *Knoxville Daily Register* could hardly keep up with the demand for advertising related to slavery. On November 8, 1862, the *Register*

$500 REWARD.— RUNAWAY FROM THE subscribers on the night of the 6th of October, four miles west of Campbell Station, Knox county, Tenn., FIVE NEGRO BOYS, viz: NED—about 34 years old, 5 feet 8 inches high, black, a low brow, with a nick out of one of his front teeth, quick spoken, great fellow to laugh, weighs about 150 pounds. FED—about 20 years old, 5 feet 10 inches high, copper color, his head unusually long and long faced, rather dull, slow spoken, rather impudent, weighs about 160 pounds. ALBERT—about 20 years old, 5 feet 9 inches high, weighs about 150 pounds, copper color, long curly hair, open countenance, slow spoken, rather impudent. LEVIS—about 21 years old, 5 feet 10 inches high, weighs about 165 pounds, black, a little stooped, slow spoken, down countenance—was raised in Clinton. HENRY—about 20 years old, weighs [...] We believe that they are aiming to get to the North or with the robbers in the mountains. We will pay the above reward for the apprehension and delivery of said boys to their owners, or one hundred for either one of them, or seventy-five each, if lodged in any jail in the State, or fifty each if lodged in any jail out of the State, so that we can get them.

NINIAN STEELE.
J. G. H. EDIN.
R. W. HARDIN.
oct1&1w

*Knoxville Daily Register*, **November 8, 1862**

published more than 10 runaway slave ads, possibly more than any single edition of a newspaper in the state's history. Most of the runaways were men, although a female slave from Jefferson County who "took with her three children" was missing as well.

Something had changed; clearly, slaves knew about the Emancipation Proclamation and were running away because of it. But slaveholders continued to buy runaway slave ads, while slave traders across East

Tennessee continued to do business as if nothing had changed.

In December 1862, a trader named W.S. Rogers advertised for sale 50 slaves "just received from Virginia and North Carolina" in downtown Knoxville. "They are of various ages, and are very valuable," the ad boasted. "They consist of house servants, field hands and mechanics." That same week, 27 slaves were sold in Loudon as part of the liquidation of an estate. In March 1863, slave traders J.A. Long and W.C. Vaughan sold 25 slaves at the McMinn County Courthouse. Trying to add some levity to the situation, Long and Vaughan asked buyers to "bring on your Confederate money, and buy a negro before Old Abe's Proclamation runs them up to Three Thousand Dollars." The next month, Latham & Howard advertised in the *Athens Post* that it would be putting up for sale 20 slaves. "Among them," the ad said, "a likely family—a man, his wife and three children—two or three good cooks and several first rate plough boys."

Many of these slaves being sold by professional traders were probably imported from Virginia and North Carolina and brought in via the East Tennessee and Virginia Railroad. But some of them may have just been bought on the courthouse steps. In a bit of historic irony, Chancery Court clerk and masters all over pro-union East Tennessee continued to sell slaves long after Lincoln's heralded Emancipation Proclamation. On December 2, 1862, a clerk and master sold four slaves in Sevierville. On May 2, 1863, a clerk and master sold three slaves in Athens. On May 9, a clerk and master sold 12 slaves in Claiborne County. On July 25, 1863, a clerk and master sold 11 slaves at the Rhea County Courthouse (then located in the community of Washington).

In Hamilton County, the *Chattanooga Daily Rebel* continued to run runaway slave ads—publishing them on February 6, March 12, March 13 and well into the summer. On July 30, 1863, the *Daily Rebel* published three runaway ads. All were purchased by members of the Confederate army. "My mulatto negro boy, Joe, was lost during the retreat on his way from Fayetteville to me at Shelbyville, Tenn.," wrote Daniel McPhail of the Texas Rangers. "The above reward will be paid for his delivery to Captain Theodore Carter, 29th Tennessee regiment, Bate's brigade."

Then came the fall of 1863, after which the runaway slave ads stop in places such as Knoxville, Athens, Loudon and Chattanooga.

So what happened? After a series of bloody, horrible battles, the Union Army took Chattanooga in November 1863 and soon controlled most of East Tennessee. Newspapers such as the *Knoxville Daily Register*, *Athens Post* and *Chattanooga Daily Rebel* ceased publication. As the Union Army took over cities, newspapers that had supported the Confederacy vanished. Most of the smaller markets in East Tennessee would have no newspapers until after the war.

Knoxville saw the return of William Brownlow, this time as the editor of a newspaper called *Brownlow's Knoxville Whig And Rebel Ventilator*. Unlike the pre-war version of *Brownlow's Knoxville Whig*, this one wouldn't publish runaway slave ads. "We confess frankly, to having no sympathy with rebels whose negroes are leaving them, and who are crying and howling over their losses," Brownlow wrote in an editorial of his new publication, sarcastically headlined "Stop the Niggers!"

When it comes to slavery ads in newspapers, Memphis appears to have been the last Tennessee holdout. Nathan Bedford Forrest, the city's most famous slave trader, had left to fight for the Confederacy. But the September 14, 1863, *Memphis Daily Appeal* published a large advertisement paid for by slave traders M.C. Cayce & Co. "Negroes and Land for Confederate Money," the item said. "1800 ACRES OF LAND AND FOURTEEN NEGROES." The same issue contained an item which offered $100 for the return of a runaway slave named John. He was said to be about 23 years old and "probably left on a

*Memphis Daily Appeal*, September 30, 1863

soldier train for Chattanooga, Tennessee, and may be with the army at that place," according to slaveholder Lewis Tumlin.

By early 1864, the Union Army was preparing to invade Georgia, the U.S. Navy had control over the Mississippi River, and the Emancipation Proclamation was more than a year old. However, slave sale ads and runaway slave ads continued to be published with regularity by the Memphis *Daily Appeal*. In January, the *Appeal* ran several ads for slave trader Robert A. Crawford, who had 40 slaves to sell and was in the market to buy "negro coopers" and "negro shoemakers." It also published an item, bought by J.C. Branson of Kingston, Georgia, seeking four runaways named Big Al, Zach, Tilman and Aleck. "The ringleader of this party is Big Al," the ad says. "There is no doubt but they are trying to get through the lines."

In April and May, the *Appeal* ran several ads offering $100 for the return of a slave named Matt. "He speaks quickly when spoken to, and is very intelligent," the ad said. "The boy is supposed to have . . . left Selma [Alabama] on the *Southern Republic* on her up trip of Wednesday, 30th." On June 11, the *Appeal* ran two more runaway ads. One offered $500 for the return of John and Anthony Scales, who had run away from the Etowah Manufacturing and Mining Company in Macon, Georgia.

**$50 REWARD !**

RAN AWAY from the undersigned, on Thursday, June 9th, my NEGRO GIRL, MARY ANN, dark mulatto, has a scar on her right foot above the toes, and slow spoken when spoken to. She formerly belonged to Mr. Winship, and is supposed to be in the city. I will give the above reward for her delivery to me or for any information so that I can get her.
S. CHAMBERLIAN,
ju17 1w
Atlanta, Ga.

*Memphis Daily Appeal,* June 21, 1864

On June 21, 1864, the *Appeal* printed what may have been the last runaway slave ad in Tennessee history. It offered a $50 reward for a slave named Mary Ann. She was a "dark mulatto, has a scar on her right foot above the toes, and slow spoken when spoken to," according to S. Chamberlian of Atlanta, who paid for the item. "She formerly belonged to Mr. Winship, and is supposed to be in the city. I will give the above reward for her delivery to me or for any information so that I can get her."

Odds are, Mr. S. Chamberlian never heard from Mary Ann again. In the fall of 1864 Tennessee Governor Andrew Johnson called for a political convention for the purpose of returning state government to civilian control. To take part in this convention, or even to vote on the delegates, voters had to take a loyalty oath to the U.S. government.

The 510 delegates elected to that convention met in January 1865, only a month after the Confederate disaster at the Battle of Nashville. Among the convention's proposals was one declaring null and void the action of the legislature on May 6, 1861, under which Tennessee severed its ties to the union. Another amendment abolished slavery.

As the referendum neared, thoughtful editorials about it appeared in the *Nashville Union.* Here are four excerpts:

February 7: "Those who desire to see the state enter upon a new career of prosperity, who wish its immense mineral and agricultural resources developed, will attend the polls and vote for the proposed amendments; while such as desire a continuance of guerilla warfare and all the inconveniences of military rule will either vote against them or remain home."

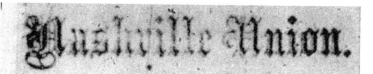

**WM. CAMERON & CO., Publishers.**

## TUESDAY, FEBRUARY 7, 1865.

### Vote for Ratification.

The 22d of February is close upon us, and on that day the people of this State will decide whether they will have law and order, or anarchy. Those who desire to see the State enter upon a new career of prosperity, who wish its immense mineral and agricultural resources developed, will attend the polls and vote for the proposed amendments; while such as desire a continuance of geurrilla warfare, and all the inconveniences of military rule, will either vote against them, or remain at home. There is no rebel so blind as not to know that their adoption by a very meagre vote will be next to equivalent to their rejection; and therefore if they remain away, they will do almost as much toward defeating them as they would by a direct negative ballot.

The necessity, then, for a large vote for the proposed amendments is im-

February 15: "Amongst those who object to the proposed amendment to the Constitution of Tennessee are some who allege that they are desirous of aiding in the removal of the stain of slavery . . . but who wish at the same time to provide for the compensation of owners for the loss of their slaves. In ordinary times this might have been a question of paramount importance . . . But not so now. Slavery in Tennessee has been *abolished by the rebellion.*"

February 16: "Immigrants from the old world will also flock hither, and at the end of one decade, Tennessee will be far more prosperous and productive than ever. Her agricultural, mineral and other resources will feel the impulse of the new and invigorating blood injected into their veins, and we will no longer bear the reproval of slothfulness and inactivity characteristic of slave states. The history of Ohio, Indiana and indeed of all the Western states proves the vast superiority of free labor."

February 22: "Do you desire to 'prop up' the tumbling, falling institution of slavery? Do you really think that it would be possible to resurrect the structure? That it is likely that the 150,000 of the 'redeemed, regenerated and disenthralled' will lay down the musket now proudly presented upon the order of their superior in arms and take up the weeding hoe, under the lash of the overseer? Or that they will labor even for kind masters without compensation?"

The slate of proposals was overwhelmingly approved by a statewide election on February 22, 1865. This date – coincidentally, George Washington's birthday – is the closest thing to an official date for the freeing of slaves in Tennessee.

"This initiates an era in the state which will make the 22nd of February doubly memorable as the birthday of the immortal Washington and of the FREE STATE OF TENNESSEE," the *Nashville Union* said. "In future years the celebration of the two events will be connected. SLAVERY IS NO MORE – the people have decreed."

There would be no more runaway slave ads in Tennessee. Advertisements requesting the leasing out of slaves would no longer be published. There would be no more sheriff-written ads asking slaveholders to claim runaways being kept in local jails. Detailed legal notice ads listing the names and ages of slaves to be sold on the courthouse steps would no longer appear in print. There would be no more ads for slave traders; no more ads that advertised the sale of carpenters, stone masons, house boys or fancy girls.

But was Tennessee completely done with slavery? Perhaps not. There were pockets of the state where slaves remained in bondage for weeks or months. Some former slaveholders gathered their slaves together and told them that they were free to leave if they wanted. Some did not.

Across Tennessee's border, in states such as Georgia, Alabama and Mississippi, the status of slaves remained uncertain for even longer—in some cases until the passage of the Thirteenth Amendment. An interesting example can be found in the memoirs of Louis Hughes, who had spent many of his years enslaved in Memphis and Hardeman Counties. In 1864, Hughes and his wife were sent away from the plantation where they lived in northwest Mississippi to work at a salt works in Alabama. After the Confederate government abandoned the salt works, Hughes and his wife were sent back to Mississippi. There they remained until June 1865—after the war ended—still living as slaves. "After we came back from Alabama we were held with a tighter rein than ever," Hughes wrote in his memoirs. "We were not allowed to go outside of the premises."

On Sunday June 26, 1865, Louis Hughes and a fellow slave named George made a break for it, passing farm after farm until they got to the railroad; then Senatobia and Hernando, Mississippi; and then Memphis (a journey that took them more than 24 hours). "I could scarcely recognize Memphis, things were so changed," he said.

On Thursday of that week, Louis and George went to see a U.S. Army officer and asked him for help retrieving their wives. The colonel wished them well but said that there was no way that he could help them. "I would be overrun with similar applications," he said, if he helped them on this errand.

The next day, Louis and George set off for Senatobia, Mississippi, to see if anyone who would help there. Along the way they met two Union soldiers who agreed to do so if paid $10 each. The next day, Louis and George, escorted by two members of the U.S. Army, rode up to the house of Jack McGee of Panola, Mississippi. It was there and then, in front of their sneering former slaveholders, that the remaining nine slaves which had been held by the McGee family grabbed what worldly possessions they could carry and hurried out the front door to the wagon—all while the two soldiers chastised the former slaveholders. "Why have you not told these men, Louis and George, that they are free men—that they can come and go as they like?" the soldiers asked.

Years later, Louis Hughes reflected on how grateful he was to these two men and how much he regretted never learning their names. "Those soldiers were brave indeed. Think of the courage and daring involved in this scheme - only two soldiers going into a country of which they knew nothing except that every white man living in it was their enemy. . . It is true that we should have been free, sooner or later; still, but for their assistance, my wife and I might never have met again. Thousands were separated in this manner - men escaping to the Union lines, hoping to make a way to return for their families; but, failing in this, and not daring to return alone, never saw their wives or children more."

Louis Hughes never forgot the reception he got when they arrived in Memphis. "Having to walk some of the way, as all could not ride in the wagon at the same time, we were all tired, dirty and rest-broken, and, on the whole, a pitiful crowd to look at, as we came into the city," he said. "One venerable old man, bent with age, whose ebony face shone with delight, came running out into the road as we appeared, exclaiming: 'Oh! here dey come, God bless 'em! Poor chil'en!'"

Tennessee was done with slavery.

The date? July 4, 1865.

APPENDIX ONE

# TENNESSEE'S RUNAWAY SLAVE ADS

*This data was obtained from newspapers on microfilm and generally only includes ads where the slaveholder was in Tennessee, although I have included some from out of state slaveholders when the slave had a connection to Tennessee. When an age range for the slave was given, I took the middle age, rounding off to the lower number.*

*For more complete information, go to the Tennessee State Library and Archives and look it up.*

| Name of Slave | Age | Date Published | Newspaper | Slave Holder | County | Special Notes |
|---|---|---|---|---|---|---|
| Thomas | 20 | Oct 6, 1792 | *Knoxville Gazette* | John Crawford | Wythe, VA | A "mulattoe fellow" and "it is probable that he may make for the Cherokee nation." |
| Jim | 25 | April 6, 1793 | *Knoxville Gazette* | Joseph Erwin | Lee, VA | "One of his thighs shorter than the other" and "laughs very hard, and is fond of children." |
| Jack | 23 | June 29, 1793 | *Knoxville Gazette* | John Shelby | Sullivan | Took with him a "smooth bord gun." |
| William Bundle | | June 29, 1793 | *Knoxville Gazette* | William Rickard | Knox | "It is supposed he made for the Clinch River." Also, "he is the property of Peter Samuel, of Kentucky." |
| Isaac | 18 | Oct 19, 1793 | *Knoxville Gazette* | John Singleton | Knox | "I expect he will attemp to make for Maryland and pass himself off as a free man." |
| Sampson | 40 | Dec. 26, 1794 | *Knoxville Gazette* | Robert Preston | Washington, VA | "Chunky well-made fellow" who "took with him one rifle gun." |
| Jack | 22 | Jan. 23, 1794 | *Knoxville Gazette* | James Piper | Washington, VA | "He talks very broken English, and speaks the French language tolerably well." |
| Jim | old | March 2, 1795 | *Knoxville Gazette* | Samuel Mc-Clung | Knox | Expected to have run toward Cumberland Settlement. |
| Dave/ Bob/Pegg | 36 | April 24, 1795 | *Knoxville Gazette* | James Richardson | Roane | Dave, Bob (38) and Pegg (40) ran away from Fort Southwest Point together. "Dave had an excellent new rifle. Bob's rifle was not too good." |
| Jemmy | 35 | May 8, 1795 | *Knoxville Gazette* | Alexander Carmichael | Knox | Has a "scar on his forehead," was apprehended by the jailer, then ran away from him. |
| Elice/ Olive/ Tora | 22 | May 3, 1796 | *Knoxville Gazette* | Daniel Stringer | Pendleton, SC | Mark on her right cheek, scar on her breast. Ran away with 2 children, ages 5 and 3. |
| Sam | | May 3, 1796 | *Knoxville Gazette* | Elijah Tucker | Virginia | Said to have "stole" Elice, Olive and Tora. |

| Name of Slave | Age | Date Published | Newspaper | Slave Holder | County | Special Notes |
|---|---|---|---|---|---|---|
| Ned | 25 | May 3, 1796 | *Knoxville Gazette* | Thomas Buckingham | Sevier | "A very sensible fellow when spoken to." |
| Henry | 27 | Nov. 14, 1796 | *Knoxville Gazette* | Benjamin White | Knox | "An artful fellow" whose "intention is to make for Pennsylvania." |
| Unnamed Male/ Female | 30 | Nov. 21, 1796 | *Knoxville Gazette* | George Jackson | Moore, NC | He reads and writes, "has a scar on one of his legs, by the cut of an axe." Both likely "heading for Maryland." |
| London | 35 | Dec. 19, 1796 | *Knoxville Gazette* | Alexander Outlaw | Jefferson | "Rather slim built and bow-legged." |
| Derry | 27 | March 6, 1797 | *Knoxville Gazette* | William Mebane | Blount | "A fize larger than a dollar" on the upper part of his head. |
| Dick | 20 | March 15, 1797 | *Knoxville Gazette* | John Sherrill | Knox | "A tolerable good scholar." |
| Jack | 25 | April 8, 1797 | *Knoxville Gazette* | Abner Witt | Knox | "Some of the toes on both his feet have been cut off." |
| Aaron | 24 | April 24, 1797 | *Knoxville Gazette* | Elias Lawrence | Knox | "I expect he will make for Northampton County, North Carolina." |
| Sampson | 25 | Feb. 2, 1798 | *Knoxville Gazette* | Thomas Brown | Washington | A blacksmith with "a small scar in the forehead and a good deal marked with the whip on the back." |
| Godfry | 35 | Sept. 11, 1798 | *Knoxville Gazette* | Abraham Maury | Davidson | Ran away on the road from Abington to Knoxville. This is the second time he tried to escape. Also, "limps in the left leg, it being larger and somewhat shorter than the other." |
| Sam | 30 | Aug. 28, 1799 | *Nashville Intelligencer* | Robert Cartwright | Davidson | Has "a wadling walk." This is the first runaway ad published in Middle Tennessee of which we are aware. |
| Ned | | Feb. 18, 1801 | *Nashville Intelligencer* | John McNairy | Davidson | "Plays well on the violin," is slim, and has a "mark on one cheek." |
| Abraham | 20 | Oct. 11, 1801 | *Knoxville Gazette* | Charles Mc-Clung | Knox | May be "heading toward Mero District, where he has a brother." |
| Jim | 21 | May 12, 1802 | *Tennessee Gazette* | Benjamin Phillips | Davidson | "His left arm appears to have been broke above the wrist." |
| Caezar | | Aug. 2, 1802 | *Knoxville Gazette* | Francis Wren | Knox | "Was stolen from Francis Wren, then residing in South Carolina" and "was found in possession of Jeff Riggs of Grainger County and from thence brought to Knoxville last week." |
| George | 22 | Dec. 18, 1802 | *Tennessee Gazette* | Thomas McClung | Knox | "Has a scar on left cheek, occasioned from a bite." Also, may be making off with man he met at Ft. Southwest Point who said that if "he traveled to the territory north of the Ohio, he would be free." |
| Spencer | 30 | June 15, 1803 | *Tennessee Gazette* | James Wilson | Davidson | "Very much pock-marked in the face." Slaveholder resides on Mill Creek. |
| Andrew | 32 | March 28, 1804 | *Tennessee Gazette* | Elizabeth Evans | Davidson | "Has a scar on top of forehead." |

| Name of Slave | Age | Date Published | Newspaper | Slave Holder | County | Special Notes |
|---|---|---|---|---|---|---|
| Cato | 28 | June 6, 1804 | *Tennessee Gazette* | Michael Dickson | Dickson | "Cooper by trade." |
| Joe | 21 | Aug. 8, 1804 | *Tennessee Gazette* | H.L. White | Knox | "Speaks bold and distinctive." |
| Lucy | 20 | Sept. 19, 1804 | *Tennessee Gazette* | Barham Newsom | Davidson | "Of a yellowish complexion, broad full face." |
| Unnamed Man | 30 | Oct. 3, 1804 | *Tennessee Gazette* | Andrew Jackson | Davidson | "Ten dollars extra for every hundred lashes any person will give him, to the amount of three hundred." |
| Peter | 25 | Jan. 30, 1805 | *Tennessee Gazette* | John Miller Isbell | Sevier | "A scar on one cheek" and it is "very probable he may have a forged pass." |
| Aaron | 22 | July 3, 1805 | *Tennessee Gazette* | Joel Childress | Sumner | Either heading to Alexandria, VA, or Ohio. |
| Peter | 23 | Jan. 14, 1806 | *Nashville IRCR* | Thomas McAlpin | Wilson | "A hole in his right jaw." |
| Jeffrey | 35 | June 14, 1806 | *Nashville IRCR* | George Blackmore | Sumner | "It is supposed he will make for Natchez." |
| Oliver | 35 | Aug. 6, 1806 | *Knoxville Gazette* | Archibald Rhea | Knox | "A thick well set fellow" who "speaks bad English." |
| Jacob | 20 | Aug. 16, 1806 | *Nashville Imp Review Cumberland Repository* | John Overton | Davidson | "Owned" by John Overton; ad published by "his agent" William Dickerson. The slave "has rather a down look when spoken to." |
| Spencer | 28 | Aug. 23, 1806 | *Nashville IRCR* | William Edwards | Sumner | "He was taken up on Duck River but made his escape." |
| Bob/Tom | old | Aug. 30, 1806 | *Nashville Imp Review Cumberland Repository* | Thomas Ryan Butler | Robertson | Ran away together and will probably head to Amelia County, Virginia, or Ohio. Tom "can spell and read a little" and is "a cunning artful fellow." |
| Philip | 28 | Nov. 8, 1806 | *Nashville Imp Review Cumberland Repository* | John Baker | Robertson | A carpenter who has a "scar over his left eye and a scar on one of his thighs" and "holds his head high when walking." Ran away from near Port Royal. |
| Ben | 30 | Feb. 21, 1807 | *Nashville IRCR* | Francis Newsom | Davidson | Works in the "mill-wright business" and "has a scar on his forehead." |
| Tom | 19 | April 4, 1807 | *Nashville IRCR* | J. Lyon | Smith | "Speech fluent." |
| Esther | 40 | April 4, 1807 | *Nashville IRCR* | Elijah Hughes | Robertson | The slave is "the property of John W. Bryan," so she was apparently leased to Elijah Hughes. |
| 5 unnamed males | | July 11, 1807 | *Nashville IRCR* | William Edwards | Sumner | Unnamed teenagers, all ran away together. |
| Lem | 25 | Aug. 15, 1807 | *Nashville Imp Review Cumberland Repository* | Henry Bryan | Robertson | "I moved to this state [to near Port Royal] from North Carolina the first of June . . . where I expect he will aim for until caught." |
| Billey | 34 | Aug. 27, 1807 | *Nashville Imp Review Cumberland Repository* | Montgomery Bell | Dickson | Ran away from Cumberland Furnace. Billey has worked in coaling business and "his countenance indicative of discontent, unless when he affects a smile." |

| Name of Slave | Age | Date Published | Newspaper | Slave Holder | County | Special Notes |
|---|---|---|---|---|---|---|
| Bob | 23 | Sept. 24, 1807 | *Nashville IRCR* | Thomas Hardeman | Williamson | "It is supposed he will aim for the Cherokee nation or state of Ohio." |
| Sandy/ Lewis | 37 | Oct. 15, 1807 | *Nashville Imp Review Cumberland Repository* | Ferdinand L. Claiborne | Adams, MS | Sandy formerly belonged to a "Mr. Ferguson" who lived near the mouth of the Cumberland. Lewis formerly lived near Nashville. "Their object will be to return to Tennessee." |
| Parmus | | Oct. 15, 1807 | *Nashville IRCR* | Robert Crockett | Rutherford | "Does not incline to talk much." Ran away from "near Ready's Mill." |
| Tom | 22 | Dec. 17, 1807 | *Nashville IRCR* | Thomas Ryan Butler | Robertson | Has a "scar or burn on the right side of his upper lip. . . has a wife at Capt. Goodrick's on Dry Creek." |
| John | 25 | Dec. 17, 1807 | *Nashville IRCR* | Nathaniel A. McNairy | Davidson | "I bought him near Norfolk in Virginia, and I suppose he will attempt to return hither." |
| Allen | | Feb. 11, 1808 | *Nashville Imp Review Cumberland Repository* | Thomas H. Holland | Maury | A fiddle player who "understands boating, has been upon sea and talks much of naval affairs." Admiral Walton of Maryland "formerly owned him and now owns his wife." |
| Beck | 32 | Feb. 25, 1808 | *Nashville Imp Review Cumberland Repository* | Nicholas Boyce | Sumner | Ranaway or was "stolen" from Station Camp plantation along with 5 slave children--Jude (11), Moses (10), Jake (4), Rachel (2) and an unnamed child (3 months). |
| Billy | 36 | March 17, 1808 | *Nashville IRCR* | Richard Winn | Davidson | "Very grey, slowful speech, down in his countenance." |
| Toby | 18 | July 16, 1808 | *Nashville Imp Review Cumberland Repository* | Hardy Murfree | Williamson | "Expect he is on his way to South Carolina." Also, he ran away from the Mississippi Territory, but Hardy Murfree of Williamson County is running the ad. |
| Jesse | 28 | July 28, 1808 | *Nashville Imp Review Cumberland Repository* | David Peeples | Montgomery | Ran away from the Yellow Creek iron works. He "will make to Stones River, and from thence to Holston to his old master, Thomas Titsworth, Sullivan [County]." |
| Lem | 27 | Sept. 15, 1808 | *Nashville Imp Review Cumberland Repository* | James Turner | Davidson | "Has a very noted scar on his upper lip" and "when spoken to, has a down look." "He was lately brought from Bertie County, North Carolina, to which place I expect he will endeavor to return." |
| Manuel | 35 | Sept. 15, 1808 | *Nashville Imp Review Cumberland Repository* | Samuel Crothers | Trousdale | "One of his hands is decrepid by reason of a cut on the back of it, which hand he cannot straighten without difficulty." Ran away with Andy. |
| Andy | 25 | Sept. 15, 1808 | *Nashville IRCR* | William Smith | Trousdale | Andy has a large scar on his forehead and ran away with Manuel. |
| Tom | 32 | Nov. 10, 1808 | *Nashville IRCR* | Robert Adams | Davidson | "Pretends to be a horse-doctor" and "was formerly the property of John Johnson of Virginia, who now resides near Gallatin." |

| Name of Slave | Age | Date Published | Newspaper | Slave Holder | County | Special Notes |
|---|---|---|---|---|---|---|
| Ned | 26 | Dec. 1, 1808 | *Nashville IRCR* | Richard Winn | Davidson | Has formerly been employed in the "house business." |
| Oston | 30 | Dec. 8, 1809 | *The [Nashville] Review* | Andrew Jackson | Davidson | Can read, and is a coachman, seamster and gardener. Has an "effeminate voice" and when he looks at a person "is in the habit of shutting his left eye." Ran away before and made it all the way to the Ohio River. |
| Unnamed Man | 30 | June 15, 1810 | *Carthage Gazette* | James Norris | Wilson | "African born" and has "long black hair." Ran away with a woman about 26 years old and "of yellow complexion." |
| Dick/ Noah | 23 | June 29, 1810 | *Carthage Gazette* | Thomas McNutt | Sumner | Brothers who ran away together; both "owned" by McNutt, Findlay & Co., but hired out. Noah is about 20 years old. |
| Adam/ Cato | 23 | Dec. 6, 1810 | *Carthage Gazette* | Alexander Ardrey | Putnam | Adam is a shoemaker and carpenter. Both ran away from South Carolina and made it to Tennessee, were apprehended and then ran away again. |
| Harry | 30 | June 11, 1811 | *Carthage Gazette* | John Tate | Overton | Held by Colonel William Roberson of Claibourne County and hired out to John Tate of Overton County. |
| Essex | 25 | April 12, 1812 | *Carthage Gazette* | Wright Bonds | Montgomery | "Can read" and "took with him some books." His right eye is "smaller than the other, occasioned by a burn." Said to be heading to North Carolina. |
| Jim | 19 | Nov. 11, 1812 | *Nashville Whig* | Felix Grundy | Davidson | "He was stolen by a certain JAMES SMITH, who was convicted of horse stealing at the last September term of the Davidson circuit court." |
| Martin | 20 | Jan. 13, 1813 | *Nashville Whig* | John Stump | Davidson | "Rather a down look when spoken to." Was raised in Jessamine County, Kentucky, and expected to head toward Lexington. |
| Abraham | 18 | May 19, 1813 | *Nashville Whig* | Captain Sample | Davidson | A cook, carriage driver, waiter and distiller who "is extremely proud; smokes segars, and walks with a considerable air." [This ad was run by John H. Eaton.] |
| Sam | 25 | June 1, 1813 | *Nashville Whig* | Michael Campbell | Davidson | A cook, waiter, understands distilling and "shows marks of the whip on back." |
| Ned | 27 | Aug. 24, 1813 | *Nashville Whig* | Frederick Stump | Davidson | A shoemaker who has "a small scar in his face, a scar on his thigh and neck, made by a rope." He may have been "taken" by a man named John D. Johnson. |
| Jesse | 27 | Aug. 31, 1813 | *Nashville Whig* | George W. Sanders | Van Buren | "Half of his right ear is cut off, and a large scar on his left cheek." Address of slaveholder is Big Bone Cave. |
| Moses | | March 23, 1814 | *Nashville Whig* | David Craig | Williamson | "Dark complexion." Slaveholder lives 6 miles east of Franklin. |
| Derry | 25 | April 27, 1814 | *Nashville Whig* | William Gillespie | Sumner | A "considerable scar on one of his arms, near his shoulder, occasioned by a burn when small." Said to be heading for Ohio or Virginia. |

| Name of Slave | Age | Date Published | Newspaper | Slave Holder | County | Special Notes |
|---|---|---|---|---|---|---|
| Anthony | 25 | June 21, 1814 | *Nashville Whig* | Thomas Eastland | Coffee | "Has a small piece out of his right ear" and "this is the third trip the said fellow has taken within a few months." Address of slaveholder is "at the stone fort." |
| Major | | July 12, 1814 | *Nashville Whig* | G.G. Washington | Davidson | "It is expected he will make for the Duck River, where he formerly lived." |
| Lewis | 35 | July 12, 1814 | *Nashville Whig* | Archer Cheatham | Robertson | A "cooper, shoemaker and carpenter" who "has a scar on one of his big toes." Purchased in North Carolina, near Murfreesborough." |
| Cary | 24 | Aug. 9, 1814 | *Nashville Whig* | Montgomery Bell | Dickson | Ran away from Cumberland Furnace. Had been bought from Reuben Paine of Dry Creek area, in Jan. 1813. |
| Tom | 45 | Aug. 9, 1814 | *Nashville Whig* | Thomas Overton | Dickson | "When spoken to smiles, and answers without hesitation; he is an artful sensitive fellow." Had been bought from Robert Harrison of Pittsylvania County, Virginia. |
| Dennis | | Dec. 6, 1814 | *Nashville Whig* | Joseph Morton | Rutherford | Has "a small scar on his throat" and "his back is very much cut with cow-hide." He is "fond of drinking, swearing and quarrelling." |
| Letty | 22 | Dec. 6, 1814 | *Nashville Whig* | John J. Zollicofer | Maury | She is about 6 months pregnant, and she may be heading to Rhea County, "from where she was brought." |
| Charles | | Jan. 23, 1815 | *Nashville Whig* | George Smith | Davidson | Was "brought up in the plastering business." His right foot is "deformed and nearly half off." |
| Jack | 21 | July 25, 1815 | *Nashville Whig* | William McDonald | Davidson | "He will probably aim for Duck River, near the three forks, as he has some relations there." |
| Solomon | 22 | Aug. 15, 1815 | *Nashville Whig* | William Rutherford | Davidson | Expected to head towards North Carolina. |
| Finch | 19 | Aug. 15, 1815 | *Nashville Whig* | Hugh McCutchan | Logan, KY | Has scars on back "from whipping." |
| Amia | 36 | Sept. 12, 1815 | *Nashville Whig* | William Donelson | Davidson | "Has a scar on the back part of her head near the edge of her hair." She may have run away with Bristol. |
| Bristol | | Sept 12, 1815 | *Nashville Whig* | Thomas Napier | Montgomery | Ran away from Yellow Creek iron works and may have run away with Amia. "Middle finger off on his right hand." |
| Ned | 25 | Sept. 19, 1815 | *Nashville Whig* | Andrew Jackson | Davidson | A good cook or body servant who has resided at the Nashville Inn for 4 or 5 years. |
| Randolph/ Solomon | 22 | Oct. 10, 1815 | *Nashville Whig* | Thomas Washington | Rutherford | Randolph is knock kneed and "walks fast." Solomon (28) has a scar on his right cheek. When he was born, "had on each hand a sixth finger, which were cut off." |

| Name of Slave | Age | Date Published | Newspaper | Slave Holder | County | Special Notes |
|---|---|---|---|---|---|---|
| Sam/ Nuncanna/ Luck | 25 | Nov. 28, 1815 | *Nashville Whig* | Stokely Hays/ Francis Sanders | Davidson | Sam, Nuncanna and Luck ran away together and all may be heading toward Augusta, GA from where they came last summer. Nuncanna and Luck are "marked in the face by the African mark." |
| Mingo | 42 | Dec. 12, 1815 | *Nashville Whig* | John Chapman | Davidson | "Is injured so as to be obliged to wear trusses." Formerly "belonged to Joseph Pitts of Robertson [County]." |
| Frank | 20 | April 2, 1816 | *Nashville Whig* | Giles Harding | Davidson | "Was bought by George Harding from Virginia a few weeks ago, and will probably attempt to return." |
| Major | | April 16, 1816 | *Nashville Whig* | Baker Wrather | Wilson | Absconded "without the least provocation." His wife is at the household of Mr. Joseph Woods. "If he will return, he shall be forgiven--I will then sell him in Nashville." |
| Sam | 27 | May 21, 1816 | *Nashville Whig* | Thomas Martin | Davidson | "The last place he was seen was at Mr. Jesse Parker's, on White's Creek, where he has a wife." Plays the hanger. |
| Gilbert | 30 | June 11, 1816 | *Nashville Whig* | Edward Hogan | Jackson | A blacksmith who "formerly worked at the business in Nashville." He "originally belonged to Mr. James Harvey of North Carolina." |
| Cary/Bob | 26 | June 2, 1816 | *Nashville Whig* | Montgomery Bell | Dickson | Both ran away from Cumberland furnace. Both may have already made it to Pennsylvania. |
| William | 25 | Sept. 3, 1816 | *Nashville Whig* | William Crawford | Sumner | Last seen at the plantation of John Nichols. |
| Sally | 25 | Sept. 24, 1816 | *Nashville Whig* | Clayton Talbot | Davidson | She was working at the Nashville Inn. Ad run by Thomas Crutcher, Clayton Talbot's agent. |
| Solomon | 35 | Nov. 12, 1816 | *Nashville Whig* | John B. Craighead | Davidson | "It is supposed will make for the lead mines, Missouri territory." |
| Coy | 22 | Dec. 11, 1816 | *Nashville Whig* | Robert Purdy | Rutherford | Has several scars on his face. "It is supposed he will make for Davidson" since he "has a wife at McClain Bend of the Cumberland River." |
| Bob/Hester/child | 28 | Dec. 25, 1816 | *Nashville Whig* | William Porter | Smith | Bob, his 18-year-old wife Hester and infant girl ran away on Christmas Day. |
| Michael | 28 | June 2, 1817 | *Nashville Whig* | John Hughes | Davidson | Ran away before, was put in jail and escaped from there. |
| Bob | 27 | April 30, 1817 | *Nashville Whig* | Matthias Murfree | Rutherford | Had a pass "signed by Roger B. Sappington, authorizing him to go to Major Dunn's, on Mansker Creek." |
| Minta/ Nancy | 18 | July 21, 1817 | *Nashville Whig* | David Marshall | Wilson | Sisters ran away together. Nancy is 15 years old. They had been purchased from Henry Kearny of Maury, who had given a mortgage on them 3 years before. |

| Name of Slave | Age | Date Published | Newspaper | Slave Holder | County | Special Notes |
|---|---|---|---|---|---|---|
| Mary | | Sept. 8, 1817 | *Nashville Whig* | Jason Thompson | Davidson | Is pregnant and has "a scar on the left side of her neck." Said to be heading for Lexington, KY, or Charlotte, VA. |
| Patience | 35 | Jan. 5, 1818 | *Nashville Whig* | Thomas Martin | Davidson | "Was taken from my house by her husband who belongs to Mr. Benjamin Philips." She "has a son who belongs to Mrs. Benton, near Franklin." |
| Randol | 26 | March 21, 1818 | *Nashville Whig* | Wood Tucker | Franklin, NC | Should have some "marks of shot" since he has been shot at several times. His wife belongs to Mr. Henry Bridges, who has moved, and "he is probably in search of her." |
| Burrill | 30 | April 14, 1818 | *Knoxville Register* | James McDonald | Knox | Can read. Ran away because of "an unwillingness to go with his master to the Alabama territory." |
| Ginny | | May 2, 1818 | *Nashville Whig* | Plummer Willis | Robertson | "Has been in the possession of Edward Daniel since the first of January." |
| Sucky/ child | | May 9, 1818 | *Nashville Whig* | D.L. Thompson | Davidson | Took with her an unnamed 2-year-old child. "Is expected to head toward one of her children who are "hired out." |
| Moses/ Ben/Dick | 23 | May 30, 1818 | *Nashville Whig* | Allen Elston | Lincoln | All ran away together. Ben is 18; Dick's slaveholder is Benjamin Short. Said to have run off with "some white man." Moses has "a notable scar above one of his eyes." |
| Jim | | June 20, 1818 | *Nashville Whig* | Charles Wilson | Davidson | "Hired to the subscriber by T.H. Fletcher [presumably the slaveholder]." |
| Prince | 50 | July 7, 1818 | *Knoxville Register* | Robert Church | Washington | Belongs to Nathanial Gordon of Wilkes County, N.C., and has been hired out to Robert Church in Jonesboro. |
| Jim | 24 | Sept. 26, 1818 | *Nashville Whig* | Samuel Hodge | Wilson | A "small black African fellow" who "has his teeth filed according to the custom of his country." Location of slaveholder is "near Pond Lick." |
| John/ Adam | 19 | Oct. 13, 1818 | *Knoxville Register* | William B. Drake | Wilson | Both "aiming" for Richmond, VA, since both were raised there. John has a scar on his upper lip. Adam is 27 and "inclined to be hump shouldered." |
| Luce | 22 | Oct. 24, 1818 | *Nashville Whig* | John Wood | Warren | Her arms and head "scarred from a scald." |
| Francis | 34 | Nov. 18, 1818 | *Nashville Whig* | George Shall | Davidson | Left with his wife Maria. "Pretends to possess a great knowledge of horses" and is "marked in the face by smallpox." |
| Maria | 26 | Nov. 18, 1818 | *Nashville Whig* | B. Poyzer | Davidson | Left with her husband Francis and has some children in the Duck River area. When spoken, she "has a smiling countenance, very much effected in her manners." |
| Jim | 22 | Jan. 5, 1819 | *Knoxville Register* | Robert Lankford | Knox | A scar "hardly perceivable" on one side of his face. Formerly lived in Lunenburg County, VA. |

| Name of Slave | Age | Date Published | Newspaper | Slave Holder | County | Special Notes |
|---|---|---|---|---|---|---|
| Harry | 40 | Jan. 30, 1819 | *Nashville Whig* | Joseph Cook | Davidson | A stone cutter. Address of the slaveholder is Stone's Lick. |
| Gere | 28 | Feb. 6, 1819 | *Nashville Whig* | William McCann | Davidson | One of his little fingers is "crooked at the first joint." |
| Jerry | 40 | Feb. 9, 1819 | *Knoxville Register* | Charles Hodge | Jefferson | Had a "12-day pass" before he ran away. |
| Eleanor | 23 | Feb. 9, 1819 | *Knoxville Register* | Richard K. Meade | Frederick, VA | Thinks she was taken by John Tipton, former overseer, whose parents live in Tennessee. |
| John | 24 | March 20, 1819 | *Nashville Whig* | F. Thornton | Robertson | "Stammers a little." |
| Bill | | March 25, 1819 | *Knoxville Register* | James Allen | Greene | Ran away from George Gordon's paper mill and was formerly held by Davens Wyly. |
| Lige | 18 | March 30, 1819 | *Knoxville Register* | Hanna Baker | Greene | Said to have been taken by James Baker. |
| Peter | 36 | April 13, 1819 | *Nashville Whig* | Riley Slocumb | Williamson | "A very good rough shoemaker." |
| Bob/Tilla | | April 20, 1819 | *Knoxville Register* | Matthias Firestone | Knox | Ran away with his wife Tilla. Both hired from a "Mrs. Newman" of Grainger County. Bob "walks a little lame." |
| Jinny | 20 | May 1, 1819 | *Nashville Whig* | T. G. Bradford | Davidson | Right arm shorter than her left. |
| Harry | | May 1, 1819 | *Nashville Whig* | Washington Pulliam | Davidson | Bow-legged and "was lately brought from Virginia, by John Criddle." |
| Lewis | 30 | May 8, 1819 | *Nashville Whig* | Robert Johnston | Davidson | "Apt to smile when spoken to and nearly shuts his eyes." Was "the property of David Beatty, deceased" and may have left Nashville with a man named Black. |
| Harry | 27 | May 22, 1819 | *Nashville Whig* | Thomas Hickman, Sheriff | Davidson | Ran away from the sheriff. |
| Daniel/3 others | 26 | May 25, 1819 | *Knoxville Register* | Israel and William Standefer | Bledsoe | Daniel, Cary, London and Louisa ran away and all may be making their way to "lower part of North Carolina, from whence they were lately purchased." |
| Edmund | 22 | Oct. 20, 1819 | *Nashville Whig* | John Camp | Giles | "Plays the fiddle and is a carpenter by trade." |
| Jacob | 18 | July 6, 1819 | *Knoxville Register* | John Nolan | Jefferson | Left slaveholder in Dandridge while he was heading toward Nashville. |
| Bill | 21 | July 6, 1819 | *Knoxville Register* | Green B. Taylor | Wilson | Purchased in Norfolk, VA. His "intention is to try to get back." |
| Patrick | 18 | July 6, 1819 | *Knoxville Register* | Joel R. Taylor | Wilson | "Stammers very much when spoken to." Purchased in Lynchburg, VA and his "intention is to try to get back." |
| Rose | 18 | July 29, 1819 | *Knoxville Register* | Eben T. Mathes | Washington | "Her left hand disfigured by a burn and a bald spot on her head about the size of a dollar." Was supposedly "stolen by a free negro named Jeffry Jackson, a blacksmith by trade." |
| James | 17 | Sept. 11, 1819 | *Nashville Whig* | J. Potts | Davidson | "Formerly the property of Mr. Cattron, attorney." |

| Name of Slave | Age | Date Published | Newspaper | Slave Holder | County | Special Notes |
|---|---|---|---|---|---|---|
| Nelly | 17 | Sept. 11, 1819 | *Nashville Whig* | Joel Dyer | Rutherford | Was "raised in Kingston and brought to Murfreesborough last summer." |
| Yorke | 28 | Sept. 14, 1819 | *Knoxville Register* | Joshua Haskell | Rutherford | "Was purchased from Major Henry Rutledge of this state . . . has a wife and three children at my house." |
| Abner | 21 | Sept. 25, 1819 | *Nashville Whig* | John Templeton | Bedford | "Rode a bay horse" when he ran away. |
| George | 26 | Oct. 27, 1819 | *Nashville Whig* | Michael Campbell | Davidson | "Has a large burn on his face . . . it was burnt with gunpowder some years ago." Also, "has a wife at Captain Sims' about five miles from Nashville." |
| Paris | 27 | Nov. 3, 1819 | *Nashville Whig* | W.B. Lewis | Davidson | He tried to escape before and was caught near Glasgow, KY. |
| Simon | | Nov. 3, 1819 | *Nashville Whig* | D. Vaughn | Davidson | "Lame in one of his hips." |
| Guilford | 17 | Dec. 1, 1819 | *Nashville Whig* | William Green | Lawrence, AL | Slaveholder was moving from North Carolina to Alabama. Guilford ran away "near the Rock Island between Sparta and McMinnville." |
| Jack | 31 | Feb. 2, 1820 | *Nashville Whig* | John Holcolmbe | Lincoln | "Excellent at whip saw or shoemaking" and has "an impediment in his speech." He "once belonged to Robert Boyd on Stone's River." |
| Aaron | 35 | March 29, 1820 | *Nashville Whig* | Jacob Adams | Smith | Has "a scar on his right side," and "three outside fingers on his right hand have been burnt so that he cannot straighten them." |
| Peter | 28 | May 10, 1820 | *Nashville Whig* | Robert Smith | Rutherford | "A very sensible, sharp and artful fellow" who "can read tolerably well and write a little." |
| Squire/ Beck | 30 | June 13, 1820 | *Knoxville Register* | Lewis Cox | Knox | Husband and wife ran away. Squire has "a scar on one of his cheeks." |
| Phill | 19 | June 28, 1820 | *Nashville Whig* | R. Goodrich | Davidson | Has a scar on the right side of his jaw. Took a bay mare with him. |
| Patrick | | July 12, 1820 | *Nashville Whig* | J.H. Hall | Williamson | Has a scar between his eyes and may go to Robertson [County] "in the neighborhood of the Forts, where he has relations." |
| Elijah | 16 | July 19, 1820 | *Nashville Whig* | William Doake | Lincoln | He is a brick moulder and "believe he on board a keel boat commanded by a Capt. Hanby, bound for New Orleans." |
| Ben/3 others | 33 | July 26, 1820 | *Nashville Whig* | John Thompson | Davidson | Ben ran away with Davy (22), Daniel (24) and Aaron (25). |
| John | 30 | Aug. 1, 1820 | *Knoxville Register* | William Trotter | Sevier | "Mulatto" man who is "very heavy built." |
| Thomas Shootman | 24 | Sept. 5, 1820 | *Nashville Whig* | N.C. Davis | White | "One of his legs has been broke and is sometimes sore." He took a horse with him and may be headed toward Powell's Valley. |
| Lem/ Betsey/ David | 27 | Sept. 12, 1820 | *Knoxville Register* | Joseph Shaw | Jackson | Lem, Betsey (26) and David (33) ran away together. Lem has a scar on his forehead. |

| Name of Slave | Age | Date Published | Newspaper | Slave Holder | County | Special Notes |
|---|---|---|---|---|---|---|
| Lawrence | 21 | Sept. 23, 1820 | *Nashville Gazette* | John Wright | Rutherford | Allegedly taken by a white man named John Coleman. |
| Pleasent | | Sept. 26, 1820 | *Knoxville Register* | William Whiteman | Knox | Has a small scar on his forehead and is thought to have gone to Dandridge, where his mother lives. |
| Dave | | Oct. 3, 1820 | *Nashville Whig* | William B. Robertson | Davidson | "Purchased at the sale of Col. John Stump, last fall." |
| Clem | | Oct. 3, 1820 | *Nashville Whig* | William B. Robertson | Davidson | "A great wrestler" who has traveled to Pittsburg, Pennsylvania, and with whom the slaveholder has "placed a lot of confidence." |
| George/ Jinney | 40 | Nov. 29, 1820 | *Nashville Whig* | Joseph Royall | Bedford | George "is fond of talking of his travels" and Jinney (35) "has a scar on the left side of the neck, like it was cut with a knife." |
| Dick | | Feb. 6, 1821 | *Knoxville Register* | J. Willborn | Wilkes, NC | "Speaks plain, and rather impudent. . . Has a wife in Murfreesborough." Ran away before and was caught in Knoxville. |
| Ellen | 20 | Feb. 9, 1821 | *Tennessee Watchman* | John Long | Green, AL | Has scars on the side of her neck and "is fond of dressing well." When spoken to, "she has a peculiar turn with the eyes." Previously lived in Franklin and has friends near Mill Creek in Nashville. |
| George | | March 18, 1821 | *Knoxville Register* | Thomas Moor | Rhea | "Fore finger on his right hand is stiff" and has a scar above his left eyebrow. |
| George | | March 17, 1821 | *Knoxville Register* | William Lyon | Knox | Has family in Hawkins, at the home of J.G. Winstons of Rogersville. |
| Merit | 18 | May 16, 1821 | *Nashville Whig* | John Davis | Davidson | Has "an awkward, careless manner of speaking." |
| Isaac | 23 | May 16, 1821 | *Nashville Whig* | James Heflin | Tuscaloosa, AL | Has a round scar on his forehead and "was raised by John Rains, near Nashville, and sold to me by his son, John Rains." |
| Elijah | 30 | May 22, 1821 | *Knoxville Register* | W. Chilton | Overton | A carpenter who is "rather slow of speech and backward in conversation." |
| Levi | 35 | July 4, 1821 | *Nashville Whig* | Austin M. Coats | Davidson | "Has the first and second fingers of one hand bit off at the first joint." |
| George | 23 | July 17, 1821 | *Knoxville Register* | B. Totten | Overton | "Has a scar on one of his cheeks." Slaveholder resides in the community of Monroe. |
| Perry | 40 | Aug. 1, 1821 | *Nashville Whig* | John Hightower | Williamson | Small scar over one of his eyes. |
| Ben | 20 | Sept. 12, 1821 | *Nashville Whig* | J. McKinley | Lauderdale, AL | Ran away before and ended up in the Nashville jail. "Will no doubt endeavor to get to Jessamine County, Kentucky, where he was raised." |
| Stephen | 40 | Oct. 9, 1821 | *Knoxville Register* | Edward Tate | Grainger | "Has a small scar below one of his eyes." Previously had lived in North Carolina and ran away "and was taken in this county." |

| Name of Slave | Age | Date Published | Newspaper | Slave Holder | County | Special Notes |
|---|---|---|---|---|---|---|
| Fanny | 35 | Oct. 10, 1821 | *Nashville Whig* | Edward Scruggs | Sumner | Ran away from near the mouth of Mansker's Creek. |
| Harry/Joe | | Oct. 17, 1821 | *Nashville Whig* | Charles Bosley | Davidson | "Said negroes were purchased by Philip Shute in Richmond and delivered to me a few days ago; no doubt but their intention is to make their way back." |
| Major | | Nov. 28, 1821 | *Nashville Whig* | David Sloan | Pendleton, SC | Ran away and was caught in Sequatchee Valley, Tennessee, a few months earlier. "He has been whipped, and I expect bears the marks." |
| Betts | 30 | Dec. 4, 1821 | *Knoxville Register* | Robert Wear | Loudon | She "has a scar a little above the elbow occasioned by a burn" and is "very artful and cunning." Slaveholder lives in Morganton [now submerged location]. |
| Patty | 29 | Dec. 18, 1821 | *Knoxville Register* | Robert King | Knox | Has a scar on one of her arms. |
| Ellick | | Jan. 22, 1822 | *Nashville Whig* | R&W Armstrong | Davidson | Formerly the "property" of Governor Carroll. |
| Jim | 37 | March 10, 1822 | *Knoxville Register* | William Deery | Sullivan | "Once belonged to Captain Salathiel Martin of Claiborne County." Ran away from Blountville. |
| Harry | | April 17, 1822 | *Nashville Whig* | R&W Armstrong | Davidson | "Was purchased from Isaac Franklin of Tennessee, where it is presumed he will aim for." |
| Henry | 20 | May 22, 1822 | *Nashville Whig* | Z. Grant | Montgomery | "Has a scar on his forehead near the hair." Bought from "Jonathan Cowly, who was on his way from Virginia to Missouri in 1819." |
| Charles | 26 | May 22, 1822 | *Nashville Whig* | Chamberlayne Jones | Davidson | Has a large scar across his forehead. "Has a wife at Mr. Alex Walker's on the north side of the Cumberland River near Haysborough." |
| Lewis | 25 | May 31, 1822 | *TN Watchman* | Anthony W. Vanleer & Co. | Montgomery | Ran away from the Tennessee iron works. Is "the property of D. Harrison, deceased, of Montgomery." His wife "owned by Mr. Morrison, who lives on the bend of the Cumberland River." |
| Daniel | 20 | May 31, 1822 | *TN Watchman* | William Bishop, jailer | Dickson | Has "rather a feminine voice" and escaped from the Dickson County jail. |
| Harry | 40 | June 1, 1822 | *Franklin Gazette* | William Yancy | Maury | "I suppose he is lurking about Nicholas P. Smith's, as he has a wife there, in Williamson County." |
| Billy | 37 | July 3, 1822 | *Nashville Whig* | Edward Jones | Sumner | "Drove a hack between Nashville and Louisville Ky. about three months last winter." Is "very fond of laughing and talking." |
| Bob | 23 | July 30, 1822 | *Knoxville Register* | James Reese | Jefferson | "Has a piece bit out of one of his ears" and "has considerable cunning but it is not forward or saucy." Slaveholder resides in Mossy Creek. |

| Name of Slave | Age | Date Published | Newspaper | Slave Holder | County | Special Notes |
|---|---|---|---|---|---|---|
| Ned | 4 | Aug. 20, 1822 | *Knoxville Register* | Thomas Clark | Monroe | Has a scar under the shirt collar " occassioned by a burn." |
| Nelson | | Aug. 20, 1822 | *Knoxville Register* | Adam Huntsman | Overton | "A scar under one of his eyes" and "another almost in the center of his forehead." He may have left with an "abandoned prostitute" named Margaret Bauldwin. |
| Sam / John | 27 | Aug. 28, 1822 | *Nashville Whig* | David M. Harding | Davidson | Sam is a fiddle player who was purchased "high up in Virginia." John (22) is from Maryland and "studders very bad when spoken to." |
| Eady/ Rachel | 23 | Sept. 3, 1822 | *Knoxville Register* | Thomas C. Hindman | Roane | Eady was "raised" by the late Robert Holt of Knoxville. Rachel (24) was purchased from James Stephenson of Knoxville. |
| George | 24 | Sept. 3, 1822 | *Knoxville Register* | Robert Bradley | Smith | "Was brought from the Eastern shore of Maryland this spring past." Slaveholder resides near Dixon's Springs. |
| John | 35 | Sept. 18, 1822 | *Nashville Whig* | Henry Robertson | Lincoln | Has some scars on his face. Previously lived in Mississippi, and prior to that, in Nashville. |
| Betty | 40 | Sept. 25, 1822 | *Nashville Whig* | John Strode | Sumner | "Light complexion and rather slender made." |
| Nimrod | 22 | Dec. 11, 1822 | *Nashville Whig* | R.H. Boston | Madison, AL | Ran away before and was caught and put in jail in Pulaski. |
| Savage | 37 | Dec. 21, 1822 | *Franklin Gazette* | William Wright | Williamson | "Twice before made the attempt." This runaway ad also signed by William Tillette, so Savage was probably hired out. |
| Lizy | 28 | Feb. 12, 1823 | *Nashville Whig* | S.V.D. Stout | Davidson | "Speaks soft when spoken to." |
| Joshua | 20 | Feb. 14, 1823 | *Knoxville Register* | John Sharp | Sevier | "Has rather a down look." |
| Kingston | 30 | Feb. 24, 1823 | *Knoxville Register* | James Sanders | Sumner | "More than ordinarily intelligent." |
| Silas | 22 | April 2, 1823 | *Nashville Whig* | John O'Neil | Davidson | "Yellowish complexion" and "very small round head." |
| Trouble/ Phillip/ July | 55 | April 30, 1823 | *Nashville Whig* | George Colbert | Chickasaw Nat | Trouble ran away with Phillip (20) and July (18). All speak English and Chickasaw. |
| Benjamin | 32 | April 30, 1823 | *Nashville Whig* | William Ward | Rutherford | Shoemaker, woodworker and flatboat maker who "speaks proper and distinct." |
| Sambo | 34 | May 30, 1823 | *Knoxville Register* | Robert Hays | Greene | A "scar on his left cheek by a cut under the eye." |
| Charles | 21 | June 11, 1823 | *Nashville Whig* | Thomas Cash | Williamson | A blacksmith who is a "keen artful fellow." He may have got on board the steam boat Pittsburgh unknown to the captain; purchased from Rev. Gideon Blackburn of Williamson." |
| Ned | | July 7, 1823 | *Nashville Whig* | Thomas Fearn | Davidson | Reads and writes; ran away before from a man who was moving from Lexington, KY, to Huntsville. |

| Name of Slave | Age | Date Published | Newspaper | Slave Holder | County | Special Notes |
|---|---|---|---|---|---|---|
| Clara/ Louise | 19 | Sept. 9, 1823 | *Jackson Pioneer* | Ms. Henrietta Jacobs | Chickasaw Bluffs | Louise is 12 years old. These slaves are "owned" by Henrietta Jacobs, "a helpless widow with three little children." Clara is "talkative when indulged." |
| Jim/Elijah | 32 | Oct. 23, 1823 | *Tennessee Watchman* | Robert Baxter | Davidson | Ran away with Elijah (40), who has "two large scars on his head, from cuts, which are perceivable unless his hat is on." |
| Bob | 30 | Jan. 19, 1824 | *Nashville Whig* | John Dorlon | Henry | "A tolerably good barber, an excellent ostler, and a very polite fellow" and who has a scar on nose and upper lip. |
| Henry | 22 | May 17, 1824 | *Nashville Whig* | Elijah Kimbrough | Rutherford | "Formerly belonged to the estate of Frederick Stump, dec'd . . . has a wife at Mr. N.A. McNairy's." |
| Morris | 40 | June 21, 1824 | *Nashville Whig* | John Hays | Davidson | A shoemaker whose wife is in Alabama. |
| Billy | 35 | Oct. 28, 1824 | *Nashville Whig* | Nathaniel A. McNairy | Davidson | An ostler, and the "same negro that has attended on the Female Academy of Nashville for several years past." |
| Fountain | 30 | Nov. 8, 1824 | *Nashville Whig* | Lysander McGavock | Williamson | "He had a pair of handcuffs on when he broke away." |
| Hugh | | Nov. 24, 1824 | *Knoxville Enquirer* | William Whiteman | Knox | It is "expected he will go to Kingston, as I purchased him of Blackwell and Martin." |
| Ezekiel/ Isaac/ Shadrach | 40 | Dec. 11, 1824 | *Jackson Gazette* | John Maness | Madison | Ran away with Isaac (30) and Shadrach (29). "They were raised, it is believed, on the eastern shore of Maryland." |
| David | | Dec. 15, 1824 | *Knoxville Enquirer* | Woodson Francis | Rhea | A blacksmith whose "intention is to get back to the state of Maryland, from whence he was recently brought." |
| Peter | | Feb. 19, 1825 | *Jackson Gazette* | Robert Clanton | Madison | "Has with him a dark bay horse." |
| Quale | | March 14, 1825 | *Nashville Whig* | Zach Wyatt | Stewart | A "first rate distiller" and blacksmith who is knock-kneed. Likely to head to Williamson County, "as he was brought from that neighborhood by Mr. Amon Johnson." |
| Ben | 27 | March 14, 1825 | *Nashville Whig* | George Smith | Madison, AL | Expected to head for Williamson County, where he used to live. |
| Henry | 22 | March 26, 1825 | *Jackson Gazette* | James Baxter | Madison | "Several scars on his face." |
| Willis | 42 | April 23, 1825 | *Nashville Whig* | John Easley | Hickman | "Professes to be a conjurer or fortune teller" and has a scar on one of his cheeks. |
| Billy | 40 | April 23, 1825 | *Nashville Whig* | John Nichols | Davidson | His wife is at Judge Whyte's in Nashville. Both of his ears have been scarred and "his countenance resembling that or any Indian." |
| Essick | 42 | May 16, 1825 | *[Paris] West Tennessean* | John Hardin | Chickasaw Nation [Mississippi] | A "scar on his forehead" and "his left thumb nearly cut off." Expected to "aim for Monroe, Kentucky, by the way of Bolivar, Paris and Dover in Tennessee." |

| Name of Slave | Age | Date Published | Newspaper | Slave Holder | County | Special Notes |
|---|---|---|---|---|---|---|
| George | 19 | July 16, 1825 | *Nashville Whig* | D.C. Ward | Davidson | Can read and is a carpenter. Has a visible scar on his forehead and his "arms occasioned by burns when small." May be heading to Smith County. |
| Charles | | July 16, 1825 | *Nashville Whig* | W.D. Whitsitt | Henry | "Purchased said boy from Dr. Jos. Minick near Nashville, last winter, and it is probable may be in that neighborhood at this time." |
| Ben | | July 30, 1825 | *Jackson Gazette* | George Todd | Madison | "Has a wife at Parson Haralson's in Haywood." |
| Bradley/4 others | 32 | Aug. 6, 1825 | *Nashville Whig* | Isaac Franklin | Sumner | Ran away with Shedrick, Bill (35), Elias (25) and Alfred (19). |
| Grace/3 others | 25 | Sept. 3, 1825 | *Jackson Gazette* | David Shropshire | Madison | Grace "was under sentence of death for murdering a child. "Henry "a bold impudent fellow." Mary had with her an infant child. All 4 ran away from jail together. |
| Eliza Kemp | | Oct. 3, 1825 | *Nashville Whig* | Peter Perkins | Williamson | "When walking steps briskly; speaks low when spoken to by a white person. . . previously belonged to the heirs of J. Camp." |
| Elijah | 35 | Oct. 3, 1825 | *Nashville Whig* | Henry Crabb | Davidson | A scar on his head. |
| Isaac/Paddy | 27 | Oct. 3, 1825 | *Nashville Whig* | Charles Bosley | Davidson | Both recently purchased from Kentucky. Isaac "has a scar in the center of his forehead resembling a cross." Paddy (20) "has the appearance of a burn." |
| Jacob | 45 | Oct. 3, 1825 | *Nashville Whig* | John Nichols | Davidson | "A carpenter by trade" who "has a scar on his forehead produced by a cut." |
| Cato | 28 | Nov. 28, 1825 | *Nashville Whig* | Daniel A. Dunham | Davidson | Ran away with Robin and Moses. Can read, is a blacksmith, and recently cut the top of his left foot with an axe. "Was purchased last spring from James Weir" of Greeneville, KY. |
| Robin | 25 | Nov. 28, 1825 | *Nashville Whig* | William E. Watkins | Davidson | Ran away with Cato and Moses. |
| Moses | 30 | Nov. 28, 1825 | *Nashville Whig* | Edwin H. Childress | Davidson | Ran away with Cato and Robin. |
| Creed | 19 | Jan. 18, 1826 | *Knoxville Enquirer* | Blake B. Jones | Tuscaloosa, AL | Raised in Chesterfield County, VA then moved to Pulaski, TN. Sold to current slaveholder in 1820. |
| Ben | 35 | April 26, 1826 | *Jackson Gazette* | John McClellan | Madison | "Pretends to be a preacher" and "has a small bit taken out of one of his ears and probably a scar on his face." |
| Jacob | 20 | July 8, 1826 | *National Banner/ Nashville Whig* | Abel Beaty | Tipton | "Speaks freely, is full of chat. . . I brought him from Rutherford, North Carolina, to which place he will probably attempt to return." |

| Name of Slave | Age | Date Published | Newspaper | Slave Holder | County | Special Notes |
|---|---|---|---|---|---|---|
| Armstead | 26 | Oct. 7, 1826 | *National Banner/ Nashville Whig* | Wiley F. Daniel | Bedford | "A stone mason by trade" who "speaks rather long and slow when spoken to. . . I have good reason to think he is conducted by a white man, Dennis Dial, of Bedford." |
| Lawson | 23 | Feb. 2, 1827 | *Hiwassee Reporter* | James Thomas | McMinn | "Has a very bad scar on his head, running with the mold thereof, and then down toward the ear, as to form an angle." |
| Ned | 25 | April 18, 1827 | *Knoxville Enquirer* | Samuel Kennedy | Knox | A tanner whose left hand injured by the bursting of a gun and "has rather a bad countenance and a down look when spoken to." |
| David | 23 | Sept. 2, 1827 | *Murfreesbor-ough Courier* | Benjamin Forbes | Rutherford | A scar on his right arm, also a small one on his forehead. "It is likely he will make for ... Caldwell County, Kentucky, where his mother lives." |
| Billy | 24 | Sept. 2, 1827 | *Murfreesbor-ough Courier* | James Irwin | Rutherford | "I have owned him but a few days" and "he was raised in the neighborhood of Washington City and brought from that place by a man named Samuel Hunter" of NC. |
| Joe/Anica | 36 | Sept. 2, 1827 | *Murfreesbor-ough Courier* | N. Partee | Rutherford | Ran away with his wife Anica (23), who is also "owned" by N. Partee. |
| Emery | 25 | Sept. 15, 1827 | *Memphis Adv WDI* | Robert Rose | Tipton | [First runaway slave ad I can find published in Memphis.] |
| Crese/ Pleasant | 16 | Nov. 5, 1827 | *Memphis Advocate and Western District Intelligencer* | Patrick Meagher | Shelby | Crese "has the ends from the third and fourth fingers of the right hand taken off by a burn" and "extremely forward and pert when spoken to." |
| Ned | 22 | Dec. 8, 1827 | *Memphis Adv WDI* | Joseph Graham | Shelby | "Has a remarkable scar behind his left shoulder blade" and is "inclined to swing in walking." |
| Orange | 35 | Jan. 12, 1828 | *Nat Banner/ Nashville Whig* | Robert Doak | Maury | Ran away with Stephen and Elijah. |
| Stephen/ Elijah | 32 | Jan. 12, 1828 | *Nat Banner/ Nashville Whig* | J. Rucks | Davidson | Ran away together. Elijah (22) "speaks rather slower than common." |
| Jeff | 18 | Jan. 19, 1828 | *National Banner/ Nashville Whig* | David Barrow | Davidson | "Belongs to the estate of H. Crabb," who is a teenager. Is "well known in and about Nashville." |
| Sally | 22 | Jan. 19, 1828 | *Nat Banner/ Nashville Whig* | Green B. Bateman | Rutherford | Is pregnant and has a small scar over one of her eyes. |
| David | 35 | Jan. 19, 1828 | *National Banner/ Nashville Whig* | Thomas S. Spencer | Maury | "Rather ugly, has one club foot" and "walks badly." Slaveholder address is Mt. Pleasant. |
| Johnson/ Isaac/ Chooker | 23 | March 1, 1828 | *National Banner/ Nashville Whig* | James Saunders | Sumner | Ran away with Isaac (57) and Chooker (37). Isaac is "very fluent in speech" and Chooker is "a shrewd , cunning fellow, artful and ingenious." |

| Name of Slave | Age | Date Published | Newspaper | Slave Holder | County | Special Notes |
|---|---|---|---|---|---|---|
| Isom | 25 | March 1, 1828 | *Nat Banner/ Nashville Whig* | Jonas Jones | Cannon | Ran away with Bob. |
| Bob | 26 | March 1, 1828 | *Nat Banner/ Nashville Whig* | Jesse Thompson | Cannon | "Slow of speech, with a down look." Ran away with Isom. |
| Orin | 29 | March 1, 1828 | *National Banner/ Nashville Whig* | Isom Robertson | Selma, AL | Purchased from the estate of the late John Robertson in Fayetteville; his mother still lives there. |
| George | 17 | March 1, 1828 | *National Banner/ Nashville Whig* | Joseph Cook | Davidson | Has a scar near his right eye and another on his forehead and "of slender made, with great activity." Was raised near Carthage "by Mrs. Goodall." |
| Sterling | 20 | March 1, 1828 | *National Banner/ Nashville Whig* | G.W. Campbell | Giles | "Was raised in Halifax County, North Carolina and brought to this state last fall . . . He will probably attempt to go back where he was raised." |
| Edmund | 35 | April 16, 1828 | *Knoxville Register* | Samuel Fowlkes | Nottoway, VA | "Has a scar on his right breast." Was caught in Rutledge, TN, before and may be on his way to Columbia in search of his wife. |
| Louis/Jack | 32 | April 19, 1828 | *National Banner/Nashville Whig* | John L. Brown | Davidson | Both were seen 4 miles north of Nashville on the road heading to Lexington. Both "purchased" 2 months ago from that place. Jack is a fiddle player. |
| Sam | 22 | April 19, 1828 | *National Banner/ Nashville Whig* | David M. Harding | Davidson | Has a scar, "I think, on his left side." Ran away from the Belle Meade Mansion and was raised near Bowling Green. |
| Nancy | 35 | April 26, 1828 | *Nat Banner/ Nashville Whig* | Ellen Kirkman | Davidson | Has lived in Nashville about 10 years. |
| Charles | 20 | April 26, 1828 | *Nat Banner/ Nashville Whig* | A.W. Norris | Williamson | "Slow motioned and slow of utterance." |
| Dave | 27 | April 26, 1828 | *National Banner/ Nashville Whig* | John Tillman | Bedford | A "considerable scar on his breast" and "has been seen frequently in the neighborhood of where the counties of Bedford, Rutherford and Warren join." Slaveholders address is Davis Mills. |
| Isham | 45 | May 28, 1828 | *Knoxville Register* | John Love | Greene | "A scar on the back of his head which is bald." |
| Reuben | | May 28, 1828 | *Knoxville Register* | William Bowen | Knox | "Frequently preaches" and "appears very humble when spoken to." |
| Hiram | 26 | July 4, 1828 | *National Banner/ Nashville Whig* | Palfrey, Dyson & Co. | Orleans, LA | An engineer and blacksmith and can read. "Is supposed to have gone off in the steamboat Emerald for Nashville." |
| Sukey Butcher | 23 | July 4, 1828 | *Nat Banner/ Nashville Whig* | Robertson Johnston | Wilson | "Rather larger than an ordinary woman." |
| Lucy/2 others | 30 | July 4, 1828 | *National Banner/ Nashville Whig* | Joseph Cotton | Fayette | Woman ran away with 2 small children, ages 2 and 1. Both children described as "mulatto," but mother is not. They may have been taken away by Samuel A. Hamner. |

| Name of Slave | Age | Date Published | Newspaper | Slave Holder | County | Special Notes |
|---|---|---|---|---|---|---|
| Ben/2 others | | July 5, 1828 | *Memphis Adv WDI* | Robinson J. Cotten | Fayette | Ran away with Joe and George. All 3 believed to be headed back to North Carolina, from where they came. |
| Robin | 30 | Aug. 16, 1828 | *National Banner/ Nashville Whig* | Benjamin Litton | Davidson | "Has a tetter in his face" and is "surley when spoken to." [This slaveholder later became a Chancery Court Clerk and Master.] |
| Mansfield | 26 | Oct. 4, 1828 | *National Banner/ Nashville Whig* | M.B. Belknap | Stewart | A bricklayer and plasterer who "talks fast, smiles whist speaking." Ran away from Dover Furnace and was purchased in Petersburg, VA; held by William Compton of Nashville. |
| Clai-borne/ Charity | 37 | Oct. 25, 1828 | *National Banner/ Nashville Whig* | James G. Martin | Davidson | Husband and wife Charity (34) ran away together. He is a shoemaker, can read and is "shrewd and artful." She is a good weaver and seamstress. |
| Cook/ Primus | 40 | Nov. 1, 1828 | *National Banner/ Nashville Whig* | John Ruff | Carroll | Ran away together; both brought from Green County, NC, last spring and may attempt to get back. Cook is a "Guinea" negro. Primus is about 38. |
| Charles | 19 | Dec. 6, 1828 | *Jackson Gazette* | John McCracken | Lawrence | "A bright mulatto, without any scars." |
| Orrison/ Lucy | 27 | Dec. 6, 1828 | *Nat Banner/ Nashville Whig* | Mary Walker | Williamson | Ran away together. Lucy is 35. |
| Phillis | 19 | Jan. 7, 1829 | *Knoxville Register* | Isaac Bass | Knox | "A scar and naked place on her head, occasioned by a burn." Slaveholder asks that Phillis be delivered to Zac Boothe. |
| Jacob | 23 | Jan. 10, 1829 | *Nat Banner/ Nashville Whig* | William Wray | Davidson | "Speaks quick and short." Slaveholder address is Neely's Bend. |
| Hardy | 25 | Jan. 29, 1829 | *National Banner/ Nashville Whig* | Rebekcah Williams | Davidson | "Was raised in Northhampton, North Carolina . . . lived several years in Raleigh." |
| Charles | | Jan. 30, 1829 | *Franklin Western Balance* | Thomas H. Perkins | Williamson | "Blacksmith by trade." |
| Payne | | Jan. 31, 1829 | *National Banner/ Nashville Whig* | Unsigned Ad | Davidson | "Yellow complexion, well grown and likely." Asks that he be delivered to the jailer. |
| Green | 25 | March 21, 1829 | *Nat Banner/ Nashville Whig* | James Brown | Williamson | "Tolerably quick spoken." |
| Anthony | 36 | March 21, 1829 | *National Banner/ Nashville Whig* | Jason W. Smith | Jackson | A scar on his left arm and "has travelled as a servant considerably in the western country." |
| Nathaniel | 27 | March 21, 1829 | *Nat Banner/ Nashville Whig* | William Liggett | Maury | A "scar under his chin" and "has a down look when talked to." |
| Bill | 45 | April 11, 1829 | *Jackson Gazette* | Duncan McIver | Tipton | A "down look when spoken to. . . he was purchased of a Mr. Reed, who owns his wife and now resides in Gibson County." |
| Dick | 23 | June 13, 1829 | *National Banner/ Nashville Whig* | John P. Wagnon | Sumner | "A blemish in one eye" and "will endeavor to get to Green County, Georgia, or to some of the free states." |

| Name of Slave | Age | Date Published | Newspaper | Slave Holder | County | Special Notes |
|---|---|---|---|---|---|---|
| Ben | 18 | June 13, 1829 | *Jackson Gazette* | Enos Rodgers | Tipton | "Sprightly look, when spoken to." |
| Frederick | 25 | Aug. 8, 1829 | *Knoxville Register* | William Cannon | Sevier | "A scar on his breast caused by a burn, cripped in one finger" and is a "keen, active fellow." |
| Joe | 37 | Sept. 2, 1829 | *Knoxville Register* | John Winton | Roane | Can read and write, is a preacher and "has a down look." Also, "it is thought he will endeavor to get to Richmond, Virginia, from whence he was brought." |
| Robert | 13 | Sept. 5, 1829 | *Nat Banner/ Nashville Whig* | Calvin Goodman | Davidson | His hair is inclinded to be "reddish." |
| Daniel | | Oct. 10, 1829 | *National Banner/ Nashville Whig* | Peter Demoville | Davidson | Ran away from George Austin's brickyard. Has a "scar on his ankle" and may be heading for Hanover County, Virginia, "having frequently threatened to return to that place." |
| Edmund | 19 | Oct. 31, 1829 | *Nat Banner/ Nashville Whig* | Joseph T. Elliston | Davidson | A scar on his forehead and took with him a pocketbook with $70 in it. |
| Jim | 30 | Dec. 29, 1829 | *National Banner/ Nashville Whig* | John Timmons | Madison, AL | An African by birth who may be coming to see his wife who is "now owned by Jason Ridley of Nashville." |
| Jack | 50 | Jan. 13, 1830 | *Knoxville Register* | Thomas Clark | Roane | Ran away with David. Jack "has a scar across his nose, extending on each cheek, made with a knife" and "speaks quickly when spoken to." |
| David | 47 | Jan. 13, 1830 | *Knoxville Register* | Isham Cox | Roane | Ran away with Jack. David is a "shrewd, cunnng fellow." |
| Willis | 23 | Jan. 26, 1830 | *Nat Banner/ Nashville Whig* | Fountain Hume | Davidson | Will "more than likely endeavor to get business at some of the landings." |
| Daniel | 32 | Jan. 30, 1830 | *Jackson Gazette* | Nathaniel W. Dandridge | Madison | The "forefinger of his right hand is off at the second joint." Also, his wife is at James Norvell's. |
| Maria | 22 | Feb. 5, 1830 | *National Banner/ Nashville Whig* | William Gill | Davidson | "Speaks slow." Slaveholder wants her returned to Wiliam D. Philips, near his residence, near White's Creek. |
| William | 23 | Feb. 5, 1830 | *National Banner/ Nashville Whig* | Peyton Fletcher | Davidson | A riverboat worker who "is known in Nashville by the name Bill Tate. It is understood that he left this place on the steamboat Traveller." |
| Reuben | | April 9, 1830 | *Nat Banner/ Nashville Whig* | William Dwyer | Davidson | "Was seen a few days since in town, where it is supposed he yet remains." |
| Stephen | 27 | June 5, 1830 | *Jackson Gazette* | Dempsey E. Brittenum | Perry | "With a pleasing countenance, and tolerably much knock kneed. . . was purchased six years ago in Anson County, N.C." |
| Robin | | June 7, 1830 | *National Banner/ Nashville Whig* | Benjamin Litton | Davidson | "Marked in the face by a tetterworm." [This slave ran away from the same man 2 years earlier.] |
| Davy | 35 | July 1, 1830 | *Knoxville Register* | Alexander McMillan | Knox | "Cringing and sycophantic in his manners." |

| Name of Slave | Age | Date Published | Newspaper | Slave Holder | County | Special Notes |
|---|---|---|---|---|---|---|
| Tom/ Charlotte | 40 | July 1, 1830 | *National Banner/ Nashville Whig* | George Ament | Davidson | Husband and wife ran away together. He is a weaver by trade who "when he is scared "stammers a bit." She is 32 and is "rather inclined to be fat." |
| Mirah/Sal | 15 | Aug. 2, 1830 | *National Banner/ Nashville Whig* | Richard A. McRee | Henderson | Slaveholder believes both girls were stolen by a white man from Maury named Joel Huggins, to whom they formerly belonged. Sal is 11 years old. |
| Isaac/ Surrey/ Toney | 30 | Sept. 6, 1830 | *National Banner/ Nashville Whig* | Edward O. Chambers | Tipton | Isaac a "cunning fellow" who came from Mercer County, KY, and "always had a desire to return." Surrey is 30. Toney (40) lost some toes and forefingers when he was a child. |
| Ephraim | 18 | Sept. 6, 1830 | *National Banner/ Nashville Whig* | Abraham Overall | DeKalb | "Has a mark on the corner of the eyebrow and a flesh cut on the inside of his left foot." Slaveholder resides in Liberty. |
| Gabriel | 28 | Sept. 6, 1830 | *Nat Banner/ Nashville Whig* | Joseph Miller | Davidson | A steward on riverboat Red Rover whose "back much marked by the whip." |
| Jerry | 30 | Sept. 22, 1830 | *Knoxville Register* | John Patterson | Hamilton | Has a "large mole or wart on the under part of his upper lip." |
| David/ wife/child | 28 | Sept. 22, 1830 | *Knoxville Register* | John Patterson | Hamilton | A blacksmith with a scar on his head who ran away with his 22-year-old wife and one-year-old child. |
| Jim | 25 | Oct. 14, 1830 | *National Banner/ Nashville Whig* | A.B. Shelby | Davidson | "Can read and write well" and ran away from the race course near Nashville. Formerly belonged to E.D. Hicks of Nashville. |
| Isaac | 25 | Oct. 14, 1830 | *National Banner/ Nashville Whig* | John S. Willis | Bedford | Has scars on his arms from being a blacksmith. Also, "when walking, hangs his head." |
| Simon | 40 | Oct. 27, 1830 | *Knoxville Register* | F.C. Boston | Roane | "Has an usually large foot" and "walks a little lame." |
| Jordan | 15 | Nov. 3, 1830 | *Knoxville Register* | Samuel Mitchell | Bedford | A "keen, artful fellow. . . no doubt is trying to make his way to the State of Virginia." |
| Wilson | 27 | Nov. 4, 1830 | *National Banner/ Nashville Whig* | James E. Browning | Madison, AL | A shoemaker and "sprightly, active fellow. . . .It is likely he is now lurking about Nashville, as he has a sister living in that place." |
| Surry | 30 | Dec. 29, 1830 | *National Banner/ Nashville Whig* | Samuel Kercheval | Giles | A plasterer who can read and write who is "easy in his address, and when spoken to, speaks low and soft." |
| David | 22 | Jan. 12, 1831 | *Knoxville Register* | M.H. Bogle | Blount | A "small scar on or near the top of his head" and has a "very pleasing countenance, inclining to smile when spoken to." |
| Gabriel | | Jan. 21, 1831 | *Nat Banner/ Nashville Whig* | Peter Vaughan | Rutherford | "Has a scar on each of his hands." Slaveholder address is Abbott's Mill. |

| Name of Slave | Age | Date Published | Newspaper | Slave Holder | County | Special Notes |
|---|---|---|---|---|---|---|
| Mike | 21 | Jan. 21, 1831 | *National Banner/ Nashville Whig* | John Mosely | Madison, AL | A large scar above one of his eyebrows. "I understand he was taken up and made his escape at the fishing ford of Duck River, Bedford, Tenn." |
| Bill | 30 | Feb. 28, 1831 | *National Banner/ Nashville Whig* | Z.H.B. Anthony | Rutherford | Is "lame in the left hip" and "was seen about Nashville a short time after he ran away." |
| Jacob | 24 | March 9, 1831 | *Knoxville Register* | James W. Wily | Greene | Has a large scar on his arm and "possesses a good countenance . . . well calculated to impose on the unsuspecting. . . Will aim to reach a horde of counterfeiters who infest Clinch mountain." |
| Bob | 40 | March 18, 1831 | *National Banner/ Nashville Whig* | Robert Newell | Davidson | "Has a wife at Mr. William Ramsey's . . . I think the said boy is lurking about the neighborhood of Nashville, or upon Mill Creek." |
| John Cartwright | 27 | April 4, 1831 | *National Banner/ Nashville Whig* | Perry Horney | Davidson | Ran away from a man who apprehended him and was heading to the Williamson jail. |
| Daniel/ Betsy | 25 | April 28, 1831 | *National Banner/ Nashville Whig* | Joseph Dunbar | Jefferson, Miss. | Previously "owned" by Col. Ward in the Choctaw Agency, then by John Rodgers of Giles. [The government of Nashville later bought these slaves.] |
| Lewis | 25 | May 20, 1831 | *National Banner/ Nashville Whig* | Benjamin Fugitt | Rutherford | Speaks "a little" French and "has holes in his ears for rings and a scar on the inside of his wrist." Ran away with Sam. |
| Sam | 29 | May 20, 1831 | *Nat Banner/ Whig* | John B. Pruitt | Bedford | "A rough square made bow-legged sluggish fellow." Ran away with Lewis. |
| Daniel/ Betsy | 25 | July 11, 1831 | *Nat Banner/ Nashville Whig* | Sam V.D. Stout, Mayor | Davidson | Ran away again, this time from the government of Nashville. |
| Tom | | July 11, 1831 | *National Banner/ Nashville Whig* | James C. Rupert | Tipton | A blacksmith whose "utterance is not very good." Was purchased from Georgia. |
| Bob | 20 | July 13, 1831 | *Knoxville Register* | George W. Porter | Sevier | "Looks very sternly at you when spoken to" and "has a large scar on one of his wrists." |
| Davy | 19 | Aug. 26, 1831 | *National Banner/ Nashville Whig* | William B. Ament | Davidson | "A skillful thief" who was bought from Mr. Nicholas Hobson and was seen lurking about the residence of Samuel Weakley. |
| Peter | 29 | Sept. 23, 1831 | *National Banner/ Nashville Whig* | James R. Bosley | Davidson | Is "supposed to be in the upper part of Williamson, on the head waters of the Harpeth River." |
| Bill | 24 | Oct. 5, 1831 | *National Banner/ Nashville Whig* | Amsel Epperson | Hickman | "Reads well and writes a little." Had been bought out of jail in Florence, Alabama, and "never would say who had owned him before." |
| Mary | 18 | Nov. 21, 1831 | *Nat Banner/ Nashville Whig* | Elizabeth Moore | Davidson | "Last owned by Mr. William Nichol and purchased from him by Gilman Moore." |

| Name of Slave | Age | Date Published | Newspaper | Slave Holder | County | Special Notes |
|---|---|---|---|---|---|---|
| Henry | 35 | Nov. 21, 1831 | *National Banner/ Nashville Whig* | Edward A. Moseley | Bedford | Was raised in Mecklenburg County, Virginia, and ran away before and was caught in Smith after which he was "kept in chains." [This ad was continuously run for more than a year.] |
| Archer | 28 | Jan. 20, 1832 | *National Banner/ Nashville Whig* | Benjamin T. Parkinson | Tipton | "Both of his feet have been frostbitten, has lost a part of one of his large toes and on his other foot some of his other toes." Was raised in Prince Edward County, VA. |
| Patrick | | Feb. 4, 1832 | *National Banner/ Nashville Whig* | Sterling H. Lester | Giles | Trained race horses and is "humble and respectful to white persons" and "when interrogated, is apt to twist or shake his shoulders." |
| Alfred | | March 6, 1832 | *(Shelbyville) West Free* | Robert Stevenson | Bedford | "I had hired him from the widow Martin." |
| Claiborne/ Lucy | 40 | March 7, 1832 | *Knoxville Register* | William E. Phillips | Knox | Husband and wife ran away together at McBee's Ferry while traveling through Knoxville on way to Huntsville, AL. Lucy (30) has 2 scars on her forehead. |
| Jerry | | March 7, 1832 | *Knoxville Register* | James Henry | Blount | "Has very large feet something like 13 inches in length." |
| Simpson | 26 | April 19, 1832 | *Nat Banner/ Nashville Whig* | Robert Doak | Maury | "When spoken to speaks rather low and slow." Slaveholder address is Little Bigby. |
| Solomon Smith | 30 | May 16, 1832 | *Knoxville Register* | Perrin Cardwell | Knox | "A barber by trade who "has a scar on his head occasioned by a burn" and "one leg longer than the other. . . He left the steam boat Knoxville at Brown's Ferry in Alabama." |
| Tom | 22 | May 19, 1832 | *Nat Banner/ Nashville Whig* | L.P. Cheatham | Davidson | [This slaveholder was later a Clerk and Master.] |
| Warren | 18 | June 13, 1832 | *Nat Banner/ Nashville Whig* | Ramon Mon. | Orleans, LA | Speaks Spanish, French and English and "is a native of Tennessee." |
| Thornton | 23 | June 23, 1832 | *Nat Banner/ Nashville Whig* | Thomson & Grant | Orleans, LA | This slave was sold by Richard Johnson of Nashville only 6 months earlier. |
| Wilson | 21 | July 5, 1832 | *Nat Banner/ Nashville Whig* | G.W. Coleman | Davidson | "Has no eyelashes on the upper side of the left eye." |
| Edom | 20 | Aug. 9, 1832 | *National Banner/ Nashville Whig* | George L. Bird | Madison, AL | "There remains some considerable scars on his breast." This slave once lived in or near Winchester with a tailor named Harril. |
| Austin | 30 | Aug. 21, 1832 | *(Shelbyville) West Free* | Flower Swift | Bedford | "Yellow, active and smart." |
| Ralph | 17 | Aug. 22, 1832 | *Nat Banner/ Nashville Whig* | Dennis Cannon | Hickman | "Low, chunky, well set." |
| Judy | 21 | Sept. 20, 1832 | *Nat Banner/ Nashville Whig* | H.R. Elgin | Rutherford | A seamstress who may have been pregnant when she ran away. |

| Name of Slave | Age | Date Published | Newspaper | Slave Holder | County | Special Notes |
|---|---|---|---|---|---|---|
| Harry/ Jenny | 35 | Oct. 16, 1832 | *National Banner/ Nashville Whig* | James Trezvant | Fayette | Husband and wife ran away together. Both "came here with me recently from Virginia." He is "shrewd and artful." She is 24, a seamstress, and pregnant. |
| Lossen | 18 | Oct. 17, 1832 | *Knoxville Register* | Archibald Cobb | Knox | Has a small scar a little above the corner of his right eye and "took with him a New Testament." |
| James | | Nov. 28, 1832 | *Knoxville Register* | A.C. Gillespie | Maury | Has a scar near his eye and "lost the first joint of the middle finger of the left hand." Has relatives in VA and used to belong to Dr. McCall of Nashville. |
| Miley/4 others | 30 | Jan. 7, 1833 | *National Banner/ Nashville Whig* | John B. Lynch | Montgom- ery | 5 ran away from Blooming Grove Creek iron furnace. Miley "has an old scar on her head and has lost part of a finger." Others include Buddy, George, Frank (a carpenter) and Cyrus (who is "awkward and stupid.") |
| Frank | 24 | Feb. 7, 1833 | *National Banner/ Nashville Whig* | Daniel Buie | Davidson | "Very pleasant appearance. . . purchased from Mr. Oliver Simpson of Rocking-ham County, North Carolina." [This ad ran for at least 6 months.] |
| John | | Feb. 7, 1833 | *National Banner/ Nashville Whig* | Elisha Clampitt | Cumberland | "Has a small lump on the back of his neck and a large scar on his thigh." Also, "his mother belongs to Mr. Matthew H. Quin" and "he was raised by Joseph T. Elliston of Nashville." |
| Bill | 35 | March 11, 1833 | *National Banner/ Nashville Whig* | C. and B.C. Robertson | Dickson | Has a large scar on his chest. Ran away from Harpeth Forge in Dickson. May have left on a boat because he "has been accustomed to follow the boating business for some years." |
| Paulina | 15 | March 30, 1833 | *National Banner/ Nashville Whig* | Jervis Cutler | Davidson | "Remarkably stout and strong for her age." Belonged to J.S. Simpson of Nashville and was presumably leased to Jervis Cutler. |
| David | 35 | April 15, 1833 | *National Banner/ Nashville Whig* | Henry C. Bell | Obion | An experienced cook on steamboats who has "one a club foot, which was burnt off where the instep joins the ankle." Slaveholder lives in Trigg County, KY, has a farm in Obion County. |
| Jim/2 others | 30 | May 8, 1833 | *Knoxville Register* | William T. Gholson | Shelby | Jim and Simson (23) were recently bought from Mr. Porter of Giles County. Michael was bought from Isaac Franklin, "and by him brought from Virginia." His arms much cut from frequent bleeding. |
| Washing-ton | 16 | May 13, 1833 | *Nat Banner/ Nashville Whig* | Henry Smith | Maury | "Has a small scar just above one of his eyes." |
| Charles | 22 | June 19, 1833 | *Knoxville Register* | John B. Crozier | Anderson | "When in a good humor, laughs very loud." Charles lived near Clinton, but Daniel Clap in Knox County "owns" his mother. |

| Name of Slave | Age | Date Published | Newspaper | Slave Holder | County | Special Notes |
|---|---|---|---|---|---|---|
| Ned | | July 5, 1833 | Nashville Republican | Andrew Cavit | Hardeman | "A similar sum for bringing the scoundrel to punishment who has seduced him off." |
| Joseph | 39 | July 19, 1833 | Nat Banner/ Nashville Whig | Jason Barret | Davidson | A weaver and shoemaker, who "reads and writes very well for a slave." |
| Caswell | 24 | Aug. 20, 1833 | National Banner/ Nashville Whig | George D. Blackmore | Davidson | Has 2 scars, one of which was "inflicted on himself during a moment of intoxication." Ran away from Dr. Shelby's mill. |
| Major | 42 | Sept. 4, 1833 | National Banner/ Nashville Whig | Charles W. Metcalfe | Robertson | "A stone cutter, stone mason and brick mason and a superior workman . . . was seen at the mouth of Cumberland River about three weeks ago, on board a keelboat." |
| Ailsey | | Sept. 4, 1833 | Nat Banner/ Nashville Whig | W.H. Moore | Robertson | "Has a pleasing countenance and a very neat appearance generally." |
| Jim | 33 | Sept. 27, 1833 | National Banner/ Nashville Whig | Peyton Robertson | Davidson | "Jim has been hired on the steamboat Nashville the last three years. . . it is supposed that he will endeavor to escape to Canada, where he has a brother who ran away 12 years since." |
| Charles | 26 | Nov. 14, 1833 | Nat Banner/ Nashville Whig | Thomas Miles | Rutherford | "Has a scar on one side of his head" and "free open countenance." |
| Squire | 26 | Nov. 14, 1833 | Nat Banner/ Nashville Whig | John Barber | Wilson | "Rather a down look." |
| Richmond | 22 | Dec. 16, 1833 | Nat Banner/ Nashville Whig | William S. King | Lincoln | Was raised by Thomas Peay of Williamson. |
| Moses | 20 | Feb. 11, 1834 | Nashville Republican | Edmond Turner | Sumner | The "second or middle finger on the right hand crooked." Was "last seen at the wharf in Nashville." |
| Granville | 25 | March 22, 1834 | Nashville Republican | Thomas B. Murphy | Madison, AL | Is "much freckled on his breast and face." He "will endeavor to make his way to Columbia, Tennessee where he has free parents." |
| Joshua | 50 | March 29, 1834 | Nashville Republican | Serene J. Hulme | Williamson | A Baptist preacher who "has a scar on one side of his face." |
| Annis | 30 | May 8, 1834 | Nashville Republican | Martha Boyd | Davidson | 4 of her upper teeth out and "scar caused by a burn on the back of her right hand." Also, "it is thought said negro left here on a steamboat." |
| John | 14 | May 10, 1834 | Nashville Republican | J.D. March | Davidson | "Very shrewd and sensible and quick spoken." |
| Jim | | June 21, 1834 | Randolph Recorder | Micajah Phelps | Tipton | "Limps very much, occasioned by a severe burn on one of his hips." |
| Jim | 24 | July 22, 1834 | Nashville Republican | Will Polk | Hardeman | "He is considerably marked on the back with the whip" and "rather a down look when spoken to." |
| Abram | | July 25, 1834 | Randolph Recorder | William Anthony | Tipton | "Has downcast looks when spoken to, and a hesitating speech especially when questioned close." Address of slaveholder is "Hatchey turnpike bridge." |

| Name of Slave | Age | Date Published | Newspaper | Slave Holder | County | Special Notes |
|---|---|---|---|---|---|---|
| Marion | 28 | Aug. 8, 1834 | *Columbia Observer* | William B. Vincent | Maury | "Has been seen in the neighborhood of Dr. G.T. Greenfield, in this county." |
| Emanuel | 35 | Aug. 12, 1834 | *Nashville Republican* | John Bass, Mayor | Davidson | Ran away from the corporation of Nashville. "Was raised by Edward Stokes of Petersburg, Va. and purchased of William Finch, Chesterfield County, Va." |
| Elijah | 22 | Sept. 6, 1834 | *Nashville Republican* | Benjamin Russell | Williamson | "Rather a stubborn countenance." Has runaway once before. |
| Mike | 35 | Sept. 16, 1834 | *Randolph Recorder* | Samuel Owen | Haywood | A "smiling countenance when addressed." |
| Granderson | 25 | Sept. 19, 1834 | *Columbia Observer* | William H. Harris | Haywood | Reads and writes. Has a "good many acquaintances" in Jackson and "a good many relations about Columbia." |
| Levi | 16 | Oct. 11, 1834 | *Murfr Central Monitor* | Booker Nevels | Maury | A "small scar in the forehead" and "I expect that he is aiming for Norfolk, Virginia." |
| Unnamed males | 20 | Nov. 7, 1834 | *Randolph Recorder* | Jonn Lawhorn, Jailer | Haywood | Unnamed runaways broke out of the Haywood County jail. |
| Sam/ Daniel | 23 | Nov. 15, 1834 | *Nashville Republican* | Thomas Talbot | Davidson | Sam "has a wife at Jonathan Wilkinson's on White's Creek" and "a scar on one side of his mouth." Daniel "was brought from Knoxville." |
| Davy/ Isam | 47 | Dec. 27, 1834 | *Nashville Republican* | Thomas Mull | Cumberland | Ran away at Crab Orchard together, having been brought from Salisbury, NC. Davy "speaks a little loud when spoken to." Isam (21) "has a rather wild look; lisps." |
| Emily | 19 | Dec. 30, 1834 | *Nashville Republican* | P.W. Davis | Davidson | "Bad countenance, down look when spoken to." |
| Lewis | 23 | Jan. 9, 1835 | *Randolph Recorder* | John Polk | Tipton | Formerly belonged to J.J. Alston of Tipton. |
| Amos | 28 | Jan. 9, 1835 | *Randolph Recorder* | Ferriday & Turner | Yazoo, MS | A shoemaker who broke out of Raleigh jail in Shelby County. |
| Tom/ Louis | 25 | Jan. 17, 1835 | *Nashville Republican* | Matthias B. Murfree | Rutherford | Tom has holes in his ears, wears earrings and "walks a little lame, has had the rheumatism." Louis (23) "stoops in his shoulders when walking." |
| Jerry | 40 | Feb. 13, 1835 | *Randolph Recorder* | Thomas Cooke | Tipton | Has "a hole in one of his cheeks from the toothache" and ran away from Portersville. |
| Stephen | 30 | Feb. 13, 1835 | *Randolph Recorder* | William McIntosh | Tipton | "Is obedient when sober but quarrelsome and inpudent when intoxicated." Ran away from the plantation of H.R.W. Hill, but apparently "owned" by William McIntosh. |
| Brister | 30 | Feb. 17, 1835 | *Nashville Republican* | Daniel Cherry | Haywood | "He was brought from North Carolina" and "has once before runaway and attempted to get to the state of Illinois." |
| Nicolas | 24 | Feb. 26, 1835 | *Nashville Republican* | John Edmonson Jr. | Williamson | "Has a fine set of razors marked Waller Cummins." |

| Name of Slave | Age | Date Published | Newspaper | Slave Holder | County | Special Notes |
|---|---|---|---|---|---|---|
| Jack | 22 | April 3, 1835 | *Randolph Recorder* | Orville Shelby | Tipton | Has "a burn under the right ear shaped like the letter O." Formerly belonged to Mr. Houston of Portersville. Ran away about 6 weeks ago and was caught in Arkansas. |
| Fanny | 17 | April 18, 1835 | *Nashville Republican* | Elizabeth Cox | Davidson | A seamstress and milliner who has a scar over one of her eyes. "Is property of William Lewis" but ran away from Elizabeth Cox, with whom she has lived and worked "at the millinery business." |
| Bob Craft | 40 | April 18, 1835 | *Nashville Republican* | L. P. Cheatham | Davidson | "Was engaged as a stone mason" and "has a scar just above one eyebrow." When talking, "looks often at the ground." |
| Shack | | May 15, 1835 | *Randolph Recorder* | George T. Tailor | Haywood | A bricklayer and plasterer who has a scar on one of his temples. Speaks "loud and bold" and "is addicted to whittling and singing." Father and mother "belong" to Orville Shelby of Tipton. |
| Lilburn | 34 | May 21, 1835 | *Nashville Republican* | Albert G. Ward | Davidson | A "first-rate shoemaker who "looks earnestly at you when spoken to." Previously lived in Todd County, KY. "It is believed that he left via steamboat Monday evening." |
| Charles | 35 | June 2, 1835 | *Nashville Republican* | Thomas G. James | Davidson | Is "accompanied by his wife, Jane Lewis, who is a free mulatto woman." |
| Hulda | 23 | June 23, 1835 | *Nashville Republican* | Thomas J. Talbot | Davidson | She "was raised by Major John Boyd" and "has lost one of her thimble fingers at the first joint." |
| Squire | 22 | Aug. 20, 1835 | *Nashville Republican* | James Ridley | Davidson | "When addressed, is polite, speaks rather quickly." His wife is at Mr. John Shute's on Richland Creek. |
| Hannah | 30 | Oct. 16, 1835 | *Randolph Recorder* | George Penn | Tipton | "Speaks low and but little." Ran away with 6 others, 4 of whom already captured in Arkansas and 2 of whom drowned. |
| Moses | 23 | Oct. 16, 1835 | *Randolph Recorder* | Orville Shelby | Tipton | "Knock kneed and inclines forward when walking." Ran away before, was caught and then ran away "while being conveyed home from Covington jail." |
| Lewis/ Sandy | 20 | Nov. 6, 1835 | *Randolph Recorder* | Miles Wagoolsley | Shelby | Lewis "was purchased from John Polk of Portersville" and "appears very humble when spoken to." Sandy "has the scald head." |
| Isaac Hatchet | 20 | Dec. 17, 1835 | *Nashville Republican* | Joseph Neibert | Adams, MS | "Brought to this place by Mr. Isaac Franklin from Virginia, in April" and is "slow to answer when spoken to." |
| Ellen | 20 | Jan. 2, 1836 | *Nashville Republican* | B.S. Rutherford | Sumner | Has a scar on one side of her face. Ran away from Rutherford's home in Hendersonville. |

| Name of Slave | Age | Date Published | Newspaper | Slave Holder | County | Special Notes |
|---|---|---|---|---|---|---|
| Isaac | | Jan. 19, 1836 | *Nashville Republican* | Thomas B. Coleman | Davidson | "Raised by Squire Ramsey of Davidson." |
| William | 35 | Jan. 19, 1836 | *Nashville Republican* | Philip Callaghan | Davidson | "Can read and write" and "his right hand cut off below the elbow." Ran away once before and made it to Canada. "It is supposed he left here on the steamboat Native." |
| Paschael | 32 | March 18, 1836 | *Randolph Recorder* | E.M. Ford | Fayette | "Has done some service on flat and steamboats" and "once belonged to L.P. Cheatham of Nashville." |
| Hiram | 18 | March 24, 1836 | *Nashville Republican* | John Hill | Davidson | "Purchased" 18 miles from Bowling Green, "on the waters of Barren River." Ran away from home near Richland Creek. |
| Mitch | 40 | April 5, 1836 | *Memphis Enquirer* | Lawson H. Bedford | Shelby | "Performs well on the violin" and is "stout and robust in his appearance." He "may have attempted to reach the Chickasaw nation." |
| Unnamed Female | 17 | April 5, 1836 | *Memphis Enquirer* | B.W. Williamson | Fayette | This slave eloped with her overseer, whose name was Bedford Easley. [According to a later ad they eventually captured the slave.] |
| Bill | 35 | April 5, 1835 | *Memphis Enquirer* | John Best | Shelby | Ad was run by Thomas Mackey, executor. The slave said to have been stolen by John Fleming of Vicksburg, MS. |
| Melinda | 23 | April 14, 1836 | *Nashville Republican* | William Wray | Davidson | Shows "slight marks of negro parentage." |
| Bill | | April 19, 1836 | *Nashville Republican* | John Hill | Davidson | "Was brought to me from a man of the name of Lynch of Simpson County, Ky." He ran away with Hiram, above. |
| Jane | 15 | May 10, 1836 | *Nashville Republican* | Moses Stevens | Davidson | Had lately been "in the employ" of Moses Stevens and "absconded without just cause." [Stevens taught at the Nashville Classical Seminary.] |
| Jim | 24 | June 22, 1836 | *Memphis Enquirer* | John B. House | Henry | Slaveholder lives "six miles north of Paris, on the Obion River." |
| Jefferson | 23 | June 9, 1836 | *Nashville Republican* | L.R. Starkes | Williamson | House servant who "has a scar under the left jaw as to be seen on the neck, one also on on the back of his head." Previously lived in Huntsville, AL, and in MS. |
| Harriet | 22 | July 8, 1836 | *Randolph Recorder* | Micajah Phelps | Tipton | Has a scar on the inside of her left wrist. "It is thought that she has been persuaded and conveyed off by some white man." |
| Solomon/ Jack | 45 | July 18, 1836 | *Nashville Republican* | Lodwick B. Beech | Williamson | Solomon is "bow-legged, with a scar on his upper lip" and has "rather a down look, fond of spirits." Jack (22) "has a bald place on one side of his head caused by a scald" and "speaks boldly when spoken to." |

| Name of Slave | Age | Date Published | Newspaper | Slave Holder | County | Special Notes |
|---|---|---|---|---|---|---|
| Priscilla/Jack | 35 | Sept. 6, 1836 | *Nashville Republican* | Nathaniel Cartmill | Wilson | Ran away together from near Spencers Creek. Jack is about 17. |
| Tom/4 others | 35 | Sept. 9, 1836 | *Randolph Recorder* | J.W. Wright | Haywood | Tom, Aggy and their 3 children ran away and took a horse with them. "Belong to the estate of Freeman, N. Carolina, and was hired by J.W. Wright for the present year." |
| Green | 26 | Sept. 27, 1836 | *Nashville Republican* | Daniel Dansbee | Maury | "A first-rate carpenter" who "on close examination, has freckles on his nose." Also, "he is a very artful fellow, and well calculated to deceive." |
| Unnamed male | 22 | Oct. 25, 1836 | *Nashville Republican* | Matthew Martin | Lincoln | Can read and "has on one of his arms, in blue marks, 'W.M. March 20, 1820.'" Also, "squints a little in the left eye" and "is very intelligent and cunning." |
| Freeman/1 other | | Nov. 10, 1836 | *Nashville Republican* | James Mc-Loughlin | Williamson | Man and woman ran away together. He "has a down look when spoken to." She, "when spoken to, speaks quick and bold." |
| Braxton | 20 | Dec. 24, 1836 | *Nashville Republican* | James Shelton & Co. | Lauderdale, AL | "His feet have been badly frostbitten which caused him to lean forward in walking." Also, "please deliver him to us in Florence or to H&J Kirkman & Co. in Nashville." |
| Fill | 35 | Jan. 19, 1837 | *Nashville Republican* | Elizabeth Braissie | Trousdale | A "small lump on the back of his neck." |
| Redden | 25 | Jan. 21, 1837 | *Memphis Enquirer* | Caro Epperson | Montgomery | Had been purchased from John Fletcher of Carroll County. |
| Jerry | 28 | Jan. 28, 1837 | *Nashville Republican* | Samuel Bunch | Grainger | Came from Buckingham County, VA. Has "some scars about the face" and is "very knock-kneed; the right is very crooked and foot turns out very much." He "has a coarse voice." |
| Unnamed Female | 42 | Feb. 11, 1837 | *Nashville Republican* | Henry Forrester | Henry | "Rather under common size, a little yellow complected." |
| Jesse | 26 | Feb. 18, 1837 | *Memphis Enquirer* | Walter Mask | Hardeman | Has "a knot on one of his ankles occasioned by a cut with an axe." Address of slaveholder is the community of Van Buren. |
| Dinah | 35 | March 11, 1837 | *Memphis Enquirer* | Thomas Halsel | Chickasaw Nation | Had been living with Mr. Doty in Shelby. "Any person who will apprehend said woman can receive the above reward upon application to Jesse Whitaker in the Nation." |
| Isham | 27 | April 8, 1837 | *Nashville Republican* | Samuel Winston | Rutherford | "A shrewd, artful fellow, and has travelled a great deal with me." |
| Dick | 23 | April 15, 1837 | *Memphis Enquirer* | Geraldus Buntyn | Shelby | "One of his arms, when small, was torn from about half way from the elbow to the wrist very badly from the teeth of a cotton gin." |

| Name of Slave | Age | Date Published | Newspaper | Slave Holder | County | Special Notes |
|---|---|---|---|---|---|---|
| Davy | 25 | May 13, 1837 | *Memphis Enquirer* | James Kimbrough | Shelby | "Rather chunky built, very dark complexion, left handed." |
| Peter | 18 | May 27, 1837 | *Memphis Enquirer* | J.H. and W.H. Bolton | Shelby | "Had an iron around his neck" when he went away. "Is particularly gifted" with "his great art of chicanery in lying." Also, he is "very fond of steamboats and often travels on them when runaway." |
| Tempy | 24 | June 24, 1837 | *Nashville Republican* | A. Russell | Davidson | A house worker who had previously lived in Jackson. |
| Sip/Wilson | 23 | June 24, 1837 | *Nashville Republican* | John Peck | Weakley | "Purchased [Sip] several years ago of Mr. Gardener of Robertson, where his father now lives and he may attempt to go back there. . . Bought [Wilson, who is 17] of Armstrong's estate, of Overton." |
| Hide | 30 | July 6, 1837 | *Nashville Republican* | Powhaten Gordon | Maury | "He will make for Cincinnati, Ohio, as he has but recently been brought from there, he has a white wife near that place." One finger on his left hand is "deformed." |
| Edmund/Ben | 30 | Jan. 15, 1838 | *Republican Banner* | Matthew Cowen | Jackson | Edmund's "father, mother and brother live in Nashville, his father is called John Pinchim, his brother Page a shoe and boot maker." Ben is also about 30. |
| Claiborne | 30 | Jan. 25, 1838 | *Daily Republican Banner* | A.A. Hall | Davidson | "The property of John H. Eaton." |
| Wilson/Emeline | 33 | Feb. 6, 1838 | *Republican Banner* | William Compton | Davidson | Husband and 22-year-old wife ran away together. Wilson is "shoemaker by trade and a good worker." |
| Martha | 13 | March 13, 1838 | *Daily Republican Banner* | Martin New | Davidson | "Heavy make, full face; her great toes about half an inch longer than the others." |
| George | 25 | April 21, 1838 | *Republican Banner* | John Saunders | Davidson | "When spoken to manifests some hesitation and embarrassment." Is "a little knock kneed." |
| Myal | 23 | April 27, 1838 | *Republican Banner* | Egbert A. Raworth | Davidson | "Is lurking about the neighborhood of Nashville, as he has some relations not far off." |
| Henry/Anthony | | April 27, 1838 | *Jackson District Telegraph* | Thomas P. Shelton | Tipton | "Purchased by me from a gentleman in Caldwell County, Ky., to which place I expect they will go." Slaveholder address is Beaver Dam Forks. |
| Adam | 22 | May 18, 1838 | *Jackson District Telegraph* | Samuel J. Taylor | Madison | Ran away "while on the road leading from Mount Pinson to Bolivar." Has been hired to Joseph B. White of Henderson County. |
| Bob/4 others | 27 | May 24, 1838 | *Republican Banner* | Gwin & Love | Perry | 5 men ran away from the Gwin & Love iron works. Four--Bob, Bob (25), Daniel (22) and Jim(22)--were bought from traders who brought them from VA or SC. Alexander, (19) "was hired of a Mr. Thompson, in Davidson." |

| Name of Slave | Age | Date Published | Newspaper | Slave Holder | County | Special Notes |
|---|---|---|---|---|---|---|
| Cy | 25 | June 8, 1838 | *(Athens) Tennessee Journal* | Thomas Crutchfield | McMinn | "All the fingers of his right hand were burnt off when young." Also, "there is reason to believe he will seek shelter in the Cherokee Nation." |
| Nelson | 25 | July 6, 1838 | *Paris West Tennessean* | Robert S. Bingham | Henry | A "scar on his breast." |
| Hampton/Tom | | July 21, 1838 | *Republican Banner* | Jesse Collins | Davidson | Hampton "was raised by Jerry Sadler, Nashville" and "stammers in his speaking." Tom "was raised in White County". |
| Sam | 15 | Sept. 10, 1838 | *Repub Banner* | Robert Lusk | Davidson | Ran away from S.C. Earl's chair factory. |
| Burton/2 others | 30 | Oct. 12, 1838 | *Jackson District Telegraph* | Daniel Cherry | Crockett | Burton's mother died "a short time since at Mills Point, Ky. and his step father still lives there" Elias (21) has a "down look when spoken to." Anderson is a blacksmith. |
| Josiah | 22 | Oct. 13, 1838 | *Republican Bannerr* | David Dickinson | Rutherford | "Can write a pretty good hand." Was confined at Morgantown, KY, but then he escaped from there. |
| Squire | 39 | Feb. 21, 1839 | *Republican Banner* | Miles M. Temple | Tipton | "Has been a house servant, barkeeper, ostler and gardener" and "generally becomes known for his attention and politeness." |
| Sam | 26 | March 5, 1839 | *Republican Banner* | J.R. Ashworth | Wilson | "Can read and spell" and has "a scar on the side of his head caused by a burn." He may try to get to Henderson County. |
| Henry | 27 | April 15, 1839 | *Republican Banner* | Robert I. Moore | Davidson | "Has a wife at H.G. Williamson's." |
| Joe | | April 15, 1839 | *Repub Banner* | James Cooper | Davidson | "Purchased him from Joseph Meek." |
| Henry | 25 | May 23, 1839 | *Republican Banner* | G.E. Franklin | Fayette | "He will make his way for Sevier [County]." |
| Jim Lace | 25 | June 22, 1839 | *Republican Banner* | Asa Jackson | Wilson | "Has once before attempted to make his escape . . . and was taken in Kentucky making his way to Illinois." |
| Ruffin/Jesse | | July 2, 1839 | *Republican Banner* | Charles Locke | Rutherford | Ruffin has a "good countenance." Jesse has a scar on one of his legs "caused by the kick of a horse." |
| Jim/George | 50 | July 9, 1839 | *Republican Banner* | Morgan Cartwright | Fayette | Escaped in Dickson while being brought from North Carolina to Fayette County. Jim "speaks very quick." George (25) "speaks very slow." |
| Ben | | Aug. 16, 1839 | *Jackson District Telegraph* | John E. Stewart | Madison | "I have purchased him from Dr. William Murchison." |
| Dan | 20 | Oct. 8, 1839 | *Greeneville Mountaineer* | D.M. Waters | Knox | "Not quickly spoken, but rather diffident when spoken to." Ran away with Frank and another Frank. |
| Frank | | Oct. 8, 1839 | *Greeneville Mountaineer* | Edward Stephens | Knox | Appears to have run away with Dan and Frank. |

| Name of Slave | Age | Date Published | Newspaper | Slave Holder | County | Special Notes |
|---|---|---|---|---|---|---|
| Frank | | Oct. 8, 1839 | *Greeneville Mountaineer* | William D. Ragin | Knox | Appears to have run away with Dan and Frank. |
| Essex | 47 | Oct. 14, 1839 | *Republican Banner* | Steward Carter | Tuscumbia, AL | A blacksmith who is "somewhat slow of speech." He "was caught . . . at Robertson's Bend, at the residence of James Bosley . . . but escaped again the same night." |
| Delpha | 30 | Nov. 1, 1839 | *Paris West Tennessean* | Zacariah Wyatt | Henry | "Quick spoken." |
| Dimbo | 40 | Nov. 4, 1839 | *Republican Banner* | Jas. W. M'Combs | Davidson | "Dark complexion, thin visage." |
| Robin | 45 | Nov. 12, 1839 | *Knoxville Argus and Commercial Herald* | Lewis Dinhins | Knox | "Has on one of his hands some severe scars, having been torn by a cotton gin" and is a "shrewd smart fellow." |
| Pleasant | 22 | Dec. 5, 1839 | *Elizabethton Tennessee Whig* | Thomas Crutchfield | McMinn | One of his fingers is missing, so wears a glove. He ran away from Cleveland, was caught in Maryville but then escaped. Was "raised" by James Guthery of Lick Creek in Greene County. |
| Israel | 22 | Feb. 20, 1840 | *Clarksville Weekly Chronicle* | Griffin Orgain | Montgomery | "Open countenance." |
| Bob | 18 | Feb. 27, 1840 | *Republican Banner* | W. Donelson | Davidson | "Walks very erect; square shouldered," and "rather serious cast of countenance." May be harbored in Nashville and "has been attempting to get on board a boat." |
| Jacob | 22 | March 23, 1840 | *Republican Banner* | Montgomery Bell | Cheatham | A blacksmith who ran away from the Narrows of the Harpeth and who ran away with Jesse. |
| Jesse | | March 23, 1840 | *Republican Banner* | Mr. Rape | Cheatham | Ran away from the Narrows of the Harpeth with Jacob. |
| Robert | 20 | April 30, 1840 | *Elizabethton Whig* | Elizabeth Carter | Carter | "Blue eyes, straight sandy hair and skin as fair as a dark skinned white man." |
| Jacob Parnell | 19 | April 30, 1840 | *Elizabethton Whig* | A.M. Carter | Carter | "Works well in a forge" and is "somewhat talkative upon an acquaintance." |
| Furney | 40 | May 14, 1840 | *Clarksville Weekly Chronicle* | W.C. Metcalf | Montgomery | "Belongs to the estate of Lewis Whitfield and will probably aim for the neighborhood of Oak Grove, Ky." |
| Jacob Crockett | 38 | May 19, 1840 | *Knoxville Argus and Commercial Herald* | Montgomery Irwin | Washington | A "first rate waggoner and excellent fiddler" who is "quick spoken and very polite." Previously "owned" by "the widow Crockett." |
| Charles | 25 | July 1, 1840 | *Republican Banner* | George O. Stovall | Stewart | Ran away from the Cumberland iron works. Can read and write and "has a brother in Nashville, [who is] owned by a man by the name of Beaty, on Water Street." |
| Dick | 35 | Aug. 1, 1840 | *Republican Banner* | James Y. Hardison | Maury | "Very stout made, has straight hair and his face slightly pock-marked." |

| Name of Slave | Age | Date Published | Newspaper | Slave Holder | County | Special Notes |
|---|---|---|---|---|---|---|
| Caroline | 28 | Aug. 6, 1840 | *Pulaski Whig Courier* | John K. Yerger | Giles | "She is no doubt harbored in the vicinity of town." |
| Washing | 35 | Sept. 25, 1840 | *Repub Banner* | Willis Boddie | Maury | "Talks much." |
| George/ Lige | 28 | Sept. 26, 1840 | *Republican Banner* | William Massengill | Jefferson | George is a bricklayer, plasterer and painter with an "assuming consequential airs when spoken to." Lige is about 26. |
| Solomon/ Fil | | Oct. 9, 1846 | *Pulaski Whig Courier* | Robert Rodes | Giles | Ran away from the plantation of John H. River, deceased. Solomon is "cross-eyed." |
| Andrew | 22 | Oct. 28, 1840 | *Jonesboro Whig* | Samuel A. Lyle | Washington | A "brickmaker by trade" who "has a prominent scar on the back of one of his hands, occassioned by the stab of a knife." |
| Joe | 37 | Nov. 28, 1840 | *Republican Banner* | Thomas Chandler | Giles | Left the plantation of J.B. Davis, near Gordonsville. |
| Charles | 32 | Dec. 3, 1840 | *Pulaski Whig Courier* | E.G. Brown | Giles | "Left me at John Neal's, on the road from Pulaski to Elkton." |
| Reuben | 23 | Jan. 7, 1841 | *Republican Banner* | Elisha White | Giles | Has a small scar over one of his eyes. His mother lives in Smithland, KY. Ran away before "and was employed on a trading boat from Cumberland River to New Orleans." |
| Harry | 24 | May 15, 1841 | *Jackson Intelligencer* | Auston Maupin | Obion | "A scar above his right eye" and "the upper part of his right ear is cut off." |
| Minerva | 38 | May 22, 1841 | *Repub Banner* | Ann Eliza Hyde | Davidson | "Mulatto girl, good size." |
| Washington | 20 | Sept. 1, 1841 | *Republican Banner* | Samuel Baker | Caldwell, KY | Has a small scar on top of his right hand and another on his forehead. Once lived in Nashville and "is very desirous to get back there." |
| Josh/3 others | 27 | Oct. 2, 1841 | *Republican Banner* | John C. Reagin | Giles | Simon (40) is a "very smart fellow." Peggy (22) is a "very large big boned stout woman." Abby is about 22. |
| Littleton | 15 | Oct. 2, 1841 | *Republican Banner* | Mark R. Cockrill | Davidson | "His face was burned a short time before he left by powder, and his lips and face show the scars." Was raised in Richmond, VA. |
| Sam | 42 | Oct. 13, 1841 | *Knoxville Argus and Commercial Herald* | Evan Parker | Hamilton | Has "a large scar on his left arm occassioned by a burn" and scar in one of his insteps caused by an axe. Ran away with Hardin. |
| Hardin | | Oct. 13, 1841 | *Knox Argus CH* | Thomas McSpadden | Walker, GA | Ran away with Sam. |
| David | 28 | Oct. 29, 1841 | *Republican Banner* | Elisha White | Giles | "His left knee is a little stiff and a scar on it." |
| Unnamed male | | Oct. 29, 1841 | *Republican Banner* | George Malone | Giles | Ran away with David; name not given. |
| Edward | 19 | Nov. 13, 1841 | *Republican Banner* | M. Hamilton | Davidson | "When interrogated closely about anything speaks fast and not distinctly." |

| Name of Slave | Age | Date Published | Newspaper | Slave Holder | County | Special Notes |
|---|---|---|---|---|---|---|
| Sephus | 18 | Dec. 23 1841 | *Republican Banner* | William Payne | Smith | "Inclinded to be knock kneed." Took a horse with him. |
| Unnamed male | 19 | July 22, 1842 | *Republican Banner* | Logan Henderson | Rutherford | "Has a large scar on his left foot across the instep, made by an axe." Also, "to converse with him quite a pleasant fellow." |
| Eli | 20 | Aug. 1, 1842 | *Republican Banner* | John Haley | Williamson | "Was brought from Mississippi about the 1st of June last, and was formerly from Virginia." Ran away from Eagleville. |
| Wilkins | 23 | Aug. 1, 1842 | *Republican Banner* | H.W. Bateman | Shelby | "Leans forward in walking" and "he has rather a sleepy look out of the eye of a large upper eyelid." Ran away from Island Number 40 on the Mississippi River. |
| Peter | 22 | Oct. 20, 1842 | *Clarksville Weekly Chronicle* | John Gilmer | Montgomery | "Has a blemish in one eye" and "stutters badly when excited." |
| Finch | 29 | Oct. 28, 1842 | *Republican Banner* | N.L. Bennett | Williamson | Has "a scar on one of his eyes, another on his head, and several on his breast" and is "very intelligent." Ran away from William P. Yarbrough's plantation, but was "owned" by heirs of Alexander Bennett. |
| Reuben | 21 | Dec. 2, 1842 | *Republican Banner* | H & J Kirkman | Davidson | "Very bright mulatto" with "prominent features." |
| Bob | 47 | Dec. 14, 1842 | *Republican Banner* | John Y. Perry | Robertson | Has 4 scars, including "a small piece out of the top of one of his ears, resembling a small swallow fork." Said to be "owned" by the estate of Joseph Perry, deceased. |
| Peter | 47 | Dec. 16, 1842 | *Republican Banner* | McKinney Dooley | Maury | "Stutters when talking." Ran away from Peter Joyce, but ad run by McKinney Dooley. |
| Abram/ Nathan | 19 | Dec. 20, 1842 | *Shelbyville Intelligencer* | Bedford Jailer | Bedford | They had been apprehended and ran away from jail. Abram had a "rifle ball through one of his thighs when he was taken this summer." |
| George | | Feb. 10, 1843 | *Republican Banner* | Samuel B. Lee | Williamson | "A scar across his nose" and had previously belonged to Dr. John Hadley of Davidson and in Giles. |
| Solomon | 35 | May 1, 1843 | *Republican Banner* | Paul & Murrell | Davidson | "A scar over one of his eyes" and "has a down look and speaks intelligently and quick." [Paul & Murrell was a brickmason.] |
| Ned | 22 | May 1, 1843 | *Republican Banner* | Benjamin W. Bradford | Pontotoe, Miss. | "Ned is known about Nashville by the name of Allen; his father and mother are free and live in Nashville." |
| Frank/ Florinda | 26 | May 8, 1843 | *Republican Banner* | Christopher Bullard | Hardeman | Frank has "a large scar on his cheek, which is at times a running sore." Florinda is about 17. |

| Name of Slave | Age | Date Published | Newspaper | Slave Holder | County | Special Notes |
|---|---|---|---|---|---|---|
| John Robinson | 18 | May 8, 1843 | *Republican Banner* | B.F. Young | Davidson | "Owned" by Charles Bosley of Nashville; ran away from the steamer *Red Rover* "somewhere in the vicinity of Canton, Ky." |
| Bowlie | 14 | July 21, 1843 | *Memphis W Appeal* | S.D. & W. Prescott | Shelby | "Belongs to the estate of Hines." |
| Isaac | 30 | Aug. 23, 1843 | *Republican Banner* | Madison H. Alexander | Rutherford | "Was taken to Mississippi from Kentucky by a trader." |
| John | 20 | Sept. 15, 1843 | *Memphis W Appeal* | Elijah Whitney | Fayette | "Bends a little in walking" and "polite and quick spoken." Ran away with Jesse from the community of Egypt. |
| Jesse | 35 | Sept. 15, 1843 | *Memphis W Appeal* | E.F. Lumsden | Fayette | Has a scar "on the left side of his chin" and is a "quick spoken and shrewd rascal." Ran away with John from the community of Egypt. |
| John | 25 | Sept 15, 1843 | *Memphis W Appeal* | William Winfrey | Shelby | A barber who is "fond of telling extravagant tales for the amusement of those that are present." |
| John | 22 | Sept. 20, 1843 | *Republican Banner* | Montgomery Bell | Cheatham | Ran away from the Narrows of the Harpeth. "Said negro was hired of the estate of William Hadley." |
| Henry | 18 | Sept. 22, 1843 | *Republican Banner* | Jason H. Kendrick | Davidson | "A little stoop shouldered." |
| David/8 others | 29 | Sept. 29, 1843 | *Memphis W Appeal* | William D. Primrose | Maury | A white man, John W. Etheridge, who trains race horses, was said to leave with 9 slaves and 9 racehorses. Slaves are David, Bill (20), Henry (20), John (17), Eli (21) and 4 unnamed. |
| George | 24 | Oct. 23, 1843 | *Republican Banner* | Henry Dickinson | Davidson | A "downcast and sullen look." |
| Demsey | | Nov. 24, 1843 | *Republican Banner* | Grant A. Bowen | Davidson | "So well known in this community that any description is deemed unnecessary." |
| Albert | 22 | Jan. 22, 1844 | *Republican Banner* | Thomas K. Handy | Williamson | "A carpenter by trade" who "can read and write and is also something of an engineer." |
| Peter | 27 | Feb. 16, 1844 | *Memphis W Appeal* | Daniel Lake | Shelby | Has a "slight impediment in his speech which is wild and pleasant. . . It is probable that he will make his way to South Alabama, where he was brought from." |
| Bill/ Henry | 23 | March 6, 1844 | *Republican Banner* | David M. Harding | Davidson | Ran away together. Henry about 18. |
| Prince | 22 | March 19, 1844 | *Clarksville Weekly Chronicle* | Elizabeth Elliott | Montgomery | "Is somewhere in the neighborhood of his wife, who lives with a man named Bell, near Vanlier's Furnace." |
| John Lewis | 19 | April 8, 1844 | *Republican Banner* | B.F. Young | Adams, MS | "Has been trepanned on the skull, where the scar is left." Also "has been lurking about Nashville for several years and passing himself as free among steamboat hands." |

| Name of Slave | Age | Date Published | Newspaper | Slave Holder | County | Special Notes |
|---|---|---|---|---|---|---|
| Charles | | May 1, 1844 | *Republican Banner* | Thomas Dannall | Sumner | A "scar on his lip" and was "previously owned by Stanfield's estate." Ran away from Cairo. |
| Peter Bell/ Charles | 25 | May 8, 1844 | *Republican Banner* | A.W. Vanleer | Dickson | Ran away from the Cumberland iron works. "Were lately purchased of a Mr. Morgan of Rutherford or Giles." Charles is about 21. |
| Sam | 27 | June 28, 1844 | *Memphis W Appeal* | S.G. Dunn | Shelby | Can read and write and "talks promptly and with good sense." Was raised in Lexington, KY, and took 2 shotguns with him. |
| Spencer | 22 | June 28, 1844 | *Memphis W Appeal* | W.M. Dunn | Shelby | "Looks down when sharply interrogated." Probably ran away with Sam, who was "owned" by W.M. Dunn's father S.G. Dunn. |
| Jane | 20 | July 9, 1844 | *Clarksville Weekly Chronicle* | John A. Withers | Montgomery | "Frequently passes herself for white." |
| Black Jim/ Yellow Jim | 29 | July 17, 1844 | *Knox Argus CH* | James W. Jones | Knox | Black Jim has "no marks recollected. " Yellow Jim (21) has a mark on one of his cheeks. Yellow Jim ran away a year ago and "was aiming for Virginia." |
| Lemuel | 33 | Sept. 25, 1844 | *Republican Banner* | Warren Jordan | Davidson | A cook and steward on steamboats. Ran away with Charles. "The last time these negroes were seen, they were together in a canoe in Cumberland River." |
| Charles | 18 | Sept. 25, 1844 | *Republican Banner* | Thomas Taylor | Davidson | Ran away with Lemuel. "The last time these negroes were seen, they were together in a canoe in Cumberland River." |
| Berry | 36 | Sept. 27, 1844 | *Republican Banner* | Andrew McClellan | Jackson | One scar on his legs and the other on his lip "caused by a bite." Tends "to look down when spoken to." |
| Ned | 12 | Nov. 4, 1844 | *Republican Banner* | John Haley | Williamson | "I have heard that he was seen at the Nashville Convention." |
| Strother | | Dec. 10, 1844 | *Clarksville Weekly Chronicle* | Stewart & Dick | Montgomery | Ran away from the Lafayette furnace. Has "a scar across his nose and another probably on the forehead." |
| Henry | 25 | Feb. 24, 1845 | *Republican Banner* | T.O. Harris | Davidson | Ran away with George. Is "smart, sprightly and intelligent." |
| George | 23 | Feb. 24, 1845 | *Republican Banner* | J.B. Carter | Davidson | Ran away with Henry. Is "smart, sprightly and intelligent." |
| Davy | 42 | April 25, 1845 | *Republican Banner* | C.R. Bass | Sumner | "Seldom looks you in the face when spoken to." Slaveholder lives at Castalian Springs and owns plantation near Princeton, MS. |
| Joe/2 others | 28 | June 25, 1845 | *Republican Banner* | Thomas N. Figures | Williamson | Ran away with wife Martha (16) and 1 year old child who is "just beginning to talk." Martha and child held by T.B. Dawson of Davidson County. |

| Name of Slave | Age | Date Published | Newspaper | Slave Holder | County | Special Notes |
|---|---|---|---|---|---|---|
| Andy | 30 | July 23, 1845 | *Republican Banner* | J.H. Greer | Bedford | A barber who was some years ago employed by Reuben Graham in Nashville, Shelbyville and Murfreesboro. "Quick of speech, and when excited lisps a little." |
| Tom/Jim | 21 | Aug. 15, 1845 | *Clarks Jeffersonian* | Montgomery Bell | Dickson | Tom is an engineer; Jim (18) a blacksmith. Ran away from Worly furnace and "two low white women left the neighborhood about the same time . . . [they] may be in company with them." |
| Davy/Jack | | Aug. 15, 1845 | *Memphis W Appeal* | W. Chase | Shelby | Davy "stoops when walking." Both were part of the estate of William Spickernagle (deceased) and had been hired out to Peter Rives in Arkansas, from whom they ran away. |
| Dick | | Sept. 12, 1845 | *Memphis W Appeal* | John D. Neville | Hardeman | The "little finger of [his] left hand has been burnt and drawn in the shape of a half circle." |
| Eliza | 40 | Oct. 3, 1845 | *Republican Banner* | Benjamin Litton (C&M) | Davidson | "A very delicate woman" who ran away "from the residence of Samuel T. Love," but was in the care of the Davidson County Clerk and Master. |
| March | 26 | Oct. 17, 1845 | *Memphis W Appeal* | Charles Jones | Shelby | "Has a limp in his walk as if one of his legs is shorter than the other" and has scars and welts on his chest. Previously held in Arkansas, before that by H.B.H. Williams of Dickson. |
| George | 32 | Nov. 1, 1845 | *(Murfreesboro) TN Telegraph* | Gordon W. Shanklin | Rutherford | Walks with a cane "owing to his knee becoming stiff and crooked." Would "pass very readily for a white man." |
| Edmund | 29 | Nov. 14, 1845 | *Memphis W Appeal* | C. Byrn | Marshall, MS | "Was raised in Wilson [County], Tenn., where he may probably attempt to go." |
| Tempy | 26 | Dec. 26, 1845 | *Memphis W Appeal* | Edward Chandler | Hardeman | "A scar on the side of her head" and "the right thumb about half in two between the joints." Ran away from Williams' store. |
| George/ Jack | 25 | Dec. 26, 1845 | *Memphis W Appeal* | Thomas Nash | Shelby | George is "good looking." Jack (23) "has a scar on back part of his head that extends half round" and is "quick spoken, intelligent." Wives of both live in Gibson County. |
| Jerry/3 others | 34 | Jan. 30, 1846 | *Memphis W Appeal* | Aaron Spivey | Haywood | Jerry "leans forward a good deal in walking." Charles (25) is "knock kneed." Robert (30) "stoops slightly and spare built." Thompson (25) "stoops a little." |
| Morgan/3 others | 25 | March 20, 1846 | *Memphis W Appeal* | F.D. Farabee | Shelby | On one of his cheeks "a spot darker than any other part of his face." Jake (17) "rather inclined to stammer." Tom (21) "stammers a little." George (17) has "rather a down look." |

| Name of Slave | Age | Date Published | Newspaper | Slave Holder | County | Special Notes |
|---|---|---|---|---|---|---|
| George | | April 7, 1846 | *Clarksville Weekly Chronicle* | William Griffey | Montgomery | "Speaks quickly when spoken to." Also, "I have reason to believe he visits Neblett's Furnace and the Bear Spring Furnace." |
| Allen | 40 | June 13, 1846 | *Clarks Jeffersonian* | Emily Wynne | Montgomery | "It is supposed that he was taken away from John L. Moore, of whom he was purchased about two years ago." |
| Bill | 25 | July 20, 1846 | *Republican Banner* | David M. Harding | Davidson | "One or two" scars on the right temple near the edge of the hair. |
| Margaret | 21 | Aug. 13, 1846 | *Memphis W Appeal* | George W. Murphy | Shelby | Speaks Cherokee and French and "almost entirely white," with blue eyes and has a "a raised scar on one of her shoulders." Was brought from Arkansas 3 months ago. |
| Charity | 23 | Aug. 25, 1846 | *Clarks Weekly Chronicle* | James Clardy | Montgomery | "A burnt scar on one of her arms above the elbow." |
| George Erwin | | Sept. 8, 1846 | *Clarksville Weekly Chronicle* | Stewart & Dick | Montgomery | Ran away from the Lafayette furnace, having been hired from J.W. Erwin of Clarksville. He is "intelligent and active." |
| Manuel | 30 | Sept. 16, 1846 | *Republican Banner* | George M. Martin | Maury | "Left handed" and is "a genteel-looking negro." |
| John | | Sept. 25, 1846 | *Republican Banner* | William J. Menzies | Decatur | "Has a scar on his upper lip." |
| John | 25 | Oct. 9, 1846 | *Memphis W Appeal* | Isaac Turnage | Tipton | "Can read tolerably well," has scars or spots on upper lip and is "quick spoken and polite in his deportment." Ran away from near Randolph. |
| Peter/ George | 30 | Nov. 27, 1846 | *Memphis W Appeal* | John Dockery | Hardeman | "Formerly owned by a Mr. Clark" who lived south of Somerville. George is about 18. |
| Anderson/ Anderson | 40 | Jan. 1, 1847 | *Republican Banner* | William P. Cannon | Williamson | Can read, is a carpenter by trade, and "has been preaching." Ran away with is 9-year-old nephew (also named Anderson) who can also read. |
| Henry | 21 | Feb. 9, 1847 | *Clarksville Weekly Chronicle* | Hugh Dunlap | Montgomery | Was recently purchased from Samuel McMichael's estate. |
| Hal | 26 | Feb. 13, 1847 | *Clarks Jeffersonian* | Peter F. Gray | Stewart | "6 foot 4 inches high, rawboned." |
| Garland | 22 | March 10, 1847 | *Republican Banner* | Thomas S. Williamson | Williamson | I "think he is in Nashville" and "will attempt to secrete himself on some steamboat." |
| Jim | 24 | March 12, 1847 | *Columbia Beacon* | Nathan Coffey | Maury | A "small scar on his right jaw." |
| Aaron | 13 | April 2, 1847 | *Memphis W Appeal* | Andrew Taylor | Shelby | Has a "slight impediment in his speech." Purchased in Memphis, from the Bibb estate. |
| Bill | 19 | April 30, 1847 | *Memphis W Appeal* | R.L. Watt | Shelby | "Yellow, sandy hair." |

| Name of Slave | Age | Date Published | Newspaper | Slave Holder | County | Special Notes |
|---|---|---|---|---|---|---|
| Foster | 19 | June 23, 1847 | *Republican Banner* | John Overton | Davidson | Foster is "quick spoken and very smart." Haywood (18) is "rather slow to speak." |
| Hazzard/4 others | 22 | July 12, 1847 | *Republican Banner* | John W. Walker | Wayne | All ran away from Wayne County furnace. Hazzard raised in South Carolina. Wesley (19) and Henderson (20) raised near Nashville. Jim (19) an engineer. George (28) from near Columbia. |
| Henry | 18 | Sept. 14, 1847 | *Clarks Weekly Chronicle* | John H. Hiter | Montgomery | "Belonging to the Hon. Cave Johnson." |
| Patrick | 21 | Sept. 19, 1847 | *Memphis Daily Eagle/Examiner* | Noah Parker | Lawrence | "Has a small scar near the crown of his head" and another "I think on the right breast." Ran away from Holly Springs, Miss., but his slaveholder lives in Lawrenceburg. |
| Jack | 17 | Nov. 16, 1847 | *Memphis Daily Eagle/Examiner* | George T. Taylor | Tipton | Has traveled much on steamboats as a waiter, is a barber and "reads well." Has a large scar on one of his hands. Had been purchased from Mansfield Ware, who had bought him from a man in Louisville, KY. |
| Henry | 24 | Jan. 10, 1848 | *Republican Banner* | Hinchey Petway | Davidson | "Almost white" but "a slight conversation with him will quickly convince a stranger that he is a slave." Has a relation in Gallatin. |
| Unnamed Female | 18 | Jan. 10, 1848 | *Republican Banner* | D.B. Turner | Davidson | "A scar caused by a burn on her left cheek." May have run away with Henry. |
| Dick/Sandy | 16 | March 31, 1848 | *Republican Banner* | Smith & Hobbs | Wilson | Both ran away near community of Salisbury. [Smith & Hobbs was a candle factory in Nashville.] |
| Cyrus | 21 | June 14, 1848 | *Republican Banner* | John Kelly | Wilson | Has done some blacksmith work and has a scar on his left hand. Also "would be apt to pass himself off for a white man if not carefully observed." |
| Bob | 15 | June 14, 1848 | *Republican Banner* | John W. Martin | Davidson | "He was raised in or about the city of Washington." |
| Simon | 22 | Sept. 27, 1848 | *Republican Banner* | Wyat Layne | Coffee | "Formerly belonged to Benjamin Prater of Roane." |
| Bob | 25 | Sept. 27, 1848 | *Repub Banner* | William N. Bilbo | Davidson | "Belongs to Mrs. Perkins of Pulaski." |
| Hazzard/Aaron/Prince | | Oct. 27, 1848 | *Republican Banner* | John W. Walker | Wayne | Ran away from Walker's furnace. "Have no doubt gone down Tennessee River in a skiff." Hazzard is "slow spoken." Left with Aaron ("bad countenance") and Prince ("half idiot"). |
| Johnston | | Nov. 1, 1848 | *Republican Banner* | John Beaty | Davidson | "A carpenter by trade" who "smiles when spoken to." He formerly belonged to George H. Burton, deceased. |
| Sanford | 27 | Nov. 24, 1848 | *Republican Banner* | B. Embry | Davidson | "Has been my waggoner for several years." Wife and mother live in Nashville. |

| Name of Slave | Age | Date Published | Newspaper | Slave Holder | County | Special Notes |
|---|---|---|---|---|---|---|
| Peter | 28 | Nov. 27, 1848 | *Republican Banner* | William McKissack | Maury | "Writes well" and "converses well, using grand language," and ran away from the City Hotel in Nashville. (Slaveholder in Spring Hill.) |
| Emily | 23 | Nov. 27, 1848 | *Republican Banner* | L. Moses | Davidson | Has a "scar on the right thumb" and "a little hard of hearing." Formerly belonged to James Diggons. |
| Haywood | 40 | Jan. 4, 1849 | *Repub Banner* | B.F. McGehee | Davidson | "Quick spoken." |
| Alfred | 21 | April 28, 1849 | *Repub Banner* | J. Field | Lawrence | "A turner by trade." |
| Wiley | 23 | May 8, 1849 | *Republican Banner* | B.D. Harris | Davidson | "A good carpenter" who is knock-kneed. Purchased from George Lincoln of Nashville, who bought him from John W. Walker of Nashville, who bought him from Gen. Brown of Maury. |
| Peter | 13 | May 9, 1849 | *Republican Banner* | John C. Webb | Davidson | "One eye is somewhat smaller than the other." |
| Jim | 21 | May 22, 1849 | *Knox Standard Reformer* | Mary R. Webb | Knox | "A bright mulatto" and "is a tanner by trade." |
| Brice | 18 | July 21, 1849 | *Brownlow's Knox Whig* | C.K. Gillespie | Washington | "Speaks slow and soft, frequently clearing his throat." |
| Bill | | Oct. 27, 1849 | *Brownlow's Knox Whig* | William Heiskell | Monroe | Has a scar on his lower jaw near his chin. "Last seen in Powell's Valley" [Virginia]. |
| Zeb | 25 | Jan. 8, 1850 | *Repub Banner* | A. Bryan | DeKalb | "An axe wound on his leg or ankle." |
| Bullet | 18 | Feb 18, 1850 | *Republican Banner* | N. Knight | Davidson | "A scar on his head near the right temple." |
| Jacob/ Mary | 57 | March 22, 1850 | *Athens Post* | A.G. Rice | McMinn | Husband and wife ran away together. Both formerly belonged to William Ainsworth. Mary is about 46. |
| Philip | 28 | April 25, 1850 | *Repub Banner* | John Rains | Davidson | "Rather a surly downcast look." |
| Jacob Joiner | 50 | June 17, 1850 | *Republican Banner* | Aaron Wright | Davidson | "Hands are rather rough from exposure on steamboats." |
| Winney | 13 | July 20, 1850 | *Republican Banner* | Alexander Williamson | Davidson | "Rather large eyes, very likely, pretty well grown." |
| Tom | 18 | July 26, 1850 | *Republican Banner* | G.W. Wright (for Dr. Waters) | Davidson | "In appearance resembles and Indian. . . I do not think Tom sufficiently intelligent to manage an escape to a free State without the cooperation of some white person." |
| Martha | | Sept. 19, 1850 | *Republican Banner* | M. Wynne | Davidson | "Had on when she left a brown calico dress." |
| Ned | 29 | Dec. 28, 1850 | *Brownlow's Knox Whig* | Allen L. Williams | Hawkins | A carpenter with scars on his left hand and on one or both of his feet. Slaveholder was on his way from VA to MS when the slave ran away. Ned "has a free wife" in Lynchburg, VA. |

| Name of Slave | Age | Date Published | Newspaper | Slave Holder | County | Special Notes |
|---|---|---|---|---|---|---|
| Isaac | 25 | Feb. 8, 1851 | *Brownlow's Knox Whig* | Thomas E.K. Young | Catoosa, GA | "When spoken to answers slow with a down look . . . this slave was raised in Washington, TN and may be on his way back there, since he was last seen at Calhoun." |
| Hannibal | 25 | Feb. 20, 1851 | *Republican Banner* | G.P. Smith | Davidson | "One or two two fingers of his right hand are contracted so that they cannot be extended." |
| Handy | 30 | May 17, 1851 | *Brownlow's Knox Whig* | Reuben Roddy | Blount | "Speaks quickly when spoken to and is quite talkative. . . was raised on Little River in Blount County." |
| George | 24 | June 12, 1851 | *Rogersville Times* | Joshua Phipps | Hawkins | Ran away from Rotherwood. |
| Charley | 26 | June 28, 1851 | *Republican Banner* | S.A.G. Noel | Davidson | A steamboat worker who "speaks well and fluently." Formerly belonged to Dr. Scruggs, "now of New Orleans." |
| Isom | 42 | July 4, 1851 | *Pulaski Gazette* | Thomas H. Lilly | Giles | "I have no doubt he will endeavor to get to Gallatin, or that neighborhood, as he has a wife there." |
| Unnamed Male | 30 | Aug. 2, 1851 | *Republican Banner* | B.H. Sheppard | Davidson | "Was heard of in the neighborhood of Lebanon a few days since, and is probably about there or Gallatin now." |
| Unnamed Female | 20 | Sept. 6, 1851 | *Clarks Jeffersonian* | Baker Degraffenreid | Stewart | "Crippled in her right knee" and ran away from near Tobacco Port. |
| Elias | 20 | Sept. 19, 1851 | *Athens Post* | James Grisham | McMinn | "Was raised near Tellico Plains" and is part of the estate of Philander Wright, deceased. |
| Dick/ Berry/ Prince | 35 | Oct. 11, 1851 | *Republican Banner* | John W. Walker | Wayne | All ran away from Wayne County furnace. Dick is "copper colored." Berry (25) has "down look." Prince (35) is very black. |
| Missouri | | Jan. 23, 1852 | *Athens Post* | Robert Stockton | Meigs | "Forcibly taken from my possession in Polk, Missouri, together with all my other property." |
| Reub | 19 | Jan. 23, 1852 | *Memphis Daily Eagle/Examiner* | J.A. Sloane | Shelby | "Had on a pair of handcuffs when he left." |
| Rube | | March 10, 1852 | *Memphis Daily Eagle/Examiner* | Wallace & Dennie | Shelby | Wallace & Dennie is an auctioneering firm. |
| Henry | 25 | March 25, 1852 | *Memphis Daily Eagle/Examiner* | J.M. White | Shelby | Ran away from the steamer Glendy Burke at Island 37 on the Mississippi River. |
| Miles Montgomery | | April 3, 1852 | *Memphis Daily Eagle/Examiner* | Q.L. Morton | Shelby | "Already been seen about Wolf Bridge and also about Raleigh." |
| Moses | 42 | April 3, 1852 | *Memphis Daily Eagle/Examiner* | A. Pattison Jr. | Shelby | "Quite a plausible fellow." |
| Willis | 28 | April 3, 1852 | *Memphis Daily Eagle/Examiner* | Abner Pitts | Lauderdale | "A scar on his under lip, caused by a bite from another negro." |

| Name of Slave | Age | Date Published | Newspaper | Slave Holder | County | Special Notes |
|---|---|---|---|---|---|---|
| Winney | 16 | May 15, 1852 | *Republican Banner* | Alexander Williamson | Davidson | Has large feet and hands. This is the same slave who tried to run away 2 years earlier. |
| Harry | | May 29, 1852 | *Brownlow's Knox Whig* | Jefferson Stone | Blount | "Quick of speech, with a slight lisp." |
| Handy | 30 | May 29, 1852 | *Brownlow's Knox Whig* | Reuben Roddy | Carter | Same slave who tried to run away a year earlier. |
| Ben/ Freeman | 18 | June 14, 1852 | *Memphis Daily Eagle/Examiner* | Isaac Russom | McNairy | "Down look when spoken to." Freeman (23) has a "scar on one of his ankles." |
| Wash | 21 | June 30, 1852 | *Memphis Daily Eagle/Examiner* | George O. Ragland | Hamilton | "An excellent bricklayer" who "might pass himself off for a white man." He "delights in comic songs and witty expressions." |
| Pheriba/ Nancy | 22 | July 19, 1852 | *Republican Banner* | Langdon Harrison | Davidson | Pherib's husband lives with Cyrus Hallam of Columbia. Nancy (10) "was raised by John W. Walker of this city." |
| Reubin | 24 | Aug. 3, 1852 | *Republican Banner* | James Bartlett | Putnam | "Speaks rather slow when spoken to" and ran away from the White Plains plantation. |
| Claiborne | | Aug. 28, 1852 | *Republican Banner* | Donelson McGregor | Rutherford | A blacksmith who "has been cut across the right hand which crooked several of his fingers." |
| Jeff | 30 | Aug. 28, 1852 | *Clarks Jeffersonian* | Hugh Dunlop | Montgomery | "Has a mean deceitful countenance" and "belongs to Gilliford Talley of this county." |
| Alfred/ Joe/ Caroline | 40 | Sept. 25, 1852 | *Republican Banner* | Samuel H. Davis | Davidson | Alfred "talks plausibly" and "was purchased by J.M. Elkin of Bedford." Joe (28) has a "don't care expression of countenance" and used to live in Memphis. Caroline (25) is Joe's wife and can read, is "good looking, intelligent countenance." |
| Sam | 35 | Oct. 12, 1852 | *Repub Banner* | W.J. Phillips | Davidson | "Reads very well." |
| John | | Oct. 22, 1852 | *Republican Banner* | D.T. Scott | Davidson | "Rather a down or confused countenance, and might pass for a white man." |
| Maria | 23 | Jan. 2, 1853 | *Memphis Daily Eagle/Examiner* | J.G. Lonsdale | Shelby | "Mulatto" and "had on a small plaid linsey dress." |
| Bob | 24 | Jan. 2, 1853 | *Memphis Daily Eagle/Examiner* | A.E. Stratton | Shelby | He is "of the Mexican or Indian complexion." |
| Nelly | 21 | Jan. 6, 1853 | *Nashville Union* | Wesley Wheless | Davidson | "Small and delicately formed, dresses neatly, speaks sprightly and steps accurately." Was "formerly owned by Charles A. Turley." |
| Margaret | 30 | Jan. 6, 1853 | *Nashville Union* | Alexander Parker | Lincoln | "Tells persons that she may chance to meet that she is free. . . Said negro was purchased in St. Louis, Mo., and will try to get back there." |

| Name of Slave | Age | Date Published | Newspaper | Slave Holder | County | Special Notes |
|---|---|---|---|---|---|---|
| Malvina | 21 | Feb. 1, 1853 | *Memphis Daily Eagle/Examiner* | B.Graham | Shelby | Ran away from the Bolton & Dickins trading yard. "One of her ears is swelled from having been lately bored." |
| Hinton | 30 | Feb. 12, 1853 | *Clarks Jeffersonian* | J.B. Green | Montgomery | "Was well known in this community having been hired for several years past by McClure &Crozier." |
| Curtis | 32 | Feb. 15, 1853 | *Republican Banner* | Lewis Allison | Smith | Has a small scar over his left eye; walks with a limp and "has an observable impediment in his speech when he talks much." Ran from near "Clinton College." |
| Luther | | March 1, 1853 | *Republican Banner* | J.H. and F.T. Webster | Maury | "Ran away without any cause" from near Williamsport. |
| Sally | 22 | March 12, 1853 | *Memphis Daily Eagle/Examiner* | William C. Baily | Fayette | "Copper colored" and "has a large mole under the right ear." |
| Jonas | 23 | March 12, 1853 | *Memphis Daily Eagle/Examiner* | N.M. Trezevant | Shelby | May be in Hickory Wythe, Germantown or Desoto County, MS. |
| Edmond | 28 | April 13, 1853 | *Memphis Daily Eagle/Examiner* | C. Church | Shelby | Used to belong to Irwin Sherrod of Tipton and his wife belongs to Dr. Clemments. Also, was caught and then (Apr. 29, 1853) broke jail. |
| Caroline | 25 | May 19, 1853 | *Memphis Daily Eagle/Examiner* | M.C. Allen | Shelby | "Is of a light copper color" and has "straight hair." |
| Jackson | 32 | May 21, 1853 | *Memphis Daily Eagle/Examiner* | John Donelson | Fayette | "Fore finger of his right hand disfigured by a bone-felon" and ran away from near Hickory Wythe. |
| Mot/ Harris | 30 | May 21, 1853 | *Memphis Daily Eagle/Examiner* | S.S. Rembert | Shelby | Ran away together from Seven Hills Plantation "without cause." Both about 30. |
| Sam | 35 | May 27, 1853 | *Memphis Daily Eagle/Examiner* | H.C. Stark | Shelby | A plasterer who had been raised in New Orleans and sold 3 times before purchased by current slaveholder. He "has had the small pox" and is "bow legged." |
| Henry/ Jack | 33 | June 27, 1853 | *Republican Banner* | A.P. Eakin | Bedford | Both escaped from the Shelbyville branch railroad. Henry has an "impediment in his speech." Jack is about 21. |
| Nat Mayson | | July 27, 1853 | *Memphis Daily Eagle/Examiner* | Hill & Forrest | Shelby | Ran away from the slave yard of Byrd Hill and Nathan Bedford Forrest. |
| Rice | 35 | Aug. 5, 1853 | *Republican Banner* | Maxey & McClure | Davidson | A tin plate workman by trade who is "badly marked with smallpox in the face." |
| Nancy | 22 | Aug. 5, 1853 | *Loudon Free Press* | William Y. Bardin | Muscogee, GA | Was "raised" near Greeneville. Has "whip marks on back, arms and thighs--some on her back are fresh." |
| Wesley Porter | | Aug. 12, 1853 | *Loudon Free Press* | J.A. Kline | Loudon | "A bright mulatto." |
| Wilson | 26 | Oct. 8, 1853 | *Nashville Union and American* | Thomas Batte | Davidson | "Can read a little." |

| Name of Slave | Age | Date Published | Newspaper | Slave Holder | County | Special Notes |
|---|---|---|---|---|---|---|
| Frank | 21 | Oct. 13, 1853 | *Nashville Union and American* | Whitworth & Taylor | Davidson | "We bought him of Mr. Jourden of Rutherford . . . [he] has the appearance of having the scurvey." |
| George | | Oct. 20, 1853 | *Nashville Union and American* | Guthridge Alford | Davidson | "Has several shot underneath the skin of one of his wrists, which can be felt on examination." |
| Wily | 35 | Dec. 16, 1853 | *Nashville Union/Amer* | W.E. Goodrich | Davidson | "Thin visage, sallow, grum look." |
| Jack | | Dec. 17, 1853 | *Nashville Union and American* | D. Searcy | Davidson | Is "well known by most of the citizens, having been here 8 or 10 years. . . left my house of business, Broadway." |
| Unnamed male | 22 | Jan. 5, 1854 | *Republican Banner* | John Word | Wilson | Is "both deaf and dumb." Ran away from near Cainsville. |
| Jim | 23 | Jan. 11, 1854 | *Republican Banner* | Thomas Johns | Rutherford | "His right forefinger partially perished in consequence of a felon." |
| Nat | 27 | March 21, 1854 | *Nashville Union and American* | James L. Bell | Davidson | "A fiddle under his arm and is a carpenter by trade. . . has an intellectual appearance." |
| Peter | 8 | April 5, 1854 | *Republican Banner* | Dabbs & Porter | Davidson | Wandered off from the auction yard. "We suppose he is lost and don't know the way back or to who he belongs to." |
| Isham | 40 | April 12, 1854 | *Republican Banner* | A. Thompson | Maury | "Is very well known about Nashville." |
| Sampson | 25 | May 18, 1854 | *Nashville Union and American* | Nelson & Donelson | Lafourche, LA | A bricklayer who "was brought from Nashville and raised by Samuel Watkins." [Watkins is mentioned in *Unwritten History of Slavery*.] |
| Tilford | | July 7, 1854 | *Republican Banner* | Berry Whitesides | Davidson | This slave has been sold 4 times and "his wife lives about 6 miles of Statesville and belongs to a gentleman by the name of Ramsey." |
| Elizabeth/ Thomas | 18 | July 18, 1854 | *Kingston Gazetteer* | John Woodfork | Morgan | She and her 2-year-old son were said to have been stolen by a white man named Robert Smith. She has a small scar on the left side of her neck, "would pass for a white woman" and is "very good looking." |
| Jerry | 40 | July 28, 1854 | *Athens Post* | J.H. Johnston | Bradley | "Three fingers on his right hand are stiff, caused by a cut on the wrist." Formerly belonged by Col. P.W. Green. |
| Sam/Ben | 24 | Aug. 16, 1854 | *Clarks Jeffersonian* | William Norsworthy | Montgomery | "Stutters in speaking." Ben (22) has a "scar on his upper lip." |
| David | | Aug. 25, 1854 | *Republican Banner* | A.C. Mayberry | Williamson | "Probably aiming for Canada, as one of his acquaintances has escaped from the same neighborhood and gone to that country." |
| Alfonso | | Aug. 28, 1854 | *Republican Banner* | H. Bridges & Son | Davidson | "Rather inclined to smile when speaking." Is "owned by Mr. Polk of Columbia" but was working for H. Bridges at Sewanee House. |

| Name of Slave | Age | Date Published | Newspaper | Slave Holder | County | Special Notes |
|---|---|---|---|---|---|---|
| Mary | 30 | Sept. 14, 1854 | *Nashville Union/Amer* | Clinton Brigance | Henderson | Was raised near Gallatin, "where she has some children now living." |
| Henry | 17 | Sept. 15, 1854 | *Athens Post* | William Terry | McMinn | "A keen active boy" who was purchased from Joseph Warren and and brought from Augusta, GA. |
| Ellick | 41 | Nov. 29, 1854 | *Nashville Union and American* | Smith Carney | Coffee | "Has two scars on the inside of the arm near the wrist--cut with a gin saw." Ran away with Reuben. |
| Reuben | | Nov. 29, 1854 | *Nashville Union/Amer* | Mrs. Jernigan | Coffee | Ran away with Ellick. |
| Ben | 40 | Dec. 9, 1854 | *Kingston Gazette* | H.G. Redman | Scott | Has a "scar across his fingers." His wife "belongs" to E.M. Dunn of Polk County and he ran away from Huntsville, Tennessee. |
| Joe Hall/ Jim | 24 | Dec. 14, 1854 | *Nashville Union and American* | Montgomery Bell | Williamson | Ran away together with a "large amount of money." Joe Hall can read and write and "has a scar on one of his cheek bones, caused by a burn." Jim is about 30. |
| John | 23 | Dec. 17, 1854 | *Nashville Union and American* | Thomas G. James | Davidson | John "speaks slow but sensibly" and has a wife at Mr. Gleaves'. Previously held by John Shoot, who lived near the Hermitage. [Thomas James is a slave trader.] |
| Levi | 25 | Dec. 29, 1854 | *Nashville Union and American* | John W. Pennington | Davidson | Has "a scar between his thumb and forefinger caused by catching a scythe" and "a peculiar way of drawing up his upper lip." |
| George | 24 | Dec. 30, 1854 | *Republican Banner* | C.D. Brien | Davidson | "Purchased him about two years ago from Mr. Heughan of Wilson." |
| Minerva | | Jan. 31, 1855 | *Nashville Union/Amer* | Thomas M. Petway | Davidson | "Has been employed in Nashville as a seamstress several years." |
| Henry | 27 | Jan. 31, 1855 | *Republican Banner* | William Penn Harding | Davidson | Teeth nearly all gone and has a scar on his nose. Previously held by D.D. Holman of Robertson. [See Emma Grisham slave narrative interview regarding William Penn Harding.] |
| John | 24 | March 18, 1855 | *Nashville Union and American* | John Smith | Maury | The "middle finger of his left hand is stiff." Also, he "was purchased by me, about three years ago, of one William Hunt of Davidson." |
| Rhoda | 25 | March 22, 1855 | *Nashville Republican* | David Ralston | Davidson | She had been hired out by the heirs of William Paradise to Martha Miller, and now both Rhoda and Martha Miller have vanished. |
| Harmon | 37 | April 27, 1855 | *Athens Post* | John Stanfield | Loudon | "Not bold, daring or impudent on conversation." |
| Albert/ Tom/ Mary | 25 | May 8, 1855 | *Republican Banner* | William L. Boyd Jr. | Davidson | Albert is "blind in the right eye" and was raised in Montgomery, Ala." Tom (23) is "a little cross eyed" and "was raised by John Webb of Davidson." Mary (20) was raised in Rutherford County. |

| Name of Slave | Age | Date Published | Newspaper | Slave Holder | County | Special Notes |
|---|---|---|---|---|---|---|
| Nelson | 19 | May 31, 1855 | *Fayetteville Observer* | Daniel Coleman | Athens, AL | A blacksmith who is "a little lame in one foot." Also, "probable he will be lurking about Fayetteville" since he was recently purchased from John Burke. |
| Adolphus | 25 | June 10, 1855 | *Nashville Union and American* | Thomas L. Yancey | Davidson | "Quick speech, and very intelligent . . . his color is so light that one would suppose him to be not more than one fourth negro." |
| George | 22 | July 27, 1855 | *Memphis Daily Eagle/Examiner* | W.P. Matthews | Shelby | Is left handed and "was bought in New Orleans about 18 months ago and says he was raised in North Carolina." |
| Jim/ Albert | 25 | Aug. 29, 1855 | *Daily Nashville Patriot* | C.L. Nelson | Davidson | Both working for Charles E.H. Martin when they ran away. Jim "was raised in Williamson by Thomas Petway" and "speaks quickly when spoken to." Albert also about 25. |
| Jane | 25 | Oct. 7, 1855 | *Republican Banner* | S. Gatking | Monroe, MS | Has a scar over one eye. "She ran away some two years ago, and was taken up in Williamson. . . and may try to get back." |
| Anthony | 27 | Oct. 30, 1855 | *Republican Banner* | Young W. Redmond | Williamson | "Purchased said negro of James Johnson, who has kept him in the warehouse of Johnson & Weaver ever since he owned him." |
| George | 28 | Nov. 16, 1855 | *Republican Banner* | John March | Lincoln | "Speaks tolerably quick, and has a very pleasing countenance." |
| Bob | 24 | Dec. 12, 1855 | *Republican Banner* | Jordan & Wood | Williamson | He was "sold in Nashville . . . by John S. Williams of Kentucky." |
| Henry | 24 | Dec. 20, 1855 | *Nashville Union/Amer* | K.L. Burditt | Bedford | "Stammers in speech." |
| Austin | 22 | Dec. 20, 1855 | *Nashville Union and American* | S.R. Kitrell | Maury | A "small scar on the right jaw." |
| Jack | 18 | Jan. 9, 1856 | *Nashville Union/Amer* | Duncan McRae | Maury | "Tolerable quick spoken." |
| Tom | 23 | Jan. 15, 1856 | *Nashville Daily Patriot* | W.G. Hight | Bedford | A "good scribe" and "good scholar." |
| Harry | | Feb. 1, 1856 | *Nashville Union and Americanic* | George C. Allen | Davidson | A carpenter by trade who was hired by Coleman & Spain, Nashville carpenters. Is "owned" by John W. Allen of New Orleans "who left him in my care this fall." Has a scar on the center of his forehead. |
| Sap | | Feb. 1, 1856 | *Nashville Union/Amer* | A.B. Montgomery | Davidson | "Soft spoken, and whines a little through his nose." |
| Richard | 30 | Feb. 16, 1856 | *Memphis Daily Appeal* | Forrest & Maples | Shelby | A carpenter from Charleston who can read and write and who escaped from the slave yard of Forrest & Maples. Reward is $500. |
| Daniel | 35 | Feb. 20, 1856 | *Republican Banner* | J.L. Bayne | Davidson | "A good Stone Mason, has been hired about Nashville to work at the trade." |

| Name of Slave | Age | Date Published | Newspaper | Slave Holder | County | Special Notes |
|---|---|---|---|---|---|---|
| Bettie | | March 15, 1856 | *Daily Nashville Patriot* | Isaac Koonce | Haywood | Has "a very bumpy face." |
| John | 27 | April 5, 1856 | *Republican Banner* | Rees W. Porter | Davidson | Ran away from the slave yard; has a scar on his lip. "John S. Gray of Hopkinsville, Ky. brought John from that neighborhood and sold him at this place last October." |
| Abram | | April 26, 1856 | *Republican Banner* | A. Thompson | Maury | "Slow spoken and rather a dull negro." |
| Emily | 31 | May 9, 1856 | *Nashville Union/Amer* | Joseph C. Rye | Maury | "Well made. . . bought her from Hinchey Petway of Davidson." |
| Edmund | 25 | May 18, 1856 | *Republican Banner* | Pointer Brothers | Wayne | "Keeps one eye partially closed." Ran away from the furnace in Wayne County. |
| John/Ned | 23 | June 8, 1856 | *Nashville Union and American* | S.R. Alexander | Maury | "Quick spoken and uses bad language." Ran away with Ned. Both "brought from Savannah, Georgia, and are no doubt trying to make their way back." |
| Ned | 23 | June 8, 1856 | *Nashville Union/Amer* | E.W. Buford | Maury | Ran away with John. Brought from Savannah, GA. |
| Mary | | June 19, 1856 | *Daily Nashville Patriot* | William L. Boyd Jr. | Davidson | "She has a free husband in Bowling Green, and also has several children belonging to a gentleman in or near that place, and will doubtless attempt to get back there." |
| Wonder | 24 | July 15, 1856 | *Nashville Union and American* | M.W. Wetmore | Davidson | "Downcast countenance and slow of speech" and "purchased" from Andrew Gerbardstein of KY. |
| Harrison Black | 35 | July 15, 1856 | *Nashville Union/Amer* | Thomas Brown | Williamson | "A scar on one of his arms near the elbow caused by a burn." Also, "quick spoken." |
| Aleck | 15 | July 15, 1856 | *Nashville Union/Amer* | B.L. Simpson | Davidson | "Small scar on the right cheek." |
| John | 29 | July 22, 1856 | *Nashville Union and American* | James M. Murrell | Davidson | "Has a very plain scar on his lip" and "resembles the real African." Also, "was raised in South Carolina or Georgia." |
| Henry | 18 | July 30, 1856 | *Nashville Union and American* | David M. Allen | Davidson | "Was raised in East Tennessee, near McMinnville. He will probably make his way back there." |
| Cyrus | 42 | Aug. 6, 1856 | *Nashville Union and American* | Dr. James B. Stone | Williamson | A tanner. "The third finger . . . presents the appearance of a stick cut half in two." Also, "very intelligent, but speaks in a slow undertone, and has a habit of clearing his throat frequently during conversation." |
| Camel | 30 | Aug. 15, 1856 | *Clarksville Weekly Chronicle* | Thomas Brame | Christian County, Ky. | "Bought said boy in Nashville last February out of Fosters' negro yard." |
| Anderson | 27 | Aug. 31, 1856 | *Nashville Union/Amer* | Tom J. Watson | Williamson | "Speaks quickly." |

| Name of Slave | Age | Date Published | Newspaper | Slave Holder | County | Special Notes |
|---|---|---|---|---|---|---|
| Toney | 24 | Sept. 14, 1856 | *Republican Banner* | R.W. Shaffer | Davidson | "Was raised in Dooly County, Georgia, and bought . . . in Macon." Also, "I understand he has been in the habit of unloading boats on Sunday." |
| Henry | 35 | Sept. 21, 1856 | *Republican Banner* | John Thompson | Davidson | A blacksmith by trade who "speaks mildly and civilly when addressed." |
| Hannibal | 24 | Oct. 22, 1856 | *Nashville Union/Amer* | W.P. Bobo | Bedford | "Last seen at Wartrace." |
| Unnamed male | 21 | Oct. 28, 1856 | *Nashville Union and American* | Zadol Motlow | Moore County | Ran away from Lynchburg and supposed to have gone off in company with a boy belonging to W.P. Bobo." (Hannibal) |
| Henry | | Oct. 29, 1856 | *Clarks Jeffersonian* | Jesse Darden | Robertson | "Black and stoutly made." Slave holder address is Turnersville. |
| Ben | 43 | Nov. 9, 1856 | *Republican Banner* | C.E. Woodruff | Davidson | "Stoop shouldered" and "downcast look." |
| Dick | 22 | Dec. 18, 1856 | *Nashville Union/Amer* | John Brown | Maury | "Quick spoken, and a rather indolent appearance." |
| 2 unnamed males | 21 | Jan. 13, 1857 | *Memphis Daily Appeal* | J.A. Mickleberry | Shelby | First male has "a scar on his right cheek." Second "has a bad delivery." Both 21; both ran away from Rosstown. |
| Violet | 55 | Jan. 23, 1857 | *Clarks Weekly Chronicle* | Henry Northington | Montgomery | "Quick spoken when addressed." Ran away from near Port Royal. |
| Jim | 19 | Feb. 10, 1857 | *Republican Banner* | J.C. Darden | Davidson | Deliver the boy to me "at the lumber yard on Broad Street." |
| William | 22 | March 2, 1857 | *Clarksville Weekly Chronicle* | James M. Radford | Christian, KY | "Has a very sulky appearance when spoken to, and is quite bushy headed." Also, "he may have a wound from a pistol shot as he was shot at twice." |
| Miles | 22 | April 3, 1857 | *Paris Sentinel* | B.C. Bradley | Henry | "Plays well on the fiddle" and has a "small scar over one eye." Ran away from near Conyersville. |
| Ben | 40 | April 4, 1857 | *Nashville Union and American* | James & Harrison | Davidson | "Very sensible and smart. . . He was raised on White's Creek, in Davidson." Ran away from the slave trading yard at 18 Cedar. |
| Unnamed male | 19 | April 17, 1857 | *Clarks Weekly Chronicle* | Jason Babb | Robertson | Ran away from the community of Black Jack. |
| Bent | | May 7, 1857 | *Memphis Daily Appeal* | B.B. Mitchell | Shelby | "Likely, smart and intelligent. . . Raised in Charleston, South Carolina, and brought from there some months since by Mr. N.B. Forrest, from whom I bought him; he will probably attempt to get back there." |
| Isabella | 31 | May 18, 1857 | *Daily Nashville Patriot* | Rees W. Porter | Davidson | "Has very keen sparkling eyes, her front teeth are very bad, she frequently wears false teeth and ear rings. . . I hired her to Mr. M.S. Allen on Broad Street for the present year." |
| Ben | 20 | May 22, 1857 | *Clarks Weekly Chronicle* | Stephen M. Ligon | Montgomery | "Has a lazy, shambling gait in walking, and has a down cast look." |

| Name of Slave | Age | Date Published | Newspaper | Slave Holder | County | Special Notes |
|---|---|---|---|---|---|---|
| Morgan/ Isaac | 35 | May 26, 1857 | Memphis Daily Appeal | H.C. Stark | Shelby | Both ran away while working on the Germantown plank road. Morgan has a small scar on the left side of his face" and is "probably marked with the whip." Isaac is about 28. |
| Jo | 33 | June 5, 1857 | Shelbyville Expositor | J.P. Dromgoogle | Bedford | "Professes to talk French." |
| Barnett/ Peter | 24 | June 18, 1857 | Fayetteville Observer | Lucius D. Suttle | Lincoln | Ran away together. from Elkton. Both about 24. |
| Henry | | July 1, 1857 | Republican Banner | David B. Hicks | Davidson | "Ran away from my brickyard on the north side of the river" and "is the property of Jane W. Campbell." His wife is free and lives on Spruce Street. |
| Tom | 35 | July 21, 1857 | Republican Banner | M.A. Parish | Davidson | "Hired him from John Thompson" and works at Johnson, Horne & Co. |
| Adam/ Fed/ Sandford | 40 | Aug. 6, 1857 | Memphis Daily Appeal | Samuel J. Neal | Fayette | All ran away from a plantion near Elkton. Adam has "a scar on his nose, and one of his knees is enlarged by a cut." Fed is about 35; Sandford about 21. |
| Joe | 40 | Aug. 20, 1857 | Memphis Daily Appeal | Thomas H. Allen | Shelby | "A spare built man." Ran away with Hugh. |
| Hugh | 26 | Aug. 20, 1857 | Memphis Daily Appeal | Mrs. M.A. Rice | Shelby | "Wears a goatee." Ran away with Joe. |
| Jim | 22 | Aug. 25, 1857 | Republican Banner | William Little | Bedford | Reads and writes well. Purchased from H.A. Defriese of Cleveland, TN. |
| George | 30 | Sept. 6, 1857 | Nashville Union and American | J.J. Abernathy | Franklin | A "small scar under his right jaw." From Nashville and "was hired last year to B. Lanier, whose warehouse he was in when it fell." His wife lived in Edgefield, at Mr. Sledge's. |
| Sam | 32 | Sept. 8, 1857 | Republican Banner | A. Thompson | Maury | Has a small scar in one of his eyebrows and "speaks a little slow or rather long when spoken to, but very pleasantly." |
| William/ James | 22 | Sept. 8, 1857 | Republican Banner | J.M. Marks | Giles | William has "rather a fine voice, stoops a little forward in walking." James (24) "has a very coarse voice, carries himself very erect." |
| Logan | 25 | Sept. 8, 1857 | Republican Banner | Thomas G. James | Davidson | Ran away "from J. Lumsden's Tan-Yard a few days ago." [Thomas G. James is a slave trader.] |
| Nelson | 19 | Oct. 8, 1857 | Fayetteville Observer | James P. Burke | Lincoln | A blacksmith who "has one or two scars on his face." |
| Louisa Walton | 22 | Oct. 10, 1857 | Daily Nashville Patriot | J.T. Walton | Davidson | She is from Alabama but the family to whom she belongs is visiting Nashville, from where she escaped. |
| Unnamed Female | 42 | Dec. 4, 1857 | Athens Post | Benjamin Huffince | Loudon | "She was bought some four years since in Atlanta, Ga., and I expect she will try to get back to that place." |

| Name of Slave | Age | Date Published | Newspaper | Slave Holder | County | Special Notes |
|---|---|---|---|---|---|---|
| Jim | 28 | Dec. 8, 1857 | *Nashville Union and American* | William D. Phillips | Davidson | "I think he is in Robertson, Sumner or perhaps in Davidson." |
| Easter | 22 | Dec. 15, 1857 | *Daily Nashville Patriot* | W.S. Stratton | Davidson | She was brought from Knoxville, has a "scar on one wrist, from a cut" and "speaks slow." |
| Lucy | 25 | Dec. 22, 1857 | *Memphis Daily Appeal* | F.S. Latham | Shelby | "Has a scar on one of her arms, above the wrist, sheped like the letter L." Also, "was bought of David Kyle, near Grenada, Miss., and is supposed to have returned in that direction, along the railroad track." |
| Bill | 14 | Jan. 12, 1858 | *Memphis Daily Appeal* | T.J. Waller | Fayette | "Has a scar on the back of one of his hands." |
| Ned/Nancy | 27 | Feb. 13, 1858 | *Memphis Daily Appeal* | John C. Weaver | Shelby | Husband and wife fan away together. Nancy is "rather delicate and smiles when spoken to." |
| Edmond | 14 | Feb. 13, 1858 | *Memphis Daily Appeal* | W.F. Long | Shelby | "Slow of speech" and "brought him from Middle Tennessee a year since." |
| Amy | | Feb. 19, 1858 | *Clarksville Weekly Chronicle* | C.W. Beaumont | Montgomery | "A bright mulatto, with large and course features." |
| Kinion | 30 | Feb. 18, 1858 | *Memphis Daily Appeal* | D.M. Witherington | Shelby | Had a scar on upper lip and a scar behind his left ear. Ran away from Hazel Flat. |
| Austin/Jordan | 26 | March 7, 1858 | *Nashville Union and American* | W.H. Wilson | Rutherford | Both were en route from Murfreesboro to MS when they ran away. Austin is a blacksmith "sold to me in Nashville." Jordan is about 22. |
| Arthur | 31 | April 9, 1858 | *Clarksville Weekly Chronicle* | Alexander Outlaw | Montgomery | Had a scar on his left wrist and "somewhat slow spoken" and "good countenance." |
| Lem | 33 | May, 2, 1858 | *Memphis Daily Appeal* | B.F. Brown | Shelby | "Nearly white." |
| Timey | 12 | May 19, 1858 | *Republican Banner* | John Browne | Davidson | "Has a mark from a burn on one side of her forehead." |
| William | 21 | June 5, 1858 | *Memphis Daily Appeal* | Maddox & Groves | Shelby | "A scar on one leg." |
| Grissey | 14 | June 26, 1858 | *Memphis Daily Appeal* | Thomas W. Preston | Shelby | House servant. |
| Levi/Isom | 25 | July 8, 1858 | *Memphis Daily Appeal* | E.M. Apperson | Fayette | Both ran away from plantation near La Grange. Levi is "dark colored, spare made." Isom (21) is "mulatto, heavy set." |
| John Payne | | July 15, 1858 | *Fayetteville Observer* | H.M. Bledsoe | Lincoln | "Understood to be lurking in this vicinity." |
| Jessie | 22 | July 22, 1858 | *Memphis Daily Appeal* | S.P. Gregory | Shelby | "Speaks quick when spoken to." Ran away before and was lodged in Henderson County jail. |
| Rachel | | July 30, 1858 | *Memphis Daily Appeal* | Sam B. Read | Shelby | "Bright color" and "rather corpulent." |

| Name of Slave | Age | Date Published | Newspaper | Slave Holder | County | Special Notes |
|---|---|---|---|---|---|---|
| Minerva | 30 | Sept. 10, 1858 | *Clarksville Chronicle* | R. Caldwell | Humphreys | "Bold and somewhat impudent in speech." |
| Pauline | 28 | Sept. 29, 1858 | *Republican Banner* | A.B. Montgomery | Davidson | "Full breasts, thick lips, large mouth, copper colored, quick spoken, and carries herself very erect. . . I think she is trying to make her way back to Virginia." |
| Charles/ Tennes-see/child | 30 | Oct. 1, 1858 | *Clarksville Weekly Chronicle* | Mitchel Trotter | Benton | Man and wife. Tennessee (22) ran away with their infant child from Trotter's Landing. |
| Marilla | 28 | Oct. 27, 1858 | *Clarksville Jeffersonian* | Elizabeth Dolan | Montgom-ery | "When questioned she is slow in answer" and "is shy when spoken to and turns her face away." |
| Dennis | 20 | Oct. 29, 1859 | *Brownlow's Knox Whig* | Guilford Cannon | Monroe | A "scar on his forehead, on the edge of his hair . . . it is supposed that he has as a pilot a white boy 16 years old" and "I suppose he will make for Cumberland Gap." |
| David | 40 | Oct. 31, 1858 | *Memphis Daily Appeal* | M.B. Baldwin | Shelby | "A plasterer by trade." |
| Adam/ Fred/ Charles | 42 | Dec. 3, 1858 | *Memphis Daily Appeal* | Samuel J. Neal | Fayette | Adam has "a scar on his nose and one knee "somewhat enlarged by a cut." Fred about 38. Charles "has rather a down look when spoken to, nonetheless very shrewd and smart." |
| Jack | | Jan. 9, 1859 | *Memphis Daily Appeal* | John McGrath | Shelby | Has a scar over one of his eyes. Also, "speaks in a fine voice" and "has a long stride when he walks." |
| John | 25 | Jan. 12, 1859 | *Nashville Union and American* | George Stroud | Warren | Is a "good boot and shoemaker" who "can read and write pretty well" and is "hard to distinguish from a white man, except by close observers." Ran away from Morrison Depot. |
| Jerry | | Jan. 18, 1859 | *Memphis Daily Appeal* | E. Ayres | Shelby | "Had locked to his right leg a pair of shackles." Was "owned" in Cleveland but worked for the Memphis and Charleston Railroad and escaped from there. |
| Dave | | Jan. 21, 1859 | *Memphis Daily Appeal* | Nathan B. Forrest | Shelby | Ran away from Forrest's slave yard. Was placed there by Dr. Robert Temple of Hernando, MS. |
| Malinda | 21 | March 15, 1859 | *Nashville Union and American* | T.F. McNish | Davidson | "Speaks quick and has a grum look." |
| Jim | 20 | March 24, 1859 | *Winch Home Journal* | J.C. Montgomery | Franklin | A "large and stout negro every way" who ran away near the [Cowan] tunnel. |
| John | 22 | April 22, 1859 | *Memphis Daily Appeal* | C. Spigel | Shelby | "Wears a little moustache." |
| Frank | 34 | April 27, 1859 | *Memphis Daily Appeal* | Bosley & Smith | Shelby | May "make his way to Grand Junction." |

| Name of Slave | Age | Date Published | Newspaper | Slave Holder | County | Special Notes |
|---|---|---|---|---|---|---|
| Manuel | 22 | April 29, 1859 | *Clarksville Chronicle* | C.H. Smith | Montgomery | "Took his fiddle with him." He was purchased from Abednego Hale, near Jonesboro, "and is probably making his way in that direction." |
| George | 24 | May 4, 1859 | *Greeneville Democrat* | Samuel W. Davis | Greene | "Has a large scar on his left forefinger caused by a straw cutter." Ran away from Camp Creek. Last seen heading to Jennings Iron Works. |
| Bill | 28 | May 5, 1859 | *Nashville Union and American* | John Casey | Davidson | "Quick motioned and speaks rather slow." |
| Arthur | 28 | May 6, 1859 | *Clarksville Chronicle* | B.J. Crowder | Stewart | [This may be the same Arthur who tried to escape from Alexander Outlaw a year earlier.] |
| Jim | 30 | May 11, 1859 | *Daily Nashville Patriot* | W.J. Martin | Hamilton | A blacksmith with a small scar on his left nostril caused by blasting rock and some on his chest caused by burns. Ran away from the Decherd Depot, but slaveholder lives in Chattanooga. |
| Joe | 22 | May 17, 1859 | *Republican Banner* | L.B. McConnico | Davidson | A painter, paper hanger and barber who "tries to show off in conversation, and his pronunciation somewhat peculiar." |
| Giles | 40 | May 26, 1859 | *Memphis Daily Appeal* | William Y. Williams | Shelby | "He plays well on the banjo." |
| Enoch/ Aleck | 27 | June 2, 1859 | *Republican Banner* | Henry Alley | Davidson | Enoch "speaks in a drawling tone." Aleck "speaks with a whining voice." |
| Clark/ Tom | 35 | June 12, 1859 | *Nashville Union and American* | William Ashly | Coffee | Brothers ran away together. Clark has his "left thumb cut off at the first joint." Tom is about 36. |
| John | 30 | June 25, 1859 | *Memphis Daily Appeal* | Henry T. Hulbert | Shelby | "Think visage, very smart." |
| Melinda | 45 | June 28, 1859 | *Republican Banner* | Thomas H. Millington | Davidson | "I purchased her from Richard Barnafield of Lebanon who, I understand, owns some of her children." |
| Hannibal | 17 | June 30, 1859 | *Republican Banner* | James G. Perry | Maury | "Said boy is supposed to be lurking about Columbia or Williamsport." |
| Edmund | 23 | Aug. 4, 1859 | *Memphis Daily Appeal* | John M. Mickelberry | Shelby | "Has a downcast look and stammers very much when spoken to." Ran away from Hazel Flat. |
| Joe | | Aug. 13, 1859 | *Memphis Daily Appeal* | John Morrison | Shelby | "My boy Joe, better known as 'Joe Grooms.'" |
| Cain | 25 | Aug. 16, 1859 | *Memphis Daily Appeal* | Edward Pickett | Shelby | A painter who "has a wife at B.W. Burch's." |
| Maria | 22 | Aug. 27, 1859 | *Memphis Daily Appeal* | Norvell, Boone & Co. | Shelby | She "may endeavor to make her way to Holly Springs, Mississippi" and left from the residence of William McKean. |
| Huston | 22 | Sept. 2, 1859 | *Clarksville Weekly Chronicle* | J.G. Foster | Christian, KY | Had on a heavy pair of handcuffs. Was raised near Buena Vista Ferry on Cumberland River and his wife at Mr. Anderson's in the same neighborhood. |

| Name of Slave | Age | Date Published | Newspaper | Slave Holder | County | Special Notes |
|---|---|---|---|---|---|---|
| Pate | 17 | Oct. 7, 1859 | *Nashville Union/Amer* | Sam B. Watkins | Rutherford | "Has a scar on his face from a burn." |
| Eliza | 38 | Oct. 15, 1859 | *Memphis Daily Appeal* | George W. Griffin | Shelby | "Blind in one eye." |
| Jack | 45 | Oct. 15, 1859 | *Memphis Daily Appeal* | Joseph Dennis | Tipton | "Was brought from Missouri, about three years since, and will probably try to return." Ran away from Randolph. |
| Eva | 17 | Oct. 26, 1859 | *Daily Nashville Patriot* | George S. Bolling | Davidson | "Had on when she left gold cross earrings and a number of finger rings." Ran away from Nashville's St. Cloud Hotel. |
| Wilson | 30 | Nov. 12, 1859 | *Republican Banner* | George Sanford | Rutherford | Father is free and named Alfred; mother belonged to the widow Maxwell of Davidson; children in Huntsville. |
| William | 23 | Dec. 15, 1859 | *Memphis Daily Appeal* | William H. Weller | Shelby | "Wears rings in his ears" and is "slightly knock kneed." |
| Flora | 17 | Dec. 16, 1859 | *Repub Banner* | H.M.M. | Davidson | "Has an impediment in her speech." |
| Charles | 24 | Dec. 22, 1859 | *Chattanooga Advertiser* | Elizabeth W. Carter | Hamilton | Has a "slight scar on one of his wrists." Was previously "owned" by William F. Carter, deceased. |
| Jesse | | Dec. 23, 1859 | *Nashville Union and American* | James E. Newsom | Davidson | "A piece bitten out of one ear" and has "rather a feminine voice and talks rather long." |
| Henry | 40 | March 2, 1860 | *Memphis Daily Appeal* | R.B. Hawley | Shelby | "While walking, swings himself a little, holds his head down on one side." May be near Clarksville. |
| Henry | 24 | March 30, 1860 | *Nashville Union and American* | John K. Taylor | Sumner | "No. 1 second rate man" and "some marks on his back or hips." He "was raised by Wiley J. Douglass of Sumner." |
| Alfred/ John | 42 | April 21, 1860 | *Nashville Union and American* | James Lewallen | Corinth, Miss | Alfred a good blacksmith who "was raised about Nashville." John (15) "was raised on Harpeth, about 12 miles from Nashville, by Mr. Demoss." |
| Charles | 30 | May 9, 1860 | *Republican Banner* | John Philips | Giles | "The scar of a burn on one of his legs above the knee." Also, "speaks slow, and stutters when excited, but uses good language." |
| Henry | 21 | May 18, 1860 | *Nashville Union/Amer* | John G. Primm | Rutherford | "No marks only his little finger, by a felon." |
| Gipson | 35 | May 19, 1860 | *Brownlow's Knox Whig* | W.M. McClellan | Knox | "Has a scar on his left cheek" and is "tolerably talkative, and pretty well informed." |
| Jourdan | 34 | May 25, 1860 | *Clarksville Chronicle* | W.H. Ellis | Stewart | Jourdan used to live in Springfield, then Port Royal, then Clarksville, then Stewart County and now with W.H. Ellis in Caleb's Valley. |
| Sol | 24 | May 26, 1860 | *Brownlow's Knox Whig* | William W. Lackey | Knox | Has been hired out for years as an ostler in a livery stable. |

| Name of Slave | Age | Date Published | Newspaper | Slave Holder | County | Special Notes |
|---|---|---|---|---|---|---|
| Ike | 38 | June 1, 1860 | *Nashville Union and American* | John Cotner | Bedford | "Reads well" and "speaks rather slow when talking." Also, "has had one of his legs broken just above the knee." |
| Dick | 25 | June 10, 1860 | *Memphis Daily Appeal* | H.S. Crawford | Shelby | "The whites of his eyes are of a reddish color." |
| Belinda | 45 | June 13, 1860 | *Memphis Daily Appeal* | N.L. Lawrence | Shelby | Has "several scars on her neck and breast." |
| Priestly | 33 | June 22, 1860 | *Clarksville Chronicle* | James N. Smith | Montgomery | "Dark mulatto color." |
| George | 28 | June 24, 1860 | *Nashville Union and American* | Richard R. Hyde | Davidson | "Face covered with beard, never shaving." |
| Mary | | July 8, 1860 | *Memphis Daily Appeal* | K.G. Ferrell | Grenada, MS | Ran away with her infant child. "She was purchased of Forrest, of Memphis." |
| Henry | 40 | Aug. 29, 1860 | *Memphis Daily Appeal* | J.C. Nelson | Haywood | "Has a very dull expression" and "has a wife at Matthew White's or J.B. Ashes' in Mississippi." |
| Bill | 16 | Oct. 17, 1860 | *Murfreesboro News* | S.B. Watkins | Rutherford | "Well grown, upright carriage." |
| Westley | 35 | Nov. 16, 1860 | *Clarksville Chronicle* | T.Y. Dickson | Montgomery | Has a scar over the left eye, "is rather intemperate, and has considerable proclivity for card playing." Slaveholder was Sol D. Raimey. Westley had been farmed out to the Antonio Furnace near Palmyra. |
| William | 28 | Nov. 20, 1860 | *Nashville Union and American* | Napolean B. Hyde | Davidson | Belongs to John Johns Jr. Has a scar "on his left foot, just back of his little toe, that was cut this year with an axe." |
| 3 Unnamed Slaves | 47 | Dec. 11, 1860 | *Nashville Union and American* | A.P. Forrester | Grundy | One is a woman who "walks a little lame." The other 2 were boys aged 11 and 12. Slaveholder resides near Altamont. |
| Rozeon | 16 | Dec. 12, 1860 | *Nashville Union and American* | Anonymous | Davidson | "Any information concerning her will be thankfully received at this office, and a suitable reward paid for delivery here." |
| Aggy/4 others | 30 | Feb. 13, 1861 | *Nashville Union and American* | J.W. Pettus | Williamson | All 5 left together from Truine with a white man named Newton Jordan. Others include an infant girl, Lizzy (30), Burton (14) and Joshua (17). |
| Nick/Bill | | May 4, 1861 | *Memphis Daily Appeal* | John C. Weaver | Shelby | Nick "has the appearance of an Indian." Bill (15) is "likely and well grown for his age." Ran away from plantation 9 miles SW of Memphis. |
| John Henry | 18 | May 4, 1861 | *Memphis Daily Appeal* | S.M. May | Shelby | "The ends of two of his fingers have been mashed off." Also, "raised in Stewart City, Tennessee, and was sold to A&N Delap of Memphis, from whom I purchased him." |
| Catherine | 20 | June 14, 1861 | *Clarksville Chronicle* | John Birney | Montgomery | "Inclined to laugh when spoken to." |

| Name of Slave | Age | Date Published | Newspaper | Slave Holder | County | Special Notes |
|---|---|---|---|---|---|---|
| Will | | Dec. 6, 1861 | *Athens Post* | David Leuty | Loudon | Lives in Roane, ran away from Loudon. |
| Charles | 27 | Dec. 14, 1861 | *Nashville Union and American* | Berry Whitesides | Wilson | Writes "well" and is a carpenter. "When he left home, carried with him his trunk and has a suit of soldier's clothes." |
| Abram | 28 | Jan. 19, 1862 | *Memphis Daily Appeal* | John D. Eastin | Tipton | "Quick spoken and very likely. . . Ranaway from the subscriber, while working on the fortifications at Fort Pillow." |
| Tennessee | 40 | Feb. 1, 1862 | *Nashville Union and American* | John and Hugh Ewing | Davidson | "Smokes tobacco and drinks whiskey; looks young." Also, "her husband Cyrus lives at Ann Richardson's in Hartsville." |
| Aaron | 15 | May 11, 1862 | *Nashville Daily Union* | John Brownlee | Davidson | "Last seen in the academy yard at Nashville." |
| Ann | 45 | May 25, 1862 | *Memphis Daily Appeal* | E.E. Dill | Shelby | "She is no doubt in the southern part of the city." |
| Pitt/Joe | 22 | June 25, 1862 | *Nashville Daily Union* | W.D. Simpkins | Davidson | Brothers who ran away together. Joe has "a scar from a cut on his left forefinger." |
| Tilmon | 28 | Aug. 8, 1862 | *Nashville Daily Union* | Robert Cato | Davidson | "[He] said he was in Murfreesboro at the time of the late battle and got slightly wounded in the hand." |
| Foster/ Edmund | 22 | Aug. 8, 1862 | *Nashville Daily Union* | William S. Cheatham | Montgomery | "Left Clarksville a few days after the Federal troops took possession of the place." "When last heard from, they were in Gen. McCook's division." Edmund is about 23. |
| Will | | Nov. 8, 1862 | *Knoxville Daily Register* | George Ferguson | Knox | "Belongs to Peter Everette of Mt. Sterling, Ky." and "I think he will endeavor to make his way back into Kentucky through Cumberland Gap." |
| Zack | 30 | Nov. 8, 1862 | *Knoxville Daily Register* | John Jackson | Knox | "Said negro has a sprinkle of gray hairs." |
| Sam | 16 | Nov. 8, 1862 | *Knoxville Daily Register* | J.W. Harris | Knox | "Very erect and likely" and "stammers." |
| Mary/3 others | | Nov. 8, 1862 | *Knoxville Daily Register* | S.D. Williams | Jefferson | Mary ran away with her 3 small children--Charlotte and Em (twins, both 7) and Hannah (1). |
| Mat | 14 | Nov. 8, 1862 | *Knoxville Daily Register* | W. Mountcastle | Knox | "May have gone westward towards Kingston with the army" and "belongs to the estate of the late Judge Welcker." |
| Ned | 34 | Nov. 8, 1862 | *Knoxville Daily Register* | Ninian Steele | Knox | Either heading to the North or "with the robbers in the mountains." Ran away with Fed, Albert, Lewis and Henry. |
| Fed/ Albert | 20 | Nov. 8, 1862 | *Knoxville Daily Register* | J.G. Hardin | Knox | Either heading to the North or "with the robbers in the mountains." Ran away with Ned, Albert and Lewis. |
| Lewis/ Henry | 21 | Nov. 8, 1862 | *Knoxville Daily Register* | R.W. Hardin | Knox | Either heading to the North or "with the robbers in the mountains." Ran away with Ned, Fed and Albert. |

| Name of Slave | Age | Date Published | Newspaper | Slave Holder | County | Special Notes |
|---|---|---|---|---|---|---|
| Evermont | 28 | Nov. 16, 1862 | *Knoxville Daily Register* | H.T. Cox | Blount | "Quite agreeable and polite in his manners." He "will probably endeavor to make his way to some military camp and engage as a cook, ostler or waiter." |
| Jacob | 25 | Nov. 16, 1862 | *Knoxville Daily Register* | William Bush | Knox | Ran away "from the courthouse hospital." |
| 2 unnamed males | 33 | Dec. 12, 1862 | *Athens Post* | James Johnson | Loudon | One is a 33 year old blacksmith. Another is about 28 and "has a wen on his right temple about the size of a partridge egg." |
| Davy/ Felix | 22 | Dec. 12, 1862 | *Athens Post* | J.L. McClary | Polk | Davy is a "bright mulatto" and "near sighted." Felix (21) is "copper colored." Ran away with Baker. |
| Baker | 28 | Dec. 12, 1862 | *Athens Post* | E.H. Dunn | Polk | "Copper colored" and ran away with Davy and Felix. |
| Mollie | 16 | Dec. 14, 1862 | *Knoxville Daily Register* | Z.L. Burson | Washington | "Bought her last February at Morristown, at the sale of Blevins & Franklin . . . her mother belongs to Dr. Drake, at Bull's Gap." |
| Edmund | 23 | Jan. 20, 1863 | *Winchester Daily Bulletin* | W.L. Rucker | Rutherford | "Dark mulatto" who "was dressed in Yankee uniform when he left" with Granville and John and ran away from Polk's Brigade, Confederate Army. |
| Granville | | Jan. 20, 1863 | *Winchester Daily Bulletin* | R.M. Rucker | Rutherford | "Mulatto" who is "slow in speech and who ran away with Edmund and John from Polk's Brigade, Confederate Army." |
| John | 16 | Jan. 20, 1863 | *Winchester Daily Bulletin* | Miles Furgerson | Rutherford | "Stammers in his speech" and ran away with Edmund and Granville from Polk's Brigade, Confederate Army." |
| Toby | 20 | Jan. 30, 1863 | *Athens Post* | John Stewart | Meigs | "At a distance would pass for a white man." |
| Harrison | 20 | Jan. 30, 1863 | *Athens Post* | Allen Dennis | McMinn | "Several scars on shoulders caused by burn" and was "purchased some six months ago; came from North Carolina." |
| Andrew | | Feb. 6, 1863 | *Chattanooga Daily Rebel* | William Snow | Hamilton | Is "rather slow of speech" and "is supposed to be making his way for Kentucky or for the lines of the federal government." |
| Dolly | 18 | Feb. 15, 1863 | *Winchester Daily Bulletin* | C.B. Austell | Franklin | "Left my house, near Cowan Depot" and "I heard of her being in the neighborhood of Decherd ten days ago." |
| Bill | 19 | Feb. 23, 1863 | *Nashville Daily Union* | E.A. Herman | Davidson | "He had a good home, and was indulged as much as possible for a servant to be." [This may have been the last runaway slave ad published in Nashville.] |
| Dave | 18 | March 11, 1863 | *Chattanooga Daily Rebel* | James M. Stewart | Sequatchie | Born in Petersburg, VA, brought to Hamburg, S.C., then bought by current slaveholder, who lives in Sequatchie Valley. |

| Name of Slave | Age | Date Published | Newspaper | Slave Holder | County | Special Notes |
|---|---|---|---|---|---|---|
| Jane | 19 | April 3, 1863 | *Winchester Daily Bulletin* | T.A. Word | Coffee | "Quick spoken, and shows her teeth quite plainly, when talking." Slaveholder lives in Decherd. |
| Laura | 25 | April 19, 1863 | *Knoxville Daily Register* | E.M. Plumlee | Knox | "Speaks quickly and rather saucy." |
| Winnie | 21 | April 19, 1863 | *Knoxville Daily Register* | Daniel Duggan | Knox | "Last seen in company with a white man who was well dressed . . . between the Big East Fork of Pigeon and the campground on Middle Creek." |
| Unnamed male | 24 | April 20, 1863 | *Knoxville Daily Register* | W.H. Smith | Grainger | "Was all through Kentucky with Morgan and Bragg during last year, and talks a good deal about his cowardice in battle, and his disposition to run under fire." |
| West | 21 | April 26, 1863 | *Knoxville Daily Register* | G.W. Vittetoe | Grainger | "Down countenance, slow spoken" and his wife lives in Merriwether County, GA. Slaveholder address is Powder Spring Gap. |
| Arch/Jim | 30 | April 29, 1863 | *Knoxville Daily Register* | William D. Browder | Monroe | 5 ran away together from Sweetwater. Arch and Jim (27) ran away with Henry, Allen and Bill. |
| Henry/ Allen | 21 | April 29, 1863 | *Knoxville Daily Register* | French Pickell | Monroe | Allen is 17. These 2 ran away fro Sweetwater with Arch, Jim and Bill. |
| Bill | 30 | April 29, 1863 | *Knoxville Daily Register* | Jason M. Browder | Monroe | Ran away from Sweetwater with Arch, Jim, Henry and Allen. |
| George/ Dick | 22 | April 29, 1863 | *Knoxville Daily Register* | John B. McLin | Washington | Ran away from a Confederate army officer passing through Jonesborough. Dick is 25. |
| George | | April 30, 1863 | *Fayetteville Observer* | John H. Steelman | Lincoln | "Rather quick spoken, a close observer will notice a slight stammering in his speech . . . said boy will probably attempt to make his way to the federal lines." |
| Alf | 30 | June 12, 1863 | *Athens Post* | F.H. Gregory | Monroe | Slaveholder residence is "Sweetwater Valley." |
| Tom/John | 30 | June 12, 1863 | *Winchester Daily Bulletin* | Hezekiah Farris | Franklin | Tom "has a wife at the place of Joseph Barker." John (26) "has a wife at Esquire Green's old place." |
| John | | July 14, 1863 | *Knoxville Daily Register* | B. Lanier | Blount | "Carried a violin with him when he left" from Montvale Springs. |
| John/ George | 19 | July 14, 1863 | *Knoxville Daily Register* | E.E. Gillenwaters | Hawkins | Ran away together and "are probably aiming for Kentucky." George (also 19) has "a little finger cut off" and "two fingers on the left hand nearly closed, caused by a burn." |
| 6 unnamed men | | July 14, 1863 | *Knoxville Daily Register* | O.M. McGhee | Monroe | "They were in company with 25 or 30 white men and negroes, making for Pack's Ferry on Holston River." |
| Jim | | July 14, 1863 | *Knoxville Daily Register* | John Nave | Carter | "Slick, black and very likely and well made." |

| Name of Slave | Age | Date Published | Newspaper | Slave Holder | County | Special Notes |
|---|---|---|---|---|---|---|
| Oliver | 18 | July 25, 1863 | *Chattanooga Daily Rebel* | Captain T.E. Powell | Bedford | The "property of Mrs. Winston" who ran away near Shelbyville from a member of General Wheeler's staff. |
| Warner | 15 | July 25, 1863 | *Chattanooga Daily Rebel* | E.O. Stafford | Coffee | Lost "during the retreat from Tullahoma" who ran away from someone in Forrest's regiment. |
| Joe | | July 30, 1863 | *Chattanooga Daily Rebel* | Daniel McPhah | Lincoln | Lost "during the retreat on his way from Fayetteville to Shelbyville" from the "Wharton's Escort, Texas Rangers." |
| Dave | 22 | July 30, 1863 | *Chattanooga Daily Rebel* | E.M. Bruce | Bartow, GA | "Previously lived near Spring Hill, to which place it is presumed he will attempt to return." |
| Joe | 20 | July 30, 1863 | *Chattanooga Daily Rebel* | M.B. Kittrell | Catoosa, GA | "Was raised near McMinnville, Tenn., to which place he will probably attempt to go." He is "quite intelligent." |
| Tom | 37 | Aug. 4, 1863 | *Knoxville Southern Chronicle* | B.R. Strong | Knox | "This negro came originally from Huntsville, Ala., where he has a wife and to which place he may be making an effort to return." |
| Albert/ Robert | | Aug. 27, 1863 | *Knoxville Southern Chronicle* | R. Harris | Knox | Has a "very large scar on his forehead" and "will probably try to pass himself off as a waiter for some soldier." Robert about 18 years old, "last seen about Dr. Crozier's quarters." |
| Jerry/Tom | 35 | Aug. 27, 1863 | *Knoxville Southern Chronicle* | William B. Smith | Knox | Ran away June 26th, "the day of the raid." Tom is about 22. |
| John | | Sept. 14, 1863 | *Memphis Daily Appeal* | Lewis Tumblin | Bartow, GA | "May be with the army at Chattanooga." |
| Charles | 25 | Sept. 30, 1863 | *Memphis Daily Appeal* | M.C. Cayce & Co. | Shelby | A cooper who ran away from a slave trader. |
| Zack | 35 | Jan. 4, 1864 | *Memphis Daily Appeal* | N.W. Steele | Shelby | Of "low stature and bow-legged." Was the "property of Mr. Watkins of North Alabama" and was left with Mr. B.D. Smith of this city to sell. |
| Levi | 24 | April 18, 1864 | *Memphis Daily Appeal* | Paul Jones | Fulton, GA | He "is supposed to be trying to get into Tennessee." |
| Mary Ann | | June 21, 1864 | *Memphis Daily Appeal* | S. Chamberlain | Fulton, GA | "Dark mulatto, has a scar on her right foot above the toes." |

APPENDIX TWO

# TENNESSEE'S CLERK AND MASTER SALES

*This data only reflects clerk and master sales which I found and can in no way be considered a complete list.*

| Date of Auction | County | Clerk | Total | Men | Women | Children | Notes |
|---|---|---|---|---|---|---|---|
| Jan. 1, 1836 | Williamson | Benjamin Litton | 3 | 3 | 0 | 0 | *B. Crichelow v. William Ramsey.* Slaves names were Jerry, Lewis and Woodley. |
| March 5, 1836 | Davidson | Benjamin Litton | 3 | UNK | UNK | UNK | Slaves named Kissey (33) and Martha and her child. |
| October 23, 1837 | Henderson | Augustus Williams | 14 | UNK | UNK | UNK | "At the late residence of John Turner" in Perry County. |
| March 12, 1838 | Davidson | James Johnson | 4 | 1 | 1 | 2 | Case of John Holoway (dec'd). Slaves were Harrison (40), wife Judy (30) and 2 children (6 and infant). |
| March 31, 1838 | Davidson | Benjamin Litton | 12 | UNK | UNK | UNK | Slaves' names were Jack, Tom, Sam, John, Maria, Violet, Martha, Louisa, Patsey, Flora and her 2 children. |
| June 16, 1838 | Davidson | Benjamin Litton | 2 | UNK | UNK | UNK | "Several valuable and likely negroes of good character--and among them is a first rate cook." |
| Dec. 15, 1838 | Williamson | Benjamin Litton | 2 | 1 | 1 | UNK | Slaves named Claiborne and Dolly. |
| June 22, 1839 | Williamson | Benjamin Litton | 2 | 2 | 0 | 0 | *Goss v Bellsnyder.* Slaves named Enoch and Ephraim |
| May 2, 1840 | Maury | S.D. Frierson | 12 | UNK | UNK | UNK | Rogal Fergusson (dec'd). Slaves included 3 men "accustomed to work about iron works," and the rest are "girls, boys and two women with children." |
| May 30, 1840 | Williamson | Benjamin Litton | 1 | UNK | UNK | UNK | *John Davis v. E.N. Phipps.* Slave named Maria. |
| Sept. 9, 1840 | Knox | M. Payne | 9 | 4 | 5 | UNK | "To wit: Fredrick, Philip, Polly, Milly, Maltha, Blount, Mary, Nancy and Robinson." |
| May 28, 1842 | Supreme Court | James P. Clark | 1 | UNK | UNK | UNK | Supreme Court case of *John W. Jones v. John Wright.* Slave named Eliza. |
| Dec. 30, 1843 | Davidson (Circuit) | Jacob McGavock | 24 | 20 | 1 | 3 | *Barrett v. Vanleer* and *Stacker v. Barrett.* "Some of them are first-rate blacksmiths and forge hands." |
| Jan. 1, 1844 | Williamson | Benjamin Litton | UNK | UNK | UNK | UNK | "Several valuable negroes of both sexes, and among them a first rate blacksmith." |
| May 18, 1844 | Hamilton (Circuit) | B.B. Cannon | 7 | 2 | 2 | 3 | Hugh Francis (dec'd). |
| June 3, 1844 | Montgomery | Periander Priestly | 37 | UNK | UNK | UNK | 37 names all listed in the newspaper, although no breakdown in terms of ages. |

| Date of Auction | County | Clerk | Total | Men | Women | Children | Notes |
|---|---|---|---|---|---|---|---|
| June 3, 1844 | Montgomery | Periander Priestly | 10 | 3 | 4 | 3 | *Barker v. Oldham.* Slaves named Big Sam, Edmund, Lindsey, Little Sam, Harriet, Jane, Betty and her three children Frank, Jim and another. |
| Feb. 12, 1845 | Supreme Court | James P. Clark | 1 | 0 | 1 | 0 | *Gookin v. Graham.* Slave named Betsey. |
| Dec. 30, 1846 | Davidson | Jackson B. White | 7 | 2 | 2 | 3 | George H. Burton, dec'd. Slaves were Lydia (70), Stephen (40), Matilda (38), Dock (25), Margaret (14), Ann (11) and Ellen (3). |
| Jan. 25, 1847 | Williamson | Benjamin Litton | 44 | UNK | UNK | UNK | At farm of Robert Whyte, dec'd, of Fayette County. |
| Feb. 8, 1847 | Davidson | Benjamin Litton | 11 | UNK | UNK | UNK | At residence in Nashville owned by Robert Whyte. |
| May 3, 1847 | Maury | George M. Martin | 35 | UNK | UNK | UNK | Archibald Campbell (dec'd). Slaves are "30 to 40 likely Negroes, consisting of men, women, boys and girls." |
| June 2, 1847 | Henry | Elridge G. Atkins | 20 | UNK | UNK | UNK | *Craige, Holmes & Co. v. James Cowan.* Slaves are "of various ages, consisting of men, women and children." |
| Dec. 1847 | Davidson | Jackson B. White | 4 | 0 | 1 | 3 | *Puckett and wife v. Beasley.* Slaves were "Caroline aged 24 years, Tom aged 12 years, Henry aged 7 years and Bob aged 2 years." |
| Feb. 12, 1848 | Davidson | Jackson B. White | 5 | 1 | 0 | 4 | *Milam v. Watkins* and *Cartwright v. Watkins.* Slaves were Francis (28), Deaderick (13), Emily (11), Mary (9) and Fanny (3). |
| April 22, 1848 | Supreme Court | James P. Clark | 1 | 1 | 0 | 0 | 1847 Supreme Court case involving Dr. E.P. Breathett (dec'd). Slave named Randall. |
| May 6, 1848 | Williamson | Jackson B. White | 1 | 0 | 0 | 1 | Case of *Ewing v. Boyd.* "Negro girl Frances, aged about 9 years." |
| Dec. 20, 1848 | Davidson | Jackson B. White | 4 | 2 | 1 | 1 | Thomas Tollbert (dec'd). Slaves were George (25), Washington (27), Anne (52) and her child Mary (9). |
| Jan. 1, 1849 | Dickson | John C. Collier | 6 | UNK | UNK | UNK | Spencer T. Hunt (dec'd). Slaves were Charles, Nancy, Jane, John, Isham and an infant girl. |
| Jan. 2, 1850 | Davidson (Circuit) | Thomas T. Smiley | 2 | 1 | 0 | 1 | Slaves named Claiborne (20) and Letty (4). |
| May 4, 1850 | Supreme Court | James P. Clark | 7 | 1 | 1 | 5 | *M.A. Kidd v. H.A. Kidd.* Daniel, Lucy and their children Nancy, Easter, Charity, Isaac and Solomon. |
| Aug. 20, 1850 | Bradley | James Berry | 22 | UNK | UNK | UNK | *Traynor v Cozby, McDonald and Ragsdale.* Sale was at Smith's Cross Roads. |
| Oct. 12, 1850 | Davidson | Thomas T. Smiley | 1 | 0 | 0 | 1 | Richard Paradise et al ex parte. Slave named Lucy (15). |

| Date of Auction | County | Clerk | Total | Men | Women | Children | Notes |
|---|---|---|---|---|---|---|---|
| Oct 19, 1850 | Meigs | John M. Lillard | 2 | UNK | UNK | UNK | Pliney Locke (dec'd). Slaves included "boy and girl." |
| Jan. 1, 1851 | Davidson | Jackson B. White | 11 | UNK | UNK | UNK | *McCampbell v. heirs/creditors of S.V.D. Stout.* Slaves named Gabe, Henry, Isaac, Mary, Letty, Ann, Drury, Georgiana, Susan and her 2 children. |
| Jan. 1, 1851 | Davidson | Jackson B. White | 1 | 1 | 0 | 0 | *Jordan v. Savis.* Slave named Andrew. |
| Jan. 1, 1851 | Davidson | Jackson B. White | 9 | 3 | 1 | 5 | *Castleman v. Ament (dec'd).* Slaves were Fayette (30, blacksmith), Albert (30, blacksmith), Bill (24), Delilah (34), Eliza (16), Mary Ann (8), Henry (6), Eliza Jane (4), Maraha (5). |
| Jan. 4, 1851 | Davidson | Jackson B. White | 5 | 0 | 2 | 3 | Martha Williams and others, ex parte. Slaves were Savannah (26) and her child Elizabeth (7), Jane (22) and her two children William (6) and Abok (3). |
| Jan. 10, 1851 | Bradley | James Berry | 3 | 2 | 1 | 0 | Samuel Easly (dec'd). |
| July 22, 1851 | Davidson (Circuit) | Thomas T. Smiley | 3 | 0 | 1 | 2 | "Negro woman, Susan, and her two children." |
| Aug. 16, 1851 | Davidson | Jackson B. White | 3 | 1 | 1 | 1 | *Huff v. McKeiver.* Slaves were Elvira (25) and John (7). |
| Aug. 16, 1851 | Davidson | Jackson B. White | 1 | 1 | 0 | 0 | *Gray v. Wiabourne.* Slave named Sam (30). |
| Oct. 13, 1851 | Montgomery | Periander Priestly | 4 | 1 | 1 | 2 | This also included the sale of the Louisa and Mount Vernon furnaces. Slave was "John Carter, a founder, together with his wife and children." |
| Nov. 28, 1851 | Giles | James McCallum | 2 | UNK | UNK | UNK | At residence of James T. Fogg, dec'd. Slaves were Lucy and Easter. |
| Dec. 30, 1851 | Giles | James McCallum | 11 | UNK | UNK | UNK | Residence of James Higgins (dec'd). 11 slaves. |
| April 10, 1852 | Davidson | Jackson B. White | 2 | 0 | 0 | 2 | Slaves named Eliza (12) and William (5). |
| April 24, 1852 | Bradley | James Berry | 2 | 0 | 1 | 1 | At residence of Francis W. Lea (dec'd). "A negro girl and her child." |
| June 5, 1852 | Davidson | Jackson B. White | 1 | 0 | 0 | 1 | *John Wright v. Joseph White.* Slave named Jane (17). |
| March 27, 1852 | Supreme Court | James P. Clark | 3 | UNK | UNK | UNK | Supreme Court case *Alfred Fullbright v. Elizabeth Clemson.* Slaves named Granville, Sylvia and Fanny. |
| Feb. 16, 1853 | Supreme Court | James P. Clark | 3 | UNK | UNK | UNK | *Jason Love's administrators v. Roberts.* Slaves named John, Sally and Henry (ages not given). |
| March 14, 1853 | Supreme Court | James P. Clark | 10 | 1 | 3 | 6 | Supreme Court case of *Planters Bank v. S.S. Mayfield.* Slaves named Leah, Bob, Mary and Lili and her 6 children. |

| Date of Auction | County | Clerk | Total | Men | Women | Children | Notes |
|---|---|---|---|---|---|---|---|
| Dec. 10, 1853 | Davidson | C.D. Brien | 2 | 0 | 0 | 2 | *John Hugh Smith v. heirs*, creditors of B.R.B. Wallace, dec'd. Slaves named Eliza (14) and William (8). |
| Dec. 28, 1853 | Davidson | F.R. Cheatham | 7 | UNK | UNK | UNK | Thomas Warmuth, dec'd. Slaves named Abner, Mary, Martha, Albert, Priscilla, Louisa and Maria. |
| Dec. 29, 1853 | Davidson | F.R. Cheatham | 1 | 0 | 1 | 0 | *Thos. J. Adams v. Mary A. Adams and others*. Slave was 50-year-old woman. |
| Dec. 30, 1853 | Davidson | F.R. Cheatham | 8 | 2 | 2 | 4 | *Hamlet v. Johnson*. Slaves were Mahala (50), Hartly (25), Nathan (23), Wiley (18), Jenny (14), Lotty (11), Andrew (11), and Jim (8). |
| Dec. 31, 1853 | Davidson | C.D. Brien | 5 | UNK | UNK | UNK | *Shapard and Bostick v. B. Childress*. Slaves named Charles, Darcas, John, Phillip and George. |
| Jan. 14, 1854 | Davidson | C.D. Brien | 5 | 1 | 2 | 2 | *Union Bank v. Thomas B. Childress (adm) of M.W. Brown, dec'd*. Slaves were Wiley, Mariah, Rachel and her two children Toby and Elizabeth. |
| Feb. 2, 1854 | Davidson | F.R. Cheatham | 12 | 1 | 2 | 9 | William Dunn, dec'd. Slaves were Isham, Eli, Druscilla, Betty, Mary, Amanda, Louisa, Emily, Elizabeth, Elbert, George and Isham. |
| Feb. 24, 1854 | Monroe | Elisha E. Griffith | 4 | UNK | UNK | UNK | A.B. Gentry, dec'd. Slaves were George, Toby, Ritter and Susan. |
| Feb. 20, 1855 | Monroe | James A. Coffin | 4 | 4 | 0 | 0 | *Robert Carter v. the widow and heirs of Garland Smith*. Slaves were Spencer, Dice, Henry and Absolum. |
| Feb. 23, 1855 | Monroe | Elisha E. Griffith | 7 | UNK | UNK | UNK | John R. Williams (dec'd). Slaves were Cal, Beck, Hunt, Harry, Phil, Isam and Betsy. |
| March 3, 1855 | Monroe | Elisha E. Griffith | 2 | 0 | 1 | 1 | *Biddy Wallis v. E.W. Hyden*. Slaves named China and her child Esther Ellen. |
| March 6, 1855 | Monroe | Elisha E. Griffith | 5 | 2 | 3 | 0 | Richard Stephens, dec'd. Slaves were Hugh, Burrell, Clarissa, Jane and Dialtha. |
| March 31, 1855 | Davidson | F.R. Cheatham | 2 | 0 | 1 | 1 | Estate of John Blair. Slaves named Violet (32) and Stephen (14). |
| Dec. 15, 1855 | Davidson | F.R. Cheatham | 12 | 0 | 3 | 9 | Residence of John M. Wright, dec'd. Slaves were Betsy (30), Sely (28), Mary (21), and children Louisa, Henry, Nancy, George, Martha, Alley, Solomon, Josiah and Harriett. |
| Dec. 21, 1855 | Polk | E.P. Douglass | 1 | 1 | 0 | 0 | Josiah Harrison, dec'd. Slave named Moses (25). |
| Jan. 5, 1856 | Davidson | C.D. Brien | 2 | 2 | 0 | 0 | *Jones v. James Newsom*. |
| Jan. 5, 1856 | Davidson | C.D. Brien | 2 | 0 | 1 | 1 | *Hamilton v. Fliza Ezell*. Slaves were Hannah (30) and Mathilda (14). |
| March 3, 1856 | Blount | W.A. Walker | 2 | 1 | 0 | 1 | Winfield Porter (dec'd). Slaves Isaac (26) and Sid (14). |

| Date of Auction | County | Clerk | Total | Men | Women | Children | Notes |
|---|---|---|---|---|---|---|---|
| Aug. 16, 1856 | Humphreys | Levi McCollum | 1 | 1 | 0 | 0 | Slave was 65-year-old man. |
| Aug. 30, 1856 | Montgomery | William Rogers | 2 | 1 | 1 | 0 | Slaves named Hawkins and Violet. |
| Oct. 10, 1856 | Davidson | F.R. Cheatham | 6 | 1 | 1 | 4 | Case of John Callendar. |
| Oct. 20, 1856 | Lincoln | R. Farquharson | 1 | 1 | 0 | 0 | Slave named Henry (35). |
| Nov. 3, 1856 | Franklin | Hugh Francis | 1 | 1 | 0 | 0 | Mathew Williams and wife, ex parte. Slave named Bill; "biddings to commence" at $900. |
| Dec. 6, 1856 | Davidson | F.R. Cheatham | 6 | 1 | 1 | 4 | John H. Callender and wife, ex parte. Slaves named Judith (50), Anderson (23), Thomas (15), William (4), Mary (2), and Judith (6 months). |
| Dec. 14, 1856 | Polk | E.P. Douglass | 1 | 1 | 0 | 0 | Josiah Harrison (dec'd). |
| Dec. 20, 1856 | Lincoln | R.S. Woodard | 1 | 1 | 0 | 0 | "In the matter of John Wood." Slave named Lloyd. |
| Dec. 25, 1856 | Henry | B.C. Brown | 1 | 1 | 0 | 0 | Elizabeth Olive and others, ex parte. Slave named Reddirck. |
| Dec. 26, 1856 | Lincoln | R.S. Woodard | 3 | 0 | 0 | 3 | William Rhea. Slaves named Jack, Ann and Puss. |
| Dec. 26, 1856 | Rutherford | David D. Wendel | 9 | UNK | UNK | UNK | John McCrary, dec'd. "Nine likely negroes." |
| Dec. 27, 1856 | Rutherford | David D. Wendel | 7 | UNK | UNK | UNK | Burrel Ward, dec'd., east of Murfreesboro. "Seven likely negroes." |
| Dec. 30, 1856 | Rutherford | David D. Wendel | 1 | 0 | 0 | 1 | Henry Atkinson v. William Atkinson and others. Slave was an 8-year-old boy. |
| Dec. 31, 1856 | Rutherford | David D. Wendel | 1 | 1 | 0 | 0 | "One valuable negro man." |
| Jan. 1, 1857 | Lincoln | R. Farquharson | 54 | UNK | UNK | UNK | *John Fulton v. Francis Fulton and others.* Slaves "consisting of house servants and field hands." |
| Jan. 1, 1857 | Lincoln | R. Farquharson | 4 | 2 | 1 | 1 | *Amos Hurley v. Absalom Davis.* Slaves "from 12 to 24 years of age." |
| Jan. 1, 1857 | Lincoln | R. Farquharson | 1 | 1 | 0 | 0 | "In the matter of William J. Galloway." Slave a "negro man named Peter." |
| Jan. 5, 1857 | Lincoln | R.S. Woodard | 4 | 0 | 1 | 3 | Fanny and her three children, Lucretia, Henry and Albert. |
| Jan. 15, 1857 | Lincoln | R.S. Woodard | 1 | 1 | 0 | 0 | Case of John T. Cunningham. |
| Feb. 13, 1857 | Rutherford | John Jones | 4 | 1 | 1 | 2 | Sarah Wade, dec'd. Slaves were "an old fellow, a woman, a likely boy and a likely girl." |
| Feb. 14, 1857 | Rutherford | John Jones | 8 | UNK | UNK | UNK | "Men, women, boys and girls" sold at New Fosterville in the case of J.R. Pucket, L.L. Pucket and others. |

| Date of Auction | County | Clerk | Total | Men | Women | Children | Notes |
|---|---|---|---|---|---|---|---|
| Feb. 20, 1857 | Polk | E.P. Douglass | 7 | 1 | 1 | 5 | Richard Kird, dec'd. Slaves are Cynthia (40), Lafayette (21), Robert (12), Elizabeth (9), Queen (7), Joseph (5) and Lewis (3). |
| March 6, 1857 | Montgomery | William Rogers | 5 | 1 | 1 | 3 | |
| April 18, 1857 | Lincoln | R. Farquharson | 11 | UNK | UNK | UNK | "In the matter of Jeff M. Stone and others." |
| April 18, 1857 | Lincoln | R. Farquharson | 15 | UNK | UNK | UNK | *Allen Johnson v. Nancy Johnson.* |
| April 18, 1857 | Lincoln | R. Farquharson | 5 | UNK | UNK | UNK | B.W.D. Carty, dec'd. |
| April 18, 1857 | Lincoln | R. Farquharson | 11 | UNK | UNK | UNK | Thomas McGaugh, dec'd. |
| April 18, 1857 | Lincoln | R. Farquharson | 7 | UNK | UNK | UNK | William Harris, dec'd. |
| April 25, 1857 | Lincoln | R.S. Woodard | 13 | 3 | 3 | 7 | In the matter of Needham Koonce and others. 13 slaves named Alfred, Washington, Beverly, Jacob, Lydia, Wallace, Emily, Jane, Harriet, Wyatt, Zoe, Rufus and Mariah. |
| July 6, 1857 | Montgomery | William G. Boyd | 1 | 1 | 0 | 0 | "In the case of John Randle." Slave named Moses. |
| Aug. 3, 1857 | Montgomery | T.J. Munford | 2 | 1 | 1 | 0 | "One negro woman, a No. one cook, washer and ironer; one negro man named Dick, a good gardener." |
| Jan. 4, 1858 | Montgomery | T.J. Munford | 10 | UNK | UNK | UNK | In the case of F.A. Hannum, guardian, ex parte. Slaves named Jo, Ned, Allen, Harriet, Anthony, Wesley, Nelson and Chaney" and "children belonging to W.S. Dick." |
| Jan. 4, 1858 | Montgomery | T.J. Munford | 5 | 0 | 3 | 2 | *L.F. Howard v. Cobb & Hannam.* "A boy about 16, a girl about 10, the balance women." |
| Jan. 4, 1858 | Lincoln | R. Farquharson | 60 | UNK | UNK | UNK | *John S. Fulton v. James M. Davidson.* Slaves "house servants and field hands." |
| Jan. 4, 1858 | Lincoln | R. Farquharson | 2 | 0 | 0 | 2 | *Smith v. James T. Davis.* Slaves Mary (15) and Joana (6). |
| Jan. 4, 1858 | Lincoln | R. Farquharson | 2 | 0 | 2 | 0 | "In the matter of Thoephilus Harris." Slaves Sally and Elizabeth. |
| Jan. 9, 1858 | Davidson | C.D. Brien | 15 | 1 | 5 | 9 | *Jo. Norvell v. Henry Norvell.* Slaves named Hester, Jack, Patsey, Harriet, Mary Ann and her 4 children, Altha and her 5 children |
| Jan. 13, 1858 | Davidson | C.D. Brien | 9 | 1 | 1 | 7 | *Mayes v. Slayden.* Slaves named Amos (48), Angeline (21), Johnson (18), Arch (8), Willis (5), Larry (8), Anne (2) and 2 children names unknown. |

| Date of Auction | County | Clerk | Total | Men | Women | Children | Notes |
|---|---|---|---|---|---|---|---|
| Jan. 13, 1858 | Davidson | C.D. Brien | 3 | 1 | 2 | 1 | *Moran v. Moran.* Slaves were Binah and Anne and their child. |
| Jan. 16, 1858 | Davidson | C.D. Brien | 1 | 0 | 1 | 0 | Slave named Lizzie. |
| Jan. 23, 1858 | Davidson | C.D. Brien | 4 | 1 | 0 | 3 | *Rivers v. Stockwell.* Slaves were Charity (20) and her infant child, Joseph (12) and Jane (9). |
| May 3, 1858 | Lincoln | R. Farquharson | 3 | 0 | 2 | 1 | *Fulton v. Davidson.* |
| July 5, 1858 | Lincoln | R. Farquharson | 8 | 2 | 1 | 5 | Slaves named Jim (28, a mechanic), Peter (33, a mechanic), Susan (26), Jack (12), Bill (7), Matt (5) and two small children. |
| Aug. 6, 1858 | Gibson | J.A. McDearman | 3 | 0 | 1 | 2 | "A likely negro woman and two children" sold at the courthouse door in Trenton. |
| Oct. 7, 1858 | Davidson | J.E. Gleaves | 11 | UNK | UNK | UNK | Delia C. King, dec'd. |
| Dec. 6, 1858 | Montgomery | T.J. Munford | 2 | 2 | 0 | 0 | Williams v. Dye. |
| Dec. 30, 1858 | Lincoln | R. Farquharson | 5 | 0 | 1 | 4 | Rachel Buchanan (dec'd). Slaves were Mariah (27), Cowan (10), Louisa (2) and an infant. |
| Jan. 1, 1859 | Stewart | C. Roberts | 18 | UNK | UNK | UNK | John Bavliss, dec'd. "Men, women and children, of all ages and sizes." Includes "mechanics, stone masons, founders and miners." |
| Jan. 7, 1859 | Montgomery | W.M. Rogers | 7 | 3 | 0 | 4 | Man (35, a carpenter), man (50), man (22), boy (17), boy (14), girl (12) and girl (10). "Sold for division among the heirs." |
| Jan. 10, 1859 | Montgomery | W.M. Rogers | 1 | 1 | 0 | 0 | Slave named Banks (31). |
| Jan. 13, 1859 | Shelby | John P. Trezevant | 7 | 0 | 1 | 6 | Slaves named Hannah (28) and her infant, Ann (8), Steph (7), Cinda (6), Frank (3) and Flora (3). |
| Jan. 22, 1859 | Davidson | F.R. Cheatham | 4 | 1 | 3 | 0 | *Tucker v. Wilson.* Slaves named Arthur (60), Saply (60), Polly (35) and Amanda (26). |
| Jan. 22, 1859 | Davidson | J.E. Gleaves | 9 | UNK | UNK | UNK | *Barnes v. Barnes and others.* Slaves and 40-acre farm near Franklin College. |
| Jan. 25, 1859 | Shelby | John G. Lanier | 41 | 9 | 9 | 23 | At the residence of Henry C. Stark, dec'd. Names and ages of all slaves listed in Dec. 25, 1858, Memphis Daily Appeal. |
| Feb. 1, 1859 | Shelby | John G. Lanier | 16 | 8 | 6 | 2 | Thomas Mull (dec'd). Slaves named Tom, Caroline, Abb, Winney, Adam, Harriet, John, Lucy, Daniel, Tom, Tom, Scy, Jerry and three others. |
| Feb. 12, 1859 | Lincoln | Done by Executors | 45 | 11 | 15 | 19 | Order of "County Court" in the case of John Clark (dec'd). Names and ages of all slaves listed in Jan. 20, 1859 Fayetteville Observer. |
| April 4, 1859 | Franklin | H.R. Estill | 1 | 0 | 1 | 0 | James Lewis (dec'd). Slave is "the negro woman Mariah." |
| May 2, 1859 | Lincoln | R. Farquharson | 2 | 2 | 0 | 0 | *Pryor Buchanan v. Mary L. Buchanan et al.* Slaves named Peter and Andrew. |

| Date of Auction | County | Clerk | Total | Men | Women | Children | Notes |
|---|---|---|---|---|---|---|---|
| May 5, 1859 | Lincoln | R. Farquharson | 9 | 2 | 2 | 5 | Thomas J. Anderson (dec'd). "Mariah and 4 children under 9 years to be sold in one lot." |
| May 6, 1859 | Lincoln | R. Farquharson | 1 | UNK | UNK | UNK | "Likely negro boy named Jim." |
| May 15, 1859 | Williamson | W.H.S. Hill | 1 | 0 | 1 | 0 | Case of Philip H. Cook and others, exparte. Slave named Dianna (18). |
| 1859 (date UNK) | Wilson | J.P. Clark | 23 | 2 | 7 | 14 | *Henry Smith v. Ingram and Deloach.* These prices were detailed in Hunt's Merchant Magazine, fall 1859 issue. |
| Jan. 17, 1860 | Blount | Samuel Pride | 4 | 0 | 1 | 3 | Sarah Bayless (dec'd). "A likely negro woman and three children." |
| Jan. 23, 1860 | Franklin | R.F. Sims | 3 | 0 | 1 | 2 | *Felix Green v. Sarah Hatchet.* |
| Jan. 24, 1860 | Franklin | R.F. Sims | 1 | 1 | 0 | 0 | *Wallace Estill v. John Chitwood.* Slave was a 24-year-old man named Henry. |
| Jan. 27, 1860 | Blount | Samuel Pride | 9 | 0 | 2 | 7 | Hugh Wear, dec'd. "One of the women has two small children and the other an infant, who will be sold in lots with their respective children." |
| March 26, 1860 | Franklin | R.F. Sims | 8 | UNK | UNK | UNK | Absalom Williams (dec'd). |
| April 2, 1860 | Franklin | H.R. Estill | 5 | UNK | UNK | UNK | *C.M. Wiseman v. Isaac Hall.* Slaves named Ellis, Mariah, Mahala, Isaac and Carter. |
| April 2, 1860 | Franklin | H.R. Estill | 2 | 0 | 1 | 1 | *Embrey v Embrey.* "Biddings for the negro woman to commence at $1,100--for the negro girl $800." |
| April 2, 1860 | Franklin | H.R. Estill | 1 | UNK | UNK | UNK | *Elliott v. Joseph Holder.* |
| April 7, 1860 | Davidson | J.E. Gleaves | 6 | UNK | UNK | UNK | *Hobson, Watson and Zimmerman v. Pitts.* Names were Louisa, Ailsey, Lucy Ann, Maria, Martha and Ellen. |
| May 7, 1860 | Dickson | H.C. Collier | 1 | 0 | 0 | 1 | *Judge Jackson v. Caleb Rooker.* "A very likely negro boy, aged about 14 years." |
| July 2, 1860 | Rhea | W.E. Colville | 1 | 1 | 0 | 0 | Slave named Dick and he was sold at the courthouse in Washington "to pay the debts of said Wright Smith Jr, deceased." |
| Aug. 20, 1860 | Shelby | John. C. Lanier | 2 | 2 | 0 | 0 | *Candee, Mix & Co. v. F. Baxter.* |
| Feb. 4, 1861 | Gibson | J.A. McDearman | 5 | 2 | 2 | 1 | Three separate cases being settled, all at the courthouse in Trenton. |
| April 20, 1861 | Davidson | J.E. Gleaves | 29 | UNK | UNK | UNK | Dr. Shelby (dec'd). |
| July 6, 1861 | Stewart | A.B. Ross | 1 | 0 | 0 | 1 | William Brandon (dec'd). |
| Aug. 10, 1861 | Rhea | W.E. Colville | 11 | 1 | 2 | 8 | Benjamin D. Smith (dec'd). Two "families" sold in lots and then a group of small kids sold individually. |
| Dec. 21, 1861 | Davidson | J.E. Gleaves | 7 | 0 | 1 | 6 | *J.E. Newman v. Fred Sloan.* |
| Sept. 2, 1861 | Stewart | H.C. Collier | 2 | 2 | 0 | 0 | *H.C. Burnett v. James Cunningham.* |

| Date of Auction | County | Clerk | Total | Men | Women | Children | Notes |
|---|---|---|---|---|---|---|---|
| Dec. 30, 1861 | McMinn | John Rogers (deputy sheriff) | 25 | UNK | UNK | UNK | *Polly Lowry v. Alexander Cleage.* |
| Jan. 4, 1862 | Bledsoe | S.C. Norwood | 6 | 1 | 1 | 4 | *Brown v. Dorsey and Swafford.* "Women and children to be sold together." |
| Feb. 13, 1862 | Hamilton | William I. Standefer | 0 | 0 | 0 | 0 | *Union Bank v. Alexander Bell's administrator.* Six slaves to be hired out (not sold). |
| Feb. 27, 1862 | McMinn | William George | 4 | 1 | 2 | 1 | John Gregory, dec'd. Slaves named Silva (30), Dark (21), Betty (20) and Ben (8 months). |
| March 17, 1862 | Lincoln | Daniel J. Whittington | 17 | 1 | 3 | 13 | Names and ages all listed in the March 13, 1862 Fayetteville Observer. Notably, one of the slaves already ran away. |
| June 27, 1862 | McMinn | John L. Bridges | 5 | 1 | 1 | 3 | At residence of T.S. Rice. |
| Oct. 30, 1862 | McMinn | William George | 1 | 0 | 1 | 0 | Slave named Kate (20). |
| Dec. 12, 1862 | Sevier | R. Lanning | 4 | 4 | 0 | 0 | William M. Bryan, dec'd. Slaves named Mike (65), Jim (18), Clib (25) and Ben (55). |
| Dec. 1862 (date unkn) | Knox | William Craig | 3 | 2 | 0 | 1 | Slaves sold at the courthouse included Carrick (27), Titus (18) and Crockett (12). |
| May 2, 1863 | McMinn | William George | 5 | 1 | 1 | 3 | Allen Dodson, dec'd. Slaves named Major (50), Matilda (23), Jim (14), Dan (13) and Tom (4). |
| May 9, 1863 | Claiborne | P.L. Lanham | 14 | UNK | UNK | UNK | "At the late residence of Hugh Jonens, dec'd, 4 miles south of Tazewell." |
| July 4, 1863 | Lincoln | Daniel J. Whittington | 3 | 0 | 1 | 2 | "In the case of Rufus Harris." Slaves included Delia (20) and her two children James (4) and Robert (8 months). |
| July 25, 1863 | Rhea | Indecipherable | 11 | 0 | 4 | 7 | Cannot read this notice clearly but it does say that this sale occurred at the courthouse in Washington. |
| Aug. 1, 1863 | Lincoln | Daniel J. Whittington | 8 | 0 | 2 | 6 | "In the case of Pleasant Halbert." Slaves named Amanda (35), Martha (6), Cordy (1), Ann (19), Tom (16), Andrew (14), Josephine (10) and Nancy (8). |
| | | TOTALS | 1,199 | 144 | 134 | 295 | |

APPENDIX THREE

# NASHVILLE'S SLAVE PURCHASES, 1830-31

*This information is on file at the Metro Nashville Archives and was logged by hand in the spring of 1831, when Nashville purchased 24 slaves from slave trader Williams Ramsey.*

*Thanks to the staff of the Metro Nashville Archives for their assistance in helping me find this information.*

| Name | Age | Height | Complexion | Physical Description | Previous Residence | Name of Previous owner |
|------|-----|--------|------------|---------------------|--------------------|------------------------|
| Ben | 39 | 5 ft, 7 in | dark | "A small scar across the upper edge of the right wrist." | Anne Arundel County, MD | Ohara |
| Emanuel | 35 | 5 ft, 3 in | dark yellow | "A small scar in his left eye brow--stout and muscular." | Stafford County, VA | William Finch |
| Jim | 30 | 5 ft, 2 in | dark brown | "A scar on the inside of the right knee, also two scars on the right arm, one below, and one above the elbow." | Stafford County, VA | Thomas Hill |
| Frank | 45 | 5 ft, 7 in | black | "Black complexion, two of his upper and all of his under front teeth out." | Campbell County, VA | German Jordan |
| Lewis | 45 | 5 ft, 9 3/4 in | black | "Black complexion, upper left eye tooth out, scar across his breast." | Campbell County, VA | German Jordan |
| Moses | 16 | 4 ft, 7 3/4 in | brown | "Thick, prominent under lip, considerable space between front teeth, small (burn) scar on his right arm." | Campbell County, VA | German Jordan |
| Salem | 22 | 5 ft, 9 in | yellow | "A small scar in his right eye brow, rather slender made, a (burn) scar on his left arm above the elbow." | Isle of Wight County, VA | Fra. J. Lawson |
| Anthony | 21 | 5 ft, 10 in | black | "A small scar under the left eye, thick lips." | Isle of Wight County, VA | Abednigo Goodrick |
| Charles | 17 | 5 ft, 9 in | black | "Large scars on his left elbow caused by a burn, long chin which projects downwards, all toes on the right foot have been injured by being frost bitten." | Washington County, VA | Susanna Hickman and Mr. Snodgrass, |
| Lucinda | | | | No information given but apparently purchased with Charles. | Washington County, VA | |
| Lilburn Henderson | | | | No information given but apparently purchased with Charles. | Washington County, VA | |
| Allen | 23 | 5 ft, 11 1/2 in | black | "Small scar across the back of the right hand, small scar in the left eyebrow." | Anne Arundel County, MD | Laikin Dorrey |
| Jim | 30 | 5 ft, 8 1/2 in | light yellow | "Upper front teetch decayed, long bushy hair." | Baltimore County, MD | Charles R. Owen |

| Name | Age | Height | Complexion | Physical Description | Previous Residence | Name of Previous owner |
|------|-----|--------|------------|---------------------|--------------------|-----------------------|
| Moses | 24 | 5 ft, 5 3/4 in | brown | "Small scar on his right arm below the elbow about an inch long, slender made." | Randolph County, VA | James Carder |
| Allen | 14 | 4 ft, 10 1/2 in | light yellow | "Slender made, large scar on his left jaw, thick lips, his back much scarred with the whip." | Campbell County, VA | Beasley |
| Isaac | 20 | 6 ft | yellow | "Small scar near the corner of the right eye, thick under lip, his front teeth irregularly out." | Montgomery County, VA | Henry Hance |
| Vincent | 22 | 5 ft, 5 in | yellow | "Heavy built, large scar on his right elbow, large scar on the right shin bone, caused by a cut with a blade." | Henrico County, VA | Mo. B. Williamson |
| Peter | 22 | 5 ft, 11 1/4 in | brown | "Thick under lip, small scar on the upper side of the right arm just above the elbow joint, heavy built, joints of the big toes large, toes turn out very much." | Sussex County, VA | John Goorum |
| Bob | 15 | 4 ft, 7 3/4 in | black | "Large front teeth, small scar near the corner of the left eye." | Stafford County, VA | Charles Bruce |
| Granville | 15 | 5 ft, 4 1/2 in | light yellow | "Long bushy hair, slender made." | Wythe County, VA | Theodore Johnston |
| John | 27 | 5 ft, 7 in | black | "Small cut on the edge of the left nostril, large face, small head and eyes." | Prince George County, VA | Simmons |
| Isaac | 26 | 5 ft, 9 1/2 in | dark brown | "A scar on left knee about size of half dollar." | Annapolis, MD | Rich J. Jones |
| John | 28 | 5 ft, 11 1/4 in | dark brown | "A small scar in his right eyebrow, rather slender made, has 12 or 13 shot in the calf of his right leg." | Annapolis, MD | Rich J. Jones |
| Jim | 30 | 5 ft, 10 1/4 in | black | "A small scar or cut on the right point on the chin, his toes too much crumpled up and his toes turn out a good deal." | Annapolis, MD | Rich J. Jones |

# SOURCES CITED

## Chapter 1

"John Donelson's Journal," *Three Pioneer Documents* (Nashville: Tennessee Historical Commission, 1964), p. 2.

*Knoxville Gazette*, Nov. 5, 1791; Feb. 11, 1792; Oct. 6 and 20, 1792; April 6, 1793; June 15 and 29, 1793; Oct. 12 and 19, 1793; May 2, 1794; June 19, 1794; Nov. 1, 1794; Dec. 26, 1794; Jan. 23, 1795; March 2 and 27, 1795; April 24, 1795; May 8 and 22, 1795; June 1, 1795; May 3, 1796; Nov. 14 and 21, 1796; Dec. 19, 1796; March 6, 15, 20 and 27, 1797; April 8, 10 and 24, 1797; May 22, 1797; Feb. 2, 1798.

## Chapter 2

Anita S. Goodstein, "Black History on the Nashville Frontier, 1780-1810." *Tennessee Historical Quarterly* 38, Number 4 (Winter 1979), p. 404.

Louis-Phillipe, King of France (1830-1848), *Diary of My Travels in America* (New York: Delacorte Press, 1977), p. 108.

W. Calvin Dickinson, *The Walton Road: A Nineteenth Century Wilderness Highway in Tennessee* (2007), p. 85.

John F. Baker Jr., *The Washingtons of Wessyngton Plantation* (Atria: New York, 2009), p. 43.

Social Sciences Department, Fisk University, *Unwritten History of Slavery* (Nashville: Fisk University, 1968), page 155.

*Tennessee Gazette*, Jan. 14, 1801; Feb. 8, 1801; Nov. 9, 1801; May 12, 1802; Dec. 18, 1802; March 23, 1803; April 13, 1803; April 27, 1803; June 15, 1803; Aug. 17, 1803; Dec. 14, 1803; Feb. 2 and 29, 1804; March 28, 1804; June 6, 1804; Aug. 8, 1804; Sept. 19, 1804; Oct. 3, 1804; Nov. 7, 1804.

*Carthage Gazette*, Aug. 17, 1809.

## Chapter 3

*Tennessee Gazette*, Sept. 14, 1804.

*Nashville Whig*, Sept. 22, 1820.

*Jackson Gazette*, Aug. 21, 1824; Sept. 11, 1824; Oct. 30, 1824; Dec. 11, 1824; Feb. 12, 19 and 26, 1825; March 26, 1825; June 4 and 11, 1825; July 9 and 30, 1825; Sept. 3 and 25, 1825; April 26, 1826; Aug. 12, 1826; Sept. 23, 1826; Dec. 23, 1826; Jan. 20, 1827; Dec. 6, 1828; April 11, 1829.

*Memphis Advocate and Western District Intelligencer*, Sept. 15, 1827; Nov. 5, 1827; Dec. 8, 1827; July 5, 1828.

*Cherokee Phoenix*, Oct. 4, 1830; Jan. 28, 1832.

*Hiwassee Reporter*, Feb. 2, 1827.

(Athens) *Tennessee Journal*, June 8, 1838.

## Chapter 4

Return J. Meigs and William F. Cooper, *A Compilation of the Statute Laws of the State of Tennessee* (Nashville: Tennessee General Assembly, 1858).

*Athens Post*, Aug. 11 and Nov. 3, 1854.

*Republican Banner and Nashville Whig*, July 2, 1850; Jan. 7 and Dec. 19, 1854.

Chase C. Mooney, *Slavery in Tennessee* (Westbrook, Connecticut: Negro Universities Press, 1957), p. 19.

## Chapter 5

*Nashville Whig*, May 19, 1813; June 1, 1813; April 16, 1816; Nov. 15, 1820; Oct. 3, 1820; July 3, 1822; April 23, 1825. July 3, 1822;
*National Banner and Nashville Whig*, Oct. 14, 1830.
*Knoxville Register*, May 22, 1821.
*Clarksville Jeffersonian*, Aug. 15, 1845.
*Impartial Review and Cumberland Repository*, Feb. 21, 1807.
*National Banner and Nashville Whig*, April 15, 1833; Sept. 4, 1833.
*Republican Banner*, Feb. 21, 1839; Sept. 26, 1840; Jan. 22, 1844; Jan. 1, 1847.
*Impartial Review and Cumberland Repository*, Feb. 11, 1808.
*Nashville Republican*, March 29, 1834; April 18, 1835; May 21, 1835; and Sept. 27, 1836.
*Memphis Weekly Appeal*, Aug. 13, 1846.
*Knoxville Argus and Commercial Herald*, May 19, 1840.
*The Review*, Dec. 8, 1809.
*Knoxville Register*, July 1, 1830; March 9, 1831.
*Randolph Recorder*, May 15, 1835.
*Memphis Weekly Appeal*, Sept. 15, 1843.
*Memphis Daily Eagle and Enquirer*, June 30, 1852.
*Nashville Union and American*, Aug. 6, 1856.
*Shelbyville Intelligencer*, Dec. 20, 1842.
*Clarksville Weekly Republican*, March 2, 1857.

## Chapter 6

*Knoxville Gazette*, Sept. 11, 1798.
*Nashville Intelligencer*, Feb. 18, 1801.
*Tennessee Gazette*, July 3, 1805.
*Impartial Review and Cumberland Repository*, Aug. 16, 1806; Sept. 24, 1807.
*Nashville Whig*, Nov. 11, 1812; Sept. 19, 1815; June 2, 1816; April 2, 1816; Jan. 30, 1822; April 30, 1823; Nov. 8, 1824; Oct. 3, 1825.
*Impartial Review and Cumberland Repository*, Aug. 23, 1806; July 16, 1808.
*Memphis Advocate*, Nov. 5, 1827.
*Daily Republican Banner*, Jan. 25, 1838.
*Republican Banner*, June 23, 1847.
*Clarksville Weekly Chronicle*, Sept. 14, 1847.
*Tennessee Gazette*, Oct. 3, 1804.
*The (Nashville) Review*, Dec. 8, 1809.
William Dusinberre, *Slavemaster President: The Double Career of James Polk* (New York, Oxford University Press, 2003), p. 32.

## Chapter 7

*Nashville Whig*, Jan. 23, 1815.
*Nashville Republican*, Jan. 19, 1836.
*Knoxville Gazette*, April 8, 1797.
*Nashville Whig*, Sept. 12, 1815; Oct. 10, 1815; July 4, 1821.

*Memphis Advocate and Western District Intelligencer*, Nov. 5, 1827.
*National Banner and Nashville Whig*, Sept. 6, 1830.
*Nashville Republican*, June 23, 1835.
*Athens Journal*, June 8, 1838.
*Elizabethton Whig*, Dec. 5, 1839.
*Memphis Daily Appeal*, May 4, 1861.
*Republican Banner*, Feb. 20, 1851.
*Knoxville Gazette*, Feb. 2, 1798.
*Nashville Whig*, June 1, 1813; Dec. 6, 1814.
*Nashville Whig*, Nov. 28, 1821.
*National Banner and Nashville Whig*, Sept. 6, 1830.
*Loudon Free Press*, Aug. 5, 1853.
*Memphis Daily Appeal*, May 26, 1857.
*Nashville Union and American*, March 30, 1860.
*Nashville Whig*, Aug. 31, 1813; June 21, 1814.
*Knoxville Register*, July 30, 1822.
*Jackson Gazette*, April 26, 1826.
*Nashville Union and American*, Dec. 23, 1859.
*Republican Banner*, Dec. 14, 1842.
*National Banner and Nashville Whig*, Oct. 14, 1830.
*Knoxville Argus and Commercial Herald*, Nov. 12, 1839.
*Knoxville Gazette*, May 3, 1796.
*Nashville Whig*, Aug. 24, 1813; Oct. 3, 1825.
*Hiwassee Reporter*, Feb. 2, 1827.
*Knoxville Register*, Jan. 13, 1830.
*Memphis Daily Appeal*, Dec. 22, 1857.
*Randolph Recorder*, April 3, 1835.
Henry Watson, *Narrative of Henry Watson, a Fugitive Slave* (Boston: Bela Marsh, 1848), p. 9.

## Chapter 8

*Tennessee Gazette*, July 30, 1804.
Knoxville *Brownlow's Whig and Independent Journal*, Aug. 18, 1849.
*Nashville Whig*, July 12, 1814.
*Knoxville Register*, May 7, 1828.
*Clarksville Weekly Chronicle*, Feb. 6, 1857.
*Knoxville Gazette*, Aug. 6, 1806.
*Carthage Gazette*, Feb. 12, 1813.
*Nashville Whig*, June 7, 1814; May 8, 1819.
*Knoxville Register*, May 8, 1833.
*Republican Banner and Nashville Whig*, May 15, 1852; Dec. 17, 1853.
*Nashville Whig*, July 19, 1820.
*Knoxville Register*, June 21, 1821.
*National Banner and Nashville Whig*, Jan. 26, 1830.
*Jackson Gazette*, March 7, 1839.
(Murfreesboro) *Tennessee Telegraph*, July 12, 1844.
*Republican Banner*, Feb. 17, 1847.
*Knoxville Register*, Feb. 14, 1823.
*National Banner and Nashville Whig*, Nov. 9, 1832.

## Chapter 9

*Knoxville Gazette*, Oct. 23, 1795.
*Tennessee Gazette*, Aug. 25, 1802.
*Nashville Whig*, Dec. 16, 1812; Nov. 5, 1816.
*Knoxville Register*, Feb. 9, 1819.
*Knoxville Enquirer*, Jan. 12, 1825.
*Columbian Western Merchant*, Dec. 20, 1828.
*Nashville Republican*, Dec. 18, 1834.
*Daily Nashville Patriot*, Dec. 22, 1855.
*Chattanooga Advertiser*, Jan. 8, 1857.
William Fletcher King, *Reminiscences* (New York: Abington Press, 1915), p. 101.
*Nashville Republican*, July 22, 1834.
*Nashville Union and American*, Jan. 25, 1856.

## Chapter 10

*Clarksville Chronicle*, April 23, 1844.
Frederic Bancroft, *Slave Trading in the Old South* (Fredrick Ungar Publishing Co., 1959), p. 348.
*Daily Republican Banner*, March 24, 1838; May 20, 1840; Dec. 28, 1846.
*Republican Banner*, Nov. 22, 1847; Jan. 28, 1848; April 28, 1848.
*Republican Banner and Nashville Whig*, Dec. 13, 1848; Dec. 9, 1850; March 17, 1852; June 3, 1852.
*Nashville Republican*, April 28, 1835.
*Athens Post*, Aug. 2, 1850.
*Loudon Free Press*, Feb. 14, 1855.
*Athens Post*, Jan. 20, 1854; Jan. 27, 1854; Feb. 16, 1855; Feb. 20, 1857.
*Fayetteville Observer*, April 9, 1857.
*Nashville Union and American*, Sept. 1, 1859.
*Nashville Daily Patriot*, Aug. 18, 1861.
*Fayetteville Observer*, Dec. 4, 1856; April 9, 1857.
*Nashville Daily Patriot*, Aug. 18, 1861; Dec. 3, 1861.
*Hunt's Merchants' Magazine and Commercial Review*, July-December 1859, p. 774.

## Chapter 11

Wendell Holmes Stephenson, *Isaac Franklin: Slave Trader and Planter of the Old South* (Baton Rouge, Louisiana University Press, 1938), p. 46.
Henry Watson, *Narrative of Henry Watson, a Fugitive Slave*, 1848.
Frederick W. Seward, *William H. Seward: An Autobiography, from 1801 to 1834* (New York, Derby and Miller, 1891), p. 271.
*Alexandria Gazette*, May 17, 1828.
*Washington Daily National Intelligencer*, March 28, 1836.
*Nashville Whig*, April 17, 1822.
*Knoxville Register*, May 8, 1833.
*Nashville Republican*, Dec. 17, 1835.
*New Orleans Weekly Delta*, Dec. 28, 1846.
*Nashville Whig*, May 1, 1819; Aug. 6, 1825.
*Republican Banner*, May 24, 1838.
*Natchez Gazette*, April 26, 1826.

Chase C. Mooney, *Slavery in Tennessee* (Westport, Connecticut: Negro Universities Press, 1959), p. 42.

## Chapter 12

*Knoxville Register*, Feb. 1, 1820; May 25, 1831.
*Nashville Republican*, April 30 through Oct.8, 1835.
*Knoxville Daily Register*, December 14, 1862; April 28 and 29, 1863;
*Athens Post*, Dec. 26, 1862; Feb. 27, 1863; March 6 and 20, 1863; April 17, 1863; June 12, 1863.
*Clarksville Chronicle*, Feb. 6 and 20, 1857; July 31, 1857.
Social Sciences Department, Fisk University, *Unwritten History of Slavery* (Nashville: Fisk University, 1945), p. 234.
*Nashville Whig*, Dec. 16, 1825.
*Nashville Republican*, Dec. 19, 1835.
William Fletcher King, *Reminiscences* (New York, Abington Press, 1915), pp. 101-103.
*Pulaski Gazette*, Oct. 31, 1851.
*Bedford Weekly Yeoman*, March 1, 1854.
Frederic Bancroft, *Slave Trading in the Old South* (New York: Frederick Ungar Publishing, 1959), p. 366.

## Chapter 13

**Robertson & Currey and others:**
*Nashville Whig*, July 12, 1814; Sept. 20 and 27, 1814; July 2, Nov. 26 and Dec. 4, 1816; May 9, 1818; Nov. 29, 1820; Feb. 5, 1823.
**L.E. Temple:**
*Republican Banner*, May 31, 1837; Oct. 8, 1838; March 29, 1839; April 20, 1839; May 31, 1839; Jan. 11, 1840; Jan. 14, 1842.
**Maddux and Dawson:**
*Republican Banner*, Feb. 12, 1847.
**A.A. McLean:**
*Republican Banner*, Jan. 7, 10 and 12, 1850; Feb. 15, 1850; April 8, 1850; July 30, 1850; Nov. 23, 1850; Dec. 4, 1850; May 17 and 30, 1851; June 11, 1852; Oct. 1, 1852.
**Glover & Boyd:**
*Nashville Union*, Feb. 24, 1853; March 16, 1853; April 9, 1853.
*Republican Banner*, March 23, 1853; Oct. 25, 1853.
**Dabbs and Porter:**
*Republican Banner and Nashville Whig*, Jan. 22, 1853; Feb. 12, 1853.
*Nashville Union*, April 25, 1853; March 30, 1854; July 27, 1854.
**Rees W. Porter:**
*Nashville Union and American*, Nov. 18, 1854; Dec. 23, 1854; Jan. 6, 1855; Feb. 1, 1855; Jan. 1, 1856.
*Republican Banner*, April 1, 5 and 26, 1856; Aug. 8, 1856; Oct. 13, 17 and 22, 1856; Sept. 20 and 21, 1856; May 6, 1856; Feb. 13 and 26, 1857.
Frederika Bremer, *Homes of the New World*, Volume II, p. 535.
**James & Harrison:**
*Republican Banner*, Dec. 2 and 12, 1856; Jan. 3 and 29, 1857; Feb. 26, 1857; March 22, 1857; May 13, 1857.
**H.H. Haynes:**
*Republican Banner*, Aug. 14, 1857; Nov. 22, 1857; March 24, 1858; Aug. 10, 1861.

*Daily Nashville Patriot*, Aug. 21, 1858, March 24, 1860; July 4, 1860.

**Lyles & Hitchings:**

*Nashville Daily Patriot*: Sept. 21, 1860; Dec. 3, 1860.

*Republican Banner*, July 28, 1858; June 7, 1859; Sept. 16, 1859; Oct. 13, 1860.

*Nashville Union and American*, April 14, 1861; June 5, 1861.

**Webb, Merrill & Co.:**

*Republican Banner*, July 22, 1859; Sept. 6, 1859; Dec. 12, 1859, Dec. 21, 1860; July 26, 1861; Nov. 19, 1861.

**William Compton:**

*Nashville Whig*, Dec. 19, 1825.

**Samuel H. Davis:**

*Republican Banner*, Aug. 16, 1850.

**Slave Interview:**

Social Sciences Department, Fisk University, *Unwritten History of Slavery (Nashville: Fisk University, 1968), page 45.*

## Chapter 14

**Early Memphis slave traders:**

*Tennessee Gazette*, Sept. 14, 1804.

*Nashville Whig*, Sept. 22, 1820.

*Memphis Commercial Appeal*, July 7, 1843; Jan. 5, 1844; Feb. 21, 1845; July 18, 1845; Feb. 27, 1846.

*Memphis Daily Eagle and Enquirer*, July 17, 1847; May 28, 1852; April 9, 1853.

**Bolton, Dickins & Co.:**

*Memphis Daily Eagle and Enquirer*, Jan. 21, 1847; March 16, 1847; Feb. 8, 1852; April 21, 1852; June 14 and 30, 1852; Jan. 8, 1853; Feb. 23, 1852; April 13, 1853; April 8, 1857.

*Memphis Daily Appeal*, June 21, 1854; July 20, 1854.

**M.C. Cayce**

*Memphis Daily Eagle and Enquirer*, Feb. 25, 1853; April 29, 1853; May 10, 1853.

*Memphis Daily Appeal*, March 11, 1859; Dec. 11, 1860.

**L. Ketchum**

*Memphis Daily Eagle and Enquirer*, March 7, 1856.

**Nevill & Cunningham**

*Memphis Daily Eagle and Enquirer*, March 7, 1856; May 2, 1857; June 4, 1858.

**Bolton murder trial**

*Memphis Appeal*, April 1 and 7, 1858.

**Hill & Forrest**

*Memphis Eagle and Enquirer*, Jan. 4, 1854.

**N.B. Forrest (freelance trader)**

*Memphis Daily Appeal*, Jan. 1, 1856; June 13, 1856; April 12, 21 and 29, 1857; May 2, 6, 9 and 14, 1857; June 12, 1857; Oct. 31, 1858.

*Memphis Eagle and Enquirer*, Jan-June 1857 (practically every issue).

*Daily Nashville Patriot*, April 30, 1859.

**Forrest & Maples**

*Memphis Appeal*, July 20, 1854.

*1855 Memphis City Directory.*

**Forrest & Jones/Forrest, Jones & Co.**

*Charleston Courier*, Jan. 23, 1860.

*Memphis Daily Appeal*, May 11, 1857; April 20 and 30; 1858; May 11, 14 and 15, 1858; Aug. 1, 3,

7, 11, 14 and 18, 1858; Nov. 23 and 29, 1858; Nov. 24, 1859.

*Nashville Union and American*, Nov. 30, 1859; December 1-31, 1859.

**Forrest and runaways associated with his businesses**

*Memphis Daily Eagle and Enquirer*, July 27, 1853.

*Memphis Daily Appeal*, Feb. 16, 1856; May 7 and 9, 1857; Jan. 21, 1859; July 8, 1860.

*Nashville Union and American*, May 17, 1856.

**Forrest's life/steamboat incident/other**

Horatio J. Eden, *Diaries, Memoirs, Etc.*, Tennessee State Library and Archives, pp. 4-5.

Louis Hughes, *Thirty Years a Slave: From Bondage to Freedom: The Institution of Slavery as Seen on the Plantation.* (Online Reprint, the University of North Carolina at Chapel Hill, 1997), pp. 91-93.

Jack Hurst, *Nathan Bedford Forrest: A Biography* (New York: Random House, 1993), pp. 33-65.

John Allan Wyeth, *That Devil Forrest: Life of Nathan Bedford Forrest* (Baton Rouge: Louisiana State University Press, 1959), pp, 17-18.

**G. N. Robinson & Co.**

*Memphis Daily Appeal*, Dec. 12, 1858.

**Byrd Hill**

*Memphis Daily Appeal*, Aug. 12, 1854; March 16, 1856; March 17 and 24, 1859; April 8 and 20, 1859.

**John Wilkerson**

*Memphis Daily Appeal*, May 13, 1860.

## Chapter 15

*Knoxville Gazette*, Dec. 1, 1792; Oct. 11, 1801.

*Impartial Review and Cumberland Repository*, July 28, 1808.

*Nashville Whig*, Dec. 6, 1814; Dec. 25, 1816; Nov. 21, 1818.

(Murfreesborough) *Central Monitor*, Oct. 11, 1834.

*National Banner and Nashville Whig*, Feb. 7, 1833.

*Nashville Republican*, June 24, 1837.

*Republican Banner*, May 30, 1851; July 7, 1854.

*Nashville Union and American*, Sept. 14, 1854.

*Memphis Daily Appeal*, May 7, 1854.

*Clarksville Chronicle*, April 29, 1859.

*Columbia Observer*, Sept. 19, 1834.

*Clarksville Weekly Chronicle*, Sept. 2, 1859.

*National Banner and Nashville Whig*, July 4, 1828.

*Knoxville Register*, Sept. 22, 1830.

*Randolph Recorder*, Sept. 9, 1836.

*Republican Banner*, June 25, 1845.

*Clarksville Weekly Chronicle*, Oct. 1, 1858.

*Memphis Daily Eagle and Enquirer*, Jan. 13, 1852.

*Athens Post*, Nov. 30, 1860.

*Knoxville Register*, Feb. 9, 1819.

*Jackson Gazette*, March 7, 1829.

*Shelbyville Western Freeman*, June 19, 1835.

*Hunt's Merchants' Magazine and Commercial Review*, July-Dec. 1859, p. 774.

*Nashville Union and American*, Dec. 16, 1853; Jan. 29, 1854; Dec. 15, 1855.

William Fletcher King, *Reminiscences* (New York, Abington Press, 1915), pp. 101-103.

*Republican Banner and Nashville Whig*, Jan. 7, 1854.

William Dusinberre, *Slavemaster President: The Double Career of James Polk* (New York, Oxford University Press, 2003), p. 21.

## Chapter 16

*Knoxville Gazette,* April 3, 1797.
*Tennessee Gazette,* Nov. 9, 1801; Feb. 22 and 29, 1804.
*Impartial Review and Cumberland Repository,* April 2, 1808; April 19, 1806; June 14, 1806.
*The Review,* Dec. 21, 1810.
*Nashville Whig,* Jan. 25, 1814; Jan. 24, 1815; May 26, 1817; Dec. 26, 1815; Nov. 10, 1817; Feb. 2, 1820; May 16, 1821; Feb. 6, 1822; July 3, 1822; Aug. 18, 1823.
*Southern Illinoisan,* Feb. 21, 2016.
*Republican Banner and Nashville Whig,* Dec. 19, 1826; May 24, 1830; May 4 and 19, 1832; June 23, 1832; Aug. 2, 1832; Nov. 9, 1832; Jan. 10, 1852.
*Clarksville Chronicle,* Nov. 12, 1858.
*Knoxville Register,* April 20, 1819.
*Impartial Review and Cumberland Repository,* April 4, 1807.
*National Banner and Nashville Whig,* Sept. 6, 1830; April 15, 1833.
*Randolph Recorder,* Sept. 9, 1836.

## Chapter 17

### Iron Manufacturing
*Tennessee Gazette,* Feb. 22 and 29, 1804.
*National Banner and Nashville Whig,* Jan. 20, 1832.
*Impartial Review and Cumberland Repository,* Aug. 27, 1807.
*Nashville Whig,* Aug. 9, 1814; June 2, 1816.
*Republican Banner,* March 23, 1840; Sept. 20, 1843.
*Clarksville Jeffersonian,* Aug. 15, 1845.
*Nashville Union and American,* Dec. 14, 1854.
*Nashville Republican and State Gazette,* July 29, 1834; Sept. 27, 1834.
*Tennessean,* Sept. 19, 1982.
*Republican Banner,* July 12, 1847; Oct. 27, 1848; Oct. 11, 1851.
Charles B. Dew, "Black Ironworkers and the Insurrection Panic of 1856," *Journal of Southern History* 41, No. 3 (August 1975), pp. 324-325.

### Other Manufacturing Work
*The Review,* Dec. 21, 1810.
*Nashville Whig,* Nov. 17, 1817; Jan. 5, 1820.
*Nashville Republican,* April 21, 1835; July 4, 1835; Aug. 25, 1835; Oct. 13, 1835.
*Republican Banner and Nashville Whig,* May 15, 1850; Dec. 19, 1853.
*Republican Banner,* Jan. 3, 1857.
*Memphis Enquirer,* April 15, 1837.
*Knoxville Argus and Commercial Herald,* Nov. 12, 1839.
*Republican Banner,* Sept. 10, 1838; March 31, 1848; July 1, 1857; Sept. 8, 1857.

### Railroads and Bridges
*Republican Banner and Nashville Whig,* March 6, 1850; July 26, 1850.
*Athens Post,* July 18, 1851.
*Republican Banner and Nashville Whig,* Dec. 17, 1853.

*Brownlow's Whig and Independent Journal*, Oct. 18, 1851.
*Athens Post*, Aug. 6, 1852; Nov. 12, 1852, Jan. 23, 1857.
**Transportation**
*Nashville Whig*, July 3, 1822.
*Daily Republican Banner*, March 16, 1840; Sept. 26, 1840; Dec. 10, 1845.
*Republican Banner and Nashville Whig*, Jan. 12, 1850.
*Nashville Union and American*, May 8, 1856.
*National Banner and Nashville Whig*, Sept. 27, 1833.

**Construction**
*Knoxville Register*, May 22, 1821.
*Republican Banner*, Feb. 20, 1856.
*Memphis Daily Appeal*, March 11, 1859.

**Miscellaneous**
*Impartial Review and Cumberland Repository*, April 20, 1806.
*Nashville Whig*, May 26, 1817; Oct. 28, 1824.
Athens *Tennessee Journal*, Aug. 22, 1838.
*Republican Banner*, July 21, 1857.
*Nashville Union and American*, March 30, 1854.

**Banking**
*Republican Banner*, April 6, 1839.
*Republican Banner and Nashville Whig*, March 23, 1853.

## Chapter 18

*National Banner and Nashville Whig*, July 11, 1831.
*Nashville Republican*, Aug. 12, 1834.
*Knoxville Gazette*, March 27, 1797; May 22, 1797.
*Tennessee Gazette*, Nov. 20, 1802.
*Impartial Review and Cumberland Repository*, June 28, 1806; Oct. 4, 1806; July 20, 1807.
*Nashville Whig*, May 17, 1814; Dec. 5, 1815; Jan. 10, 1821; Sept. 5, 1821.
*Knoxville Register*, March 2, 1819; April 20, 1819; Jan. 11, 1820.
*Memphis Enquirer*, Nov. 1, 1836; April 1, 1837; May 13, 1837; May 18, 1837; May 2, 1844; Nov. 1, 1844; Jan. 24, 1845; June 12, 1846; May 15, 1847.
*Republican Banner*, Oct. 27, 1848.
*Daily Republican Banner*, Jan. 24, 1838.
Log book entitled *City of Nashville, Agreements, Loans and Slaves, November 2, 1830 to September 20, 1851* (on file at the Metro Archives).
*National Banner and Nashville Whig*, July 27, 1831.
Chase C. Mooney, Slavery in Tennessee (Westport, Connecticut: Negro Universities Press, 1957), page 213 (footnote number 38).
Wilbur Creighton, *The Building of Nashville* (self-published, 1969), p. 46.
Bobby Lovett, *African American History of Nashville, Tennessee* (Fayetteville, Arkansas: University of Arkansas Press, 1999), 20.
*Clarksville Weekly Chronicle*, April 2, 1844; May 28, 1844; July 2, 1844.
*National Banner and Nashville Whig*, April 19, 1832.
*Memphis Enquirer*, Aug. 12, 1837.
*Knoxville Gazette*, May 2, 1794; June 19, 1794; Aug. 7, 1799.

*Nashville Republican*, March 31, 1836.
*Republican Banner*, Dec. 11 and 16, 1846; May 7, 1847; Oct. 23, 1848.

## Chapter 19

*The Emancipator*, April through October 1820.
*Genius of Universal Emancipation*, 1822-23.
*Susquehanna Democrat*, June 2, 1820.
*Knoxville Gazette*, May 2, 1794; June 19, 1794; Nov. 1, 1794.
*Carthage Gazette*, Aug. 17, 1809.
*Nashville Republican*, March 31, 1836; April 14, 1836; May 5, 1836.
*Knoxville Gazette*, Aug. 6, 1806.
*Nashville Whig*, July 12, 1814; July 23, 1820.
*Memphis Advocate*, Dec. 9, 1827.
*Rogersville Railroad Advocate*, Dec. 10, 1832.
*Louisville Daily Courier*, Dec. 29, 1856.
*Republican Banner*, Nov. 27, 1856.
*Franklin Western Review*, Dec. 5, 1856.
*Clarksville Jeffersonian*, Nov. 26, 1856; Dec. 3, 1856.
*Brownlow's Knoxville Whig and Independent Journal*, July 1849; Oct. 27, 1849; Dec. 28, 1850; Feb. 8, 1851; May 17, 1851; May 29, 1852; Oct. 29, 1859; May 19 and 26, 1860.

## Chapter 20

Note: There are many references in this chapter to items or facts referenced in previous chapters (especially the list of place names at the end). Please see those chapters and the appendix for a more detailed list of sources.
*Memphis Enquirer*, July 29, 1837; Aug. 12, 1837.
*Republican Banner and Nashville Whig*, July 26, 1850; Oct. 7, 1850.
*Athens Post*, July 18, 1851.
Knoxville *Brownlow's Whig and Independent Journal*, Oct. 18, 1851; Nov. 27, 1852.
*Athens Post*, Jan. 23, 1857.
*Republican Banner*, Oct. 23, 1848.
*Athens Post*, Dec. 26, 1862; April 17, 1863; June 12, 1863.

## Chapter 21

J.W. Loguen, *The Rev. J.W. Loguen, as a Slave and as a Freeman: A Narrative of Real Life* (Syracuse, New York: J.G.K. Truair & Co, 1859).
Louis Hughes, *Thirty Years a Slave: From Bondage to Freedom: The Institution of Slavery as Seen on the Plantation.* (Online Reprint, the University of North Carolina at Chapel Hill, 1997).
Millie Simpkins interview, Slave Narratives (Online, Library of Congress website).
Social Sciences Department, Fisk University, *Unwritten History of Slavery* (Nashville: Fisk University, 1945), pp. 86-103, pp. 283-291, pp. 309-322.

## Chapter 22

*Tennessee Gazette*, March 31, 1802; July 23, 1802.
*Nashville Whig*, March 30, 1814; Aug. 14, 1819.
*Memphis Enquirer*, April 5, 1836.

Bill Carey, "The Mystery of the Land Pirate's Missing Thumb," in *Tennessee Magazine* (April 2017).
*Republican Banner*, March 31, 1843; Dec. 4, 1850.
*Athens Post*, April 11, 1851.
*Murfreesboro Telegraph*, Jan. 29, 1852.
*Nashville Union and American*, March 30, 1854.
*Nashville Union and American*, May 13, 1854.
*Loudon Free Press*, Nov. 8, 1854.
*Nashville Daily Patriot*, Aug. 4, 1855.
*Athens Post*, Nov. 3, 1854.
*Nashville Union and American*, Dec. 5, 1854.
*Daily Nashville Patriot*, Oct. 16, 1855.
*Nashville Union and American*, Nov. 28, 1858.
*Nashville Union and American*, Sept. 19, 1859.
*Fayetteville Observer*, Sept. 15, 1859.
*Republican Banner*, Sept. 19, 1859; Feb. 5, 1861.

## Chapter 23

Sally Jenkins, "How the Flag Came to be Called Old Glory," *Smithsonian* magazine, October 2013.
*Daily Nashville Patriot*, Aug. 7, 1861.
*Memphis Daily Appeal*, Jan. 19, 1862.
*Nashville Daily Patriot*, March 21, 1860; March 7, 1861; May 17, 1861.
*Republican Banner*, Oct. 10 and 17, 1861.
*Clarksville Chronicle*, June 7, 1861.
*Nashville Daily Patriot*, Aug. 18, 1861; Dec. 3, 1861.
*Nashville Union and American*, Feb. 1, 1862.
*Daily Nashville American*, May 11, 1862.
*Nashville Daily Union*, June 25, 1862; Aug. 8, 1862; Sept. 7, 9, 11 and 12, 1862.
Emancipation Proclamation (available online).
*Nashville Daily Union*, Feb. 22 and 27, 1863; Oct. 13, 1863.
Bill Carey, "State Law, not Federal Law, Freed Tennessee's Slaves," *Tennessee Magazine*, July 2008.
(Murfreesboro) *Daily Rebel Banner*, Dec. 23, 1862.

## Chapter 24

*Athens Post*, April 17, 1863; Feb. 27, 1863; March 6 and 20, 1863; June 12, 1863; July 17, 1863.
*Winchester Daily Bulletin*, Feb. 15, 1863; April 3, 1863; June 12, 1863.
*Knoxville Daily Register*, Nov. 8 and 16, 1862; Dec. 14, 1862; April 19, 26, 28 and 29, 1863; July 14, 1863.
*Knoxville Southern Chronicle*, Aug. 27, 1863.
*Chattanooga Daily Rebel*, Jan. 31, 1863; March 12 and 13, 1863; July 30, 1863.
*Brownlow's Knoxville Whig and Rebel Ventilator*, Nov. 11, 1863.
*Memphis Daily Appeal*, Sept. 14, 1863; Jan. 7, 1864; April 29, 1864; May 1, 1864; June 11 and 21, 1864.
*Nashville Daily Union*, Jan. 17, 1865; Feb. 7, 14, 15, 16 and 21, 1865
*Nashville Union*, Feb. 22, 1864.
Louis Hughes, *Thirty Years a Slave: From Bondage to Freedom: The Institution of Slavery as Seen on the Plantation*. (Online Reprint, the University of North Carolina at Chapel Hill, 1997).

# BIBLIOGRAPHY

## Newspapers

The following newspapers routinely published runaway slave ads, slave sale ads and other types of paid advertisements associated with slavery. The years shown are the years I searched.

Microfilm is not easily searched. I did my best, but I'm sure I missed quite a bit. Also, while in some cases the Tennessee State Library and Archives has every issue ever published of the newspapers shown here, in others, TSLA only has a couple of issues per year.

*Athens Post* (1850-1863)
(Athens) *Tennessee Journal* (1838-1839)
*Bedford Weekly Yeoman* (1853-1855)
*Brownlow's Knoxville Whig and Independent Journal* (1849-1855)
*Carthage Casket* (1848-1849)
*Carthage Gazette* (1810-1824)
*Chattanooga Advertiser* (1857-1858)
*Clarksville Chronicle* (1857-1862)
*Chattanooga Daily Rebel* (1862-1864)
*Chattanooga Gazette* (1839-1861)
*Clarksville Jeffersonian* (1843-1863)
(Clarksville) *Tennessee Watchman* (1821-1823)
*Columbia Beacon* (1847)
*Columbia Chronicle* (1816)
*Columbian* (1825)
*Columbia Observer* (1834)
*Clarksville Weekly Chronicle* (1842-1847 and 1857-1861)
*Daily Nashville Patriot* (1856-1859)
*Elizabethton Tennessee Whig* (1839-1840)
*Fayetteville Observer* (1851-1863)
*Franklin Gazette* (1822)
(Franklin) *Western Balance* (1829)
*Greeneville Democrat* (1858-1860)
*Greeneville Mountaineer* (1839)
*Hiwassee Patriot* (1839 to 1841)
*Hiwassee Reporter* (1837)
(Jackson) *District Intelligencer and Southern Standard* (1841)
(Jackson) *District Telegraph and State Sentinel* (1838)

*Jackson Gazette* (1824-1829)
(Jackson) *Pioneer* (1822-1824)
*Jonesboro Whig* (1840-1841)
*Kingston Gazetteer* (1854-1856)
*Knoxville Argus and Commercial Herald* (1839-41)
*Knoxville Daily Register* (1861-63)
*Knoxville Southern Chronicle* (1863)
*Knoxville Enquirer* (1792-1818)
*Knoxville Gazetteer* (1854-1855)
*Knoxville Register* (1816-1839
*Knoxville Republican* (1832)
(Knoxville) *Western Chonicle* (1829-1830)
*Loudon Free Press* (1852-1855)
*Maryville East Tennessean* (1856)
*Memphis Advocate and Western District Intelligencer* (1827-1828)
*Memphis Daily Appeal* (1857-1864)
*Memphis Daily Eagle and Enquirer* (1851-1858)
*Memphis Enquirer* (1836-1851)
*Memphis Weekly Appeal* (1843-1847)
(Murfreesboro) *Daily Rebel Banner* (1862)
(Murfreesboro) *Tennessee Telegraph* (1845-1846)
(Murfreesborough) *Central Monitor* (1833-1835)
*Murfreesborough Courier* (1814-1827)
(Murfreesborough) *National Vidette* (1828)
*Nashville Daily Patriot* (1855-1861)
*Nashville Gazette* (1819-1827)
*Nashville Impartial Review and Cumberland Repository* (1805-1809)
*Nashville Republican* (1824-1830; 1834-1837)
*Nashville Republican Banner* (1854-1864)
*Nashville Union* (1835-1837)
*Nashville Union and American* (1853-1864)
*Nashville Whig* (1812-1826)
*National Banner and Nashville Whig* (1826-1837)
*Nashville Union and American* (1853-1864)
*Paris Analysis* (1847-1848)
*Paris Sentinel* (1857)
*Paris Weekly Patriot (1856)*
(Paris) *West Tennessean* (1825, 1839)
*Pulaski Gazette* (1851)
*Pulaski Whig Courier* (1840)
*Randolph Recorder* (1834-1836)

(Rogersville) *East Tennessean* (1839-1840)
*Rogersville Times* (1850-1856)
*Shelbyville Expositor* (1850-1861)
*Shelbyville Intelligencer* (1842-1843)
*Shelbyville Western Freeman* (1831-1835)
*Sparta Review* (1824-1825)
*Tennessee Gazette and Mero District Advertiser* (1803-1807)
*Trenton Journal* (1841)
(Trenton) *Southern Standard* (1861)
*Winchester Daily Bulletin* (1862-1863)
*Winchester Home Journal* (1856-1861)

**Issues of the following newspapers were found not to publish runaway slave ads, slave sale ads and other types of paid advertisements associated with the institution of slavery.**

(Jonesboro) *Emancipator* (1822)
(Greeneville) *Genius of Universal Emancipation* (1822-23)
*Rogersville Railroad Advocate* (1831-32)

## Published Books and Articles

Baker, John F. Jr. *The Washingtons of Wessyngton Plantation: Stories of My Family's Journey to Freedom*. New York: Simon & Schuster, 2009.

Bancroft, Frederic. *Slave Trading in the Old South*. 1931. Reprint, New York: Frederick Ungar Publishing, 1959.

Bremer, Fredrika. *Homes of The New World: Impressions of America*. New York: Harper & Brothers, 1853.

Clements, Paul. *Chronicles of the Cumberland Settlements: 1779-1796*. Self-published, 2012.

Creighton, Wilbur. *Building of Nashville*. Self-published, 1969.

Daily American Book and Job Printing Office. *The Nashville, State of Tennessee and General Commercial Directory*. Nashville, 1853.

Daily American Book and Job Printing Office. *The Nashville, State of Tennessee and General Commercial Directory*. Nashville, 1857.

Dew, Charles B. "Black Ironworkers and the Insurrection Panic of 1856." *Journal of Southern History*. Vol. 41, No. 3 (Aug. 1975).

Dickinson, Calvin. *The Walton Road: A Nineteenth Century Wilderness Highway in Tennessee*. W. Calvin Dickinson, 2007.

Durham, Walter T. *Nashville: The Occupied City*. Nashville, Tennessee Historical Society, 1985.

Durham, Walter T. *Reluctant Partners: Nashville and the Union*. Nashville: Tennessee Historical Society, 1987.

Dusinberre, William. *Slavemaster President: The Double Career of James Polk*. New York, Oxford University Press, 2003.

Folmsbee, Stanley J., Corlow, Robert E. and Mitchell, Enoch L. *Tennessee: A Short History*. Knoxville: University of Tennessee Press, 1969.

Gallay, Alan. *Voices of the Old South: Eyewitness Accounts*. Athens, Georgia: University of Georgia Press, 1994.

Goodstein, Anita S. *Nashville 1780-1860: From Frontier to City*, Gainesville, Florida: University of Florida Press, 1989.

Goodstein, Anita S. "Black History on the Nashville Frontier, 1780-1810. *Tennessee Historical Quarterly*. Volume 38, Number 4 (Winter 1979).

Hughes, Louis. *Thirty Years a Slave: From Bondage to Freedom: The Institution of Slavery as Seen on the Plantation*. Online Reprint, the University of North Carolina at Chapel Hill, 1997.

Hurst, Jack. *Nathan Bedford Forrest: A Biography*. New York: Random House, 1993.

Johnson, Walter (editor). *The Chattel Principle: Internal Slave Trades in the Americas*. New Haven, Connecticut: Yale University Press, 2004.

King, William Fletcher. *Reminiscences*. New York: Abingdon Press, 1915.

Loguen, J.W. *The Rev. J.W. Loguen, as a Slave and as a Freeman: A Narrative of Real Life*. Syracuse, N.Y.: J.G.K. Truair & Co, 1859.

Lovett, Bobby L. *The African American History of Nashville, Tennessee*. Fayetteville, Arkansas: University of Arkansas Press, 1999.

Meigs, Return J. and Cooper, William F. *The Code of Tennessee Enacted by the*

*General Assembly of 1857-58*. Nashville: Eastman and Company, 1858.

Mooney, Chase C. *Slavery in Tennessee*. Westport Connecticut: Negro Universities Press, 1957.

Olmsted, Frederick Law. *A Journey in the Back Country*, 1860. Reprint, Williamstown, Massachusetts: Corner House Publishers, 1972.

Olmstead, Frederick Law. *Slave States*. New York: G.P. Putnam's Sons, 1959.

Patterson, Caleb Perry. *The Negro in Tennessee, 1790-1865*. 1922. Reprint, New York: Greenwood Publishing Corp, 1968.

Pilkington, James Penn. *The Methodist Publishing House: A History (Volume I)*. Nashville, Abingdon Press, 1968.

Ray, Kristofer. *Middle Tennessee: 1775-1825*. Knoxville: University of Tennessee Press, 2007.

Rothrock, Mary U., editor. *The French Broad-Holston Country: A History of Knox County, Tennessee*. Knoxville: East Tennessee Historical Society, 1946.

Seward, Frederick W. *Autobiography of William H. Seward*. New York: D. Appleton and Company, 1877.

Social Sciences Institute, Fisk University. *Unwritten History of Slavery*. Nashville: Fisk University, 1945.

Stephenson, Wendell Holmes. *Isaac Franklin: Slave Trader and Planter of the Old South*. Baton Rouge: Louisiana State University Press, 1938.

Watson, Henry. *Narrative of Henry Watson, a Fugitive Slave*. Boston: Bela Marsh, 1848.

Wyett, John Allan. *That Devil Forrest: Life of General Nathan Bedford Forrest*. Baton Rouge: Louisiana State University Press, 1989.

## Other Sources

Rhea, Matthew. "A Map of the State of Tennessee Taken from Survey, 1832"

# INDEX

*Names are indexed in cases where we know a person's first and last names, or the last name and first initial. Names are not indexed if we only know the first name. Therefore, slaves identified by only their first names are not indexed.*

*The appendices are not indexed.*

*Bill Carey*

CPSIA information can be obtained
at www.ICGtesting.com
Printed in the USA
BVHW03*0911060818
523683BV00008B/37/P